Lecture Notes in Computer Science 14308

Founding Editors

Gerhard Goos
Juris Hartmanis

Editorial Board Members

The series Lecture Notes in Computer Science (LNCS), including its subseries Lecture Notes in Artificial Intelligence (LNAI) and Lecture Notes in Bioinformatics (LNBI), has established itself as a medium for the publication of new developments in computer science and information technology research, teaching, and education.

LNCS enjoys close cooperation with the computer science R & D community, the series counts many renowned academics among its volume editors and paper authors, and collaborates with prestigious societies. Its mission is to serve this international community by providing an invaluable service, mainly focused on the publication of conference and workshop proceedings and postproceedings. LNCS commenced publication in 1973.

Yi Li · Sofiène Tahar
Editors

Formal Methods and Software Engineering

24th International Conference
on Formal Engineering Methods, ICFEM 2023
Brisbane, QLD, Australia, November 21–24, 2023
Proceedings

 Springer

Editors
Yi Li 🆔
Nanyang Technological University
Singapore, Singapore

Sofiène Tahar 🆔
Concordia University
Montreal, QC, Canada

ISSN 0302-9743 ISSN 1611-3349 (electronic)
Lecture Notes in Computer Science
ISBN 978-981-99-7583-9 ISBN 978-981-99-7584-6 (eBook)
https://doi.org/10.1007/978-981-99-7584-6

Preface

This volume contains the papers presented at ICFEM 2023: 24th International Conference on Formal Engineering Methods, held on November 21–24, 2023 in Brisbane, Australia.

The International Conference on Formal Engineering Methods (ICFEM) is a premier conference for research in all areas related to formal engineering methods. Since 1997, ICFEM has been serving as an international forum for researchers and practitioners who have been seriously applying formal methods to practical applications. Researchers and practitioners, from industry, academia, and government, were encouraged to attend, present their research, and help advance the state of the art. ICFEM is interested in work that has been incorporated into real production systems, and in theoretical work that promises to bring practical and tangible benefit. In recent years, ICFEM has taken place in Madrid, Spain (2022), Singapore (2021, corresponding to ICFEM 2020, postponed due to the COVID-19 pandemic), Shenzhen, China (2019), Gold Coast, Australia (2018), Xi'an, China (2017), Tokyo, Japan (2016), and Paris, France (2015).

There were 34 full research paper submissions to the main track of ICFEM 2023. Each paper was reviewed by at least three Program Committee members. The committee decided to accept 13 papers. The program also included 3 keynotes and 5 invited talks. The keynotes were given by Graeme Smith from the University of Queensland, Australia, Yuxi Fu from Shanghai Jiao Tong University, China, and Yamine Ait Ameur from the Toulouse National Polytechnique Institute, France. The main event was preceded by the 2nd International Workshop on Formal Analysis and Verification of Post-Quantum Cryptographic Protocols (FAVPQC 2023). The program of ICFEM 2023 also featured a Doctoral Symposium (chaired by Yulei Sui, UNSW Sydney, Australia), which accepted eight doctoral research submissions, included as short papers in the ICFEM 2023 proceedings.

We would like to thank the numerous people who contributed to the success of ICFEM 2023: the General Chairs, Guangdong Bai from the University of Queensland, Australia, and Jin Song Dong from the National University of Singapore, the Steering Committee members, the PC members, and the additional reviewers for their support in selecting papers and composing the conference program. We are grateful to all authors and invited speakers for their contributions without which, of course, these proceedings would not exist. We would also like to thank Springer for their help during the production of this proceedings volume and the EasyChair system for supporting the submission, review, and volume preparation processes.

ICFEM 2023 was organized and supported by the University of Queensland, Brisbane, Australia. We would like to thank the Local Organizing Committee for their hard work in making ICFEM 2023 a successful and exciting event.

September 2023

Yi Li
Sofiène Tahar

Organization

General Co-chairs

Jin Song Dong   National University of Singapore, Singapore
Guangdong Bai   University of Queensland, Australia

Program Co-chairs

Yi Li   Nanyang Technological University, Singapore
Sofiène Tahar   Concordia University, Canada

Finance Chair

Zhe Hou   Griffith University, Australia

Publicity Chairs

Cheng-Hao Cai   Monash University at Suzhou, China
Neeraj Kumar Singh   IRIT-ENSEEIHT, Toulouse, France

Journal First Co-chairs

Mark Utting   University of Queensland, Australia
Guowei Yang   University of Queensland, Australia

Doctoral Symposium Chair

Yulei Sui   UNSW Sydney, Australia

Workshop Chair

Xiaofei Xie   Singapore Management University, Singapore

Publication Chair

Xiaodong Qi   Nanyang Technological University, Singapore

Sponsorship Chair

Kailong Wang   Huazhong University of Science and Technology,
                                            China

Local Co-chairs

Naipeng Dong   University of Queensland, Australia
Guowei Yang   University of Queensland, Australia

Web Chair

Hao Guan   University of Queensland, Australia

Program Committee

Yamine Ait Ameur   IRIT/INPT-ENSEEIHT, France
Behzad Akbarpour   NVIDIA, USA
Étienne André   Université de Lorraine, France
Cyrille Valentin Artho   KTH Royal Institute of Technology, Sweden
Guangdong Bai   University of Queensland, Australia
Christel Baier   TU Dresden, Germany
Richard Banach   University of Manchester, UK
Luís Soares Barbosa   University of Minho, Portugal
Hadrien Bride   Griffith University, Australia
Ana Cavalcanti   University of York, UK
Dipankar Chaki   University of New South Wales, Australia
Marsha Chechik   University of Toronto, Canada

Yean-Ru Chen	National Cheng Kung University, Taiwan
Yu-Fang Chen	Academia Sinica, Taiwan
Yuting Chen	Shanghai Jiao Tong University, China
Ranald Clouston	Australian National University, Australia
Florin Craciun	Babes-Bolyai University, Romania
Ana De Melo	University of São Paulo, Brazil
Thi Thu Ha Doan	Freiburg University, Germany
Naipeng Dong	National University of Singapore, Singapore
Aaron Dutle	NASA Langley Research Center, USA
Yassmeen Elderhalli	Synopsys, Canada
Santiago Escobar	Universitat Politècnica de València, Spain
Ruitao Feng	Singapore Management University, Singapore
Flavio Ferrarotti	Software Competence Centre Hagenberg, Austria
Marc Frappier	Université de Sherbrooke, Canada
Lindsay Groves	Victoria University of Wellington, New Zealand
Osman Hasan	National University of Sciences & Technology, Pakistan
Xudong He	Florida International University, USA
Zhe Hou	Griffith University, Australia
Fuyuki Ishikawa	National Institute of Informatics, Japan
Eun-Young Kang	University of Southern Denmark, Denmark
Tsutomu Kobayashi	Japan Aerospace Exploration Agency, Japan
Mark Lawford	McMaster University, Canada
Jiaying Li	Microsoft, China
Yi Li (Chair)	Nanyang Technological University, Singapore
Yuekang Li	University of New South Wales, Australia
Shang-Wei Lin	Nanyang Technological University, Singapore
Guanjun Liu	Tongji University, China
Si Liu	ETH Zurich, Switzerland
Zhiming Liu	Southwest University, China
Brendan Mahony	DSTO, Australia
Frederic Mallet	Université Cote d'Azur, France
Panagiotis Manolios	Northeastern University, USA
Heiko Mantel	TU Darmstadt, Germany
Narciso Marti-Oliet	Universidad Complutense de Madrid, Spain
Dominique Mery	Université de Lorraine, France
Stephan Merz	Inria Nancy, France
Stefan Mitsch	Carnegie Mellon University, USA
Magnus Myreen	Chalmers University, Sweden
Shin Nakajima	National Institute of Informatics, Japan
Masaki Nakamura	Toyama Prefectural University, Japan
Michael Norrish	Australian National University, Australia

Peter Ölveczky	University of Oslo, Norway
Jun Pang	University of Luxembourg, Luxembourg
Yu Pei	Hong Kong Polytechnic University, China
Shengchao Qin	Teesside University, UK
Silvio Ranise	University of Trento and Fondazione Bruno Kessler, Italy
Elvinia Riccobene	University of Milan, Italy
Adrian Riesco	Universidad Complutense de Madrid, Spain
Subhajit Roy	Indian Institute of Technology Kanpur, India
Rubén Rubio	Universidad Complutense de Madrid, Spain
David Sanan	Singapore Institute of Technology, Singapore
Valdivino Santiago	Instituto Nacional de Pesquisas Espaciais, Brazil
Yulei Sui	University of New South Wales, Australia
Jing Sun	University of Auckland, New Zealand
Meng Sun	Peking University, China
Xiaoyu Sun	Australian National University, Australia
Sofiène Tahar (Chair)	Concordia University, Canada
Elena Troubitsyna	KTH, Sweden
Ionut Tutu	Simion Stoilow Institute of Mathematics of the Romanian Academy, Romania
Mark Utting	University of Queensland, Australia
Bow-Yaw Wang	Academia Sinica, Taiwan
Hai H. Wang	Aston University, UK
Hsu Myat Win	RMIT University, Australia
Guowei Yang	University of Queensland, Australia
Naijun Zhan	Chinese Academy of Sciences, China
Min Zhang	East China Normal University, China
Xiaoyi Zhang	University of Science and Technology Beijing, China
Yongwang Zhao	Zhejiang University, China

Additional Reviewers

Bu, Hao
Eshghie, Mojtaba
Feng, Nick
Feng, Shenghua
Kalita, Pankaj Kumar
Kumar, Ankit
Lahiri, Sumit
Luan, Xiaokun
Proença, José

Walter, Andrew
Wen, Cheng
Yang, Jialin
Yang, Min

Abstracts of Invited Talks

Compositional Reasoning at The Software/Hardware Interface

Graeme Smith

The University of Queensland, Australia
g.smith1@uq.edu.au

Abstract. Rely/guarantee reasoning provides a compositional approach to reasoning about multi-threaded programs. It enables local reasoning about a thread by abstracting the thread's environment to a *rely condition* on shared resources that is guaranteed by all other threads.

This approach is sound under the assumption that the individual threads execute in a sequentially consistent manner. However, this is not the case on modern multicore processors which routinely employ out-of-order execution for efficiency gains. This loss of sequential consistency has no effects on the functionality of high-level programs that are data-race free, and for those programs rely/guarantee reasoning remains sound. However, data races may be introduced by programmers inadvertently, or for reasons of efficiency, as seen in non-blocking algorithms. These algorithms appear regularly in the low-level code of operating system routines and programming library data structures.

This presentation explores the effects of out-of-order execution on such code and how soundness of rely/guarantee reasoning can be restored by using additional checks over pairs of instructions. Such checks are presented for *multicopy atomic* processors, such as x86-TSO, ARMv8 and RISC-V, where a thread's writes become observable to all other threads at the same time, and *non-multicopy atomic* processors, such as POWER and older versions of ARM, where this is not necessarily the case. The presentation also looks at how these checks apply to reasoning about low-level security vulnerabilities, such as Spectre.

Compositional Reasoning at The Software/Hardware Interface

Graeme Smith

The University of Queensland, Australia

Separation of Concerns for Complexity Mitigation in System and Domain Formal Modelling – A Dive into Algebraic Event-B Theories

Yamine Ait Ameur

IRIT - National Polytechnique Institute - CNRS, France
yamine@enseeiht.fr

Abstract. Formal methods have shown their ability and efficiency in the design, analysis and verification of safety critical complex software systems. A crucial challenge for formal methods nowadays is to make them reasonably accessible, as to foster a wider adoption across system engineering, and make their implementation and deployment more operational for non-expert engineers and researchers alike. From our point of view, promoting the reuse and sharing of explicitly formalised elements such as models, theories, proofs, etc. contributes, undoubtedly, to the dissemination of these methods. As a result, reuse mechanisms must be defined and integrated into development processes such as refinement, abstraction, composition/decomposition, etc.

In this talk, we will discuss state -based formal methods, namely the Event-B method. We report on our findings about the definition of algebraic theories that are utilised within Event-B model refinement chains. In our method, Event-B models borrow operators, axioms, theorems, proof and rewrite rules from these theories. Relying on their well-definedness, these operators, axioms, theorems and proof and rewrite rules are useful to discharge the proof obligations generated for these models, and contribute to reducing development efforts, as theorems of the theories are proved once and for all. The approach is illustrated on the generation of new proof obligations and on system models conformance to engineering standards.

This work has been partly supported by BMK, BMAW, and the State of Upper Austria in the frame of the SCCH competence center INTEGRATE (FFG grant no. 892418) part of the FFG COMET Competence Centers for Excellent Technologies Programme and by the EBRPRodinPlus French ANR grant (ANR-19-CE25-0010).

A Foundation for Interaction

Yuxi Fu

Shanghai Jiao Tong University, China
fu-yx@cs.sjtu.edu.cn

Abstract. Concurrency theory has found applications in a wide range scenarios. The foundations of the concurrency theory have been studied in several frameworks. In this talk we present one such foundation, the Theory of Interaction. The theory builds upon four postulates, and develop the equality theory and expressiveness theory in a model independent manner. A thesis for interaction is proposed for interactability. The well-known concurrency models are studied and compared in the Theory of Interaction.

Practical Verified Concurrent Program Security

Toby Murray

University of Melbourne, Australia
toby.murray@unimelb.edu.au

Abstract. We entrust programs to keep our most precious secrets. The quest to prove that they do so securely has been ongoing for at least half a century. In that time, we have learned that doing so *practically* involves overcoming an array of challenges. Firstly, secrets can unintentionally leak via various mechanisms, many of which are below the level of abstraction at which the software was designed. Side-channel leakage via microarchitectural mechanisms is a prime example. Therefore, *implementation-level reasoning* is crucial to meaningfully verify program security. This kind of reasoning is necessarily challenging in the age of shared-memory concurrent systems software, requiring reasoning about low-level details including pointers and even compilation. Secondly, real programs that manage real secrets often implement complex security policies. Answers to questions such as "which data are secret?", "under which circumstances?", and "at which times?" are not only intertwined with each other but also with the application's functionality. For a trivial but illustrative example, in the popular game of Wordle the information that is allowed to be revealed to a particular player about the ith character of the secret word depends on the rules of the game and that player's guesses so far. Therefore, in general meaningful security cannot be verified in the absence of *functional correctness*. Moreover, it requires a general-purpose verification approach able to encompass a wide range of security policy specifications, applicable to a wide array of programs. Finally, the verification approach should also aim to maximise *usability* and the use of automation, while minimising the learning curve. This is especially true when proving confidentiality properties which, being *hyperproperties*, require reasoning about pairs of program executions.

In this talk I will describe the COVERN project (https://covern.org), which set out to overcome these challenges in 2015. Its efforts have culminated in the creation of a highly practical method for verifying the security of concurrent programs. This method is underpinned by the carefully-designed *security concurrent separation logic* (SECCSL), plus a specification and verification methodology that together address each of the aforementioned challenges, proved sound in Isabelle/HOL. Our approach supports implementation-level reasoning against complex security policies while presenting a familiar Hoare-logic style user interface to the human verification engineer. It is embodied in a program verification tool that implements the *auto-active* paradigm (as popularised by tools like Dafny, VeriFast and Why3). I will illustrate its power and versatility with the aid of a range of verified exemplar programs.

On Analysing Weak Memory Concurrency

Subodh Sharma

Indian Institute of Technology Delhi, India
svs@iitd.ac.in

Abstract. Over the past decade, the field of software engineering has seen the advent of weak memory programming models, including C/C++11 and its derivatives such as RC11. These models have not only gained considerable attention but have also been implemented in real-world applications, including but not limited to Bitcoin-core, TensorFlow, and web browsers like Firefox and Chromium. Despite their widespread usage, these programming models come with a set of complex (and sometimes nonintuitive) semantics, complicating the development of correct and reliable programs. The complexity inherent in these models makes both program development and debugging highly challenging endeavors. In this presentation, I will elucidate some of our recent efforts aimed at the efficient analysis of programs using weak memory models, as well as the automated program repair.

Certified Proof and Non-Provability

Dirk Pattinson

The Australian National University, Australia
dirk.pattinson@anu.edu.au

Abstract. A simple yes/no answer is often not a sufficient output of an automated reasoning tool. We also demand verifiable evidence, either of provability or refutability of a formula. A (formal) proof satisfies this requirement for provability. Countermodels can evidence refutability, but have drawbacks: there may not be an agreed upon notion of semantics, and the mathematical details of countermodels vary widely depending on the underlying logic. Proofs, on the other hand, have a very uniform representation. We therefore complement the syntactic notion of proof with a syntactic (coinductively defined) notion of refutation. Our main theorem then states that "every statement either has a proof or a refutation" (terms and conditions apply). We discuss both on the notion of refutation in general, and highlight the challenges encountered in fully verifying the above theorem.

Proofs are finite, often inductively defined, certificates that demonstrate truth. This includes e.g. derivations as evidence that a string is in the language of a grammar, the validity of a formula in a structure for first order logic, or a formula being derivable in a system of proof rules. Non-provability is therefore the complement of an inductively defined type, and can therefore be captured as the greatest fixpoint of a monotone operator. For an item to be non-derivable, each proof rule must have (at least) one non-derivable premiss. As a greatest fixpoint, this can continue ad infinitum. We conceptualise and generalise the inductive notion of proof as a *bipartite graph* where one type of nodes (called sequents) are the facts that we seek to establish, and the other type (called rules) are the justifications. A sequent is linked to all rules that justify it, and a rule connects to all its premisses. On top of this structure, we define mutually inductive types of *witnessed provable sequents* (there is a rule with all provable premisses) and *witnessed proving* rules (all premisses are provable). This allows us to define a dual, coinductive type of refutable sequents and refutable rules. The formalised main theorem then states that every sequent either has a proof, or a reputation.

Our work is an example of a mathematically trivial theorem that requires very elaborate proof techniques in an interactive theorem prover. We have implemented the proof in Coq, mainly because of the relatively

This work is done in collaboration with Cláudia Nalon (University of Brasilia, Brazil, nalon@unb.br).

mature support of coinductive types. The proof of the main theorem relies on termination of fixpoint iteration which requires elaborate wellfoundedness proofs. Dually, syntactic guardedness requirements require intricate formulation of auxiliary functions. The extraction of a decision procedure from the proof of the main theorem requires to distinguish proof-relevant from proof-irrelevant detail and hand-crafted code to guarantee a modicum of efficiency.

Verifying Compiler Optimisations

Ian J. Hayes

The University of Queensland, Australia
Ian.Hayes@uq.edu.au

Abstract. Compilers are a vital tool but errors in a compiler can lead to errors in the myriad of programs it compiles. Our research focuses on verifying the optimisation phase because it is a common source of errors within compilers. In programming language semantics, expressions (or terms) are represented by abstract syntax trees, and their semantics is expressed over their (recursive) structure. Optimisations can then be represented by conditional term rewriting rules. The correctness of these rules is verified in Isabelle/HOL. In the GraalVM compiler, the intermediate representation is a sea-of-nodes graph structure that combines data flow and control flow in the one graph. The data flow sub-graphs correspond to term graphs, and the term rewriting rules apply equally to this representation.

Contents

Doctoral Symposium Papers

Invited Paper

Verifying Compiler Optimisations
(Invited Paper)

Ian J. Hayes[✉], Mark Utting, and Brae J. Webb

The University of Queensland, Brisbane, Australia
{Ian.Hayes,M.Utting,B.Webb}@uq.edu.au

Abstract. Compilers are a vital tool but errors in a compiler can lead to errors in the myriad of programs it compiles. Our research focuses on verifying the optimisation phase because it is a common source of errors within compilers. In programming language semantics, expressions (or terms) are represented by abstract syntax trees, and their semantics is expressed over their (recursive) structure. Optimisations can then be represented by conditional term rewriting rules. The correctness of these rules is verified in Isabelle/HOL. In the GraalVM compiler, the intermediate representation is a sea-of-nodes graph structure that combines data flow and control flow in the one graph. The data flow sub-graphs correspond to term graphs, and the term rewriting rules apply equally to this representation.

1 Introduction

This paper overviews our research on verifying expression optimisations used in the GraalVM compiler developed by Oracle.[1] The compiler supports multiple source languages (Java, Scala, Kotlin, JavaScript, Python, Ruby, ...) and multiple target architectures (AMD64 and ARM) and has variants for both just-in-time and ahead-of-time compilation. It has front ends that generate an intermediate representation (IR) of the program being compiled from the source programming language. The compilation process includes multiple optimisation phases that transform the IR representation of a method/program to a more efficient version, also expressed in the IR. The final phase generates machine code for the target architecture from the optimised IR representation of the program.

Why Verify Compilers? Compilers for programming languages are an indispensable part of the trusted base of a software development platform. Their correctness is essential because an error in a compiler can lead to errors in any of the myriad of programs it compiles.

Why Focus on the Optimiser? For a multi-lingual, multi-target compiler, the machine-independent optimiser is common to all source programming languages and all target machine architectures and hence correctness of the optimiser affects all source languages and all target architectures.

---

[1] https://github.com/oracle/graal.

Y. Li and S. Tahar (Eds.): ICFEM 2023, LNCS 14308, pp. 3–8, 2023.
https://doi.org/10.1007/978-981-99-7584-6_1

The optimiser is a common source of errors within compilers. In a study of
C compilers, Yang et al. [7] found that for GCC, with optimisation turned off
only 4 bugs were found but with optimisation turned on 79 bugs were found,
and for Clang, with optimisation turned off only 19 bugs were found but with
optimisation turned on 202 bugs were found.

Errors in an optimiser are often due to subtle edge cases that may not be
covered by testing, whereas verification addresses all possible cases. For example,
a quirk of two's complement arithmetic is that the most negative 32-bit signed
integer $MinInt = -2^{31}$, when negated gives back $MinInt$ (because the largest
representable positive integer is $2^{31} - 1$ and hence $-MinInt = 2^{31}$ is not representable as a 32-bit signed integer and the negation of $MinInt$ "overflows" and
gives back $MinInt$). One consequence of this is that the absolute value function when applied to $MinInt$ gives $MinInt$, a negative value! Hence a plausible
optimisation that replaces $0 \leq abs(x)$ with $true$ is invalid if x is $MinInt$.

Overview. The GraalVM IR for a method consists of a graph structure that
combines both control-flow and data-flow nodes [3]. In this paper we overview our
approach to verifying the optimisation of data-flow sub-graphs, which represent
expressions in the source language. We have developed a model of the IR in
Isabelle/HOL [1] and then given the IR a semantics [6] (see Sect. 2). Expression
optimisations are given as a set of conditional term rewriting rules (see Sect. 3).
Proving the rules correct then corresponds to showing that they preserve the
semantics (see Sect. 4). Generating efficient code for an optimiser from a set of
rewriting rules is overviewed in Sect. 5.

2   Data-Flow Sub-graphs

GraalVM IR data-flow sub-graphs are,

  side-effect free – side effects are factored out into the control-flow part of
  the graph,
  well-defined in context – runtime exceptions such as divide by zero or
  index out of range are guarded in the control flow graph, so that for example,
  a divide node cannot be reached if its divisor is zero, and
  share common sub-expressions – if the same sub-expression, e, is used in
  multiple places in an expression f, a single sub-graph representing e is shared
  by all references to e within f.

Sharing common sub-expressions is essential for generating efficient code but it
means that the representation of a term (i.e. a programming language expression)
is not a conventional abstract syntax tree but rather a directed acyclic graph
structure with a single root node, commonly known as a *term graph* [2]. Figure 1
gives an example of both a conventional tree and (maximal sharing) term-graph
representation of the term $x * x + x * x$. Note that in the term-graph representation, the node representing x is shared in the sub-graph representing $x*x$, and
the root node of $x * x$ is shared in the whole expression $x * x + x * x$. Also note

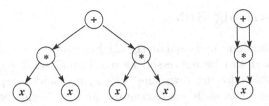

Fig. 1. Abstract syntax tree and term-graph representations of $x * x + x * x$.

that the same sharing occurs if x is a single node or a term graph representing a more complex shared sub-expression.

Each leaf node of a term represents either a constant, a parameter to the method in which the expression occurs, or a control-flow node, such as a method call node, where at runtime the value associated with that node will have already been calculated by the control-flow execution, e.g. the result of a method call.

The semantics of expressions is defined over their abstract syntax tree (or tree for short) form. Term-graphs are a (more efficient) representation of a tree (i.e. a data refinement). For any term graph there is a unique corresponding tree and hence the semantics of a term graph is defined as the semantics of the corresponding tree. Our Isabelle/HOL semantics for an expression, e, is parametrised with respect to a context consisting of a list, p, of *parameters* of the method in which e occurs and a *method state*, m, consisting of a mapping from control-flow node identifiers (e.g. for a method call node) to their (pre-computed) values. The following relation represents evaluating term e in a context consisting of method state m and parameters p to value v.

$$[m, p] \vdash e \mapsto v \tag{1}$$

In Isabelle/HOL this is a (deterministic) relation, rather than a function; if the value of e in context $[m, p]$ is not well defined, the relation does not hold.

Values may be integers, object/array references or the special undefined value.[2] The semantics needs to take into account the bit width of integer values (e.g. 32 or 64) because unbounded integers do not have the same semantics. For integers, their values are represented by a 64-bit value (using the HOL Word library) plus a bit-width b, where $0 < b \leq 64$; only the low-order b bits of the 64-bit word are significant. In two's complement arithmetic, for an expression such as $(x + y) - y$, the calculation of $x + y$ may overflow but subtracting y then "underflows" the value back to x, allowing $(x + y) - y$ to be replaced by x, even with the presence of overflow.

To validate our semantics we have developed a tool that translates GraalVM test cases written in Java to their Isabelle/HOL representation. Each test case is run in Java and its result compared with the value determined by our executable Isabelle/HOL semantics (see [4] for more details).

---

[2] GraalVM IR handles floating point numbers but we have not addressed those as yet.

3   Term Rewriting Rules

Expression optimisations are based on the algebraic properties of the expressions, e.g. $x * 0 = 0$, and can be expressed as conditional term rewriting rules [5], for example, in the following rewriting rules x, y, t and f represent arbitrary expressions, c represents an integer constant, and $\ll$ is the left shift operator. The compiler performs static analysis that tracks the lower and upper bounds of a node, which are stored in the node's *stamp* so that for Rule 6 if the upper bound for x is less than the lower bound for y, $x < y$ must be true in that context. A division node within the graph can only be reached after a (control-flow) check that the divisor is non-zero, otherwise an exception is raised.[3] That allows an optimisation like Rule 3 to be valid because the case when x is zero cannot occur.

$$x * 0 \longmapsto 0 \tag{2}$$

$$x/x \longmapsto 1 \tag{3}$$

$$(x + y) - y \longmapsto x \tag{4}$$

$$x * c \longmapsto x \ll \log_2 c \quad \textbf{when} \ \ isPower2 \ c \tag{5}$$

$$x < y \longmapsto true \qquad \textbf{when} \ \ upper(stamp(x)) < lower(stamp(y)) \tag{6}$$

$$\neg false \longmapsto true \tag{7}$$

$$(true \, ? \, t : f) \longmapsto t \tag{8}$$

The rewriting rules can be applied to any sub-term and in any order. In practice, it is better to optimise all sub-terms of a term e before applying rules to optimise e itself. An exception is when optimising a conditional $(b \, ? \, t : f)$, in which case it is better to first optimise b (e.g. using Rule 6 or Rule 7) because if Rule 8 can then be applied then f is eliminated from the expression and then only t needs to be optimised.

4   Verifying Term Rewriting Rules

This section briefly overviews the verification of rewriting rules (for more details see [5]). We say term e_1 is *refined by* term e_2 if and only if for all contexts $[m, p]$, if e_1 evaluates to a well-defined value v, so does e_2.

$$e_1 \sqsupseteq e_2 = (\forall m \ p \ v \, . \, [m, p] \vdash e_1 \mapsto v \implies [m, p] \vdash e_2 \mapsto v) \tag{9}$$

To show a rewriting rule, $e_1 \longmapsto e_2$ when *cond*, is correct, we show that if *cond* holds e_1 is refined by e_2.

$$cond \implies (e_1 \sqsupseteq e_2) \tag{10}$$

For Rule 2, the right side (i.e. 0) is valid in all contexts but the left side (i.e. $x * 0$) is only well defined in contexts where x is well defined. For the division

---

[3] Our treatment of the semantics assumes that all division nodes are so guarded.

node, the semantics defines $0/0$ to be a special undefined value, and hence Rule 3 is valid because the values of the two sides of a rewriting rule only need to be equal if the left side is well defined.

Verifying optimisations as term rewriting rules is much simpler on the tree representation than on the term-graph representation because, in a term graph, a replaced node may be referenced in multiple places in the graph. To show that term-graph rewriting is correct, we make use of a theorem that shows that if $e_1 \sqsupseteq e_2$ and a term graph matching e_1 is replaced by the corresponding term graph for e_2, then the semantics of the overall graph is preserved.

5 Generating Code for Optimisations

The approach described above represents optimisations as a set of rewriting rules. One could naively translate each rule to code and apply them repeatedly until no rule was applicable.[4] We are currently developing an approach to generate an efficient optimiser from sets of rewriting rules. In practice, there is often overlap between rules in the matching process, for example, all rules with the same node at the top-level of their pattern will perform the same initial match. In practice there are many rewriting rules for each kind of top-level node and hence in generating code we would like to factor out such matching so it is only done once. The factoring can also be applied to sub-expressions of the pattern.

To handle code generation we need to introduce more basic matching primitive, match $e\,p$, that matches term e with pattern p; it takes an initial substitution s and if the match succeeds, returns s updated with instantiations for the free variables within p. Matches can be composed using, $m_1 \,\text{\textfractionsolidus}\, m_2$, to form a combined match that takes a substitution, s, and returns s updated for both matches, if they both succeed, but if either fails their combination fails. For a condition C, test C, fails is C does not hold for its input substitution s, otherwise it passes through s. Alternative rules can be combined using, $r_1 \,\text{else}\, r_2$, meaning take the result of r_1 if it succeeds, otherwise try r_2. For example, (Rule 2 else Rule 5) expands to,

(match $e\,(x * y)$ ⁏ match $y\,(\text{con}\,c)$ ⁏ test$(c = 0)$ ⁏ apply 0) else

(match $e\,(x * y)$ ⁏ match $y\,(\text{con}\,c)$ ⁏ test$(isPower2\,c)$ ⁏ apply$(x \ll \text{eval}(\log_2 c)))$

which after factoring out the initial matches becomes the following.

match $e\,(x * y)$ ⁏ match $y\,(\text{con}\,c)$ ⁏ ((test$(c = 0)$ ⁏ apply 0) else

$\qquad\qquad\qquad\qquad$ (test$(isPower2\,c)$ ⁏ apply$(x \ll \text{eval}(\log_2 c))))$

Generating efficient code in a programming language, such as Java, from rewriting rules expressed using these primitives is relatively straightforward.

For many rewriting rules (e.g. Rule 4), if all sub-expressions of the left side (e.g. x and y) have already been optimised, then a successful application of the rewriting rule results in a term that cannot be further optimised and hence the optimisation of that term is complete.

---

[4] Each set of rewriting rules is given a measure function to ensure rewriting terminates.

6   Conclusions

Conditional term rewriting rules allow one to succinctly formalise expression optimisations. Each rule can be separately verified to show that it preserves the semantics of an expression, whenever the rule is applicable. In the context of the GraalVM compiler the rewriting rules can also be applied to its term-graph representation of expressions. Given a set of valid conditional rewriting rules, each representing individual optimisations, the challenge is then to combine them to form an efficient optimiser by factoring out common matches and avoiding applying rules in situations where they cannot possibly succeed.

Acknowledgements. Mark Utting's position and Brae Webb's PhD scholarship are both funded in part by Oracle Labs. Our thanks go to Paddy Krishnan, Andrew Craik and Gergö Barany from Oracle Labs Brisbane for their helpful feedback, and to the Oracle GraalVM compiler team for answering questions. Thanks also to honours students that have contributed to advancing the project.

References

1. Nipkow, T., Wenzel, M., Paulson, L.C.: Isabelle/HOL: A Proof Assistant for Higher-Order Logic. LNCS, vol. 2283. Springer, Heidelberg (2002). https://doi.org/10.1007/3-540-45949-9
2. Plump, D.: Essentials of term graph rewriting. Electron. Notes Theor. Comput. Sci. **51**, 277–289 (2002). https://doi.org/10.1016/S1571-0661(04)80210-X
3. Stadler, L., Würthinger, T., Simon, D., Wimmer, C., Mössenböck, H.: Graal IR: an extensible declarative intermediate representation. In: Proceedings of the Asia-Pacific Programming Languages and Compilers Workshop. APPLC '13, pp. 1–9, February 2013
4. Utting, M., Webb, B.J., Hayes, I.J.: Differential testing of a verification framework for compiler optimizations (case study). In: FormaliSE 2023. IEEE (2023)
5. Webb, B.J., Hayes, I.J., Utting, M.: Verifying term graph optimizations using Isabelle/HOL. In: Proceedings of the 12th ACM SIGPLAN International Conference on Certified Programs and Proofs. CPP 2023, pp. 320–333. Association for Computing Machinery, New York, NY, USA (2023). https://doi.org/10.1145/3573105.3575673
6. Webb, B.J., Utting, M., Hayes, I.J.: A formal semantics of the GraalVM intermediate representation. In: Hou, Z., Ganesh, V. (eds.) ATVA 2021. LNCS, vol. 12971, pp. 111–126. Springer, Cham (2021). https://doi.org/10.1007/978-3-030-88885-5_8
7. Yang, X., Chen, Y., Eide, E., Regehr, J.: Finding and understanding bugs in C compilers. In: Proceedings of the 32nd ACM SIGPLAN Conference on Programming Language Design and Implementation. PLDI '11, pp. 283–294. Association for Computing Machinery, New York, NY, USA (2011). https://doi.org/10.1145/1993498.1993532

Regular Papers

An Idealist's Approach for Smart Contract Correctness

Tai D. Nguyen[1]([✉]), Long H. Pham[1], Jun Sun[1], and Quang Loc Le[2]

[1] Singapore Management University, Singapore, Singapore
{dtnguyen.2019,hlpham,junsun}@smu.edu.sg
[2] University College London, London, UK
loc.le@ucl.ac.uk

Abstract. In this work, we experiment an idealistic approach for smart contract correctness verification and enforcement, based on the assumption that developers are either desired or required to provide a correctness specification due to the importance of smart contracts and the fact that they are immutable after deployment. We design a static verification system with a specification language which supports fully compositional verification (with the help of function specifications, contract invariants, loop invariants and call invariants). Our approach has been implemented in a tool named ICONTRACT which automatically proves the correctness of a smart contract statically or checks the unverified part of the specification during runtime. Using ICONTRACT, we have verified 10 high-profile smart contracts against manually developed detailed specifications, many of which are beyond the capacity of existing verifiers. Specially, we have uncovered two ERC20 violations in the BNB and QNT contracts.

1 Introduction

"After this decade, programming could be regarded as a public, mathematics-based activity of restructuring specifications into programs."

(Edsger W. Dijkstra, 1969)

And it didn't happen. Worse yet, the idea of having a formal specification either before or alongside with a program has become unimaginable for ordinary programmers nowadays.

We however may not have the luxury NOT to have a correctness specification when it comes to smart contracts. Smart contracts are programs that run on top of blockchain. They are often used to implement financial applications and increasingly other critical applications. A bug in a smart contract thus could result in a massive loss of valuable digital assets, which has been demonstrated time and time again [8,22]. More importantly, due to the immutability of blockchain (which is one of its fundamental properties), a smart contract cannot be patched once it is deployed. In other words, once deployed, a bug in the smart contract would make it forever vulnerable. We thus must make sure a smart contract is correct before it is deployed.

Existing approaches on tackling the correctness of smart contracts can be roughly categorized into two groups, i.e., those approaches which target common vulnerabilities and those which support (manually specified) full correctness specification. The former includes an extensive list of approaches and tools on static analysis (such as Mythril [18], Oyente [16] and Securify [28]), fuzzing (such as sFuzz [20], Echidna [13], and ConFuzzius [27]), as well as runtime monitoring (such as sGuard [19], Solythesis [15], and Elysium [12]). While the approaches are different, what is common across these approaches is that they all focus on a collection of generic bugs (such as reentrancy, overflow or underflow, frontrunning and frozen funds). While these approaches are undoubtedly useful, they are incapable of identifying contract-specific bugs or showing their absence.

In this work, we propose ιCONTRACT, a fully compositional verification system for verifying and enforcing the correctness of smart contracts. ιCONTRACT supports a rich specification language which allows developers to specify not only the traditional loop invariants and function specifications but also contract invariants (for contract-level specification) and call invariants (for specification of external function calls). We remark that designing a specification language that is relatively easy to use (which is essential in practice), expressive, and makes verification easy is nontrivial. For instance, a smart contract often interacts with other contracts via interfaces. Mishandling such interfaces (e.g., assuming that no contract states are modified by such interfaces or contracts states can be modified arbitrarily) would hinder the verification of contracts. In this work, we annotate external function calls with call invariants (so that we can quantify the behavior of the external function call using a correctness logic formula as well as an incorrectness logic formula). These call invariants can be validated at the runtime and relied upon as assumptions when we verify the calling function.

To evaluate the effectiveness and applicability of ιCONTRACT in practice, we apply ιCONTRACT to verify 10 real-world high-profile contracts. For each contract, a full specification of its correctness is first developed manually, with a total of 1 PhD-month. ιCONTRACT is then applied to verify each of the contracts. The results show that ιCONTRACT not only is scalable for verifying real-world contracts but also uncovering contract-specific bugs. The results are encouraging as it shows that developing a specification for critical but relatively simple programs such as smart contracts is entirely feasible.

To sum up, our main contributions are as follows. First, we propose an approach for the correctness specification of smart contracts which facilitate completely compositional verification, including revert specification (i.e., specifications that capture explicit reverts) as well as call invariants for frame conditions. Second, we develop an implementation of the compositional verification approach for real-world Solidity smart contracts. Lastly, we conduct an evaluation using 10 real-world high-profile smart contracts (with a full specification of their correctness).

2   Overview

2.1   Smart Contracts

The concept of smart contracts was first proposed by Nick Szabo in 1997 [26]. However, it only became a reality after the creation of Ethereum [30] in 2015. An Ethereum smart contract implements a set of rules that aim to manage digital assets in Ethereum accounts including externally owned accounts and contract accounts. Despite a large variety of contract programming languages (e.g., Solidity [5], Vyper [7], and Bamboo [1]), Solidity is the most dominant one for implementing smart contracts. It is a Turing-complete, object-oriented, and statically-typed programming language. A smart contract in Solidity is similar to a class in object-oriented programming languages such as Java or C#. It contains storage variables that stores persistent data and functions. While public functions can be invoked from other accounts to modify storage variables, private functions are internally invoked by other functions. An example of contract written in Solidity is shown in Fig. 1.

2.2   Vulnerability and Correctness

Same as traditional programs, smart contracts can have bugs. For instance, a long list of common bugs have been identified [6], some of which have been exploited and huge financial losses have occurred [8]. Making sure that a smart contract does not repeat the same mistakes merely constitutes the first step towards contract correctness.

An ideal approach for smart contract correctness verification must satisfy the following requirements. First, it must support a rich notion of correctness. This is because each contract is designed for a unique purpose and thus is expected to satisfy a contract-specific specification. Existing approaches that are designed to verify smart contracts against common general vulnerabilities are thus insufficient. Second, it must be fully compositional, i.e., given a contract, we should be able to establish its correctness without relying on external contracts. Furthermore, each functional unit, such as a function or even a loop, should have its own specification so that any kind of global reasoning (even at the contract level) could be avoided. In so doing, the verification system could achieve scalability. Third, it must be fully automatic once the specification is provided. Lastly, it must guarantee that the smart contract satisfies its specification, either through static verification (ideally) or runtime verification (if necessary).

We obviously must pay some price to achieve the above-mentioned goals. Our approach is thus based on two assumptions. First, we make the strong assumption that developers are either requested or required (by stakeholders or certification boards) to provide a correctness specification. While it was sadly proven too strong an assumption for ordinary programs, it may be justifiable for smart contracts due to the reasons mentioned above. Second, we make the assumption that developers are willing to pay some reasonable amount of additional fee (i.e., for runtime checking) in order to guarantee that the smart contract satisfies the specification.

2.3 An Illustrative Example

In the following, we illustrate how our goals are achieved by ICONTRACT through an example. Figure 1 shows a token-issuing smart contract (written according to the ERC20 standard [11]), which is a simplified version of a real-world smart contract named HEALTH[1]. The contract includes global variables *burnFee, devFee, bFee, uniswapV2*, and *balances*. It supports (through a public function) *transfer* of HEALTH tokens (hereafter h-tokens) from account *from* (a.k.a. sender) to account *to* (a.k.a. receiver). Note that the sender is charged with some fee for the transfer. Furthermore, in some cases, it burns (subtracts) an amount (proportional to *value*) of the h-tokens hold by *uniswapV2*, which is a service that swaps h-tokens with BNB (i.e., a token which is often used for token exchange services) or vice versa. Particularly, first, at lines 8–12 if the receiver is *uniswapV2*, the contract swaps *numTokensSell* h-tokens for BNB (line 9). Second, at lines 13–19, if the sender is not *uniswapV2*, the contract burns some h-tokens from *uniswapV2* (line 15). Lastly, at lines 20–26, the contract charges development fee (line 25), burns token (line 26), and transfers the remaining (line 24) to receiver.

To verify the contract, we start with developing a correctness specification. For instance, lines 3–4, 10–11 and 18 constitute the correctness specification of the function _ *transfer*. The specification relies on a set of pre-defined functions, such as reverts_if(p), modifies($\overline{x}$), ensures(p, q), call_modifies($\overline{x}$) and call_inv(p, q). Intuitively, reverts_if(p) says that the transaction reverts if p is satisfied; modifies($\overline{x}$) (respectively call_modifies($\overline{x}$)) says that the function (respectively the external call) only modifies those variables in $\overline{x}$; ensures(p, q) is equivalent to the Hoare triple $\{p\}s\{q\}$ where s is the function body; and call_inv(p, q) right after a function call is a call invariant, where p is a precondition of the call and q is expected to be satisfied after the call. We remark that modifies($\overline{x}$), call_modifies($\overline{x}$) can be regarded as syntactic sugars of certain special cases of ensures(p, q) and call_inv(p, q).

In particular, the specification at line 4 demands that when *value* = 0, no token should be burned. This is important as burning h-tokens reduces the total supply and, thus, increases the price of h-tokens. If h-tokens can be burned unintentionally (e.g., when *value* = 0), attackers could potentially use the function to manipulate the market price. According to the call_modifies($\overline{x}$) at line 11, only variables _ *balances[this]* and _ *balances[uniswapV2]* are modified. The call invariants at lines 10–11 state that the function call at line 9 transfers *numTokensSell* h-tokens from address *this* to address *uniswapV2*. In particular, the *balances[this]* is reduced and *balances[uniswapV2]* is increased by the same amount (i.e., *numTokenSell*). By default, all global variables could be modified in the called function. Line 18 specifies that no variables are modified by the external call.

Once the specification is given, ICONTRACT systematically verifies the contract against the specification. It reports that the specification at line 4 is falsified with a counterexample, i.e., if the sender is not *uniswapV2* and *value* is

---

[1] deployed at BNB chain address 0x32b166e082993af6598a89397e82e123ca44e74e.

```
1  contract Health {
2   ...
3   /// reverts_if(_balances[from] < value)
4   /// ensures(to != uniswapV2 && value == 0 && _balances[from] >= value, _balances
          [_burnAddress] == old(_balances[_burnAddress]))
5   function _transfer(address from, address to, uint value) private {
6     require(_balances[from] >= value);
7     // require(value > 0);
8     if (to == uniswapV2) {
9       UniswapRouter(uniswapV2).swapAndLiquify(numTokensSell);
10      /// call_inv(_balances[this] >= numTokensSell, _balances[this] == old(
              _balances[this] - numTokensSell && _balances[uniswapV2] == old(
              _balances[uniswapV2]) + numTokensSell)
11      /// call_modifies(_balances[this], _balances[uniswapV2])
12    }
13    if (from != uniswapV2) {
14      uint burnValue = _balances[uniswapV2].mul(burnFee).div(1000);
15      _balances[uniswapV2] = _balances[uniswapV2].sub(burnValue);
16      _balances[_burnAddress] = _balances[_burnAddress].add(burnValue);
17      IPancakePair(uniswapV2).sync();
18      /// call_modifies()
19    }
20    uint devValue = value.mul(devFee).div(1000);
21    uint bValue = value.mul(bFee).div(1000);
22    uint newValue = value.sub(devValue).sub(bValue);
23    _balances[from] = _balances[from].sub(value);
24    _balances[to] = _balances[to].add(newValue);
25    _balances[address(this)] = _balances[address(this)].add(devValue);
26    _balances[_burnAddress] = _balances[_burnAddress].add(bValue);
27  }
28
29  function transfer(address to, uint value) public returns(bool) {
30    _transfer(msg.sender, to, value);
31    return true;
32  }
33 }
```

Fig. 1. A sample contract

0, h-tokens are burned from *uniswapV2* on line 15. In other words, this contract could be exploited by abusing the function _transfer to burn h-tokens and manipulate its price, i.e., an attacker first buys some h-tokens, repeatedly calls _transfer as described above, and sells his h-tokens at a higher price.

With the verification result, we can prevent the manipulation by adding one statement *require(value > 0)* at line 7. Afterwards, ICONTRACT reports that the specification is successfully verified. This is because if *value* = 0, the function is reverted. Furthremore, if the user wish to verify the revert, he could annotate another specification as reverts_if(value=0) and invoke ICONTRACT to verify it. Indeed, our system could verify the revert scenario successfully. Alternatively, if the user chooses to conduct runtime verification, ICONTRACT automatically translates the above-mentioned unverified specification into an assertion, which is then validated every time the function is invoked. Note that in the latter case, additional gas will be paid (for executing the assertion) for the correctness.

3   Specification Language

3.1   High-Level Overview

In the following, we present our specification language which is designed to support fully compositional verification of smart contracts at the function level. At a high-level, our specification is composed of function specifications, loop invariants, (external) call invariants and contract invariants.

Function Specifications: Ideally, a user would be able to read the function specification and be fully aware of what the function does. Given a function f, a function specification takes the form of multiple ensures(p, q) statements (at the beginning of the function body), where p and q are predicates that we shall define shortly. Each ensures(p, q) statement represents a Hoare triple $\{p\}f(\overline{x})\{q\}$, i.e., any reachable state at the end of the function (i.e., without reverting) from a state satisfying p must satisfy q. In other words, q is an over-approximation of the states reachable from p.

Loop Invariants: It is well known that loops are difficult when they come to program verification. While there are many existing approaches on synthesizing loop invariants [10,17], for now, we make the assumption that loop invariants are provided as a part of the specification. A loop invariant takes the form of multiple loop_inv(q) statements at the beginning of the loop. Given a loop *while b do s*, loop_inv(q) at the beginning of the loop represents a Hoare triple $\{b \wedge q\}s\{\neg b \wedge q\}$.

Call Invariants: Smart contracts often rely on other smart contracts through external function calls. To avoid global analysis, we assume that each external call is associated with a specification in the form of multiple call_inv(p, q) statements and multiple achieves(p, q) statements. These help to ensure the function call behaves expectedly, i.e., they serve as the minimal requirements on the external contracts that are needed to guarantee the correctness of this contract. Given a function call $m(\overline{e})$, a statement call_inv(p, q) forms a triple $\{p\}m(\overline{e})\{q\}$. If p is satisfied before the call, q is always satisfied after the execution of the function call. Such statements can be used to prevent the well-known reentrancy vulnerability. A statement achieves(p, q) forms a specification in the incorrectness logic [21], which intuitively means that if p is satisfied, it is possible to satisfy q by making the external call.

Contract Invariants: A contract invariant takes the form of multiple cinv(p) statements at the top of the contract and is expected to be satisfied after executing the constructor and every public function in the contract. Although technically it can be captured using function specifications (for both the constructor and every public function), it is typically used to capture contract-level behaviors that are expected to hold always regardless of the functionalities provided

Table 1. Core features of Solidity

Func m	$m(\bar{v}) = s$
Stmt s	s_A | $s; s$ | if e then s else s | while e do s | require(p) | assert(p) | skip
Atom s_A	$v := e$ | $v.m := e$ | $v[e] := e$
Expr e	l | v | $v.m$ | $v[e]$ | $e \oplus e$ | $\odot e$ | $m(\bar{e})$

in the contract.

In addition, ιCONTRACT supports a number of syntactic sugars which ease the writing of specification. For instance, for each function, loop, or external function call, we assume that all global variables may be modified unless a modifies($\bar{x}$) statement is put in place (e.g., function definitions, function calls), which specifies that all except those variables in $\bar{x}$ remain unchanged. Additionally, when variable x is a mapping, we allow users to write modifies($x[a]$) where a is constant value to state that only the value at location a of x is modified, while the values at other locations are not.

In terms of specifying the expected behaviors of smart contracts, our specification language has mulitple advantages over existing approaches [14,23,25]. First, our specification language is designed to avoid global reasoning with the help of call invariants. Second, the reverts_if(p) statements allow us to easily capture explicit reverts which are very common in smart contracts in the form of *require, revert()* and so on. Note that this feature is missed from approaches such as Solc-verify and as a result, those respective tools often generate false alarms, i.e., reporting violation of postcondition on transactions that ought to be reverted. Last, our specification is mostly based on well-known and well-founded concepts which makes it easy to adopt.

3.2 Formalization

In the following, we provide the necessary formalization of our specification language as well as smart contracts so that we can present precisely how our approach works. Note that since all our verification effort (including static verification and runtime verification) takes place at the function-level, all we need to formalize are smart contract functions and function-level specification.

Defining Smart Contracts: To ease the discussion hereafter, we model Solidity's core (function-level) features using the language presented in Table 1. A function m includes parameters $\bar{v}$, and a body statement s. A statement s is an atomic statement s_A, a conditional statement, a while loop, an assertion, revert statement, and it also can be a sequence of statements (according to the definition shown in Table 1). An atomic statement s_A is an assignment to a variable ($v := e$), an assignment to member of a variable ($v.m := e$), or an assignment to an array element ($v[e] := e$). An expression e is a literal l, a variable v, a member access $v.m$, an index access $v[e]$, a binary expression $e \oplus e$, a unary expression $\odot e$, or a call $v.m(\bar{e})$ of a local function (in the same contract) or an external function (in a different contract). We use rev as a preserved variable for revert condition: It is true if the contract has been reverted. Note that we can simply transform other Solidity features into our core language features such as the statement $require(a)$ is equivalent to the statement i) $assert(a \wedge \neg rev)$ in verifying code against a function variant or ii) $revert(\neg a \wedge rev)$ in the verification of reverts_if(...).

To define the semantics of smart contracts, we define a set Var contains all the variables in the contract, a set Mem contains all the members of the data structures in the contract, a set of mapping for arrays A, and data structures (where $A \cap Var = \emptyset$), a set Loc contains all the memory locations, a set Val contains all non-memory values (i.e., $Val = Int \cup Float \cup Bool \cup Str$, with Int, $Float$, $Bool$, and Str are the sets containing integer, floating-point, boolean, and string literals). We use two mapping functions $S \in Stacks$ and $H \in Heaps$ to keep track of the execution environment. Consequently, a program state $\sigma_c \in States$ is defined by a pair of stack and heap, as follows.

$$
\begin{aligned}
S \in Stacks &=_{\text{def}} Var \to (Val \cup Loc) \\
H \in Heaps &=_{\text{def}} Loc \to (Type \to (Mem \cup Int) \to (Val \cup Loc)) \\
\sigma_c \in States &=_{\text{def}} Stacks \times Heaps
\end{aligned}
$$

where the set $Type$ contains all the data structure types defined in the contract as well as the array type.

We define a standard small-step operational semantics of smart contracts (based on the semantics of Solidity). A configuration C is a pair (s, σ_c) where s is a program and σ_c is a program state (i.e., the valuation of both S and H). The semantics is given by a binary relation, $\leadsto$, on configurations. Its intended interpretation is that $(s, \sigma_c) \leadsto (s', \sigma_c')$ holds if the execution of the statement in the configuration (s, σ_c) can result in the new program configuration (s', σ_c'). An execution (of s) is a possibly infinite sequence of configurations $(C_i)_{i \geq 0}$ with $C_0 = (s, \_)$ such that $C_i \leadsto C_{i+1}$ for all $i \geq 0$. We define $\leadsto^*$, the reflexive-transitive closure of $\leadsto$, to capture finite executions $(C_i)_{0 \leq i \leq n}$. The details of the small step semantics is present in Fig. 2.

Defining the Specification Language: Our specification language is constituted of predicates defined using the syntax below.

$$
\begin{aligned}
\Phi, p, q &:= \Psi \mid \Phi \vee \Phi \qquad \Psi := a \otimes a \mid \Psi \wedge \Psi \\
a &:= e \mid a \oplus a \mid \odot a \quad e := l \mid v \mid v[a] \mid v.m \mid old(v) \mid g(v)
\end{aligned}
$$

In general, a predicate Φ is a disjunction with one or multiple conjunctions Ψ. Each conjunct in Ψ is a relational predicate with $\otimes$ is a relational operator (i.e., $>, \geq, =, \neq, <, \leq$). The left-hand side and right-hand side of a relational predicate are arithmetic expressions. An arithmetic expression may have one atomic expression or multiple of them connected by binary operators $\oplus$ (i.e., $+, -, *, /$) or unary operators $\odot$ (i.e., $\neg, -$). An atomic expressions includes

$$\frac{}{\langle S,H\rangle \vdash l \Downarrow l}\;\text{Const} \qquad \frac{S(v)=l \quad H(l)=(type(v),m,k)}{\langle S,H\rangle \vdash v.m \Downarrow k}\;\text{Access}$$

$$\frac{}{\langle S,H\rangle \vdash v \Downarrow S(v)}\;\text{Var} \qquad \frac{S(v)=l \quad S(e)=i \quad H(l)=(type(v),i,k)}{\langle S,H\rangle \vdash v[e] \Downarrow k}\;\text{Select}$$

$$\frac{\langle S,H\rangle \vdash e_1 \Downarrow k_1 \quad \langle S,H\rangle \vdash e_2 \Downarrow k_2}{\langle S,H\rangle \vdash e_1 \oplus e_2 \Downarrow k_1 \oplus k_2}\;\text{Binary} \qquad \frac{\langle S,H\rangle \vdash e \Downarrow k_1}{\langle S,H\rangle \vdash \odot e \Downarrow \odot k_1}\;\text{Unary}$$

$$\frac{}{\langle S,H\rangle, \text{revert}; s_2 \rightsquigarrow \langle S_0,H_0\rangle, \text{skip}}\;\text{Revert} \qquad \frac{}{\langle S,H\rangle, \text{skip}; s_2 \rightsquigarrow \langle S,H\rangle, s_2}\;\text{Skip}$$

$$\frac{\langle S,H\rangle, s_1 \rightsquigarrow \langle S_1,H_1\rangle, s_{1'}}{\langle S,H\rangle, s_1; s_2 \rightsquigarrow \langle S_1,H_1\rangle, s_{1'}; s_2}\;\text{Seq} \qquad \frac{\langle S,H\rangle, s_1 \rightsquigarrow \langle S_1,H_1\rangle, \text{abort}}{\langle S,H\rangle, s_1; s_2 \rightsquigarrow \langle S_1,H_1\rangle, \text{abort}}\;\text{Seq-Err}$$

$$\frac{\langle S,H\rangle \vdash e \Downarrow k \quad S_1 = S[v \leftarrow k]}{\langle S,H\rangle, v := e \rightsquigarrow \langle S_1,H\rangle, \text{skip}}\;\text{Assign-1} \qquad \frac{\langle S,H\rangle \vdash v \Downarrow k \quad k \notin dom(H)}{\langle S,H\rangle, v.m := e \rightsquigarrow \langle S,H\rangle, \text{abort}}\;\text{Err1}$$

$$\frac{\langle S,H\rangle \vdash v \Downarrow k \quad k \in dom(H) \quad \langle S,H\rangle \vdash e \Downarrow k_1 \quad H_1 = H[(k,type(v),m) \leftarrow k_1]}{\langle S,H\rangle, v.m := e \rightsquigarrow \langle S,H_1\rangle, \text{skip}}\;\text{Assign-2}$$

$$\frac{\langle S,H\rangle \vdash v \Downarrow k \quad \langle S,H\rangle \vdash e_1 \Downarrow k_1 \quad \langle S,H\rangle \vdash e_2 \Downarrow k_2 \quad H_1 = H[(k,Array,k_1) \leftarrow k_2]}{\langle S,H\rangle, v[e_1] := e_2 \rightsquigarrow \langle S,H_1\rangle, \text{skip}}\;\text{Assign-3}$$

$$\frac{\langle S,H\rangle \vdash v \Downarrow k \quad k \notin dom(H)}{\langle S,H\rangle, v[e_1] := e_2 \rightsquigarrow \langle S,H_1\rangle, \text{abort}}\;\text{Err2} \qquad \frac{\langle S,H\rangle \vdash e_1 \Downarrow k_1 \quad k_1 \notin size(v)}{\langle S,H\rangle, v[e_1] := e_2 \rightsquigarrow \langle S,H_1\rangle, \text{abort}}\;\text{Err3}$$

$$\frac{\langle S,H\rangle \vdash b \Downarrow True}{\langle S,H\rangle, \text{if } b \text{ then } s \text{ else } s' \rightsquigarrow \langle S,H\rangle, s}\;\text{If-T} \qquad \frac{\langle S,H\rangle \vdash b \Downarrow False}{\langle S,H\rangle, \text{if } b \text{ then } s \text{ else } s' \rightsquigarrow \langle S,H\rangle, s'}\;\text{If-F}$$

$$\frac{\langle S,H\rangle \vdash b \Downarrow True}{\langle S,H\rangle, \text{while } b \text{ do } s \rightsquigarrow \langle S,H\rangle, s; \text{while } b \text{ do } s}\;\text{Loop-T}$$

$$\frac{\langle S,H\rangle \vdash b \Downarrow False}{\langle S,H\rangle, \text{while } b \text{ do } s \rightsquigarrow \langle S,H\rangle, \text{skip}}\;\text{Loop-F}$$

$$\frac{v.m(\bar{p}) = s \quad \langle S,H\rangle \vdash \bar{e} \Downarrow \bar{k} \quad S' = S[\bar{p} \leftarrow \bar{k}]}{\langle S,H\rangle \vdash v.m(\bar{e}) \rightsquigarrow \langle S',H\rangle, s}\;\text{Call}$$

Fig. 2. Small-step operational semantics of the smart contract language, given by the binary relation $\rightsquigarrow$ over $Stacks \times Heaps$

a literal l, a variable v, a member access $v.m$, and an index access $v[a]$. The expression $v.m$ accesses the value stored in the member m of a struct v, whereas the expression $v[a]$ accesses the value at key a of a mapping v. In addition, we provide a function $old(v)$ which returns the value of variable v at the beginning of the function (for function specifications) or the loop (for loop invariant) or before an external function call (for call invariants). Moreover, we support a library of externally defined function $g(v)$. One example is the sum function, which, given a mapping v, computes the sum of all values stored in v.

$$
\begin{aligned}
S, H &\models \Phi_1 \vee \Phi_2 &&\textbf{iff } (S, H \models \Phi_1) \vee (S, H \models \Phi_2)\\
S, H &\models \Psi_1 \wedge \Psi_2 &&\textbf{iff } (S, H \models \Psi_1) \wedge (S, H \models \Psi_2)\\
S, H &\models a_1 \otimes a_2 &&\textbf{iff } (S, H \models a_1 = k_1) \wedge (S, H \models a_2 = k_2) \wedge (k_1 \otimes k_2)\\
S, H &\models a_1 \oplus a_2 = k &&\textbf{iff } (S, H \models a_1 = k_1) \wedge (S, H \models a_2 = k_2) \wedge (k_1 \oplus k_2 = k)\\
S, H &\models \odot a = k &&\textbf{iff } (S, H \models a = k_1) \wedge (\odot k_1 = k)\\
S, H &\models l = l &&\textbf{iff true}\\
S, H &\models v = k &&\textbf{iff } S(v) = k\\
S, H &\models v[a] = k &&\textbf{iff } S(v) \in dom(H) \wedge 0 \geq S(a) < size(v) \wedge H(S(v)) = (Array, S(a), k)\\
S, H &\models v.m = k &&\textbf{iff } S(v) \in dom(H) \wedge H(S(v)) = (type(v), m, k)\\
S, H &\models old(v) = k &&\textbf{iff } S_0, H_0 \models v = k\\
S, H &\models sum(v) = k &&\textbf{iff } type(v) = Array \wedge S(v) \in dom(H) \wedge \sum_{i=0}^{size(v)}\{v[i]\} = k
\end{aligned}
$$

Fig. 3. Specification formula semantic where $dom(f)$ returns the domain of function f, $size(v)$ the range of index of the array v.

The semantics is defined according to a satisfaction relation $S, H \models \Phi$ which is defined in a common way, as shown in Fig. 3. Next, we define the correctness in our specification language. First, regarding contract invariants, given a contract c associated with multiple cinv(p) statements, the contract is correct if and only if each ensures(p, p) is satisfied by all the public functions including the constructor. Second, regarding function specifications, given a function $m(\overline{v}) = s$ associated with multiple ensures(p, q) and reverts_if(p') statements, the function is correct iff for each ensures(p, q) statement, the following is satisfied.

$$
\forall \sigma_c, \sigma'_c.\ \sigma_c \models p \wedge (s, \sigma_c) \rightsquigarrow^* (\text{skip}, \sigma'_c) \implies \sigma'_c \models q
$$

Furthermore, for each reverts_if(p') statement, the following is satisfied

$$
\forall \sigma_c, \sigma'_c.\ \sigma_c \models p' \wedge (s, \sigma_c) \rightsquigarrow^* (\text{require}(b), \sigma'_c) \implies \sigma'_c \models \neg b
$$

Third, regarding loop invariants, given a loop *while b do s* associated with an loop_inv(q) statement at the beginning, the following must be satisfied where L is a function that filters states satisfying b.

$$
\forall \sigma_c, \sigma'_c.\ \sigma_c \models q \wedge (s, L(\sigma_c, b)) \rightsquigarrow^* (\text{skip}, \sigma'_c) \implies \sigma'_c \models q
$$

Fourth, for each achieves(p, q), the following must be satisfied.

$$
\forall \sigma'_c. \exists \sigma_c.\ \sigma'_c \models q \implies \sigma_c \models p \wedge (s, \sigma_c) \rightsquigarrow^* (\text{skip}, \sigma'_c)
$$

Lastly, regarding call invariants, given an external function call $m(\overline{e})$ associated with multiple call_inv(p, q), for any implementation s of $m(\overline{e})$, the following must be satisfied: $\forall \sigma_c, \sigma'_c.\ \sigma_c \models p \wedge (s, \sigma_c) \rightsquigarrow^* (\text{skip}, \sigma'_c) \implies \sigma'_c \models q$.

4 Verification

We present our compositional verification algorithm by first defining an encoding function $post(\sigma_i, s_i)$ and illustrating how to utilize it to validate function specification ensures(p, q) and revert specification reverts_if(p). We remark that we abuse the notation σ_i to represent a symbolic state where its syntax is similar to our specification language. Furthermore, we provide encoding rules that substitute loops and function calls with their specifications.

4.1   Function Validation

We define an encoding function $post(\sigma_i, s_i)$ that takes a pre-state σ_i and a statement s_i as inputs, and procedure post-states σ_k as output. Given a function $m(\overline{v}) = s$ which may contain loops as well as internal and external function calls, our validations are defined as follows. A function specification ensures(p, q) with implementation s is verified if $post(p, s)$ returns σ such that $\sigma \Rightarrow q$. The execution $post(p, s)$ indicates that the encoding process starts with pre-state p. After processing the statement s, the validation formula $\sigma \Rightarrow q$ means that if the function is not reverted then the encoding starts with p implies the post-condition q. Similarly, a specification reverts_if(p) is verified if $post(p, s)$ returns the post-state $\sigma \wedge rev$ at exits. Note that the procedure of verifying ensures(p, p) utilizes the encoding rule REVERT-1. On the other hand, other REVERT rules, such as REVERT-2 and REVERT-3, are employed for the verification of reverts_if(p).

4.2   Generating Proof Obligations

We define encoding function $post(\sigma_i, s_i)$ using encoding rules, each of which is of the following form.

$$\frac{premise_0 \quad ... \quad premise_i}{\sigma_i, s_i \leadsto \sigma_k}$$

This transition rule means given a pre-state σ_i, a statement s_i, it executes $premise_0$, ..., $premise_i$ to obtain the post-state σ_k. The encoding rules are shown in Fig. 4. Note that the encoding transforms the code into the predicates supported by off-the-shelf SMT solver Z3. While most of the syntax is self-explanatory, we use the notation $v[a \rightarrow l]$ to represent an array with $v[a \rightarrow l][a'] = v[a']$ when $a' \neq a$ and $v[a \rightarrow l][a] = l$.

The rules are divided into three groups, i.e., rules for local operations, rules for external function calls, and rules for revert. Rules for local operations include SEQ, ASSIGN-1, ASSIGN-2, ASSIGN-3, IF and LOOP. They are similar to the traditional Hoare rules. In the ASSIGN-2 and ASSIGN-3, we substitute v before the assignment with x, and set the current v as the result of update value $e[x/v]$ to the value located at index $m[x/v]$ or property m. In the ASSIGN-2, for each write operation to $v[m]$, we compute sum(v) by adding the current sum u to the difference between the new value e and the old value $v[m]$, i.e., $u' = u + e - v[m]$. The LOOP substitutes the loop with its invariant and exiting condition (i.e., $\neg b$).

Rules for revert include REVERT-1 (the non-revert condition is part of the pre-condition), REVERT-2 (the revert condition met) and REVERT-3 (the revert condition is not met). The idea is that the function is reverted if any of the condition leading to revert is satisfied. If the revert condition is satisfied, the

$$\frac{\sigma, s_1 \rightsquigarrow q_1 \quad q_1, s_2 \rightsquigarrow \sigma_2}{\sigma, s_1; s_2 \rightsquigarrow \sigma_2} \text{ SEQ} \qquad \frac{\sigma' = \exists x.\ \sigma[x/v] \wedge v = e[x/v]}{\sigma, v := e \rightsquigarrow \sigma'} \text{ ASSIGN-1}$$

$$\frac{u' = u + e - v[m] \quad \sigma' = \exists x.\ \sigma[x/v] \wedge v = x[m[x/v] \to e[x/v]]}{\sigma \wedge \mathrm{sum}(v) = u, v[m] := e \rightsquigarrow \sigma' \wedge \mathrm{sum}(v) = u'} \text{ ASSIGN-2}$$

$$\frac{}{\sigma \wedge rev, s \rightsquigarrow \sigma \wedge rev} \text{ REV-PROP} \qquad \frac{\sigma' = \exists x.\ \sigma[x/v] \wedge v = x[m \to e[x/v]]}{\sigma, v.m := e \rightsquigarrow \sigma'} \text{ ASSIGN-3}$$

$$\frac{\sigma \wedge b, s_0 \rightsquigarrow \sigma_1 \quad \sigma \wedge \neg b, s_1 \rightsquigarrow \sigma_2}{\sigma, \text{if } b \text{ then } s_0 \text{ else } s_1 \rightsquigarrow \sigma_1 \vee \sigma_2} \text{ IF} \qquad \frac{\sigma \Rightarrow q}{\sigma, \mathrm{assert}(q) \rightsquigarrow \sigma} \text{ ASSERT}$$

$$\frac{\sigma' = \sigma \wedge p}{\sigma, require(p) \rightsquigarrow \sigma'} \text{ REVERT-1} \qquad \frac{\sigma \Rightarrow \neg p}{\sigma, require(p) \rightsquigarrow \sigma \wedge rev} \text{ REVERT-2}$$

$$\frac{\sigma \not\Rightarrow \neg p}{\sigma, require(p) \rightsquigarrow \sigma} \text{ REVERT-3}$$

$$\frac{\sigma' = \exists \bar{x}.\ \sigma[\bar{x}/\bar{v}] \wedge p \wedge \neg b}{\sigma, \mathrm{modifies}(\bar{v}); \mathrm{loop\_inv}(p); \text{while } b \text{ do } s \rightsquigarrow \sigma'} \text{ LOOP}$$

$$\frac{\mathrm{reverts\_if}(p) \in \mathrm{SPEC}(m(\bar{e})) \quad \sigma, require(\neg p); m(\bar{e}) \rightsquigarrow \sigma'}{\sigma, m(\bar{e}) \rightsquigarrow \sigma'} \text{ REVERT-INTER}$$

$$\frac{\sigma \Rightarrow p \quad \sigma' = \exists \bar{x}.\ \sigma[\bar{x}/\bar{v}] \wedge q}{\sigma, \mathrm{modifies}(\bar{v}); finv(p,q); m(\bar{e}) \rightsquigarrow \sigma'} \text{ CALL-SPEC}$$

Fig. 4. Encoding rules (where $finv(p,q)$ is ensures(p, q) or call_inv(p, q)) (Color figure online)

value of *rev* is set, and after that our system skips all the remaining statements by using rule REV-PROP.

Rules for external function calls include CALL-SPEC, which replaces function calls using either function specifications (if it calls for a local function) or call invariants (if it calls for an external function). This rule updates modified variables $\bar{v}$ through the substitutions $\sigma[\bar{x}/\bar{v}]$. Note that, to propagate the reverts_if(p) back to the caller, via rule REVERT-INTER, we simply convert it to $require(\neg p)$ before the function call is encoded. Moreover, each ensures(p, q) is lifted to the context of the current function by substituting free variables appearing on parameters with their corresponding arguments.

Note that the correctness specification may be over-approximating and thus our verification may lead to false alarms and spurious counterexamples. Instead of running test cases with extra costs, the incorrectness specification associated with external function calls is used to construct counterexamples. According to the concrete values from counterexamples, we first determine an execution path leading to the violation, and then use the achieves(p, q) statements associated with the involved external function calls to check whether the counterexample is real. We develop another predicate $post_U(p, s)$ to compute under-approximating post-states for the implementation s, then our system confirms the bug described in the spec if $q \Rightarrow \sigma$. In term of encoding for $post_U$, dropping execution paths is allowed in incorrectness logic. Therefore, the number of loop iterations can be freely chosen. Only the true-branch or the false-branch is selected while encoding an if-statement. If there is an execution path that satisfies the incorrectness specification then the counterexample is determined to be a real violation. Finally, to handle function call $m(\overline{e})$; modifies$(\overline{v})$; achieves(p', q') at the calling states σ, it first tests $p' \Rightarrow \sigma$. If this test succeeds, it produces $\sigma[\overline{x}/\overline{v}] \wedge q'$ as the post-states. Otherwise, if $\overline{v} \cap \textsc{FreeVars}(\sigma) = \emptyset$, it checks $\textsc{Sat}(p' \wedge \sigma)$. If it is satisfied, it produces $\sigma[\overline{x}/\overline{v}] \wedge q'$ as the post-states. The soundness of the former comes from Consequence rule and the later is from Constancy rule in incorrectness logic.

5   Implementation and Evaluation

5.1   Implementation

iContract is implemented with around 1K lines of Python code. It supports most features of Solidity version 0.5.1 including inheritance and important built-in functions (e.g., *send*, and *call*). iContract uses a locally installed Solidity compiler to compile a user-provided Solidity file into a JSON file containing the typed abstract syntax tree (AST). Then, iContract analyzes the AST to encode contracts into predicates using the Z3 library. We leverage NatSpec [4] format to define our own specifications.

The encoding is mostly straightforward except some relevant details that we discuss below. We use SMT Integer to model int/unsigned and int/address and so on[2]. To support contract inheritance, we implement a symbol table which allows us to query global variables and functions of parent contracts using inheritance tree provided by the Solidity compiler. We also take into account function overriding and variable hiding.

Our current implementation has several limitations. First, it does not support low-level API calls including inline assembly, Application Binary Interface functions, and bitwise operations. Second, iContract does not compute gas consumption to determine out-of-gas exceptions. Last, iContract analyzes contracts without the presence of aliasing. Note that although Solidity allows two variables reference to the same data location (i.e., aliasing), it is not very common in Solidity and we leave it to future work.

5.2   Experimental Evaluation

In the following, we design and conduct multiple experiments to answer the following research questions (RQ).

- RQ1: Can iContract verify real-world smart contracts?
- RQ2: How does iContract compare with Solc-verify [14], a state-of-the-art tool for verifying function-level properties?

---

[2] Note that runtime checking for arithmetic overflow has been introduced since Solidity 0.8 and thus no longer an issue.

Table 2. Statistics on verified contracts

Project	#Contracts	#Functions	#Ifs	#Specifications	LOC	#Transactions (mil)
BAT	4	16	20	17	179	3.97
BNB	2	13	22	25	150	1.00
HT	4	13	4	2	127	0.67
HOT	3	22	29	28	279	0.95
IOTX	8	32	28	35	500	0.28
QNT	5	24	13	16	239	1.21
MANA	11	28	21	70	282	2.50
ZIL	9	35	42	70	353	0.44
NXM	3	37	36	40	448	0.12
SHIB	4	33	12	33	448	9.5

RQ1 aims to evaluate whether ICONTRACT is useful for some practical smart contracts. RQ2 aims to evaluate whether ICONTRACT's approach (in particular, its specification language) can achieve its goals better than existing approaches.

In the following, we present the evaluation results and answer the questions. All our experiments are conducted on a single processor running an Ubuntu 16.04.6 LTS machine with Intel(R) Core(TM) i9-9900 CPU @ 3.10 GHz and 64 GB of memory. The timeout is set to be 5 min for verifying the specification. Our implementation and the verified contracts are available online [2].

RQ1: To answer this question, we identify a set of 10 high-profile projects from EtherScan [3]. The relevant statistic of these contracts is shown in Table 2. The table shows the name of each project. For each project, it shows the number of contracts (#Contracts), the number of functions (#Functions), the number of if-statements (#Ifs), the number of specification statements (#Specifications), line of codes (LOC), and the number of transactions (#Transactions) in millions. Most of them have over 200 lines of code and 20 functions. Each project is associated with a Solidity file, which typically contains multiple contracts including a main one as well as library or parent contracts. Since not all smart contracts are written in the same Solidity versions, we have to convert them to a fixed version (i.e., 0.5.1). This is necessary to ensure the consistency of our verification results. All specifications are manually written by the authors and directly injected into the Solidity files. The specifications are written in such a way that they describe the logic of each function as precise as possible. There are 124 reverts_if(), 2 contract invariants, 4 call invariants, 206 function specifications.

The verification results for each project is shown in Table 3 under column ICONTRACT. The column #V shows the number of specifications that were successfully verified. The column #F shows the number of falsified specifications. The column Time shows the average verification time in seconds. Since we group our specifications into a single specification to compare with Solc-verify, the column #Sp is less than the one shown in Table 2. Most of the projects are

```
1 /// reverts_if(_amount == 0);
2 function mint(address _to, uint256 _amount) private {
3   // Guard against overflow
4   require(balances[_to] + _amount > balances[_to]);
5   balances[_to] = balances[_to].add(_amount);
6 }
```

Fig. 5. An example illustrating the effectiveness of reverts_if() in identifying incorrect require statements

verified within 5 s. Among 336 specification statements, 3 of them are falsified. After manually investigating them, we confirm that ICONTRACT exposes contract invariant violations in HOT, QNT and BNB. First, BNB stores the frozen tokens in a mapping called *freezeOf*. When tokens are frozen, they are not subtracted from *totalSupply*. As a result, sum(*balances*) $\neq$ *totalSupply*. Second, the *totalSupply* of QNT remains unchanged even when refresh QNT is created by calling the function *mint*. Again, sum(balances) $\neq$ *totalSupply*. Third, as shown in Fig. 5, HOT has the following *require* statement at line 4 which is meant to prevent overflow according to the documentation. However, it also prevents non-overflow cases such as when $\_amount = 0$.

RQ2: To answer RQ2, we compare ICONTRACT against Solc-verify, a state-of-the-art tool for verifying function-level properties of smart contracts [14]. Solc-verify is selected as it shares much similarity with ICONTRACT, i.e., it supports contract, function and loop invariants. Other verifiers either do not support user-defined specification (such as Verismart [24]), or restrict their specification in specific forms (e.g., linear temporal logic such as in Verx [23] and SmartPulse [25]), which are not expressive enough to capture the specification required to verify the correctness of the contracts used in our experiments. We first translate all specifications written in our language to the ones supported by Solc-verify. The translation is not straightforward due to the fact that Solc-verify does not support reverts_if(p) and call invariants. We thus remove the call invariants, reverts_if(p) and convert our ensures(p, q) statements into Solc-verify's specifications. The results are summarized in Table 3 under the column *Solc-verify*. While Solc-verify does verify most of the contracts, results inconsistent with ours are reported for 3 contracts, as shown in column #Consistent. All of them are falsified by Solc but are verified by ICONTRACT. Our investigation shows that the reason is the missing specifications for external function calls, i.e., the call invariants. In the ZIL project, the external function call *token.transfer* (*owner, amount*) transfers tokens to the *owner*. Solc-verify assumes that all global variables are modified after the call and thus sum(balances) = *totalSupply* is falsified. In contrast, our call invariants indicate that the variable *balances* is unchanged and the specification sum(balances) = *totalSupply* is preserved. In the BAT and BNB projects, well-known external functions call such as *send()* and *transfer()* are not properly handled in Solc-verify. We remark that besides supporting specification features such as reverts_if(p) and call invariants, ICON-TRACT works on Solidity code directly without converting it to another language

Table 3. Comparison against Solc-verify

Project	# Sp	ICONTRACT			Solc-Verify			
		#V	#F	Time (s)	#V	#F	Consistent	Time (s)
BAT	13	13	0	4.93	12	1	×	4.51
BNB	15	14	1	7.20	13	2	×	4.00
HT	2	2	0	1.10	2	0	✓	2.77
HOT	17	17	0	1.41	17	0	✓	4.38
IOTX	23	23	0	2.09	23	0	✓	4.26
QNT	11	10	1	1.33	10	1	✓	4.69
MANA	42	42	0	3.94	42	0	✓	6.63
ZIL	40	40	0	4.61	39	1	×	7.13
NXM	22	22	0	2.24	22	0	✓	6.31
SHIB	23	23	0	1.76	23	0	✓	5.95

for verification. This makes verification of the falsified specification statements straightforward in ICONTRACT, i.e., by transforming the respective undefined functions into assertions.

6   Related Work and Conclusion

The verification for smart contracts has been the interests of multiple researchers. The systems that are closely related to ours are Solc-verify [14] and MVP [9]. Solc-verify translates Solidity contracts into the Boogie intermediate language, and relies on the Boogie system for verification. It supports contract invariant, loop invariant, and pre-/post conditions. In particular, Solc-verify assertion language targets the safety of low-level properties (e.g., the absence of overflows) and high-level contract invariants (e.g., the sum of user balances equates to the total supply). Similarly, Dill *et al.* recently proposed MVP, a static verifier based on the Boogie verifier, for smart contracts in the Move language [9]. MVP supports both contract invariants and functional invariants via pre/post conditions. It also generates global invariants for runtime checking. MVP enables an alias-free memory model through reference elimination which relies on borrow semantics. MVP was deployed for continuous verification on Move code and Diem blockchain. ICONTRACT supports all the features supported by Solc-verify and MVP, and additionally supports features like revert and call invariants that are designed to handle dynamic dispatching on unknown function calls.

There are several other verification systems for smart contracts developed in the last few years, e.g., VeriSmart [24], SmartACE [29], and VerX [23]. VeriSmart [24] focuses on intra-procedural analysis for verifying arithmetic (over- and under-flows) safety. The main contribution of their work is an algorithm that could refine transaction invariants of arbitrary transactions. These invariants boost the precision of such verification. However, VeriSmart lacks inter-procedural reasoning. SmartACE [29] is a framework that can verify user-annotated assertions by running multiple independent analysers. It models smart contract library and transforms the verification problem into off-the-self analysers like constrained Horn clause solving (e.g., SeaHorn) for correctness verification. In contrast, ICONTRACT presents a built-in static analyser for a rich specification. Finally, VerX [23] focuses on temporal properties of Ethereum contracts. It reduces the temporal safety verification to reachability verification and applies the state-of-the-art reachability checking technique. While temporal logic based specification is useful for specifying global properties, we believe that our specification language is better for supporting the motto of "specification is law" and has its advantage on compositional verification.

To conclude, in this work, we design a static verification system with a specification language which supports fully compositional verification. Using ICONTRACT, we have verified 10 high-profile smart contracts against manually developed detailed specifications, many of which are beyond the capacity of existing verifiers. In the future, we intend to improve the performance of ICONTRACT further with optimization techniques.

References

1. Bamboo: a language for morphing smart contracts. https://github.com/pirapira/bamboo
2. Dataset. https://anonymous.4open.science/r/zero1-0DEE/
3. Etherscan. https://etherscan.io/
4. Natspec format. https://docs.soliditylang.org/en/v0.8.17/natspec-format.html
5. Solidity - Solidity documentation. https://docs.soliditylang.org/en/stable/
6. swcregistry. https://swcregistry.io/
7. Vyper - Vyper documentation. https://docs.vyperlang.org/en/stable/
8. Daian, P.: DAO exploit. https://hackingdistributed.com/2016/06/18/analysis-of-the-dao-exploit/
9. Dill, D., Grieskamp, W., Park, J., Qadeer, S., Xu, M., Zhong, E.: Fast and reliable formal verification of smart contracts with the move prover. In: TACAS 2022. LNCS, vol. 13243, pp. 183–200. Springer, Cham (2022). https://doi.org/10.1007/978-3-030-99524-9_10
10. Ernst, M.D., et al.: The Daikon system for dynamic detection of likely invariants. Sci. Comput. Program. 69(1–3), 35–45 (2007)
11. Fabian Vogelsteller, V.B.: EIP-20: token standard, November 2015. https://eips.ethereum.org/EIPS/eip-20
12. Ferreira Torres, C., Jonker, H., State, R.: Elysium: context-aware bytecode-level patching to automatically heal vulnerable smart contracts. In: Proceedings of the 25th International Symposium on Research in Attacks, Intrusions and Defenses, pp. 115–128 (2022)
13. Grieco, G., Song, W., Cygan, A., Feist, J., Groce, A.: Echidna: effective, usable, and fast fuzzing for smart contracts. In: Proceedings of the 29th ACM SIGSOFT International Symposium on Software Testing and Analysis, pp. 557–560 (2020)
14. Hajdu, Á., Jovanović, D.: SOLC-VERIFY: a modular verifier for solidity smart contracts. In: Chakraborty, S., Navas, J.A. (eds.) VSTTE 2019. LNCS, vol. 12031, pp. 161–179. Springer, Cham (2020). https://doi.org/10.1007/978-3-030-41600-3_11

15. Li, A., Choi, J.A., Long, F.: Securing smart contract with runtime validation. In: Proceedings of the 41st ACM SIGPLAN Conference on Programming Language Design and Implementation, pp. 438–453 (2020)
16. Luu, L., Chu, D.H., Olickel, H., Saxena, P., Hobor, A.: Making smart contracts smarter. In: Proceedings of the 2016 ACM SIGSAC Conference on Computer and Communications Security, pp. 254–269 (2016)
17. Mariano, B., Chen, Y., Feng, Y., Lahiri, S.K., Dillig, I.: Demystifying loops in smart contracts. In: 2020 35th IEEE/ACM International Conference on Automated Software Engineering (ASE), pp. 262–274 (2020)
18. Mueller, B.: Smashing ethereum smart contracts for fun and real profit. HITB SECCONF Amsterdam **9**, 54 (2018)
19. Nguyen, T.D., Pham, L.H., Sun, J.: SGUARD: towards fixing vulnerable smart contracts automatically. In: 42nd IEEE Symposium on Security and Privacy, SP 2021, San Francisco, CA, USA, 24–27 May 2021, pp. 1215–1229. IEEE (2021). https://doi.org/10.1109/SP40001.2021.00057
20. Nguyen, T.D., Pham, L.H., Sun, J., Lin, Y., Minh, Q.T.: sFuzz: an efficient adaptive fuzzer for solidity smart contracts. In: Proceedings of the ACM/IEEE 42nd International Conference on Software Engineering, pp. 778–788 (2020)
21. O'Hearn, P.W.: Incorrectness logic. Proc. ACM Program. Lang. **4**(POPL) (2019). https://doi.org/10.1145/3371078
22. Palladino, S.: The parity wallet hack explained, July 2017. https://blog.openzeppelin.com/on-the-parity-wallet-multisig-hack-405a8c12e8f7/
23. Permenev, A., Dimitrov, D., Tsankov, P., Drachsler-Cohen, D., Vechev, M.: VerX: safety verification of smart contracts. In: 2020 IEEE Symposium on Security and Privacy (SP), pp. 1661–1677 (2020). https://doi.org/10.1109/SP40000.2020.00024
24. So, S., Lee, M., Park, J., Lee, H., Oh, H.: VERISMART: a highly precise safety verifier for ethereum smart contracts. In: 2020 IEEE Symposium on Security and Privacy (SP), pp. 1678–1694 (2020)
25. Stephens, J., Ferles, K., Mariano, B., Lahiri, S., Dillig, I.: SMARTPULSE: automated checking of temporal properties in smart contracts. In: 2021 IEEE Symposium on Security and Privacy (SP), pp. 555–571. IEEE (2021)
26. Szabo, N.: Formalizing and securing relationships on public networks. First Monday (1997)
27. Torres, C.F., Iannillo, A.K., Gervais, A., State, R.: ConFuzzius: a data dependency-aware hybrid fuzzer for smart contracts. In: 2021 IEEE European Symposium on Security and Privacy (EuroS&P), pp. 103–119. IEEE (2021)
28. Tsankov, P., Dan, A., Drachsler-Cohen, D., Gervais, A., Buenzli, F., Vechev, M.: Securify: practical security analysis of smart contracts. In: Proceedings of the 2018 ACM SIGSAC Conference on Computer and Communications Security, pp. 67–82 (2018)
29. Wesley, S., Christakis, M., Navas, J.A., Trefler, R., Wüstholz, V., Gurfinkel, A.: Verifying SOLIDITY smart contracts via communication abstraction in SMARTACE. In: Finkbeiner, B., Wies, T. (eds.) VMCAI 2022. LNCS, vol. 13182, pp. 425–449. Springer, Cham (2022). https://doi.org/10.1007/978-3-030-94583-1_21
30. Wood, G., et al.: Ethereum: a secure decentralised generalised transaction ledger. Ethereum Proj. Yellow Paper **151**(2014), 1–32 (2014)

Active Inference of EFSMs Without Reset

Michael Foster[1]([⊠])(iD), Roland Groz[2]([⊠])(iD), Catherine Oriat[2]([⊠])(iD),
Adenilso Simao[3]([⊠])(iD), Germán Vega[2]([⊠])(iD), and Neil Walkinshaw[1]([⊠])(iD)

[1] Department of Computer Science, The University of Sheffield, Sheffield, UK
{m.foster,n.walkinshaw}@sheffield.ac.uk
[2] LIG, Université Grenoble Alpes, CNRS, Grenoble INP, Grenoble, France
{roland.groz,catherine.oriat,german.vega}@univ-grenoble-alpes.fr
[3] Universidade de São Paulo, ICMC, São Carlos, São Paulo, Brasil
adenilso@icmc.usp.br

Abstract. Extended finite state machines (EFSMs) model stateful systems with internal data variables, and have many software engineering applications, including system analysis and test case generation. Where such models are not available, it is desirable to reverse engineer them by observing system behaviour, but existing approaches are either limited to classical FSM models with no internal data state, or implicitly require the ability to reset the system under inference, which may not always be possible. In this paper, we present an extension to the hW-inference algorithm that can infer EFSM models, complete with guards and internal data update functions, from systems without a reliable reset, although there are currently some restrictions on the type of system and model.

1 Introduction

Accurate models of software behaviour are useful for a wide range of software engineering tasks, including checking system correctness [12], identifying sequences of test inputs [7], and comparing differences in behaviour between software versions [8]. Reactive systems—systems that respond to their environment, their users, or other systems—are commonly modelled as (Extended) Finite State Machines ((E)FSMs), and such models form the basis of many testing and verification techniques [16].

Despite their value, models can be neglected during development, or may not exist at all. In such situations, we need to *reverse engineer* them from existing systems, and the task of inferring (E)FSM models has been the subject of a considerable amount of research. A popular strategy here is the minimally adequate teacher framework [3], in which a model is inferred by posing a series of *queries* to the system under inference (aka SUL, System Under Learning). However, existing inference techniques [11,14,15,23] tend to implicitly require the ability

---

The authors acknowledge the support of ANR project PHILAE (ANR-18-CE25-0013) and ACHAR project from LIG. Michael Foster and Neil Walkinshaw are funded by the EPSRC CITCoM project (EP/T030526/1). Adenilso Simao would like to thank the CEPID-CeMEAI/ICMC-USP (FAPESP grant 2013/07375-0).

Y. Li and S. Tahar (Eds.): ICFEM 2023, LNCS 14308, pp. 29–46, 2023.
https://doi.org/10.1007/978-981-99-7584-6_3

to return the system to some known "initial" state from which to execute a trace, which is not always feasible. While inference approaches have been developed to minimise resets [13,20], these do not give adequate consideration to how data values affect the behaviour of the SUL.

In this paper, we present the ehW-inference algorithm (the e standing for "extended") to infer EFSM models of systems with internal, data-dependent behaviour without the need for resets. Our main contributions are as follows:

- An extension to the hW-inference algorithm [13] called ehW-inference, which incorporates the ability to infer internal registers and the constraints and functions that determine how the data states within the system change in response to inputs.
- A "proof of concept" demonstration of ehW-inference being applied to a small example system.

The rest of the paper is structured as follows. Section 2 presents a motivating example and a brief overview of the relevant background upon which our contribution is based. Section 3 presents our ehW-inference algorithm. Section 4 provides a walk-through of the algorithm, showing how it can be applied to our motivating example from Sect. 2. Finally, Sect. 5 concludes the paper and discusses potential future work.

2   Background and Related Work

We first introduce a running example to illustrate the type of model we use and our inference method. We compare our model and approach with existing work. We then formally define EFSMs and discuss the semantics of the model and the operations that can be applied.

2.1   Running Example

To illustrate our approach, we use a vending machine, modelled on Fig. 1a. Starting from state s_0, a user can *select* a drink (e.g., tea or coffee), then insert a *coin*. The price of a drink is 100 (there are coins of values 20, 50, 100, and 200). The machine will reject any initial payment less than the value of the drink, but a user may choose to enter more coins. Every time a coin is accepted, the running total is displayed. After paying, the user can press a *vend* button to be served the selected drink, and the balance in excess of the cost of a drink will be reset. An example execution is shown in Fig. 1b. The formal semantics of this are detailed in Sect. 2.3.

In Fig. 1a, inputs are separated from outputs by a "/" on the label of a transition. As shown in Fig. 1a, our models can have parametric inputs, such as *select*, which carries an enumerated type for the choice of drink, or *coin*, which carries the integer value of the coin. Outputs can also bear parameters: this is the case for all three outputs in our model (*Reject*, *Display*, and *Serve*, which we subsequently abbreviate to R, D, and S). Our models are capable of storing

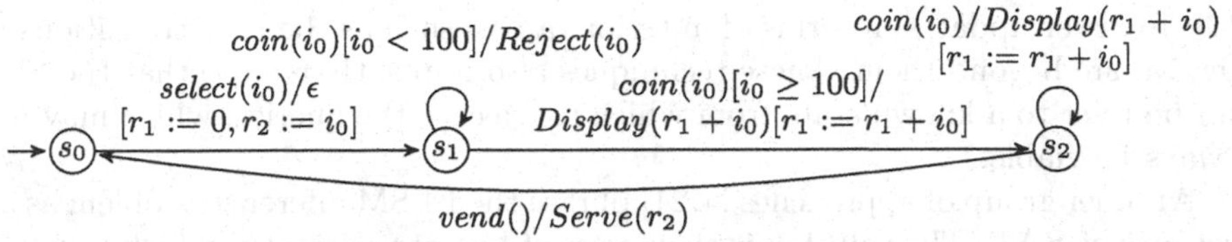

(a) EFSM representing the vending machine.

$$\langle select(tea)/\epsilon, coin(50)/Reject(50), coin(100)/Display(100),$$
$$coin(50)/Display(150), vend()/Serve(tea)\rangle$$

(b) An example execution of the simple vending machine, in which an event is denoted *input(parameters)/output(parameters)*.

Fig. 1. The vending machine EFSM and an example trace.

values in registers, which are typed variables. In our example, r_1 will store the total value of coins inserted and r_2 will store the drink that was selected.

Although simple, this example illustrates the various inference challenges that we are faced with. We are not able to observe the register state when interacting with the machine. We do not know how many (if any) registers exist, or how they affect the sequential behaviour and output parameters of the machine. The only data visible to us are the input and output parameters. There is no "reset" function. We do not presume the prior existence of some representative set of example executions from which we can seek to derive the underlying model. The only thing we know is the signature of the interface (inputs and outputs) so that we are able to interact with the system.

2.2   Related Work

Although there are several existing EFSM inference approaches in the literature, none of them has the capability of addressing this combined set of challenges. One technique [10] allows users to provide *data abstraction heuristics* to facilitate the introduction of registers during the inference process, but this requires the user to have a prior understanding of the system, which means that this technique cannot be applied to truly black-box inference scenarios.

Another technique, MINT [23], uses genetic programming (GP) to infer update functions for variables. However, MINT cannot discover data dependencies between different transitions, for example, between *select* and *vend* in Fig. 1a, nor can it discover internal registers like r_1 and r_2 in Fig. 1a. Work presented in [9,11] overcomes this by allowing the GP to introduce latent registers to output expressions and inferring update functions in a second pass of GP.

The above techniques are *passive*; they infer models from a predefined set of traces. There are also many *active* inference techniques in the literature [2,5,22], which infer models by querying the SUL, but these techniques only support updates in the form of simple assignments, or they do not support updates at all

[17]. Register updates in terms of anterior values, such as the *coin* transitions in Fig. 1a, are beyond them. These techniques also implicitly require that the SUL can be reset to a known state from which to execute the queries, which may not always be viable.

Another group of approaches [4,21] phrase the EFSM inference problem as an instance of SAT. The solution is then a set of boolean variables, which together represent the automaton. Unfortunately, these approaches only consider boolean data values and do not support internal variables, so have limited applicability.

2.3   Definitions

Extended Finite State Machines. State machine inference approaches such as Angluin's $L*$ method [3] infer deterministic automata, which do not incorporate data. In this paper, we use EFSMs [6], which do.

Definition 1. *An EFSM M is a tuple[1] $M = (S, \mathcal{R}, I, O, P_I, P_O, T)$ where S is a finite set of states, $\mathcal{R}$ is a cartesian product of domains, representing the type of registers. A domain is a set of values, such as int, float or string. I is a finite set of (abstract) inputs. O is a finite set of (abstract) outputs. P_I is a mapping from I to a product of domains which are the type of parameters of the inputs. The type can be empty if the input has no parameter. P_O is a mapping from O to a product of domains, which are parameters of the outputs. Outputs may also have no parameter. T is a finite set of transitions.*

Each transition $t \in T$ is a tuple (s, x, y, G, F, U, s') where $s, s' \in S$, $x \in I$, $y \in O$, $G : P_I(x) \times \mathcal{R} \to \mathbb{B}$ is the transition guard, $F : P_I(x) \times \mathcal{R} \to P_O(y)$ is the output function that gives the value of the output parameters, $U : P_I(x) \times \mathcal{R} \to \mathcal{R}$ is the update function that gives the value of the registers after the transition.

Given an EFSM M as above, its *control FSM* is the FSM M' defined as $M' = (S, I, O, T')$ where $T' = \{(s, x, y, s') \mid \exists t \in T, t = (s, x, y, G, F, U, s')\}$.

An EFSM is *deterministic* iff for any state s and input x, any value of the registers $(r_0, ...r_k)$, and any value of input parameters $(p_0, ...p_j)$, there is at most one transition $t \in T$ such that $G((p0, ...p_j), (r_0, ...r_k)))$ holds. An EFSM is *complete* iff under the same conditions there is at least one such transition.

Semantics. A *trace* is a sequence of events, as exemplified in Fig. 1b, where an *event* is an instance of the observable part of a transition. As in Figure 1b we denote this as $i(v)/o(v')$, for example the event $coin(100)/Display(100)$. For each event, we have $i \in I, o \in O, v \in P_I(i)$ and $v' \in P_O(o)$. Further, we refer to $i(v) \in \mathcal{I}$, as a *parametrized input* (or concrete input) for $(i, v) \in I \times P_I(i)$ and $\mathcal{I} = \bigcup_{i \in I} \{i\} \times P_I(i)$. Similarly, we call $o(v') \in \mathcal{O}$ a *parametrized output* and have $(o, v') \in O \times P_O(o)$ and $\mathcal{O} = \bigcup_{o \in O} \{o\} \times P_O(o)$. We denote the absence of an observable output by ϵ, which does not bear parameters.

---

[1] Our definition is more detailed than Cheng and Krishnakumar's [6] to enable internal register variables and externally visible data parameters to be distinguished. We also do not have an initial state as this does not make sense for no-reset inference.

As an EFSM executes a trace, transitions update registers and move the model between states. A *configuration* of an EFSM is a pair (s, r) of a state s and an n-tuple of values r, representing the values of each register $r_1, \ldots, r_n$. For example, when executing the trace in Fig. 1b, after performing the *select(tea)* event, we have the configuration $(s_1, (tea, 0))$. An *execution step* of the EFSM from (s, r), denoted as $(s, r) \xrightarrow{i(v)/o(v')} (s', r')$, is such that $\exists (s, i, o, G, F, U, s') \in T, G(v, r) \wedge v' = F(v, r) \wedge r' = U(v, r)$. An *execution* of the EFSM from (s, r) is a sequence of execution steps such that the posterior configuration of each step is the anterior configuration of the next step.

A configuration (s, r) is reachable from an arbitrary initial configuration (s_0, r_0) if there exists an execution ending in (s, r). An EFSM is *strongly connected* iff, given a reachable configuration (s, r) and a state s', there exists an execution from (s, r) ending in state s'.

Depending on the nature of the SUL, certain inputs may be invalid from a given state (e.g., a button in a GUI might be rendered inactive). For such systems, the underlying EFSM is inherently incomplete. To denote that input i is not available from state s, we use a special output symbol Ω, and "complete" the EFSM with transitions of the form $(s, i, \Omega, \top, \{\}, \{\}, s)$, which leave the model configuration unchanged.

Operations. Similar to FSM functions associated with transition triggers (state and input), we define the output function λ and configuration update δ for an EFSM as follows.

$$\lambda((s, r), (x, v)) = \begin{cases} (y, v'), & \text{if } \exists (s, x, y, G, F, U, s') \in T, G(v, r) \wedge v' = F(v, r) \\ \Omega, & \text{otherwise} \end{cases}$$

$$\delta((s, r), (x, v)) = \begin{cases} (s', r'), & \text{if } \exists (s, x, y, G, F, U, s') \in T, G(v, r) \wedge r' = U(v, r) \\ (s, r), & \text{otherwise} \end{cases}$$

These will be lifted to sequences of parametrized inputs in the usual way, and we also define $\delta_s((s, r), (x, v))$ as the first element of $\delta((s, r), (x, v))$.

We also define projections that abstract from *output* parameters. For $(o, v) \in O \times P_O(o)$, $\pi(o, v) = o$. Projections are lifted to sequences of parametrized outputs. Moreover, we slightly abuse the notation and consider that, when applied to a parametrized input, $\pi(i, v) = (i, v)$. Thus, when applied to a trace in $(\mathcal{IO})^*$, the projections will result in a trace in $(\mathcal{IO})^*$.

2.4 Inferring Functions with Genetic Programming

When inferring an EFSM, there are two dimensions to the inference challenge. On the one hand, there is the challenge of inferring the potential sequential behaviours of the model. On the other hand, there is the task of inferring the "data-state" of the machine – of inferring the presence of registers, and of how they and output parameters are updated during execution.

One approach adopted in previous EFSM inference approaches [9,11,23] is Genetic Programming (GP) [19]. Here, a GP engine is supplied with the elementary components of a function—operators and operands—as well as a sample of input and corresponding output values. This takes the form of a table where columns represent the different variables and rows represent different execution instances. Candidate functions are typically represented by their parse tree, which is the representation we use for our technique in Sect. 3. The GP engine then searches through different combinations of operators and operands with the aim of finding one which is able to approximate the given set of data-points. This search follows the principles of Genetic Algorithms; solutions are combined and mutated iteratively, and the best solutions are chosen according to a fitness function, in this case the error-margin between the observed outputs and the outputs computed by the inferred functions.

3 The *ehW*-Inference Algorithm

Our goal is to infer EFSM models, complete with guards and data transformations, of black-box systems which we cannot arbitrarily reset. This section presents our *ehW*-inference algorithm and the assumptions associated with it.

3.1 Assumptions

EFSMs introduce a particular inference challenge as the same set of behaviours can be modelled in a variety of ways. For example, conditional behaviour can either be encoded as guards on states, or can be directly encoded into separate states. We subsequently assume that the SUL can be modelled by an EFSM that has the required properties. This constrains the style of EFSM inferred and also fundamentally assumes that there is a finite state "control" model.

For our investigation of the *ehW*-inference algorithm, we have started from a relatively restrictive set of assumptions about the target model. These are collectively intended to ensure that the SUL is controllable, and that its transitions between different states are observable.

Connectivity. The control FSM of the EFSM is strongly connected. In a state machine without a reset, we assume that the inference process is always able to reach any state from any other state. Otherwise, we would only be able to infer a strongly connected component.

Determinism. The EFSM is deterministic. This is a classical and essential assumption in inference approaches from traces, to be able to recognize different configurations by the fact that they yield different observations.

Observability. An EFSM is *observable* iff any two distinct transitions $t = (s, x, y, G, F, U, s')$ and $t' = (s, x, y', G', F', U', s'')$ that share the same starting state and (abstract) input have different (abstract) outputs, i.e. $y \neq y'$.

We also introduce two assumptions which allow us to infer guard, output, and update functions.

Register domain observability. Values assigned to registers by update functions should be visible at some point as an input or an output parameter. This need not occur at the transition where the register assignment occurs.

Guard visibility. Guards can only use input parameters of the transition, and not registers. In other words, registers can only contribute to the computation of parameter outputs (e.g. to display the total value of coins inserted in our example). They cannot, however, be used to condition state transitions.

Guard visibility is a limitation of our current ehW-inference algorithm. Where a system produces outputs that depend on internal stored variables (such as, counters), the EFSM our algorithm builds would have as many different states as reachable values of the (vector of) variables. This means that, for the algorithm to infer an EFSM for a system whose decisions are based on internal variables, the system would need a finite control state space.

3.2 Homing and Characterizing

Since we do not presume the existence of a reset function, the ehW-inference algorithm must compensate for this during the learning process. We achieve this with the help of "homing" and "characterizing" sets. Intuitively, a homing sequence is an input sequence whose tail state is uniquely determined by the observed output sequence. A characterizing set is a set of input sequences that provide a unique response for every state in the system, thus enabling each state to be uniquely identified. Previous work [13] has shown how these notions can be incorporated into a learning setting to enable the inference of conventional FSMs without reset functions. To enable this here, we provide definitions of homing sequences and characterizing sets that are specific to EFSMs.

A sequence $h \in \mathcal{I}^*$ is *homing* iff $\forall (s, s', r, r') \in S^2 \times R^2, \pi(\lambda((s,r), h) = \pi(\lambda((s',r'), h) \Rightarrow \delta_s((s,r), h) = \delta_s((s',r'), h)$. This means that the sequence of (non-parametrized) outputs uniquely defines the state reached at the end of the sequence. Thus, by applying h and observing the outputs, it is possible to ascertain the state reached at the end of h. A set $W \subset \mathcal{I}^*$ is *characterizing* iff $\forall (s, s') \in S^2, s \neq s', \exists w \in W, \forall (r, r') \in R^2, \pi(\lambda((s,r), w)) \neq \pi(\lambda((s', r'), w))$. Thus, a state can identified by the (unique) response to every sequence in W.

3.3 Inputs and Data Structures

We assume we are given:

- An input set I with associated parameters P_I.
- A SUL whose behaviour can be modelled by an EFSM with these inputs, satisfying the assumptions in Sect. 3.1, to which we can apply sequences of parametrized inputs and observe the corresponding parametrized outputs.
- A tentative homing sequence $h \in \mathcal{I}^*$. This may be empty (ϵ).
- A tentative characterizing set $W \subset \mathcal{I}^*$. This may be the empty set.

- For each domain of input parameters, an ordered list of values. We further require that those values must include all values appearing in h and W, and that they should appear at the beginning of the lists of their domains. We denote I_1 a set of inputs parametrized with at least the first value in each domain. And we denote I_s the set of all (sampled) parametric inputs that can be created using the provided list of values.

As we are in the active inference setting, we also require a means of interacting with the SUL, commonly referred to as a driver [13] or a mapper [1,2]. This serves as a bridge between the inference engine and the system, and can be used to map low level inputs and outputs from the software to more abstract tokens better suited to the inference process, for example to convert network packets into a more abstract or readable format in line with the desired modelling style. It is therefore critical for inference that any such abstractions applied by the interface fulfil the assumptions set out in Sect. 3.1 as this is how the inference engine will perceive the system. However, since this work is more concerned with establishing the theoretical foundations of ehW-inference, we do not give this further consideration here.

During learning, the trace observed at any given moment is represented by ω. This is extended whenever we apply an input and observe the corresponding output. The algorithm will record deduced information in the following sets:

- $Q \subset 2^{W \to O^+}$ denote states, defined by their characterization. Each state is named by traces recording its responses to the input sequences from W.
- $\Delta : Q \times \mathcal{I} \to Q$ and $\Lambda : Q \times \mathcal{I} \to 2^O$ record transitions. With guard visibility, the abstract output sequence and state reached from a given state by applying a parametrized input sequence is unique and does not depend on the value of registers, so $\Delta(s, (x, v)) = s'$ and $(y, v') \in \Lambda(s, (x, v))$ iff $\exists (s, x, y, G, F, U, s') \in T, \exists r \in \mathcal{R}, G(v) \wedge v' = F(v, r)$. Δ, Λ are lifted to sequences, and as usual, for an empty input sequence ϵ, the output sequence is also ϵ and $s' = s$.

3.4 ehW-Inference Backbone

The ehW-inference algorithm, detailed in Algorithm 1, has four core parts. The first part, called the *backbone*, follows what is in-effect the basic hW-inference backbone algorithm [13]. Our backbone infers an FSM transition structure using only a single parameter value for each input, so we do not need registers or transition guards. The second part of the algorithm, *sampling*, is responsible for traversing the inferred structure using different parameter values for the inputs, the aim being to gather data for part three of our algorithm, *generalisation*, which infers the registers, output functions, and transition guards within an EFSM. The final part, *counterexample processing*, again comes from [13] and involves searching for inconsistencies between the conjecture model and the SUL.

Algorithm 1 ehW algorithm

1: Inputs: $I, I_1 \subset I_s \subset \mathcal{I}, h \in I_s^*, W \subset I_s^*$
2: **repeat**
3:     $Q, \Delta, \Lambda, q \leftarrow \perp$
4:     **repeat**
5:        $\omega, Q, \Delta, \Lambda \leftarrow$ BACKBONE $(I_1, h, W, \Delta, \Lambda)$ ▷ *Learn the structure*
6:        **for** $t \in \Delta, i \in I_s$ **do** ▷ *Apply sampling to learn data values for generalisation*
7:           **if** $\pi(t(i)) \notin \Lambda(t(i))$ **then**
8:              **break**
9:     **until** No inconsistency
10:     **repeat**
11:        $M \leftarrow$ GENERALISE$(\omega, h, Q, I, O, P_I, P_O, \Delta, \Lambda)$ ▷ *Generalise into an EFSM*
12:        $(\omega, CE) \leftarrow$ GETCOUNTEREXAMPLE(M, SUL)
13:     **until** ¬ (CE is a data CE)
14:     **if** CE found **then** ▷ *Present conjecture to oracle and process resulting counterex.*
15:        $(W, I_1, I_s) \leftarrow$ PROCESSCOUNTEREXAMPLE
16: **until** no counterexample found
17: **return** M

Backbone. It is the job of the backbone hW-inference algorithm (line 5) to identify the basic control structure of the model. This is done in the same way as in [13], but using only one input parameter for each abstract transition. The basic idea is to learn states by first applying the homing sequence h to reach a known location and then sequences in W to distinguish the destination state. Transitions are learned by applying (parametrised) events in I and then sequences in W to discover the destination.

The backbone runs until we end up with a graph structure that contains a strongly connected component using a single input parameter value for each transition. Then, we can run sampling, call the generalisation procedure, and ask the oracle for a counterexample, as explained later. However, this is predicated on the fact that the h and W sets provided are correct – i.e. that h is genuinely a homing sequence, and that W is characterizing. If this is not the case, this will manifest itself through various inconsistencies which, when detected, indicate that the h or W sets need to be extended and the backbone restarted.

Sampling. The main purpose of sampling (lines 6–8) is to enrich the set of values for each transition so as to be able to generalise concrete values into symbolic output and update functions (Line 11). The basic idea is to fire every transition learned by the backbone hW-inference algorithm with every input parameter in its domain[2] and observe the corresponding output. This then forms the training set for GP. However, in doing this, we may observe inconsistencies between (abstract) transitions.

---

[2] Variable domains do not have to be finite, although we can obviously only execute finite samples of infinite domains. Where counterexamples require a data value not in the observed sample, the oracle (Sect. 3.6) is free to include these, and they are added to the sampled domain as part of counterexample processing.

For example, in learning the simple drinks machine, the backbone may use 50 as its input to the *coin* transitions. In this case, the algorithm can only observe *Reject*(50) as an output, since the first coin to be input must be 100 or greater. During sampling, we then observe *coin*(100)/*Display*(100). This is inconsistent with what we have observed so far as *Reject* and *Display* clearly represent different output behaviour. Thus, we have discovered an inconsistency and can return to backbone hW-inference inference with an updated h and W.

Inconsistencies. Inconsistencies (line 9) can be detected as soon as we apply a sequence and observe differing output symbols from those expected from the partial machine. These can manifest themselves in various ways.

If h is not homing, it is possible that the same response leads to two different states, which would be considered by the algorithm as a single one. This can give rise to apparent non-determinism, which we call h-ND inconsistency. h-ND inconsistencies occur when we have observed previously $h/a.\beta/v.x/y$ and then apply $h/a'.\beta/v'.x'/y'$ s.t. $\pi(a.v) = \pi(a'.v')$ yet $\pi(y') \neq \pi(y)$ and ($x = x'$ or $y = \Omega$ or $y' = \Omega$).

Since we assume we are learning an observable EFSM satisfying guard visibility, the difference in outputs implies the control states s and s' reached after h/a and h/a' are different. Thus, h is not homing, and extending it with the prefix of β up to the first differing output symbol will distinguish two more states.

Similarly, if W is not characterizing, two different control states could be confused as a single one; the algorithm would associate outgoing transitions and sequences from those two states to the single reconstructed one.

A W-ND inconsistency occurs when we previously observed $h/a.\alpha/u.\beta/v.x/y$ and then observe $h/a'.\alpha'/u'.\beta/v'.x'/y'$ (where $\alpha, \alpha' \in \mathcal{I}^*$, $\beta \in \mathcal{I}^*$ and $x, x' \in \mathcal{I}$) s.t. $\pi(a) \neq \pi(a')$ or $\alpha \neq \alpha'$ but $\Delta(H(\pi(a)), \alpha) = \Delta(H(\pi(a')), \alpha')$, $\pi(v') = \pi(v)$ and $\pi(x') = \pi(x)$ yet $\pi(y') \neq \pi(y)$ and ($x = x'$ or $y = \Omega$ or $y' = \Omega$). In this case, $\Delta(H(\pi(a)), \alpha)$ and $\Delta(H(\pi(a')), \alpha')$ can in fact be distinguished by $\beta.x'$, so $\beta.x'$ can be added to W.

As in the case of the FSM hW-inference algorithm, we can remark that all states traversed while applying β can be distinguished by some suffix of β. We can extend W with any such suffix that is not yet in W. However, we would refrain from adding all suffixes into W as the cardinal of W acts as a multiplicative factor on the complexity of the learning [13].

Generalisation. The role of generalisation (Line 11) is to infer symbolic output and update expressions which account for the concrete output and update values observed during the backbone and sampling phases. In essence, we want to take the collected values for each (i, o) pair of input and output types and infer a general expression F for that pair. However, a complication is that the output values may be influenced by the values of unobservable registers. We need our technique to infer this, along with any updates U to the registers to ensure they evaluate to the correct values. Additionally, where the model contains data-dependent behaviour, we need to infer symbolic guards to distinguish this. This enables us to predict how the inferred model might behave when faced with unseen inputs. To do this, we apply a technique based on GP, similar to in [9,11]. We present the details of this in Sect. 3.5.

Counterexamples. Once we have found a strongly connected FSM and generalised it to an EFSM, we look for a discrepancy between outputs from the EFSM and the SUL. We first need to synchronise the EFSM with the SUL which can be done by re-running the past trace on the EFSM model from the earliest occurrence of a homing sequence. The trace can be extended using one of the usual strategies (such as random walk, bounded model checking) to look for discrepancies. As soon as an output differs between EFSM and SUL, the extended trace is returned as a counterexample.

3.5   Generalisation

We here lay out the details of our generalisation step described above. The goal here is take the concrete data values observed in the backbone and sampling phases and infer symbolic expressions which account for them, thereby enabling the model to be used to predict the output from the system when executed with unseen input parameters. We may also need to infer symbolic guards to distinguish data-dependent behaviour.

To do this, we apply a technique based on GP, similar to in [9,11]. This is shown in Algorithm 2, which defines the GENERALISE function from Algorithm 1. There are five main steps. First, we convert the abstract data structures of the backbone algorithm into an initial EFSM (line 2). Next, we group together instances of transitions that we would like to generalise to the same F and U (Line 3). For each group, we use GP to produce an output function which satisfies the observed input/output pairs (line 5). This may introduce a new register to the model for which we need to infer updates (lines 7–9) to ensure it holds the correct value when evaluated. Finally, we drop literal input guards on transitions (e.g., $i_0 = 50$, line 13) and resolve any resulting nondeterminism (line 14).

Algorithm 2 Outline of our generalisation.

1: **function** GENERALISE(ω, h, $Q,I,O,P_I,P_O,\Delta,\Lambda$)
2:     $efsm \leftarrow$ EFSM($Q, I, O, P_I, P_O, \Delta, \Lambda, h, \omega$)▷ *Convert the abstract data structures into a concrete EFSM*
3:     $groups \leftarrow$ GROUPTRANSITIONS(Λ, ω)
4:     **for** $g_1 \in groups$ **do**
5:         $fun \leftarrow$ INFEROUTPUTFUN(g_1) ▷ *Use GP to infer functions that predict outputs for each group, introducing registers if required.*
6:         $newEFSM \leftarrow$ REPLACELITWITHFUN($efsm, g_1, fun$) ▷ *Replace literal outputs with inferred functions.*
7:         **for** $r_n \in fun.latentVars$ **do** ▷ *Infer updates for any new registers.*
8:             **for** $g_2 \in groups$ **do**
9:                 $newEFSM \leftarrow$ INFERUPDATEFUNS(g_2, TARGETVALUES($newEFSM, r_n$))
10:        **if** ACCEPTS($newEFSM, \omega$) **then** ▷ *Check that inferred functions are compatible with traces. If not the efsm remains unchanged.*
11:            $efsm \leftarrow newEFSM$
12:        $efsm \leftarrow$ STANDARDISE(e) ▷ *Unify transition groups split by history.*
13:    $efsm \leftarrow$ DROPGUARDS($efsm$)
14:    $efsm \leftarrow$ RESOLVENONDETERMINISM($efsm, \omega$)
15:    **return** $efsm$

EFSM Construction. The first step of generalisation, EFSM (line 2), is to convert the abstract data structures to a concrete EFSM model where transitions guard for the observed input parameters and produce the observed concrete outputs. This is a fairly trivial process, except that we must drop all events in ω before the first occurrence of the current (lastly used) h as we do not know where we are, meaning we cannot reliably group transitions from before this point.

Transition Grouping. We use the name GROUPTRANSITIONS (line 3) to be consistent with [9,11], but what we are actually doing here is grouping events in ω by their corresponding transition in Δ as this is known here. These groups then form the training sets for GP. As in [9,11], though, there is the additional need to split groups by their *history* (the preceding groups) to account for any side effects of other transition groups on unobserved register values.

Output and Update Inference. Output functions are inferred using GP as detailed in [9,11]. In short, GP uses a series of crossover and mutation operations to combine a predefined set of operators and operands into an expression which maps the observed input parameters to the observed output parameters as discussed in Sect. 2.4. This may introduce new registers to the model for which update expressions must be inferred to ensure that they hold the correct values when they are evaluated. Details of this process can be found in [9,11].

Standardisation. Where groups are split by their respective histories, the GP may infer different output and update functions for the separate subgroups.

Because we know these subgroups are in fact instances of the same transition, we need to unify the output and update expressions of the various subgroups. This is what standardisation does. Full details of this are published in [9,11].

Resolution of Nondeterminism. Having inferred symbolic output and update expressions, we can now drop the guards (line 13) which prevent transitions from responding to unobserved input parameters. As in [9,11], this leads to nondeterminism which must be resolved. There are two potential sources of this. The first is duplicated behaviour, which is introduced to the model when we sample different data values for the same (abstract) transition. As in [9,11], this can be trivially resolved by merging the offending (concrete) transitions, which should be identical because of the standardisation step.

The other source of nondeterminism, which is not considered in [9,11], is data-dependent behaviour. This cannot be resolved by merging as the behaviours are different. Algorithm 3 shows how we resolve this by calling GP a third time to infer guard functions that distinguish pairs of nondeterministic transitions. For each nondeterministic pair of transitions (line 3), we walk the trace in the model (lines 6–12) recording the input and register values when either transition is taken (lines 8 and 10). We then call GP to find a boolean guard expression which evaluates to *true* for one transition and *false* for the other.

Algorithm 3 Resolving nondeterminism.

1: **function** RESOLVENONDETERMINISM($efsm, \omega$)
2: **while** $efsm$ is nondeterministic **do**
3:   $t_1, t_2 \leftarrow$ GETNONDETERMINISTICPAIR($efsm$)
4:   $took_1, took_2 \leftarrow \emptyset, \emptyset$ ▷ *Initialise the training sets for each transition*
5:   $state, registers \leftarrow$ INITIALISE($efsm$)
6:   **for** $event \in \omega$ **do**▷ *Walk the trace in the model.*
7:    **if** CORRESPONDSTO($event, t_1$) **then** ▷ *If we took t_1, add the inputs and registers to the training set for t_1.*
8:     $took_1 \leftarrow took_1 \cup (event.inputs, r)$
9:    **if** CORRESPONDSTO($event, t_2$) **then** ▷ *If we took t_2, add the inputs and registers to the training set for t_2.*
10:     $took_2 \leftarrow took_2 \cup (event.inputs, r)$
11:    $r \leftarrow$ UPDATEREGISTERS($r, event$)
12:    $s \leftarrow$ UPDATESTATE($s, event$)
13:   $guard \leftarrow$ INFERGUARD($took_1, took_2$) ▷ *Call GP to infer a guard to distinguish the two transitions based on the input and register values they were fired with.*
14:   $efsm \leftarrow$ ADDGUARDTOTRANSITIONS($guard, t_1, t_2$)

3.6 Oracle Procedure

With nondeterminism resolved, we can then present the EFSM to the oracle, which attempts to extend the trace to end with an output from the SUL which differs from the conjecture EFSM. If the output type is different, then we have observed an inconsistency as described above, and need to revise the structure of the control FSM. However, if the difference is only on the output parameter values, this means the functions computed by the generalisation were incorrect. We call this a *data counterexample*. To resolve data counterexamples, we can simply rerun our generalisation procedure with the new data. As in other approaches that learn models from unbounded black box systems, only an approximate oracle can be implemented. If the oracle cannot find a counterexample, the model is assumed to be equivalent to the system.

Note that our EFSM may not be strongly connected if, during inference, we get "trapped" in a state. In this case, the oracle may extend the set of input parameter values (as well as output parameter values) make it possible to reach states that are not reachable with the current set of values. The oracle may also extend the sets of input and output parameter values to elicit data counterexamples which could not be revealed otherwise.

4   Inferring a Vending Machine Controller

We now illustrate the execution of ehW-inference on our running example from Sect. 2.1. We start with $h = \epsilon, W = \{\}, I_1 = \{coin(50), select(tea), vend\}$. As h and W are empty, the backbone will just learn a "daisy" (single state) automaton with each input X from I_1.

$$(s_0, \langle\rangle) \underbrace{\xrightarrow{coin(50)/\Omega} 1}_{h=\epsilon \ \ w=\{\} \ \ X=coin(50)} (s_0, \langle\rangle) \underbrace{\xrightarrow{select(tea)/\epsilon} 2}_{w=\{\} \ \ h=\epsilon \ \ X=select(tea)} (s_1, \langle tea, 0\rangle) \underbrace{}_{w=\{\}}$$

$$\underbrace{\xrightarrow{vend/\Omega} 3}_{h=\epsilon \ \ X=vend} (s_1, \langle tea, 0\rangle) \underbrace{\xrightarrow{coin(100)/D(100)} 4}_{w=\{\} \ \ sampling} (s_2, \langle tea, 100\rangle)$$

We sample with $I_s = I_1 \cup \{coin(100), select(coffee)\}$. As soon as we apply $coin(100)$, we spot nondeterminism, leading us to revise $h = coin(100)$, $W = \{coin(100)\}$ and $I_1 = \{coin(100), select(tea), vend\}$. We restart the backbone.

$$(s_2, \langle tea, 100\rangle) \underbrace{\xrightarrow{coin(100)/D(200)} 5}_{h} (s_2, \langle tea, 200\rangle) \underbrace{\xrightarrow{coin(100)/D(300)} 6}_{w} (s_2, \langle tea, 300\rangle)$$

We now know that applying h with response D leads to q_0, characterized by $coin(100) \mapsto D$, but we have not yet learnt Δ for $(q_0, coin(100))$, so we need to home again before proceeding. This leaves us still in q_0, so we can now learn a transition from it, with $\alpha = \epsilon$ (no transfer needed), and we use $X = coin(100)$ as it is used in h and W.

$$(s_2, \langle tea, 300\rangle) \underbrace{\xrightarrow{coin(100)/D(400)} 7}_{h} \underbrace{\xrightarrow{coin(100)/D(500)} 8}_{X} \underbrace{\xrightarrow{coin(100)/D(600)} 9}_{w} (s_2, \langle tea, 600\rangle)$$

We just learnt $\Delta(q_0, coin(100)) = q_0$, so we know we remain in q_0, and can continue learning other inputs. Thus, we learn that the transition for *select* is an Ω self-loop transition, and *vend* outputs $Serve(tea)$ and goes to a state where W gives Ω. Thus we learn a new state $q_1 = \{coin(100) \mapsto \Omega\}$. After further steps to learn all transitions from state q_1 and sampling with inputs from I_s, we reach step 25 where we have found a two state machine with q_0 (a merged state of s_1 and s_2 in the SUL) and q_1 (corresponding to state (s_0), and transitions on all inputs from I_s. This graph is strongly connected, so the backbone ends with the model in Fig. 2a. The generalisation will infer a two state EFSM, shown in Fig. 2b, and the algorithm will ask the oracle for a counterexample.

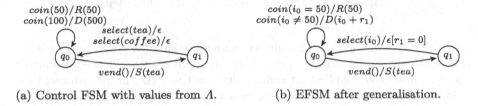

(a) Control FSM with values from Λ.   (b) EFSM after generalisation.

Fig. 2. Conjecture built from $\omega, h, \Delta, \Lambda$ after 25 steps.

A simple counterexample is obtained by sending $coin(50)$ to the SUL, which at this point is in configuration $(s_2, \langle coffee, 100 \rangle)$, so will respond with $D(150)$ whereas the conjecture would respond $R(50)$. Since output types D and R differ, this is not a data counterexample but W-ND, so we add $coin(50)$ to W and restart the backbone with $h = coin(100)$ and $W = \{coin(100), coin(50)\}$.

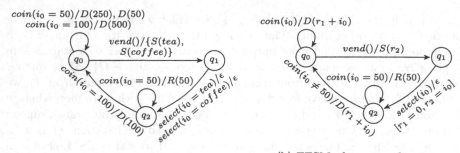

(a) Control FSM with values from Λ.

(b) EFSM after generalisation.

Fig. 3. Conjecture built from $\omega, h, \Delta, \Lambda$ after 67 steps.

As h has not changed, we can implement a dictionary (as proposed in previous learning methods [18]), viz. the outputs of any input sequence of the form $h\alpha X w$ that was previously applied (at some point) on the SUL can be assumed to be valid and can be reused to fill structures without reapplying the input sequence. However, as W changed, we need to completely re-learn the set of states Q.

Since h is homing and W is now characterizing, this application of the backbone will discover all the states of the SUL in 17 extra steps (up to step 43), and all transitions on inputs from I_1 when we reach step 59. Sampling makes it possible to learn the last transition, $coin(50)$ from state $s1$ at step 67, leaving the model shown in Fig. 3a.

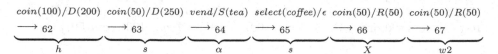

As before, we can then apply the generalisation procedure to infer a full EFSM model. This is shown in Fig. 3. As can be seen from the two $q_2 \xrightarrow{coin}$ transitions, the guard distinguishing them is rather simplistic. Because of this, our oracle is able to return the counterexample $coin(20)/R(20)$ (step 68). This brings a new input parameter, 20, into play.

This counterexample differs only in terms of its data values, and there is no h or W nondeterminism. Thus, it is a data counterexample, indicating we need only rerun generalisation on the newly extended trace. This gives the same model as in Fig. 3b, but with guards $i_0 \leq 50$ and $i_0 > 50$ where we previously had $i_0 = 50$ and $i_0 \neq 50$, and the output $R(i_0)$ instead of $R(50)$. Given the input domain of $coin$, this is equivalent to Fig. 1a as there is no coin with a value between 50 and 100. Thus, we learnt an accurate model of our vending EFSM by executing just 68 events, although this is dependent on the stochastic outcome of GP. Running the algorithm again using a different random seed for GP may produce different generalisations to Figs. 2b and 3b, so may require additional steps to infer the target model.

5 Conclusions and Future Work

In this paper we have presented the ehW-inference algorithm. It is based on the hW-inference algorithm by Groz *et al.* [13], which enables the inference of conventional FSMs from systems without a reset functionality. However, we incorporate into this the GP-driven capability to infer registers and functional relationships between data-states, based on work by Foster *et al.* [11].

Our future work will go in two primary directions. Firstly, our approach currently operates under several relatively restrictive assumptions (Sect. 3.1). Some of these assumptions may be relaxed, and our future work will set out to establish the extent to which this is the case. Secondly, we have so far only presented a single running example, without delivering any insight into the scalability of the approach. This will be investigated in a more comprehensive empirical study, with models of varying size and complexity.

References

1. Aarts, F.: Tomte: bridging the gap between active learning and real-world systems. Ph.D. thesis, Radboud University Nijmegen (2014)
2. Aarts, F., Heidarian, F., Kuppens, H., Olsen, P., Vaandrager, F.: Automata learning through counterexample guided abstraction refinement. In: Giannakopoulou, D., Méry, D. (eds.) FM 2012. LNCS, vol. 7436, pp. 10–27. Springer, Heidelberg (2012). https://doi.org/10.1007/978-3-642-32759-9_4
3. Angluin, D.: Queries and concept learning. Mach. Learn. **2**(4) (1988)
4. Buzhinsky, I., Vyatkin, V.: Automatic inference of finite-state plant models from traces and temporal properties. IEEE Trans. Ind. Inf. **13**(4) (2017)
5. Cassel, S., Howar, F., Jonsson, B., Steffen, B.: Learning extended finite state machines. In: Giannakopoulou, D., Salaün, G. (eds.) SEFM 2014. LNCS, vol. 8702, pp. 250–264. Springer, Cham (2014). https://doi.org/10.1007/978-3-319-10431-7_18
6. Cheng, K.-T., Krishnakumar, A.S.: Automatic functional test generation using the extended finite state machine model. In: 30th ACM/IEEE Design Automation Conference. IEEE (1993)
7. Choi, W., Necula, G., Sen, K.: Guided GUI testing of android apps with minimal restart and approximate learning. ACM SIGPLAN Not. **48**(10) (2013)
8. Damasceno, C.D.N., Mousavi, M.R., da Silva Simao, A.: Learning to reuse: adaptive model learning for evolving systems. In: Ahrendt, W., Tapia Tarifa, S.L. (eds.) IFM 2019. LNCS, vol. 11918, pp. 138–156. Springer, Cham (2019). https://doi.org/10.1007/978-3-030-34968-4_8
9. Foster, M.: Reverse engineering systems to identify flaws and understand behaviour. Ph.D. thesis, University of Sheffield, September 2020
10. Foster, M., Brucker, A.D., Taylor, R.G., North, S., Derrick, J.: Incorporating data into EFSM inference. In: Ölveczky, P.C., Salaün, G. (eds.) SEFM 2019. LNCS, vol. 11724, pp. 257–272. Springer, Cham (2019). https://doi.org/10.1007/978-3-030-30446-1_14
11. Foster, M., Derrick, J., Walkinshaw, N.: Reverse-engineering EFSMs with data dependencies. In: Clark, D., Menendez, H., Cavalli, A.R. (eds.) IFIP International Conference on Testing Software and Systems. Springer, Cham (2022). https://doi.org/10.1007/978-3-031-04673-5_3

12. Groce, A., Peled, D., Yannakakis, M.: Adaptive model checking. In: Katoen, J.-P., Stevens, P. (eds.) TACAS 2002. LNCS, vol. 2280, pp. 357–370. Springer, Heidelberg (2002). https://doi.org/10.1007/3-540-46002-0_25
13. Groz, R., Bremond, N., Simao, A., Oriat, C.: hW-inference: a heuristic approach to retrieve models through black box testing. J. Syst. Softw. **159** (2020)
14. Howar, F., Steffen, B., Jonsson, B., Cassel, S.: Inferring canonical register automata. In: Kuncak, V., Rybalchenko, A. (eds.) VMCAI 2012. LNCS, vol. 7148, pp. 251–266. Springer, Heidelberg (2012). https://doi.org/10.1007/978-3-642-27940-9_17
15. Isberner, M., Howar, F., Steffen, B.: Learning register automata: from languages to program structures. Mach. Learn. **96**(1) (2014)
16. Lee, D., Yannakakis, M.: Principles and methods of testing finite state machines-a survey. Proc. IEEE **84**(8) (1996)
17. Lin, S.-W., André, É., Dong, J.S., Sun, J., Liu, Y.: An efficient algorithm for learning event-recording automata. In: Bultan, T., Hsiung, P.-A. (eds.) ATVA 2011. LNCS, vol. 6996, pp. 463–472. Springer, Heidelberg (2011). https://doi.org/10.1007/978-3-642-24372-1_35
18. Niese, O.: An integrated approach to testing complex systems. Ph.D. thesis, University of Dortmund (2003)
19. Poli, R., Langdon, W.B., McPhee, N.F.: A Field Guide to Genetic Programming. lulu.com (2008)
20. Rivest, R.L., Schapire, R.E.: Inference of finite automata using homing sequences. In: Proceedings of the Twenty-First Annual ACM Symposium on Theory of Computing (1989)
21. Ulyantsev, V., Tsarev, F.: Extended finite-state machine induction using sat-solver. In: 2011 10th International Conference on Machine Learning and Applications and Workshops, vol. 2 (2011)
22. Vaandrager, F., Midya, A.: A Myhill-Nerode theorem for register automata and symbolic trace languages. In: Pun, V.K.I., Stolz, V., Simao, A. (eds.) ICTAC 2020. LNCS, vol. 12545, pp. 43–63. Springer, Cham (2020). https://doi.org/10.1007/978-3-030-64276-1_3
23. Walkinshaw, N., Hall, M.: Inferring computational state machine models from program executions. In: 2016 IEEE International Conference on Software Maintenance and Evolution (ICSME). IEEE (2016)

Learning Mealy Machines with Local Timers

Paul Kogel[1]([✉]), Verena Klös[2], and Sabine Glesner[1]

[1] Software and Embedded Systems Engineering, TU Berlin, Berlin, Germany
{p.kogel,sabine.glesner}@tu-berlin.de
[2] Centre for Tactile Internet with Human-in-the-Loop (CeTI), TU Dresden, Dresden, Germany
verena.kloes@tu-dresden.de

Abstract. Active automata learning (AAL) algorithms infer accurate automata models of black box applications, letting developers verify the behavior of increasingly complex *real-time systems* (RTS). However, learning models of larger RTS often takes very long or is not feasible at all. We introduce *Mealy machines with local timers*, a new class of Mealy machines that permit multiple location-bound timers and that can be learned efficiently. We design an efficient learning algorithm for them and validate our method across diverse case studies ranging from automotive systems to smart home appliances, where we drastically reduce runtimes compared to the state-of-the-art approach, thus, making AAL available for a wide range of RTS.

Keywords: active automata learning · real-time systems · timer-based Mealy machines

1 Introduction

Understanding and verifying the behavior of complex *real-time systems* (RTS) requires accurate and up-to date models. Such models, though, are often unavailable for legacy components, while increasingly rapid iterations prevent developers from maintaining them for new systems. *Active automata learning* (AAL) methods could fill this gap. They infer accurate automata models of black box systems by observing their output for well-chosen inputs, making them perfectly suited for RTS, which are often deterministic, state-based, and event-driven. AAL methods for RTS traditionally focused on learning timed automata with clocks and guards. As RTS typically implement time-sensitive behavior with timers, [12] recently proposed in a seminal work to learn deterministic Mealy machines with a single timer (MM1Ts) instead. Although improving runtimes significantly, this approach still takes very long for larger systems with multiple time-triggered events, making it inapplicable to many RTS in practice.

We address this problem by introducing *Mealy machines with local timers* (MMLTs), a new class of timer-based Mealy machines that allow multiple location-bound timers and that can be learned efficiently. We also create a new learning algorithm for them that we base on the efficient Rivest-Schapire [9]

The original version of this chapter was revised: in Section 4.1 and the Figure 4 has been displayed incorrectly. This was corrected. The correction to this chapter is available at https://doi.org/10.1007/978-981-99-7584-6_23

Y. Li and S. Tahar (Eds.): ICFEM 2023, LNCS 14308, pp. 47–64, 2023.
https://doi.org/10.1007/978-981-99-7584-6_4

approach. Our method has two key advantages. First, it is **efficient**, as it drastically reduces runtimes compared to the MM1T learner in practice. Second, it is **widely applicable**, as MMLTs easily express typical behavior of RTS from different domains and our learner operates efficiently in realistic black box settings, where only minimal information about the target system is available.

We implement our MMLT learner in *LearnLib*[1] and show that it drastically reduces runtimes compared to the state-of-the-art approach across diverse case studies from the fields of automotive systems, network protocols, wireless sensor networks, and smart home appliances.

The rest of this paper is structured as followed. First, we give an overview of related work (Sect. 2). Then, we establish notation related to Mealy machines and provide background on the *RS*-algorithm (Sect. 3). Afterwards, we introduce MMLTs (Sect. 4) and describe our efficient MMLT learner (Sect. 5). We follow with our practical evaluation (Sect. 6) and conclude with a summary and an outlook (Sect. 7).

2   Related Work

Learning automata with real-time behavior has been attracting sustained interest for many years. In the following, we only consider related methods that actively interact with the target system and omit methods that learn models from previously collected traces, as these are usually less accurate.

Real-time systems have been traditionally modelled with timed automata. However, learning these efficiently is difficult. An et al. [3] simplify this problem by learning timed automata with one clock only. Xu et al. [14] improve this approach with a more efficient identification of timer resets. Moreover, they adapt their method to learn Mealy machines with one clock, which is often more efficient. Like [3], though, they rely on internal information about the target to achieve reasonable runtimes. For instance, they assume to know which inputs are available at which times during their evaluation. This dependence makes their method inapplicable in many realistic scenarios. Grinchtein et al. [4] and Henry et al. [5] learn different types of *event recording automata*, a different class of timed automata. Like the previous learners, their approaches still require the complex inference of guards. Aichernig et al. [1], finally, use a genetic algorithm to learn timed automata with guards and multiple clocks. While their approach is effective for smaller models, it does not guarantee to find an accurate model.

Instead of timed automata, Vaandrager et al. [12] learn Mealy machines with a single timer (MM1Ts). This timer may be reset by almost any transition and raises an event on expiration. The authors show that their method outperforms the learners from [1,3] in realistic case studies. As MM1Ts only support a single timer, though, they need many states to describe more complex real-time behavior, increasing learning times. Moreover, identifying timer resets becomes increasingly costly in systems with more states and larger input alphabets.

Hence, despite significant recent advances, none of the above approaches can learn automata models of more complex RTS efficiently in practice.

---

[1] https://learnlib.de.

3   Preliminaries

In this section, we establish notation related to Mealy machines and recap the Rivest-Schapire algorithm on which our learner is based. We use ϵ as the empty word, $\cdot$ as concatenation, and $s^n = s \cdot s \cdot \ldots$ as $n \in \mathbb{N}^{>0}$ repetitions of s.

3.1   Mealy Machines

Mealy machines are an essential concept in Computer Science. In this work, we learn deterministic Mealy machines and extensions of these.

Definition 1. *A deterministic Mealy machine is a tuple* $\mathcal{M} = \langle Q, q_0, I, O, \delta, \lambda \rangle$, *where Q is a finite set of states, $q_0 \in Q$ is the initial state, I is a finite set of inputs, O is a finite set of outputs, $\delta : Q \times I \to Q$ is a transition function, and $\lambda : Q \times I \to O$ is an output function.*

We add the automaton name $\mathcal{M}$ as subscript to Q, q_0, I, O, δ and λ when needed. As usual, we assume that we can detect silent outputs $void \in O$. Moreover, we extend the transition function δ and the output function λ to words s.t. $\delta(q, w)$ gives the state that we reach when we trace the sequence $w \in I^*$ from $q \in Q$ and $\lambda(q, w)$ gives the concatenated outputs of this trace. We let a trace begin in q_0 when omitting q. Thus, $\delta(w) := \delta(q_0, w)$ and $\lambda(w) := \lambda(q_0, w)$. We extend the first parameter of λ to words s.t. $\lambda(w', w) := \lambda(\delta(w'), w)$, where $w' \in I^*$. We define equivalence between Mealy machines similarly to [13].

Definition 2. *The Mealy machines* $\mathcal{M}_1, \mathcal{M}_2$ *with* $I_{\mathcal{M}_1} = I_{\mathcal{M}_2} = I$ *are equivalent, written* $\mathcal{M}_1 \approx \mathcal{M}_2$, *iff* $\forall w \in I^* : \lambda_{\mathcal{M}_1}(w) = \lambda_{\mathcal{M}_2}(w)$.

Intuitively, two Mealy machines with the same input alphabet are equivalent if they produce the same outputs for any input sequence.

3.2   The Rivest-Schapire Algorithm

The Rivest-Schapire algorithm (RS) [9] is an efficient method for *active automata learning* (AAL). We describe *RS* for Mealy machines in the following.

Like other AAL methods, *RS* uses a setup with a *learner* and a *teacher*. The goal of the learner is to learn an unknown Mealy machine $\mathcal{M}$ that has the known input alphabet I. We also call $\mathcal{M}$ *system under learning* (SUL). The learner maintains a *hypothesis* $\mathcal{H}$ that only contains the initial state q_0 at the beginning. The learner may ask the teacher two types of questions to improve $\mathcal{H}$. An *output query* asks for the output of a word $w \in I^*$, while an *equivalence query* checks $\mathcal{M} \approx \mathcal{H}$. The latter is usually approximated with tests of semi-random input sequences. When $\mathcal{M} \not\approx \mathcal{H}$, the teacher returns a *counterexample* $c \in I^*$ s.t. $\lambda_{\mathcal{M}}(c) \neq \lambda_{\mathcal{H}}(c)$. Thus, c is an input sequence that yields different output in $\mathcal{H}$ and $\mathcal{M}$. The learner uses c to further refine $\mathcal{H}$. Once done, it submits a new equivalence query. Learning concludes when $\mathcal{M} \approx \mathcal{H}$.

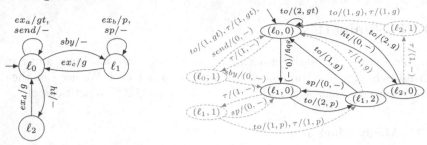

(a) MMLT with $\theta(a) = \theta(b) = \theta(d) = 2$, $\theta(c) = 3$, $\rho(\ell_0, send) = \rho(\ell_1, sp) = \top$ (b) Expanded form and reduced expanded form (black subgraph)

Fig. 1. Sensor data collector (parallel transitions separated by comma)

RS identifies states with a set of stored prefixes $S \subset I^*$. A *prefix* $s \in S$ of a state $q \in Q_{\mathcal{H}}$ is a word that always leads to q. Thus, $\delta_{\mathcal{H}}(s) = q$. The *prefix function* $\lfloor q \rfloor$ defined by [7] gives the stored prefix of q. Its extension $\lfloor w \rfloor, w \in I^*$ gives the prefix of the state $\delta_{\mathcal{H}}(w)$. When learning begins, $\mathcal{H}$ only contains the initial state q_0 with $\lfloor q_0 \rfloor = \epsilon$.

A key component of *RS* is its advanced counterexample analysis. A counterexample signals that $\mathcal{H}$ misses at least one state to match the behavior of $\mathcal{M}$. *RS* identifies such a missing state by *decomposing* the counterexample c to $c = u \cdot s \cdot v$ s.t. $\lambda_{\mathcal{M}}(\lfloor u \rfloor \cdot s, v) \neq \lambda_{\mathcal{M}}(\lfloor u \cdot s \rfloor, v)$, where $u, v \in I^*, s \in I$. A decomposition intuitively shows that the successor of a state $\delta_{\mathcal{H}}(u)$ for the input s in $\mathcal{H}$ is incorrect because it deviates from the respective successor in $\mathcal{M}$ in the input v. Consequently, *RS* refines $\mathcal{H}$ by adding the missing state.

Having described the key steps of *RS*, we introduce our new MMLT model next before presenting our efficient *RS*-based learner for them afterwards.

4   Mealy Machines with Local Timers

In the following, we introduce *Mealy machines with local timers* (MMLTs), a new model for real-time systems that is optimized for efficient learning. We motivate its key ideas, define it formally, and introduce two expanded forms that let us compare the output behavior of MMLTs during learning.

We base our MMLT design on two main observations. First, time-sensitive behavior in RTS is typically implemented with multiple timers. These timers raise an event when reaching a specific time. Second, deterministic Mealy machines with a single timer (MM1Ts) can be learned much more efficiently than timed automata [12]. Exploiting these observations, our MMLTs extend deterministic Mealy machines with multiple timers and constrain their use to common RTS behavior, e.g., by limiting the scope of a timer to a single location.[2] Using multiple timers lets us express complex real-time behavior with

---

[2] As in timed automata, locations in MMLTs can represent multiple system states.

small models, making it easy to learn. Our carefully chosen constraints make the learning of MMLTs highly efficient without sacrificing their practical applicability.

We further introduce MMLTs with an example. Consider the MMLT model of a sensor data collector in Fig. 1a. For readability, we write − for silent outputs and omit most silent self-loops in this and all following figures. After startup, our collector samples a sensor (output gt) every two time units. When receiving $send$, it transmits the collected data and restarts the collection, whereas the input ht halts the collection and starts it again after two time units, producing g. sby enters standby (location ℓ_1), where the system prepares to wake up two time units later, outputting p, and restarts the collection one time unit afterwards, resulting in the output g. Receiving sp during standby restarts this process.

We model this behavior with the timers a, b, c, and d. Each timer in an MMLT has an internal *timeout symbol* that is triggered when this timer expires. This expiration time is defined by θ. For example, a expires when it reaches $\theta(a) = 2$, which triggers ex_a. Timers in MMLTs are *local*, i.e., they can only expire in one location and can only be reset at transitions that target this location. We implicitly reset all local timers when entering a location from a different location. For instance, entering ℓ_0 at startup or from ℓ_1 or ℓ_2 resets a. Local timers and implicit resets are a key feature of MMLTs. They make efficient learning of Mealy machines with multiple timers feasible, while improving runtimes compared to MM1Ts even when just learning models with a single timer per location.

As in most RTS, timers in MMLTs may either be periodic or expire once (*one-shot*). Each location can have an arbitrary but limited number of periodic timers and up to one one-shot timer. The timers a and b in our example are periodic, as their timeout-transitions loop. Thus, ex_a implicitly resets a s.t. it expires every two time units. c and d are one-shot timers, as their timeout-transitions do not loop. One-shot timers in MMLTs must always trigger a change to a different location, resembling the classic timeout behavior found for example in network protocols.

We only let non-timeout inputs reset timers explicitly. We also let them only reset all timers at once. For instance, sp resets the timers b and c in ℓ_1 in our example. This is indicated by the value ⊤ of the local reset function ρ.

Allowing multiple timers and constraining MMLTs with local timers, implicit resets, one-shot and periodic timers, and local resets let us learn them drastically faster than MM1Ts, as we demonstrate in our evaluation. Moreover, MMLTs still easily express the real-time behavior of diverse applications ranging from automotive systems to smart home appliances. In the next section, we formally define the syntax and semantics of MMLTs.

4.1   Syntax and Semantics

MMLTs extend deterministic Mealy machines. We define them as follows.

Definition 3. *An MMLT is a tuple* $\mathcal{M} = \langle L, \ell_0, I, I^T, O, \delta, \lambda, T, \bar{T}, \gamma, \theta, \rho \rangle$, *where L is a finite set of locations, $\ell_0 \in L$ is the initial location, I is a finite set* *of non-timeout inputs, I^T is a finite set of internal timeout symbols, O is a finite set of outputs, $\delta : L \times (I \cup I^T) \to L$ is a transition function, $\lambda : L \times (I \cup I^T) \to O$ is an output function, T is a finite set of timers, $\bar{T} \subseteq T$ is a set of periodic timers, $\gamma : L \to T^*$ is a local timer function, $\eta : T \to I^T$ is a timeout-symbol function, $\theta : T \to \mathbb{N}^{>0}$ is a timeout function, and $\rho : L \times I \rightharpoonup \{\top, \bot\}$ is a local reset function.*

Our *local timer function* γ assigns each location a finite set of *local timers* that may be empty. These assignments constitute a disjoint partition of $T_{\mathcal{M}}$. Our *timeout function* θ assigns each timer an expiration time. These expiration times must be chosen s.t. a periodic and a one-shot timer never expire simultaneously and thus, the successor location at a timeout is never ambiguous. Our learner ensures this side condition when assigning timers to locations during *timer queries* and *timed counterexample analysis*. The *timeout-symbol function* η gives each timer a unique *timeout symbol*. Each timeout symbol must trigger exactly one transition. We require that $I^T \cap I = \emptyset$ to identify these timeout-transitions unambiguously. Timeout transitions only have an effect if their timeout symbol belongs to a local timer of their source location. Otherwise, they form silent self-loops. As in MM1Ts, timeouts in MMLTs must be observable, thus, timeout-transitions must not be silent. Our *local reset function* ρ returns $\top$ for transitions that reset all timers. It is only defined for non-timeout inputs that cause a self-loop. We constrain MMLTs s.t. the behavior of two locations must not only differ in their local resets. This lets us use the reduced form defined below. Also, if a sequence of locations in an MMLT visited during subsequent timeouts cannot be expressed with a single location (ignoring incoming external transitions), this must also not be possible when replacing their non-timeout transitions that target locations of this sequence with self-loops and ignore ρ.

We define the semantics of an MMLT $\mathcal{M}$ with an infinite transition system that defines the transitions between all configurations of $\mathcal{M}$. A *configuration* is a tuple (ℓ, t) that identifies a current state of $\mathcal{M}$, where $\ell \in L$ is the current location and $t \in \mathbb{N}^{\geq 0}$ the elapsed time in ℓ. We call $(\ell, 0)$ the *initial configuration* of ℓ. We transition between the configurations of $\mathcal{M}$ with non-timeout inputs and discrete time steps of size one. We define these transitions with the following rules. We represent a time step with the input symbol τ. For all $i \in (I \cup I^T), o \in O, t \in \mathbb{N}^{\geq 0}$, $\ell, \ell', \ell'' \in L$ with $\ell \neq \ell'$,

$$\frac{\ell \xrightarrow{i/o} \ell,\ i \in I,\ \rho(\ell, i) = \bot}{(\ell, t) \xrightarrow{i/o} (\ell, t)} \quad (1) \qquad \frac{\ell \xrightarrow{i/o} \ell,\ i \in I,\ \rho(\ell, i) = \top}{(\ell, t) \xrightarrow{i/o} (\ell, 0)} \quad (2) \qquad \frac{\ell \xrightarrow{i/o} \ell',\ i \in I}{(\ell, t) \xrightarrow{i/o} (\ell', 0)} \quad (3)$$

$$\frac{\exists e \in (\gamma(\ell) \cap \bar{T}) : mod(t + 1,\ \theta(e)) = 0}{(\ell, t) \xrightarrow{\tau/\lambda'(\ell, t+1)} (\ell, t + 1)} \quad (4) \qquad \frac{\forall e \in \gamma(\ell) : mod(t + 1, \theta(e)) \neq 0}{(\ell, t) \xrightarrow{\tau/void} (\ell, t + 1)} \quad (5)$$

$$\frac{\ell \xrightarrow{i/o} \ell'',\ i \in I^T,\ \exists e \in (\gamma_{\mathcal{M}}(\ell) \setminus \bar{T}) : \theta(e) = t + 1 \wedge \eta(e) = i}{(\ell, t) \xrightarrow{\tau/o} (\ell'', 0)} \quad (6)$$

Listing 1. Pseudocode for λ'

```
def λ'(ℓ ∈ L, t ∈ ℕ≥⁰):
    timers = [e for e in γ(ℓ) if mod(t, θ(e)) = 0]
    outputs = sort_alphabetically([λ(ℓ, η(e)) for e in timers])
    return outputs.concat_with('·')
```

A loop at a non-timeout input does not advance time (1), while a local reset sets t to zero (2). A location-change at a non-timeout input resets all timers of the target location (3). Rule (4) describes a time step that triggers at least one periodic timer. Periodic timers always expire when the current location time reaches a multiple of their expiration time, as they reset on expiration. This is expressed by the modulo operator mod. We allow multiple periodic timers to expire simultaneously. $\lambda'(\ell, t+1)$, as defined in Listing 1, returns their alphabetically-sorted and concatenated output. Hence, the resulting output is deterministic. Time steps that cause no timer expiration advance the current location time (5). This also applies to locations without timers. Finally, (6) describes a time step that triggers a one-shot timer. This must cause an output, a change to a different location, and a reset of all local timers of the entered location. We temporarily allow $\ell = \ell''$ during learning when $\mathcal{M}$ is a hypothesis automaton and we have not discovered the correct successor location yet. Still, we reset all timers in ℓ in this case.

The above syntax and semantics precisely describe our new MMLTs. In the next section, we introduce two additional representations of MMLT behavior and define equivalence of MMLTs.

4.2   Expanded Forms and Equivalence

During learning, we need to compare the output behavior of two MMLTs independently from their internal timeout symbols. We achieve this with two *expanded forms* that we define in the following.

Definition 4. *The expanded form $\mathcal{M}^+$ of an MMLT $\mathcal{M}$ is a finite and deterministic Mealy machine $\mathcal{M}^+ = \langle Q, q_0, I, O, \delta, \lambda \rangle$, where the states in Q represent configurations of $\mathcal{M}$, q_0 represents the initial configuration of $\mathcal{M}$, I is a finite set of inputs, O is a finite set of outputs, $\delta : Q \times I \to Q$ is a transition function, and $\lambda : Q \times I \to O$ is an output function. I consists of the non-timeout symbols of $\mathcal{M}$ and $\{to, \tau\}$. The state labels are the represented configurations of $\mathcal{M}$. The input symbol τ models a single time step and to represents a delay until the next timeout. Transition outputs $o \in O$ are tuples (t, o'), where $t \in \mathbb{N}^{\geq 0}$ is the time at which the transition is taken and $o' \in O_{\mathcal{M}}$ is sent. Hence, the output of all τ-transitions is sent at $t = 1$.*

As in Sect. 3.1, we extend δ and λ to words and use subscripts to distinguish elements from different expanded forms when needed. We construct $\mathcal{M}^+$ by exploring the transition system of $\mathcal{M}$ successively. Although this system may be infinite, we can group the configurations of an MMLT into a finite set of equivalence classes, making it only necessary to explore these.

Definition 5. *Two configurations of an MMLT are equivalent w.r.t. their output behavior iff they yield the same outputs for any input sequence $w \in (I \cup I^T)^*$.*

Theorem 1. *The number of equivalence classes of output-equivalent configurations of an MMLT is finite.*

This is backed by the following lemma.

Lemma 1. *Any configuration (ℓ, t) of a location ℓ with $\gamma(\ell) = \emptyset$ and $t \in \mathbb{N}^{\geq 0}$ is equivalent to $(\ell, 0)$. Moreover, any configuration (ℓ', t') of a location ℓ' that has only periodic timers is equivalent to $(\ell', mod(t', \kappa))$, where $t' \in \mathbb{N}^{\geq 0}$ and κ is the least common multiple of the initial expiration times of the timers in $\gamma(\ell')$.*

Exploiting the above theorem and lemma, we devise a straightforward exploration algorithm to construct the expanded form of an MMLT that operates as follows. First, we create the initial state q_0 of $\mathcal{M}^+$ that represents $(\ell, 0)$, add it to a list of known configurations, and mark it for exploration. Then, we identify all direct successor configurations of $(\ell, 0)$ in our transition system. If an identified successor is not equivalent to any known configuration, we create a new state for it in $\mathcal{M}^+$ and mark it for exploration. Otherwise, we add a transition to the known state representing the identified successor. In both cases, we copy the original transition input, which is either τ or a non-timeout symbol, and wrap the original output in a tuple, as defined above. We subsequently continue with the next unexplored configuration until there is no further configuration to explore. This process eventually terminates, as the number of classes of configurations with different output behavior in an MMLT is finite (see Theorem 1). Finally, we add an outgoing *to*-transition to each created state, which provides us a shortcut to the next timeout during learning. We never observe timeouts in states that represent locations without timers. Hence, we let their *to*-transitions self-loop and output $(\infty, void)$.[3]

Figure 1b (page 4) shows the expanded form of our sensor data collector. Here, $(\ell_0, 0)$, $(\ell_0, 2)$, $(\ell_0, 4)$ etc. are reduced to $(\ell_0, 0)$. Moreover, there is a *to*-transition in $(\ell_1, 0)$, for example, that triggers a delay until the next timeout, leading to $(\ell_1, 2)$. As shown, our expanded form does not contain the original internal timeout symbols of $\mathcal{M}$. Hence, it describes the output behavior of an MMLT abstracted from these. Thus, two MMLTs have the same *abstracted output behavior* if their expanded forms behave equivalently.

Definition 6. *The MMLTs $\mathcal{M}_1, \mathcal{M}_2$ with the non-timeout inputs $I_{\mathcal{M}_1} = I_{\mathcal{M}_2}$ are equivalent w.r.t. their abstracted output behavior iff $\mathcal{M}_1^+ \approx \mathcal{M}_2^+$.*

---

[3] We usually abort an observation after some maximum waiting time Δ during learning, thus, giving these transitions the output $(\Delta, void)$ in practice.

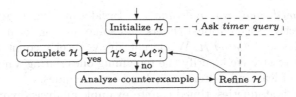

Fig. 2. MMLT learning process

We can also describe all MMLT behavior except for some local resets using a smaller model.

Definition 7. *The reduced expanded form of an MMLT M is a finite and deterministic Mealy machine $M^\diamond$ constructed from M^+ by first omitting all transitions triggered by τ and then removing all now unreachable states.*

Again, we extend δ and λ of $M^\diamond$ to words. The black subgraph in Fig. 1b is the reduced expanded form of our sensor data collector. As shown, it is significantly smaller than M^+, while capturing all of its behavior except for the local reset at *send* in ℓ_0. We exploit this smaller size during learning by using $M^\diamond$ instead of M^+ for counterexample search, reducing the search space considerably. We identify the local resets not captured by $M^\diamond$ with a new *completion* step to ensure that our learned model fully describes M^+. We present our new algorithm for learning MMLTs in the following sections.

5   Learning MMLTs Efficiently

After introducing *Mealy machines with local timers*, we now describe our method for learning them efficiently. We give an overview, describe its main components, and conclude by analyzing its output query complexity.

Our goal is to learn an unknown MMLT M with a known set of non-timeout inputs efficiently. We assume that our SUL is a black box that hides internal timeout symbols, to make our approach applicable in many different scenarios. Hence, our SUL behaves like M^+ and we must find an MMLT with the same abstracted output behavior as M. We achieve this goal with a new efficient learner that is based on the *RS*-algorithm. We choose *RS* as foundation due to its efficiency [13] and mature support in the established framework *LearnLib*.

Figure 2 gives an overview of the operation of our new MMLT learner. At the beginning, we *initialize* our hypothesis MMLT $\mathcal{H}$ by adding the initial location ℓ_0. Then, we create its outgoing transitions and use our new *timer query* to identify its local timers. Once done, we construct $\mathcal{H}^\diamond$ and ask an *equivalence query* $\mathcal{H}^\diamond \approx M^\diamond$. We use the reduced expanded forms of $\mathcal{H}$ and M instead of asking $\mathcal{H}^+ \approx M^+$ to reduce the search space for counterexamples, as $\mathcal{H}^\diamond$ and $M^\diamond$ are usually much smaller than $\mathcal{H}^+$ and M^+. This step lets our learner perform well even in more complex systems. We access $M^\diamond$ by omitting τ in queries to M^+. Assume that we receive a counterexample. We analyze counterexamples with our new *timed counterexample analysis*. Besides missing locations, this also gives us incorrectly assigned local timers and some missing local resets. We fix these inaccuracies by *refining* $\mathcal{H}$. We do not always receive counterexamples for all missing local resets. We identify the remaining ones during a new *completion* step at the end of learning. Afterwards, learning concludes.

We describe timer queries, timed counterexample analysis, hypothesis refinement, and completion in detail in the following.

5.1   Timer Queries

We use timer queries to assign periodic and one-shot timers to locations. We describe our implementation of these queries in the following.

As we assume a black box setting, we must assign timers based on observed outputs. A periodic timer and successively expiring one-shot timers, though, may produce identical outputs. This fact makes it often impossible to infer a timer type based on observations. We overcome this challenge with an opportunistic approach. Our key idea is to associate timeouts with periodic timers as long as possible w.r.t. the observed outputs. This strategy avoids redundant one-shot timers, and thus, changes to redundant locations. We apply it as follows. We set the SUL to the prefix of the queried location, repeatedly proceed a single time step, and associate all observed timeouts with periodic timers until we either reach some maximum waiting time Δ or miss a timeout from a supposed periodic timer. In the latter case, we change the last-added periodic timer to a one-shot timer. We pick an earlier timer if the new one-shot timer expires at the same time as another timer, to keep our hypothesis deterministic. Note that we may name timers that we add to our hypothesis MMLT arbitrarily, as long as there are not two timers with the same name s.t. we satisfy Definition 3.

The above opportunistic approach leads to small hypotheses and thus, small runtimes in practice, as we show in our evaluation. However, it only detects periodic timers that need to be one-shot timers up to Δ. We detect the remaining ones with counterexamples, as we discuss next.

5.2   Timed Counterexample Analysis

Missing one-shot timers, missing locations, and some missing local resets in the hypothesis $\mathcal{H}$ cause output deviations between $\mathcal{H}^\diamond$ and $\mathcal{M}^\diamond$, resulting in counterexamples. We describe our approach for identifying these deviations and their causing inaccuracies in $\mathcal{H}$ in the following sections. We use $u, v \in I_{\mathcal{M}}^*$ and $s \in I_{\mathcal{M}}$ as the components of a counterexample $c = u \cdot s \cdot v$ and the prefix function from Sect. 3.2 to retrieve stored prefixes for states in $\mathcal{H}^\diamond$. We also refer to a configuration where we mean the state representing it in $\mathcal{H}^\diamond$.

Identifying Missing Locations. Missing locations cause incorrect successors in $\mathcal{H}^\diamond$. We identify these by counterexample decomposition, similarly to how *RS*

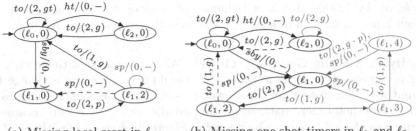

(a) Missing local reset in ℓ_1 (b) Missing one-shot timers in ℓ_1 and ℓ_2

Fig. 3. Reduced expanded forms of inaccurate hypotheses of the sensor data collector (inaccuracies in red, expected behavior dashed) (Color figure online)

identifies missing states. Different to *RS*, we also find decompositions in counterexamples that result from missing one-shot timers and missing local resets. We ensure that a decomposition corresponds to a missing location as follows. Let $\delta_{\mathcal{H}^\diamond}(u) = (\ell, t)$, where $t \in \mathbb{N}^{\geq 0}$ and $\ell \in L_{\mathcal{H}}$. We infer a missing location at $\delta_{\mathcal{H}^\diamond}(u, s)$ iff $\lambda_{\mathcal{M}^\diamond}(\lfloor(\ell, 0)\rfloor \cdot s, v) \neq \lambda_{\mathcal{M}^\diamond}(\lfloor(\ell, 0) \cdot s\rfloor, v)$ due to the following. Both correct and incorrect location changes must occur in all configurations of ℓ. Due to potentially missing one-shot timers, we do not know for sure that all configurations that are currently associated with ℓ in $\mathcal{H}^\diamond$ actually belong to it. We only know that $(\ell, 0)$ belongs to ℓ because this configuration is always entered during a location change due to our transition rules. Therefore, we test for an incorrect successor in $(\ell, 0)$.

Identifying Missing Local Resets. Some missing local resets also lead to incorrect successors in $\mathcal{H}^\diamond$. Again, we identify these incorrect successors with counterexample decomposition. Consider the hypothesis of our sensor data collector (cf. Fig. 1a) with a missing local reset in Fig. 3a and the counterexample $c = sby \cdot to \cdot sp \cdot to$. We can decompose c to $u = sby \cdot to$, $s = sp$, and $v = to$. This means that the state $\delta_{\mathcal{H}^\diamond}(u) = (\ell_1, 2)$ has an incorrect successor at sp. Indeed, sp should be a local reset in ℓ_1 and cause a transition to $(\ell_1, 0)$ instead of $(\ell_1, 2)$. An incorrect successor may also result from a missing location or a missing one-shot timer. Neither of these cases applies iff we do not detect a missing location at $\delta_{\mathcal{H}}(\ell_1, sp)$ (cf. previous section), sp triggers a self-loop in $\mathcal{H}$ that does not already cause a reset, and sp behaves like a reset. We test the latter similarly to [12] by verifying that $\lambda_{\mathcal{M}^+}(\lfloor\ell_1\rfloor, to) = \lambda_{\mathcal{M}^+}(\lfloor\ell_1\rfloor \cdot \tau \cdot sp, to)$. Thus, the additional time step must not reduce the offset to the first timeout in ℓ_1 when sp causes a reset. We also require that s from the decomposition is a non-timeout input and that the elapsed time in $\delta_{\mathcal{H}^\diamond}(u)$ is greater than zero, as timeouts cannot cause resets and resets have no effect in initial location configurations, eliminating them as cause for an incorrect successor.

We detect all missing local resets that yield counterexamples with the above approach. Some local resets, though, are not captured by our reduced expanded form and thus, give no counterexample. We identify these missing resets during *completion* by testing the reset behavior of self-loop transitions with a non-timeout input at the end of learning. We cover this step later in detail.

Identifying Missing One-Shot Timers. We miss a one-shot timer when our timer query assigns a periodic timer that should actually cause a change to a different location. Note that the converse case, where our timer query would assign a one-shot timer that should be periodic, does not occur because we initially consider all timers to be periodic. Figure 3b shows a hypothesis of our sensor data collector (cf. Fig. 1a) that misses one-shot timers in ℓ_1 and ℓ_2. Here, $\mathcal{H}^\diamond$ transitions from $(\ell_1, 2)$ to $(\ell_1, 3)$ at *to*, while the SUL moves to $(\ell_0, 0)$ instead. Moreover, $\mathcal{H}^\diamond$ stays in $(\ell_2, 0)$ at *to* instead of entering $(\ell_0, 0)$.

We can detect the missing one-shot timer in ℓ_2 with decomposition directly. Consider the counterexample $c_1 = ht \cdot to^2$ that decomposes to $u = ht$, $s = to$, and $v = to$. Here, $\mathcal{M}^\diamond$ transitions from $\delta_{\mathcal{M}^\diamond}(\lfloor u \rfloor) = (\ell_2, 0)$ to $(\ell_0, 0)$ at *to*, while $\mathcal{H}^\diamond$ remains in $\delta_{\mathcal{H}^\diamond}(u) = \delta_{\mathcal{H}^\diamond}(u, s) = (\ell_2, 0)$. Such an incorrect successor at a *to*-transition may also result from a missing location. Then, the *to*-transition in $\mathcal{H}$ models a timeout of a one-shot timer that causes an incorrect location-change. *to* in $(\ell_2, 0)$, though, belongs to a periodic timer in $\mathcal{H}$. Therefore, our output deviation must result from a missing one-shot timer triggered at *to* or earlier. Hence, we infer such a missing timer in ℓ_2 expiring at two time units or earlier.

In contrast to that, we cannot identify the missing one-shot timer in ℓ_1 with decomposition directly. Take the counterexample $c_2 = sby \cdot to^3$. We would expect to decompose c_2 to $u = sby \cdot to$, $s = to$, and $v = to$, as *to* leads to the incorrect successor $(\ell_1, 3)$ in $\delta_{\mathcal{H}^\diamond}(u) = (\ell_1, 2)$. However, this incorrect transition is part of the prefix of $(\ell_1, 3)$ in $\mathcal{H}^\diamond$. Hence, $\lfloor u \rfloor \cdot s = \lfloor u \cdot s \rfloor$ and thus, the decomposition condition $\lambda_{\mathcal{M}^\diamond}(\lfloor u \rfloor \cdot s, v) \neq \lambda_{\mathcal{M}^\diamond}(\lfloor u \cdot s \rfloor, v)$ is not satisfied. Despite that, we can still infer that ℓ_1 misses a one-shot timer from c_2. Observe that $\lambda_{\mathcal{M}^\diamond}(\lfloor sby \cdot to^2 \rfloor, to) \neq \lambda_{\mathcal{H}^\diamond}(sby \cdot to^2, to)$. Thus, the outgoing *to*-transition in $\delta_{\mathcal{H}^\diamond}(sby \cdot to^2) = (\ell_1, 3)$ appears to have an incorrect output. We identify such incorrect transition outputs with our method from [8]. First, we cut c_2 after the first output deviation. Then, we check for an output deviation at the last input of the cut c_2. In our example, we find a deviation for *to* in $(\ell_1, 3)$. Hence, we miss a one-shot timer in ℓ_1 that expires at three time units or earlier.

Consider a different counterexample $c_3 = sby \cdot to^2 \cdot sp \cdot to$. In this example, we cannot detect the missing one-shot timer in ℓ_1 with the previous method because $\lfloor sby \cdot to^2 \cdot sp \rfloor = sby$ and $\lambda_{\mathcal{M}^\diamond}(sby, to) = \lambda_{\mathcal{H}^\diamond}(sby, to)$. Still, we can infer a missing one-shot timer from c_3 through decomposition. c_3 decomposes to $u = sby \cdot to^2$, $s = sp$, and $v = to$, as $\mathcal{H}^\diamond$ transitions from $\delta_{\mathcal{H}^\diamond}(u) = (\ell_1, 3)$ to $(\ell_1, 0)$ at *sp*, while $\mathcal{M}^\diamond$ remains in $\delta_{\mathcal{M}^\diamond}(u) = \delta_{\mathcal{M}^\diamond}(u, s) = (\ell_0, 0)$. Such an incorrect successor at a non-timeout transition may also result from a missing location or a missing local reset. However, their respective preconditions (cf. previous sections) do not hold in our example. Thus, we infer a missing one-shot timer in ℓ_1. Due to $\delta_{\mathcal{H}^\diamond}(u) = (\ell_1, 3)$, this timer must expire at three time units or earlier.

The three methods described above detect locations with missing one-shot timers and the maximum time up to which these timers must expire across

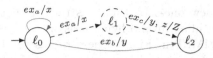

Fig. 4. MMLT hypothesis with $\theta(a) = 2$, $\theta(b) = 3$, $\theta(c) = 1$ (inaccuracies in red, expected behavior dashed) (Color figure online)

differently structured counterexamples. However, we must still choose periodic timers that should become one-shot timers. As in Sect. 5.1, we choose the timers with the highest expiration time possible, to keep $\mathcal{H}$ small.

Algorithm. We combine the approaches from the previous sections in our new algorithm for timed counterexample analysis. We design the following analysis process for a hypothesis $\mathcal{H}$, a target $\mathcal{M}$, and a counterexample $c \in I_{\mathcal{M}^\diamond}^*$:

1. Cut c after the first output deviation between $\mathcal{H}^\diamond$ and $\mathcal{M}^\diamond$ and only keep the first part as new c.
2. Set $c = u \cdot s$, $(\ell, t) \leftarrow \delta_{\mathcal{H}^\diamond}(u)$, where $s \in I_{\mathcal{M}^\diamond}, u \in I_{\mathcal{M}^\diamond}^*, t \in \mathbb{N}^{\geq 0}, \ell \in L_{\mathcal{H}}$. Iff $\lambda_{\mathcal{M}^\diamond}(\lfloor u \rfloor, s) \neq \lambda_{\mathcal{H}^\diamond}(u, s)$: identify missing one-shot timer in ℓ and terminate.
3. Decompose c to $c = u \cdot s \cdot v$ s.t. $\lambda_{\mathcal{M}^\diamond}(\lfloor u \rfloor \cdot s, v) \neq \lambda_{\mathcal{M}^\diamond}(\lfloor u \cdot s \rfloor, v)$, where $s \in I_{\mathcal{M}^\diamond}, u, v \in I_{\mathcal{M}^\diamond}^*$. Then, set $(\ell, t) \leftarrow \delta_{\mathcal{H}^\diamond}(u)$, where $t \in \mathbb{N}^{\geq 0}$ and $\ell \in L_{\mathcal{H}}$.
   - If $s = to$: iff s models the timeout of a one-shot timer in (ℓ, t), stop and signal missing location. Iff s models the timeout of one or more periodic timers in (ℓ, t), stop and identify missing one-shot timer in ℓ.
   - Iff $\lambda_{\mathcal{M}^\diamond}(\lfloor (\ell, 0) \rfloor \cdot s, v) \neq \lambda_{\mathcal{M}^\diamond}(\lfloor (\ell, 0) \cdot s \rfloor, v)$: stop and signal missing location at $\delta_{\mathcal{H}}(\ell, s)$.
   - Iff $t > 0$, $\delta_{\mathcal{H}}(\ell, s) = \ell$, $\rho_{\mathcal{H}}(\ell, s) = \bot$, and $\lambda_{\mathcal{M}^+}(\lfloor \ell \rfloor, to) = \lambda_{\mathcal{M}^+}(\lfloor \ell \rfloor \cdot \tau \cdot s, to)$: stop and signal missing local reset at s in ℓ.
   - Identify missing one-shot timer in ℓ.

Like RS, we use binary search to decompose counterexamples efficiently. Counterexamples often result from multiple inaccuracies in $\mathcal{H}$. Therefore, we analyze the same counterexample repeatedly after refining $\mathcal{H}$ until it causes no more output deviations. This saves expensive equivalence queries and makes our method even more efficient. We describe the refinement of $\mathcal{H}$ in the following section.

5.3 Hypothesis Refinement

We refine our hypothesis $\mathcal{H}$ after counterexample analysis to fix the identified inaccuracies. We describe this process in the following.

We add missing locations and set transitions that miss a local reset to perform a reset in $\mathcal{H}$. We fix a missing one-shot timer by changing the type of the identified timer from periodic to one-shot. A one-shot timer always causes a location change in an MMLT. Therefore, we also remove local timers that only expire after our new one-shot timer, as they do not have an effect anymore. This step may yield an invalid hypothesis, as we illustrate next. Consider the hypothesis of an MMLT in Fig. 4, where ℓ_0 has the local timers a, b with the timeout symbols ex_a, ex_b, ℓ_1 is yet unknown, and ex_b is the prefix of ℓ_2. Assume that we discovered the missing one-shot timer at ex_a and thus remove ex_b when refining $\mathcal{H}$. This makes ℓ_2 inaccessible via its stored prefix ex_b, violating a fundamental assumption of RS. We resolve this issue by removing all locations recursively that no longer can be accessed via their stored prefix. In our example, we remove ℓ_2 from $\mathcal{H}$. As a result, we need to rediscover ℓ_2 later, introducing additional queries. In practice, however, we have only observed removals in tests with randomly generated MMLTs yet.

We repeatedly fix inaccuracies in $\mathcal{H}$ with refinement until our learner receives no more counterexamples. Then, we complete $\mathcal{H}$ to identify potentially missing resets, as we describe next.

5.4   Hypothesis Completion

Some missing local resets may not yield counterexamples. We identify these resets during *completion*, as we describe in the following.

Consider our sensor data collector from Fig. 1a. *send* causes a local reset in ℓ_0 and thus, a change from $(\ell_0, 1)$ to $(\ell_0, 0)$ in the expanded form of the collector (cf. Fig. 1b). The reduced expanded form of an MMLT, though, represents specific locations with a single configuration only. In our example, it models ℓ_0 solely with $(\ell_0, 0)$. Hence, a local reset like *send* behaves like a normal self-loop in this form[4], and thus, yields no counterexample in an equivalence query.

We identify local resets in locations of $\mathcal{H}$ that are only represented by a single configuration in $\mathcal{H}^\circ$ by testing the reset behavior of all their self-looping non-timeout transitions. Like in Sect. 5.2, we find a reset in a candidate location ℓ at a self-loop with the input $s \neq to$ iff $\lambda_{\mathcal{M}^+}(\lfloor \ell \rfloor, to) = \lambda_{\mathcal{M}^+}(\lfloor \ell \rfloor \cdot \tau \cdot s, to)$, with $\mathcal{M}$ as the SUL. We perform these tests at the end of learning, as this ensures that all transition targets and assigned timers are correct, and thus, eliminates redundant reset tests.

Having identified the remaining missing resets, learning concludes. In the next section, we analyze the output query complexity of our learner.

5.5   Output Query Complexity

In the following, we analyze the output query complexity of our learner. This is a common metric in active automata learning and describes the worst-case number of output queries sent to the SUL $\mathcal{M}$.

We first assume no location removals when refining the hypothesis $\mathcal{H}$. As for RS, the query complexity of our learner is composed of the complexity of analyzing all counterexamples and the complexity of the remaining learner actions. In contrast to RS, our learner also analyzes counterexamples from missing resets

---

[4] We omit this loop in Fig. 1b for readability because its output is silent.

Table 1. Case studies with key properties

	AKM	CAS	PC	TCP	Oven	SCTP	WSN
States in $\mathcal{M}^+$	5	8	8	11	89	41	63
Non-timeout input symbols	5	4	9	8	5	12	4
Maximum timeout in learned MMLT [s]	2.5	270.0	10.0	20.0	300.0	1.0	3600.0
Locations in MM1T	4	8	8	11	89	41	63
Locations in learned MMLT	5	8	8	11	4	41	4

and one-shot timers. All timers and local resets are associated with an input symbol in $\mathcal{H}$. Thus, the complexity of analyzing all counterexamples in our learner grows linearly to the number of input symbols of $\mathcal{H}$, in addition to increasing linearly to the maximum size of $\mathcal{H}$ and logarithmically to the length of the received counterexamples, like RS [6]. The query complexity of the remaining actions of our learner is identical to that of RS, and thus increases linearly to the number of input symbols of $\mathcal{H}$ and quadratically to its maximum size.

Location removals make learning more costly. We remove a location when it is no longer accessible via its stored prefix. Then, we must relearn this location via a different prefix later. With repeated location removals, we must at worst rediscover each location once via each of its possible stored prefixes. The total number of different prefixes stored by $\mathcal{H}$ increases at worst exponentially with the maximum size of $\mathcal{H}$. Thus, the worst-case query complexity of our learner grows exponentially with the maximum size of $\mathcal{H}$ when removing locations.

Hence, our learner performs well unless we repeatedly remove locations. In practice, though, we have only encountered location removals in tests with random automata yet. Moreover, we can avoid redundant queries with a cache. We present the detailed results of our evaluation next.

6   Practical Evaluation

We have compared the actual efficiency of our method across diverse case studies to that of the state-of-the-art learner MM1T [12]. We present our evaluation setup and results in the following.[5]

We have chosen seven diverse case studies ranging from automotive systems to smart home appliances to validate the broad applicability of our approach, including all real-life systems from the original evaluation of the MM1T learner [12]. We have simulated these systems with models, as usual. We have also simulated the waiting times for the outputs of *to-* and τ-transitions s.t. the learner must wait until these outputs occur. Table 1 shows their key properties. From the domain of automotive systems, we have used a *car alarm system* (CAS) [1] and a *particle counter* (PC) that counts particles in exhaust gases [1]. From the area of network protocols, we have included a model of the connection handling in TCP [12], a model of the Wi-Fi authentication used by Android (AKM)

---

[5] Models and MMLT learner available at git.tu-berlin.de/pkogel/mmlt-learning.

Table 2. Evaluation results

	SUL Resets			SUL Inputs			SUL Delay [d:hh:mm:ss]		
	MM1T	MMLT	Ratio	MM1T	MMLT	Ratio	MM1T	MMLT	Ratio
AKM	1503.60	296.20	5.08	8895.20	1625.00	5.47	0:00:41:15	0:00:10:05	4.09
CAS	1519.20	368.80	4.12	9937.30	2130.90	4.66	3:14:02:58	1:03:36:03	3.12
PC	3035.80	905.90	3.35	18591.00	4685.80	3.97	0:06:06:20	0:00:40:00	9.16
TCP	4300.20	1252.60	3.43	30729.00	7803.80	3.94	0:15:37:12	0:02:15:44	6.90
Oven	41665.20	240.30	173.39	150183.90	1324.90	113.35	96:01:03:55	0:19:22:30	118.97
SCTP	20687.60	7568.10	2.73	87111.90	30368.50	2.87	1:04:14:51	0:10:04:42	2.80
WSN	27539.70	209.10	131.71	67758.40	1446.10	46.86	1732:11:57:24	8:00:37:12	215.87

[12], and a model of an endpoint for the emerging *Stream Control Transmission Protocol* (SCTP) [10]. Finally, we have added two models from our own collection that resemble major applications of RTS. These comprize a wireless sensor node (WSN) that collects and transmits data at fixed rates, and an *oven* with a time-controlled baking program and a heater.

We have implemented our MMLT learner in the established framework *Learn-Lib* and have compared it to the reference implementation of the MM1T learner. We have slightly adapted this implementation for a full black box setting. The original learner assumes that self-loops without an effect produce a special *undefined* output, letting it avoid many redundant queries. We model these transitions as normal silent self-loops instead. We have set up our MMLT learner with a query cache and a *random Wp* counterexample finder, due to its outstanding performance in practice [2]. Since we assume a realistic black box setting, we do not know the most efficient *random Wp* parameters per case study. Therefore, we have chosen a configuration that is efficient across all case studies. The MM1T learner integrates a cache by design. It can also use different learning algorithms. Like [12], we have tested it with the *RS* and *TTT* [7] algorithms and a *random words* and a *Wp* counterexample finder. We have also performed tests with a *random Wp* finder. Again assuming a realistic black box setting, we have chosen a configuration with *RS* and a *random Wp* finder as baseline for our learner, as this has been the most efficient on average across all case studies. We have observed that all tested counterexample finders fail on the *Oven, SCTP*, and *WSN* models in all experiments. This is because parts of these systems only show a change in behavior after many timeouts. *Random Wp* and *random words*, though, find counterexamples by testing semi-random input sequences, making it unlikely to find a sequence with many subsequent timeouts. *Wp* tests all input combinations up to a specific length in each hypothesis state and thus, could find counterexamples for above systems. Adjusting these input lengths for our models, though, increases runtimes excessively. Therefore, we have used a modified *random Wp* finder for the MMLT learner that, after observing a timeout, samples a subsequent timeout with higher probability. For MM1T, we have instead manually provided one additional counterexample per affected model, as its learner design makes an efficient implementation of our modified *random Wp* finder difficult.

We have measured the efficiency of the MMLT and MM1T learners with the common metrics *resets*, *inputs*, and *delay* [1]. *Resets* are all resets of the SUL, *inputs* are all symbols except for *to* and τ executed by the SUL, and *delay* is the total delay from single time steps with τ and waiting for timeouts. We have also counted the locations that our MMLT learner has removed during hypothesis refinements. However, we have not observed any such removals, clearly indicating that they only rarely affect runtimes in practice. Table 2 shows the remaining results. All values are averages over 10 runs. *Ratio* corresponds to *baseline/value*. Thus, ratios above one indicate an improvement over the MM1T learner.

As shown, our MMLT learner has drastically outperformed the MM1T learner in all efficiency metrics across all case studies. The resulting runtime savings become most immediately apparent in the accumulated delay, as this is hardware independent. Here, our learner has saved at least 30 min when learning *AKM*, 13 h when learning *TCP*, and at least 18 h for *SCTP*. For *CAS*, we have reduced the delay even by more than 48 h. Combined with the drastic reductions in resets and inputs, these improvements make our method well suited for regular use in practice.

We have saved even more time for the *Oven* and *WSN* models, where the learned MMLT has been significantly smaller than the respective MM1T (cf. Table 1). Here, our learner has used drastically fewer SUL resets, inputs, and delay than the MM1T learner. This effect is most significant in the *WSN* model, where the MM1T learner would have waited for at least 4.5 years, while our learner would have only delayed the SUL for about eight days.

Hence, our method does not only reduce runtimes drastically compared to the state-of-the-art learner MM1T in practice but thereby also opens automata learning to a wide range of applications that were unable to use it before.

7 Conclusion and Future Work

We have introduced *Mealy machines with local timers* (MMLTs), a new class of Mealy machines that permit multiple local timers and constrain timer use to enable efficient learning of real-time systems. We have also presented a new efficient learning algorithm for MMLTs that is based on the Rivest-Schapire method. We have described our model and learner in detail and demonstrated across diverse case studies ranging from automotive systems to smart home appliances that our method drastically reduces runtimes compared to the state-of-the-art approach, hence, making active automata learning feasible for a wide range of real-time systems, including systems that were unable to use it before.

We see several exciting possibilities to improve the efficiency of our method even further. First, we plan to explore modifications of the MMLT semantics that enable even smaller models, like multiple one-shot timers per location. We also intend to exploit imprecise knowledge of the SUL, as this often reduces runtimes significantly [8]. Finally, we would like to investigate methods for counterexample search that specifically target MMLTs, as efficient comparison of real-time behavior promises significant further savings [11].

References

1. Aichernig, B.K., Pferscher, A., Tappler, M.: From passive to active: learning timed automata efficiently. In: Lee, R., Jha, S., Mavridou, A., Giannakopoulou, D. (eds.) NFM 2020. LNCS, vol. 12229, pp. 1–19. Springer, Cham (2020). https://doi.org/10.1007/978-3-030-55754-6_1

2. Aichernig, B.K., Tappler, M., Wallner, F.: Benchmarking combinations of learning and testing algorithms for active automata learning. In: Ahrendt, W., Wehrheim, H. (eds.) TAP 2020. LNCS, vol. 12165, pp. 3–22. Springer, Cham (2020). https://doi.org/10.1007/978-3-030-50995-8_1

3. An, J., Chen, M., Zhan, B., Zhan, N., Zhang, M.: Learning one-clock timed automata. In: TACAS 2020. LNCS, vol. 12078, pp. 444–462. Springer, Cham (2020). https://doi.org/10.1007/978-3-030-45190-5_25

4. Grinchtein, O., Jonsson, B., Leucker, M.: Learning of event-recording automata. Theor. Comput. Sci. **411**(47) (2010)

5. Henry, L., Jéron, T., Markey, N.: Active learning of timed automata with unobservable resets. In: Bertrand, N., Jansen, N. (eds.) FORMATS 2020. LNCS, vol. 12288, pp. 144–160. Springer, Cham (2020). https://doi.org/10.1007/978-3-030-57628-8_9

6. Howar, F., Steffen, B.: Active automata learning as black-box search and lazy partition refinement. In: In: Jansen, N., Stoelinga, M., van den Bos, P. (eds.) A Journey from Process Algebra via Timed Automata to Model Learning. LNCS, vol. 13560. Springer, Cham (2022). https://doi.org/10.1007/978-3-031-15629-8_17

7. Isberner, M., Howar, F., Steffen, B.: The TTT algorithm: a redundancy-free approach to active automata learning. In: Bonakdarpour, B., Smolka, S.A. (eds.) RV 2014. LNCS, vol. 8734, pp. 307–322. Springer, Cham (2014). https://doi.org/10.1007/978-3-319-11164-3_26

8. Kogel, P., Klös, V., Glesner, S.: TTT/IK: learning accurate mealy automata efficiently with an imprecise symbol filter. In: Riesco, A., Zhang, M. (eds.) Formal Methods and Software Engineering, vol. 13478, pp. 227–243. Springer, Cham (2022). https://doi.org/10.1007/978-3-031-17244-1_14

9. Rivest, R., Schapire, R.: Inference of finite automata using homing sequences. Inf. Comput. **103**(2) (1993)

10. Stewart, R., Tüxen, M., Nielsen, K.: Stream Control transmission protocol. Technical report (2022). https://doi.org/10.17487/rfc9260

11. Tang, X., Shen, W., Zhang, M., An, J., Zhan, B., Zhan, N.: Learning deterministic one-clock timed automata via mutation testing. In: Bouajjani, A., Holík, L., Wu, Z. (eds.) ATVA 2022, vol. 1350, pp. 233–248. Springer, Cham (2022). https://doi.org/10.1007/978-3-031-19992-9_15

12. Vaandrager, F., Ebrahimi, M., Bloem, R.: Learning Mealy machines with one timer. Inf. Comput. (2023)

13. Vaandrager, F., Garhewal, B., Rot, J., Wißmann, T.: A new approach for active automata learning based on apartness. In: TACAS 2022. LNCS, vol. 13243, pp. 223–243. Springer, Cham (2022). https://doi.org/10.1007/978-3-030-99524-9_12

14. Xu, R., An, J., Zhan, B.: Active learning of one-clock timed automata using constraint solving. In: Bouajjani, A., Holík, L., Wu, Z. (eds.) ATVA 202. LNCS, vol. 13505, pp. 249–265. Springer, Cham (2022). https://doi.org/10.1007/978-3-031-19992-9_16

Compositional Vulnerability Detection with Insecurity Separation Logic

Toby Murray[1](✉), Pengbo Yan[1], and Gidon Ernst[2]

[1] University of Melbourne, Melbourne, Australia
toby.murray@unimelb.edu.au, pengpoy@student.unimelb.edu.au
[2] LMU Munich, Munich, Germany
gidon.ernst@lmu.de

Abstract. Memory-safety issues and information leakage are known to be depressingly common. We consider the compositional static detection of these kinds of vulnerabilities in first-order C-like programs. Indeed the latter are *relational* hyper-safety violations, comparing pairs of program executions, making them more challenging to detect than the former, which require reasoning only over individual executions. Existing symbolic leakage detection methods treat only non-interactive programs, avoiding the challenges of nondeterminism. Also, being whole-program analyses they cannot be applied one-function-at-a-time, thereby ruling out incremental analysis. We remedy these shortcomings by presenting Insecurity Separation Logic (INSECSL), an under-approximate relational program logic for soundly detecting information leakage and memory-safety issues in interactive programs. Importantly, INSECSL reasons about pairs of executions, and so is relational, but purposefully resembles the non-relational Incorrectness Separation Logic (ISL) that is already automated in the Infer tool. We show how INSECSL can be automated by bi-abduction based symbolic execution, and we evaluate two implementations of this idea (one based on Infer) on various case-studies.

1 Introduction

Almost all program logics are for proving the correctness of programs. Hoare logic is a classic example, whose judgements have the form $\{P\}\ c\ \{Q\}$ for a program command c and pre- and postconditions P and Q. This judgement means that when executed from an initial state satisfying P that after command c finishes, Q is guaranteed to hold. In this sense postcondition Q *over-approximates* the final states that command c can reach from an initial P-state. Recently, interest has emerged in program logics for proving *incorrectness* [16], i.e., for diagnosing bugs in programs with a true-positives guarantee. Such logics inherit the *under-approximate* structure of Reverse Hoare Logic [8]. Their judgements $[P]\ c\ [Q]$ mean that for all final states t satisfying Q, there exists an initial P-state from which Q can execute to terminate in state t. Thus Q under-approximates the final states that command c can reach from an initial P-state.

© The Author(s), under exclusive license to Springer Nature Singapore Pte Ltd. 2023
Y. Li and S. Tahar (Eds.): ICFEM 2023, LNCS 14308, pp. 65–82, 2023.
https://doi.org/10.1007/978-981-99-7584-6_5

While the two approaches are roughly equivalent for deterministic programs, under-approximate reasoning is necessary to accurately diagnose vulnerabilities in *nondeterministic* programs, including those that allocate memory or interact with an outside environment or user. Incorrectness Separation Logic [12,17] (ISL) is such an under-approximate logic, which has proved especially useful for automatic memory-safety bug detection because program analysis in the logic can be carried out automatically via bi-abduction based symbolic execution [5,17], and supports compositional and incremental program analysis [12].

All such under-approximate logics to-date, however, reason only about individual program executions. They can therefore detect only those bugs that can be observed in this way, like assertion failures (as in Incorrectness Logic [16]) or memory-safety errors like null-pointer dereferences and use-after-free errors (as in Incorrectness Separation Logic [17]). Yet, vulnerabilities come in many kinds, beyond memory-safety issues. In this paper we focus on the *automatic detection of information leakage vulnerabilities*. These are especially interesting as they are very common and can be devastating. But since information leakage is semantically expressed as a hyperproperty [6], which compares *pairs* of program executions, it is out of scope for the existing under-approximative logics.

Can we design an under-approximate logic for reasoning about such vulnerabilities which inherits the nice property that all defects which are flagged are true positives? If so, can analysis using this logic be automated to produce a compositional vulnerability analysis method?

Contribution: We answer both of these questions in the affirmative. In this paper, we present Insecurity Separation Logic (INSECSL, Sect. 4), an under-approximate separation logic for diagnosing information leakage and memory-safety vulnerabilities. INSECSL reasons about pairs of program executions but purposefully closely resembles the (single execution) logic ISL [17]. We show in Sect. 5 how reasoning in INSECSL can be automated via bi-abduction based symbolic execution by formalising and proving that the same symbolic execution procedure as is used for ISL is also sound for INSECSL. We demonstrate the practicality of our ideas by implementing them in two different tools (Sect. 6), including an extension of the Infer tool in which we adapt Infer's ISL implementation to diagnose information leakage vulnerabilities via INSECSL. We evaluate our implementations (Sect. 7) by applying them to a range of case studies. Soundness theorems (namely Theorem 1 for INSECSL and Theorem 2 for symbolic execution respectively) have been mechanised in Isabelle/HOL. All artifacts are available online with the extended version of this paper: https://covern.org/insecurity.html.

2   Motivation

We use the program in Fig. 1 to both motivate and explain our approach. This program implements the core of a simple *sealed-bid* auction server. In a sealed-bid auction, all information about bids must be kept secret until after the auction is finished, at which point only the winning bid is announced.

```
struct bid_t { int id; int qt; };          void update_max(struct bid_t *a,
                                                           struct bid_t *b)
void run_auction() {                        {
  struct bid_t highest = /* init */;          /* branching on secrets: */
  while (/* still going */) {                  if (b->qt > a->qt) {
    struct bid_t bid;                            a->id = b->id;
    get_bid(&bid);                               a->qt = b->qt;
    update_max(&highest, &bid);                  /* potentially slow: */
  }                                              log_current_max(a->id, a->qt);
  announce_winner(&highest);                   }
}                                           }
```

Fig. 1. The core of a sealed-bid auction server, adapted from a case-study in SecC: https://bitbucket.org/covern/secc/src/master/examples/case-studies/auction.c.

Bids in this auction are pairs of ints: (id, qt) where id identifies the bidder who submitted the bid, and qt is the amount (or $quote$) submitted in the bid. The C struct type bid_t pairs these two values together. The top-level function run_auction() maintains the current maximum bid highest, and a temporary bid used to store newly submitted bids, which are received via the get_bid() function. Each new bid is then compared to the current highest one using the function update_max(), which potentially updates the current highest bid and persists a record about this fact via log_current_max. Note that get_bid() is inherently nondeterministic: It may return arbitrary values, since it is the interface between the program and its environment. This puts it outside the scope of Relational Symbolic Execution [11] as implemented in tools like Binsec/Rel [7].

Unfortunately, update_max() is insecure. As it updates the maximum bid only when the newly submitted bid is larger than the current maximum, its *timing* depends on whether the branch is taken or not. This timing leak can be exploited by auction participants to game the auction. In particular if log_current_max incurs a notable delay—writing to disk or even network storage synchronously may be slow—they might be capable to infer whether the bid they have submitted is greater than the current maximum or not. Moreover, the call to announce_winner() is potentially insecure under the premise that we only want to disclose the winning bid. If highest has not been computed correctly, then we may accidentally reveal sensitive information about another bid.

Challenge: The question of whether a *potential* information leak in a program becomes critical therefore strongly depends on the context in which functions like update_max() and announce_winner() are called. A compositional underapproximative analysis like that of INSECSL must therefore be capable of tracking such relationships *precisely* to be sound, i.e., to avoid false positives.

As an example, the security-related summary inferred for update_max(), shown below, expresses that each potentially insecure final state as marked by *insec* is guaranteed to be reachable under the sufficient presumption that parameters a and b are valid pointers. Assertion $(bqt > aqt) \not\vdash \ell$ denotes that this insecurity occurs if within a given calling context the outcome of the conditional $bqt > aqt$ is *not already known to the attacker* of security level ℓ (cf. Sect. 3 and Sect. 4).

$$[\&b\text{->}qt \mapsto bqt * \&a\text{->}qt \mapsto aqt]$$
$$\texttt{update\_max(a,b)}$$
$$[insec\colon (bqt > aqt) \not\curlywedge \ell * \&b\text{->}qt \mapsto bqt * \&a\text{->}qt \mapsto aqt]$$

Note that this summary is beyond the scope of type systems like [19] which just capture whether information flow happens or not, but which fail to adequately reason about logical conditions like $(bqt > aqt) \not\curlywedge \ell$.

3   Attacker Model

We imagine that the execution of the program in question is being observed by an *attacker*, who has certain observational powers and initial knowledge and is trying to deduce secret information that the program is trying to protect. An information leak occurs if the attacker can deduce some secret information that they did not already know initially before the program was executed.

As standard, the attacker is assumed to know the program being executed and certain initial values in memory as specified by assertions characterising pre-states. The program may perform inputs and outputs during its execution and the attacker is assumed to be able to observe some of these. All other information is considered *secret*, and information flow security requires that the attacker can never learn any new information above that which they were assumed to know initially. As usual, we therefore define what an attacker can observe with the help of a security lattice comprised of labels ℓ which are comparable by a binary relation $\sqsubseteq$ with **low** and **high** being the least resp. greatest elements, modeling public and fully sensitive information, respectively. A channel at level ℓ' is observable by an ℓ-attacker if $\ell' \sqsubseteq \ell$, e.g., the **low** channel is observable publicly.

As motivated in Sect. 2, the security property for INSECSL is *timing-sensitive*. This means that the attacker can not just observe inputs and outputs on certain channels, but also at what times they occur. As is typical, time is measured in terms of the number of small-steps of execution in the language's small-step operational semantics. Following the standard *program counter (PC) security model* [13], the security property targeted by INSECSL assumes an attacker who is able to observe at each point in time (i.e. after each small-step of the semantics) the program code that is running. This implies that e.g. when executing an if-conditions **if** e **then** c_1 **else** c_2 **endif** where $c_1 \neq c_2$, that the attacker can infer some information about e (namely whether it evaluated to true or not), since they will be able to tell in the subsequent execution step whether c_1 or c_2 is being executed. A similar argument applies to while-loops. While not as strong as *constant-time security* [3], INSECSL can be easily extended to cover the stronger attacker model of constant-time security if desired (see the extended version of this paper [14]).

We emphasize that the choice of this attacker model is a trade-off: under this attacker model it is not possible to verify programs that have if/while conditions that depend on secrets, even if leakage from such conditions is considered acceptable in certain situations. On the other hand, a PC-security security guarantee requires one to consider only "matched" executions, as exploited by SECCSL [10] and also by INSECSL, which drastically simplifies the logic and its automation in comparison to product constructions like [9].

4 Insecurity Separation Logic (INSECSL)

Insecurity Separation Logic (INSECSL) is the relational analogue of ISL [17] and the underapproximative dual to Security (Concurrent) Separation Logic (SECCSL) [10]. Judgements in INSECSL are written as

$$\vdash_\ell [P]\ c\ [\epsilon:\ Q] \tag{1}$$

where relational assertions P characterizes the pre-states ("presumption") and Q characterize reachable final states ("result"), ℓ is a security level, c is a program command, and ϵ is a status flag that indicates whether the command has terminated normally ($\epsilon = ok$), whether a runtime error has occurred ($\epsilon = err(L)$), or whether an insecurity has been detected ($\epsilon = insec(L)$). The latter two track a program location L that points to the cause of the defect.

The capability to precisely characterise insecurity for nondeterministic programs is what distinguishes INSECSL from prior logics. As an example, INSECSL allows us to derive that the output of the value of an expression e to a channel of security level ℓ' can be potentially witnessed as insecure without further presumptions in any (pair of final) state(s) in which e is secret wrt. ℓ', written $e \not\sim \ell'$, under the assumption of an ℓ-attacker (which implies $\ell' \sqsubseteq \ell$):

$$\frac{}{\vdash_\ell [\textbf{emp}]\ L\colon \textbf{output}(\ell', e)\ [insec(L)\colon e \not\sim \ell']}\text{OUTINSEC} \tag{2}$$

Judgement (1) is defined relative to a relational semantics of assertions like $e \not\sim \ell'$ and **emp**, written $(s, h)\ (s', h') \models_\ell P$ where s, s' are stores (mappings from variables to values) and h, h' are heaps (mappings from addresses to values), and a small-step program semantics $k_1 \xrightarrow{\sigma} k_2$ where configurations k are either a running program $k_1, k_2 = \langle \textbf{run } "c"\ s\ h \rangle$, a terminated execution $k_2 = \langle \textbf{stop } s\ h \rangle$ or a program error $k_2 = \langle \textbf{abort } s\ h \rangle$, where the latter two correspond to a final status ϵ of ok and $err(L)$, respectively.

As a hyperproperty, security cannot be defined solely by looking at the final state of a single execution, comprised of the store s and heap h in $\langle \textbf{stop } s\ h \rangle$ configurations. Instead, we have to compare what is *observable* between possible pairs of executions. To capture this notion, execution steps additionally keep track of relevant events as a schedule σ, which records for example input events $in\langle \ell', v \rangle$ and outputs events $out\langle \ell', v \rangle$ to track a value v together with the security level ℓ' of the respective communication channel. The key issue for defining a security logic like INSECSL (and also SECCSL) and proving soundness of rules like (2) is therefore to connect the three ingredients, namely the judgements (1), observations σ, and the assertions P, Q encountered throughout a derivation. It is based on the following semantic notion:

Definition 1 (Execution Witness). *Presumption P and result Q witness an execution of program c against the ℓ-level attacker and a given status ϵ when for all final states s, h, s', h' such that (s,h) (s',h') $\models_\ell Q$, there exist initial states s_0, h_0, s_0', h_0', and σ, σ', k, k' such that (s_0,h_0) (s_0',h_0') $\models_\ell P$ and $\langle \mathbf{run}\ \text{``}c\text{''}\ s_0\ h_0 \rangle \xrightarrow{\sigma}{}^* k$ and $\langle \mathbf{run}\ \text{``}c\text{''}\ s_0'\ h_0' \rangle \xrightarrow{\sigma'}{}^* k'$, where σ and σ' have equal lengths and are input-equivalent for the ℓ-level attacker (Definition 2), and the final store and heap of k are respectively s and h and likewise for k', s' and h'. Moreover,*

If $\epsilon = ok$ resp. $\epsilon = err(L)$ then
- *σ and σ' are output-equivalent to the ℓ-level attacker (Definition 2),*
- *and k and k' must both be **stop**ped resp. **aborted**.*

If $\epsilon = insec(L)$ then
- *either σ and σ' are not output-equivalent to the ℓ-level attacker,*
- *or k and k' both denote **run**ning configurations with different commands.*

Witnessing an insecure behaviour therefore violates the standard security condition of program counter (PC) security [13]. Also note that the conditions are mutually exclusive, i.e., an execution witness can uniquely be classified into an ok behavior, an erroneous behavior, or an insecure one.

Theorem 1 (True Positives). INSECSL *guarantees that if $\vdash_\ell [P]\ c\ [\epsilon\colon Q]$ is derivable via the rules, shown in Fig. 2, then there is an execution witness for P, Q, c, and ϵ wrt. an ℓ-attacker, according to Definition 1.*

Assertions. INSECSL assertions are *relational* [10, 20]; pure assertions ρ and spatial assertions P, Q are defined according to the following grammar:

$$\rho ::= e \mid \rho \Longrightarrow \rho \mid e :: e_\ell \mid e \nmid e_\ell$$
$$P, Q ::= \mathbf{emp} \mid \rho \mid e \mapsto e' \mid e \nmapsto \mid P * Q \mid \exists x.\ P \mid P \Longrightarrow Q$$

where e ranges over pure expressions, including boolean propositions (first case of ρ), similarly, e_ℓ ranges over pure expression that denote security labels of some designated data type that models the security lattice and includes constants **low** and **high** but is not further specified here.

Semantically, assertions are evaluated over *pairs* of states, written $s\ s' \models_\ell \rho$ and $(s,h)\ (s',h) \models_\ell P$ for stores s, s' and heaps h, h', where the unprimed resp. primed states come from the two executions being compared. Stores are mappings from variable names to values as usual, whereas heaps $h\colon Val \rightharpoonup Val \cup \{\bot\}$ are partial functions that include an additional $\bot$ element as in ISL, where $p \in dom(h)$ and $h(p) = \bot$ means that pointer p is definitely invalid in contrast to $p \notin dom(h)$, which means we do not currently have access resp. own p.

The key definitions are as follows (see [14] for the full list):

$$s\ s' \models_\ell e \iff [e]_s = \mathbf{true} \wedge [e]_{s'} = \mathbf{true} \tag{3}$$
$$s\ s' \models_\ell e :: e_\ell \iff [e_\ell]_s \sqsubseteq \ell \wedge [e_\ell]_{s'} \sqsubseteq \ell \implies [e]_s = [e]_{s'} \tag{4}$$
$$s\ s' \models_\ell e \nmid e_\ell \iff [e_\ell]_s \sqsubseteq \ell \wedge [e_\ell]_s \sqsubseteq \ell \wedge [e]_s \neq [e]_{s'} \tag{5}$$

where we define (s, h) $(s', h') \models \rho$ iff s $s \models \rho$ and $h = h' = \emptyset$, and $[e]_s$ denotes the evaluation of pure expression e in store s, and $\sqsubseteq$ is the partial order between security labels. Conditions $[e_\ell]_s \sqsubseteq \ell$ and $[e_\ell]_{s'} \sqsubseteq \ell$ therefore mean that e_ℓ denotes a security label that is relevant wrt. the "current" ℓ-attacker from $\models_\ell$ resp. (1).

We can assert a pure boolean expression e if it is known to hold in both states s and s' (3). Assertion $e :: e_\ell$ denotes *agreement* of value e with respect to the security label denoted by e_ℓ, i.e., the value of e is the same in both s and s' (4). It coincides with $\mathbb{A}\, e$ of [2] for $e_\ell = \mathbf{low}$ but just as in SecCSL [10], e_ℓ can be a more complex expression, not just a constant. It expresses that an e_ℓ-attacker knows the value of e, specifically $e :: \mathbf{low}$ means that e is public. Dually, *disagreement* $e \not\lessdot e_\ell$ formalises that an attacker who can observe level e_ℓ has some uncertainty about e (5). Semantically, $s, s' \models_\ell e \not\lessdot e_\ell$ requires that it is possible for the expression e to take two *different* values in the two stores s and s' being compared. Therefore, leaking the value of e to an e_ℓ-visible output channel is insecure because the attacker can learn whether the system is actually in state s or in s' by observing the value of e.

The second feature for bug-detection is the assertion $e \not\mapsto$ from ISL [17], which expresses that e is known to be an invalid pointer, so that dereferencing e is necessarily incorrect. This is dual to the standard points-to assertion $e \mapsto e'$ which states that memory location e is valid and contains value e'.

We point out that relational implication $\Longrightarrow$ is distinct from pure implication at the level of expressions (not shown here). All other connectives intuitively mean the same as in a non-relational setting, e.g., $\mathbf{emp}$ denotes an empty heap and $P * Q$ asserts P and Q on two disjoint parts of the heap, but of course technically these have to be lifted to the relational setting semantically.

Commands and Semantics. Commands c in the language are as follows, where e is a pure expression that can mention program variables x:

$$
\begin{aligned}
c \ ::= \ & \mathbf{skip} \mid x := e \mid x := [e] \mid [e] := e' \mid x := \mathbf{alloc}(e) \mid \mathbf{free}(e) \mid \\
& L\colon c \mid c_1; c_2 \mid \mathbf{if}\ e\ \mathbf{then}\ c_1\ \mathbf{else}\ c_2\ \mathbf{endif} \mid \mathbf{while}\ e\ \mathbf{do}\ c\ \mathbf{done} \mid \\
& \mathbf{output}(e, e') \mid x := \mathbf{input}(e)
\end{aligned}
$$

Here $[e]$ denotes dereferencing pointer e and e.g. in C would be written $*e$. As in ISL [17], commands in INSECSL carry an optional label L that is used for error-reporting, written $L\colon c$. Most commands are standard, except $x := \mathbf{input}(e_\ell)$ and $\mathbf{output}(e_\ell, e)$. Command $x := \mathbf{input}(e_\ell)$ means input a value from the channel denoted by e_ℓ and assign the inputted value to the variable x; command $\mathbf{output}(e_\ell, e)$ means to output the value denoted by the expression e on the output channel denoted by the expression e_ℓ.

The language of INSECSL is given a small-step semantics $k_1 \xrightarrow{\sigma} k_2$, allowing judgements to talk about partial executions ending in **running** non-final states (cf. $insec(L)$ case in Definition 1). Importantly, this semantics records the values and security labels of input and output commands as part of schedule σ, which is necessary to state the formal security properties used for INSECSL's soundness result in Theorem 1 via Definition 2 below.

The schedule is a list of events $e ::= \tau \mid \text{in}\langle \ell, v \rangle \mid \text{out}\langle \ell, v \rangle \mid \text{allocate}\langle v \rangle$ for security level ℓ and value $v \in Val$. Event τ represents a single, non-**input**, non-**output**, non-**alloc** step of computation, i.e., τ steps are not critical for security. Event $\text{in}\langle \ell, v \rangle$ records that value v was input at security level ℓ and $\text{out}\langle \ell, v \rangle$ records that value v was output at security level (i.e. on the output channel) ℓ, while $\text{allocate}\langle v \rangle$ records that address v was dynamically allocated. It is simply included as a convenience to ensure that all non-determinism can be resolved by the schedule σ. Some key rules are shown below, the full listing is in [14].

$$\frac{a = [p]_s \qquad h(a) = v}{\langle \textbf{run } ``x := [p]" \ s \ h \rangle \xrightarrow{\ [\tau]\ } \langle \textbf{stop } s(x := v) \ h \rangle}$$

$$\frac{a = [p]_s \qquad a \notin dom(h) \vee h(a) = \bot}{\langle \textbf{run } ``x := [p]" \ s \ h \rangle \xrightarrow{\ [\tau]\ } \langle \textbf{abort } s \ h \rangle}$$

$$\langle \textbf{run } ``x := \textbf{input}(e_\ell)" \ s \ h \rangle \xrightarrow{\ [\text{in}\langle [e_\ell]_s, v \rangle]\ } \langle \textbf{stop } s(x := v) \ h \rangle$$

$$\langle \textbf{run } ``\textbf{output}(e_\ell, e)" \ s \ h \rangle \xrightarrow{\ \text{out}\langle [e_\ell]_s, [e]_s \rangle\ } \langle \textbf{stop } s \ h \rangle$$

The first rule shows a load via pointer expression p from a valid address a, the corresponding value in the heap is then assigned to variable x in the updated store $s(x := v)$. Notice that we can observe memory errors in this semantics directly by transitions to $\langle \textbf{abort } s \ h \rangle$ configurations, as it is for example when the pointer expression p instead evaluates to an unknown address $a \notin dom(h)$ or one that is definitely not allocated $h(a) = \bot$ (second rule). Reading from an input channel returns a non-deterministic value v that is assigned to x in the successor state. However, information leakage can only be observed by comparing pairs of executions in terms of their schedules (cf. Definition 1).

As an example, $\textbf{output}(e_\ell, e)$ with $[e_\ell]_s = \ell'$ and $[e_\ell]_{s'} = \ell'$ in a pair of executions with stores s and s' respectively, will expose two schedules $\sigma = [\text{out}\langle \ell', v \rangle]$ and $\sigma' = [\text{out}\langle \ell', v' \rangle]$, where $v = [e]_s$ and $v' = [e]_{s'}$ are the values that are output over the channel in the two runs. If $\ell' \sqsubseteq \ell$, i.e., the channel is visible to the attacker, then an information leak occurs if $v \neq v'$ and we have an execution witness according to Definition 1 and Eq. (5) for result $[insec: e \not\swarrow \ell']$. Input- and output-equivalence which Definition 1 relies on is therefore as follows:

Definition 2 (Input and Output Equivalence). *Two schedules are are input resp. output equivalent for the ℓ-level attacker when all inputs resp. outputs observable to that attacker are identical in each, i.e., after projecting the schedules to those input resp. output events, $\text{in}\langle \ell', v \rangle$ or $\text{out}\langle \ell', v \rangle$ for which $\ell' \sqsubseteq \ell$.*

Proof Rules and Soundness. The proof rules of INSECSL are in Fig. 2. Rules analog to those of ISL [17] are included, those rules that mention value classification (e.g. in INPUT) and those with insec result are specific to INSECSL.

$$\frac{}{\vdash_\ell [x = x']\; x := \mathbf{input}(e)\; [ok\colon x :: e[x'/x]]}\textsc{Input} \qquad \frac{}{\vdash_\ell [x = x']\; x := e\; [ok\colon x = e[x'/x]]}\textsc{Assign}$$

$$\frac{}{\vdash_\ell [P]\; \mathbf{skip}\; [ok\colon P]}\textsc{Skip} \qquad \frac{}{\vdash_\ell [x = x' * p \mapsto e]\; x := [p]\; [ok\colon x = e[x'/x] * p \mapsto e[x'/x]]}\textsc{LoadOK}$$

$$\frac{}{\vdash_\ell [p \mapsto e]\; [p] := e'\; [ok\colon p \mapsto e']}\textsc{StoreOK} \qquad \frac{}{\vdash_\ell [p \not\mapsto]\; L\colon x := [p]\; [err(L)\colon p \not\mapsto]}\textsc{LoadErr}$$

$$\frac{}{\vdash_\ell [p \not\mapsto]\; L\colon [p] := e\; [err(L)\colon p \not\mapsto]}\textsc{StoreErr} \qquad \frac{}{\vdash_\ell [emp]\; x := \mathbf{alloc}(e)\; [ok\colon x \mapsto e]}\textsc{Alloc1}$$

$$\frac{}{\vdash_\ell [p \not\mapsto]\; x := \mathbf{alloc}(e)\; [ok\colon x = p * p \mapsto e]}\textsc{Alloc2} \qquad \frac{}{\vdash_\ell [p \mapsto e]\; \mathbf{free}(p)\; [ok\colon p \not\mapsto]}\textsc{FreeOK}$$

$$\frac{}{\vdash_\ell [p \not\mapsto]\; L\colon \mathbf{free}(p)\; [err(L)\colon p \not\mapsto]}\textsc{FreeErr} \qquad \frac{}{\vdash_\ell [emp]\; \mathbf{output}(\ell', e)\; [ok\colon e :: \ell']}\textsc{OutOK}$$

$$\frac{}{\vdash_\ell [emp]\; L\colon \mathbf{output}(\ell', e)\; [insec(L)\colon e \not\preceq \ell']}\textsc{OutInsec}$$

$$\frac{\vdash_\ell [b * P]\; c_1\; [\epsilon\colon Q]}{\vdash_\ell [P]\; \mathbf{if}\; b\; \mathbf{then}\; c_1\; \mathbf{else}\; c_2\; \mathbf{endif}\; [\epsilon\colon Q]}\textsc{IfTrue} \qquad \frac{\vdash_\ell [\neg b * P]\; c_2\; [\epsilon\colon Q]}{\vdash_\ell [P]\; \mathbf{if}\; b\; \mathbf{then}\; c_1\; \mathbf{else}\; c_2\; \mathbf{endif}\; [\epsilon\colon Q]}\textsc{IfFalse}$$

$$\frac{c = L\colon \mathbf{if}\; b\; \mathbf{then}\; c_1\; \mathbf{else}\; c_2\; \mathbf{endif} \qquad c_1 \neq c_2}{\vdash_\ell [(b = \mathbf{true}) \not\preceq \ell * F]\; c\; [insec(L)\colon (b = \mathbf{true}) \not\preceq \ell * F]}\textsc{IfInsec}$$

$$\frac{\vdash_\ell [b * P]\; c;\mathbf{while}\; b\; \mathbf{do}\; c\; \mathbf{done}\; [\epsilon\colon Q]}{\vdash_\ell [P]\; \mathbf{while}\; b\; \mathbf{do}\; c\; \mathbf{done}\; [\epsilon\colon Q]}\textsc{WhileTrue}$$

$$\frac{}{\vdash_\ell [\neg b * F]\; \mathbf{while}\; b\; \mathbf{do}\; c\; \mathbf{done}\; [ok\colon \neg b * F]}\textsc{WhileFalse}$$

$$\frac{}{\vdash_\ell [(b = \mathbf{true}) \not\preceq \ell * F]\; L\colon \mathbf{while}\; b\; \mathbf{do}\; c\; \mathbf{done}\; [insec(L)\colon (b = \mathbf{true}) \not\preceq \ell * F]}\textsc{WhileInsec}$$

$$\frac{\vdash_\ell [P]\; c_1\; [ok\colon Q] \qquad \vdash_\ell [Q]\; c_2\; [\epsilon\colon R]}{\vdash_\ell [P]\; c_1; c_2\; [\epsilon\colon R]}\textsc{SeqOK} \qquad \frac{\vdash_\ell [P]\; c_1\; [err(L)\colon Q]}{\vdash_\ell [P]\; c_1; c_2\; [err(L)\colon Q]}\textsc{SeqErr}$$

$$\frac{\vdash_\ell [P]\; c_1\; [insec(L)\colon Q]}{\vdash_\ell [P]\; c_1; c_2\; [insec(L)\colon Q]}\textsc{SeqInsec} \qquad \frac{\vdash_\ell [P]\; c\; [\epsilon\colon Q] \qquad mod(c) \cap fv(R) = \emptyset}{\vdash_\ell [P * R]\; c\; [\epsilon\colon Q * R]}\textsc{Frame}$$

$$\frac{P' \overset{\ell}{\Rightarrow} P \qquad \vdash_\ell [P']\; c\; [\epsilon\colon Q'] \qquad Q \overset{\ell}{\Rightarrow} Q'}{\vdash_\ell [P]\; c\; [\epsilon\colon Q]}\textsc{Cons} \qquad \frac{\vdash_\ell [P_1]\; c\; [\epsilon\colon Q_1] \qquad \vdash_\ell [P_2]\; c\; [\epsilon\colon Q_2]}{\vdash_\ell [P_1 \vee P_2]\; c\; [\epsilon\colon Q_1 \vee Q_2]}\textsc{Disj}$$

$$\frac{\vdash_\ell [P]\; c\; [\epsilon\colon Q] \qquad x \notin fv(c)}{\vdash_\ell [\exists x.\; P\; x]\; c\; [\epsilon\colon \exists x.\; Q\; x]}\textsc{Ex}$$

Fig. 2. The rules of INSECSL.

Rule LoadErr captures the case when loading via pointer p leads to an error, which is reachable from a presumption $p \not\mapsto$, i.e., states in which p is definitely an invalid pointer [17]. It is formulated as a "small axiom" as typical for separation logic which is put into larger context by the standard frame rule (which is valid in our setting). We remark that sequential composition, too, works as expected.

Rule INPUT derives that the new value of variable x in the result can be classified with respect to e_ℓ—auxiliary variable x' is just a technical artifact to lift e over the assignment to x if e depends on x. Input commands can never be insecure, instead, manifest the domain assumption that only e_ℓ-attackers can observe the value that has been stored in x so that x is rightly classified by the level denoted by e_ℓ. Soundness of the rule therefore considers whether $x::e_\ell[x'/x]$ holds in a given trace, i.e., whether $[x]_{s(x:=v)} = v$ equals $[x]_{s'(x:=v')} = v'$ in case e_ℓ is ℓ-visible (via (4)), and if not, this pair of traces can be neglected as respective schedule-fragments $\sigma = [\text{in}\langle[e_\ell]_s, v\rangle]$ and $\sigma' = [\text{in}\langle[e_\ell]_{s'}, v'\rangle]$ from the small-step semantics are not input equivalent (cf. Definition 1).

In comparison, there are two rules for the output command, one for a secure output, OUTOK, and one for an insecure output, OUTINSEC shown in (2). If one wants to prove for a given case study that the insecure outcome $e \not\cong e_\ell$ is unreachable, one can check the result and presumption wrt. a frame assertion P that captures the path condition of the context in which the output was made, so that if $P * e \not\cong e_\ell$ is unsatisfiable the result is demonstrated to be unreachable.

Moreover, there are rules that expose branching on secrets as the test of **if** and **while** statements, and rule SEQINSEC propagates an insecurity in the first part of a sequential composition similarly to an error.

5   Symbolic Execution

INSECSL's careful design, as a relational logic that resembles the non-relational ISL, means that its application can be automated via bi-abduction [5] based symbolic execution method for automatically deriving INSECSL judgements.

We formalise the symbolic execution method for ISL, atop INSECSL, proving that it yields a sound analysis method for automatically inferring INSECSL judgements. Ours is the first such symbolic execution method, for an under-approximate logic, to enjoy a mechanised proof of soundness.

To define our symbolic execution, it helps to introduce an extra program command **assume**(e). This command is not a "real" command in the sense that it cannot appear in program text. Instead, it is used to remember, during symbolic execution, which conditional branches have been followed along the current execution path. As we will see, our symbolic execution maintains a *trace* that records the execution path followed so far, in which assume commands **assume**(e) can appear. Their semantics is to evaluate the condition e and, if e holds to act as a no-op but otherwise execution gets stuck.

Our symbolic execution method stores the path followed so far. Doing so allows it to provide detailed information to the user when a vulnerability is detected (e.g. to tell precisely along which path the vulnerability arises). Doing so is also necessary to prove the soundness of our method, as explained later. The current path is stored as a *trace*, which is a list of pairs (c, P) where c is a program command and P an INSECSL assertion. For convenience, traces are stored in *reverse* order. Each element (c, P) is understood to mean that command c was executed from symbolic state P, i.e. P represents the state before c was executed. We write the empty trace $[]$ (which represents that there has been no preceding symbolic execution), and the trace whose head is x and whose tail is xs as $x : xs$.

When a new spatial assertion F is inferred to make forward progress in symbolic execution, it is then *back-propagated* along the trace tr, causing F to be added into each of the assertions P in each element (c, P) of F. Given an assertion F, back-propagating it over trace tr produces the transformed trace tr', and operates in the expected way by successively appealing to the FRAME rule. We define the procedure $\mathsf{backprop}_\ell(F, tr, tr')$ for doing this.

Definition 3 (Backprop). *For any assertion F, any security level ℓ, and any traces tr and tr' where each of them is a list of command-assertion pairs,* $\mathsf{backprop}_\ell(F, tr, tr')$ *holds if and only if:* $tr = tr' = [] \lor (\exists c\ P\ F\ F'\ tr_2\ tr_2'.\ tr = (c, P) : tr' \land tr' = (c, P * F) : tr_2' \land mod(c) \cap fv(F) = \emptyset \land \mathsf{backprop}_\ell(F', tr_2, tr_2'))$

Symbolic execution is then defined as follows. We define a judgement $\mathsf{symex}_\ell(tr,\ JQ,\ c,\ tr',\ JQ')$. Here c is a command, tr and tr' are traces, while JQ and JQ' are judgement *post assertions*, i.e. have one of the following forms each for some assertion Q: $ok\colon Q$, $err\colon Q$, or $insec\colon Q$. Trace tr and JQ represent the current state of symbolic execution before command c is executed, in the sense that tr is the trace followed up to this point and JQ represents the symbolic state immediately before c is executed. Executing c necessarily extends the trace (possibly also transforming it via back-propagation), yielding an updated trace tr' and a new post assertion JQ'.

The symbolic execution rules are shown in Fig. 3. When encountering branching, symbolic execution will flag insecurity (SEIFINSEC) if the branch condition b is secret ($b = \mathbf{true} \not\nearrow \ell$); however it can also proceed (e.g. SEIFTRUE) by assuming the branch condition (implicitly assuming it is non-secret). The rule SEOUTINSEC detects insecure outputs. Rules for inferring spatial predicates via bi-abduction follow their counterparts in ISL [12].

Theorem 2 (Soundness of Symbolic Execution). *For all commands c, security levels ℓ, post-assertions JQ and JQ' and all traces tr, produced by symbolic execution, i.e.,* $\mathsf{symex}_\ell([],\ JQ,\ c,\ tr,\ JQ')$ *holds, we have tr is not empty. Furthermore, letting (c, P) denote the last element of tr, we have $\vdash_\ell [P]\ c\ [JQ']$.*

As mentioned earlier, the trace tr is not merely a user convenience but a necessary ingredient to prove soundness of the structural rules, like SEIFTRUE above. Soundness of this rule for instance requires deducing a judgement $\vdash_\ell [P]\ c_0; c'\ [\epsilon\colon Q]$ given premise $\vdash_\ell [P]\ c_0; c\ [\epsilon\colon Q]$ and inductive hypothesis $\forall P\ Q.\ \vdash_\ell [P]\ c\ [\epsilon\colon Q] \implies \vdash_\ell [P]\ c'\ [\epsilon\colon Q]$. Unfortunately the premise is not strong enough to deduce some intermediate assertion R for which $\vdash_\ell [P]\ c_0\ [\epsilon\colon R]$ and $\vdash_\ell [R]\ c\ [\epsilon\colon Q]$ as required to instantiate the inductive hypothesis. Inclusion of trace tr allows us to express the necessary strengthening of the theorem. This construction was not necessary for the pen-and-paper soundness proof of

$$\frac{}{\mathsf{symex}_\ell(tr,\ [ok:P],\ \mathbf{skip},\ (\mathbf{skip},P):tr,\ [ok:P])}\text{SESKIP}$$

$$\frac{}{\mathsf{symex}_\ell(tr,\ [ok:P],\ \mathbf{assume}(b),\ (\mathbf{assume}(b),P):tr,\ [ok:P*b])}\text{SEASM}$$

$$\frac{}{\mathsf{symex}_\ell(tr,\ [ok:P],\ \mathbf{output}(el,e),\ (\mathbf{output}(el,e),P):tr,\ [ok:P*e::el])}\text{SEOUT}$$

$$\frac{c=(\mathbf{output}(el,e))}{\mathsf{symex}_\ell(tr,\ [ok:P],\ L:c,\ (L:c,P):tr,\ [insec(L):P*e\not\sim el])}\text{SEOUTINSEC}$$

$$\frac{x'\notin fv(P)}{\mathsf{symex}_\ell(tr,\ [ok:P],\ x:=e,\ (x:=e,P):tr,\ [ok:P[x'/x]*x=e[x'/x]])}\text{SEASSIGN}$$

$$\frac{x'\notin fv(P)}{\mathsf{symex}_\ell(tr,\ [ok:P],\ x:=\mathbf{input}(e),\ (x:=\mathbf{input}(e),P):tr,\ [ok:P[x'/x]*x::e[x'/x]])}\text{SEINPUT}$$

$$\frac{x'\notin fv(P)}{\mathsf{symex}_\ell(tr,\ [ok:P],\ x:=\mathbf{alloc}(e),\ (x:=\mathbf{alloc}(e),P):tr,\ [ok:P[x'/x]*x\mapsto e[x'/x]])}\text{SEALLOC}$$

$$\frac{\mathsf{backprop}_\ell(M,tr,tr')\quad x'\notin fv(Frame)\quad p\mapsto e*Frame\overset{\ell}{\Longrightarrow}P*M}{\mathsf{symex}_\ell(tr,\ [ok:P],\ x:=[p],\ (x:=[p],P*M):tr',\ [ok:x=e[x'/x]*(p\mapsto e*Frame)[x'/x]])}\text{SELOAD}$$

$$\frac{\mathsf{backprop}_\ell(M,tr,tr')\quad p\not\mapsto *Frame\overset{\ell}{\Longrightarrow}P*M}{\mathsf{symex}_\ell(tr,\ [ok:P],\ L:x:=[p],\ (L:x:=[p],P*M):tr',\ [err(L):p\not\mapsto *Frame])}\text{SELOADERR}$$

$$\frac{\mathsf{backprop}_\ell(M,tr,tr')\quad p\mapsto e*Frame\overset{\ell}{\Longrightarrow}P*M}{\mathsf{symex}_\ell(tr,\ [ok:P],\ [p]:=e',\ ([p]:=e',P*M):tr',\ [ok:p\mapsto e'*Frame])}\text{SESTORE}$$

$$\frac{\mathsf{backprop}_\ell(M,tr,tr')\quad p\not\mapsto *Frame\overset{\ell}{\Longrightarrow}P*M}{\mathsf{symex}_\ell(tr,\ [ok:P],\ L:[p]:=e',\ (L:[p]:=e',P*M):tr',\ [err(L):p\not\mapsto *Frame])}\text{SESTOREERR}$$

$$\frac{\mathsf{backprop}_\ell(M,tr,tr')\quad p\mapsto e*Frame\overset{\ell}{\Longrightarrow}P*M}{\mathsf{symex}_\ell(tr,\ [ok:P],\ \mathbf{free}(p),\ (\mathbf{free}(p),P*M):tr',\ [ok:p\not\mapsto *Frame])}\text{SEFREE}$$

$$\frac{\mathsf{backprop}_\ell(M,tr,tr')\quad p\not\mapsto *Frame\overset{\ell}{\Longrightarrow}P*M}{\mathsf{symex}_\ell(tr,\ [ok:P],\ L:\mathbf{free}(p),\ (L:\mathbf{free}(p),P*M):tr',\ [err(L):p\not\mapsto *Frame])}\text{SEFREEERR}$$

$$\frac{c=(\mathbf{if}\ b\ \mathbf{then}\ c1\ \mathbf{else}\ c2\ \mathbf{endif})\quad c1\neq c2}{\mathsf{symex}_\ell(tr,\ [ok:P],\ L:c,\ (L:c,P*b=\mathbf{true}\not\sim\ell):tr,\ [insec(L):P*b=\mathbf{true}\not\sim\ell])}\text{SEIFINSEC}$$

$$\frac{\mathsf{symex}_\ell(tr,\ [ok:P],\ \mathbf{assume}(b);c_1,\ tr',\ Q)}{\mathsf{symex}_\ell(tr,\ [ok:P],\ \mathbf{if}\ b\ \mathbf{then}\ c_1\ \mathbf{else}\ c_2\ \mathbf{endif},\ tr',\ Q)}\text{SEIFTRUE}$$

Fig. 3. Symbolic execution rules.

ISL [12,17] because for any single state there exists an ISL assertion that precisely describes that state, and hence the existence of the intermediate assertion R is trivial in ISL. The same is not true for INSECSL because INSECSL's assertions, while resembling unary ones, are evaluated relationally (cf. Sect. 4).

Our symbolic execution as described can be applied to the body of a function to infer INSECSL judgements that describe its internal behaviour. Such judgements must be transformed into summaries that describe the function's external behaviour. To do so we follow the same approach as in ISL [12]. For instance, consider the trivial function `void func(int x){ x = x + 1; }` that uselessly increments its argument x. Its internal behaviour is captured by the judgement $\vdash_\ell [x = v]$ `x = x + 1` $[ok\colon v' = v * x = v' + 1]$, where the logical variable v captures the initial value of x. Transforming this internal judgement into an external summary (after simplification) yields the summary $\vdash_\ell$ **[emp]** `func(x)` $[ok\colon \mathrm{emp}]$.

6 Implementation

We implemented the symbolic execution procedure for automating the application of INSECSL in two tools: UNDERFLOW and PULSE-INSECSL. UNDERFLOW implements the entirety of INSECSL via *contextual, top-down* inter-procedural symbolic execution. PULSE-INSECSL on the other hand is a modification of the existing non-contextual, *bottom-up* inter-procedural symbolic execution method for ISL that is implemented in the Pulse-ISL plugin for Infer [12], which we modify to implement a useful subset of the INSECSL logic.

UNDERFLOW is a proof-of-concept tool, which we built by modifying an existing verifier for the over-approximate security separation logic SECCSL [10]. UNDERFLOW implements a top-down inter-procedural analysis in which individual functions (procedures) are analysed using the symbolic execution method of Sect. 5 to derive summaries for their behaviours.

When analysing a function $f()$ that calls another $g()$ UNDERFLOW attempts to apply all summaries known about $g()$. If none of them are applicable (i.e. applying them yields an inconsistent state), UNDERFLOW performs a contextual analysis of $g()$ to compute new summaries applicable at this callsite. To perform a contextual analysis of callee $g()$ from caller $f()$ we take the current symbolic state R and filter it to produce a state R' that describes only those parts of R relevant to the call. UNDERFLOW's present implementation does so using a fixed-point computation that identifies all pure formulae from R that mention arguments passed to $g()$ and values (transitively) related to those arguments by such pure formulae. It identifies all spatial assertions in R that describe parts of the heap reachable from those values, filtering everything else as irrelevant.

In contrast to Infer [12,17], UNDERFLOW does not unroll loops to a fixed bound. Instead it controls symbolic execution using two mechanisms. Firstly, for each program point it counts the number of paths that have so far passed through that point during analysis. When that number exceeds a configurable bound, additional paths are discarded. Additionally it monitors the latency of symbolically executing each program statement. When this latency gets too high (exceeds a configurable timeout), the current path is discarded. The former bound is reached only when unfolding relatively tight loops, while the latter attempts to maintain reasonable symbolic execution throughput. When analysing a function UNDERFLOW will avoid generating multiple summaries that report the same problem for a single program point. UNDERFLOW reports *unconditional* (aka *manifest* [12]) bugs whose presumptions are **true**.

UNDERFLOW encodes all non-spatial formulae to SMT via a relational encoding which directly encodes their relational semantics [14]. Doing so necessarily duplicates each variable, meaning that SMT encodings of formulae are often relatively large. While this can impede scalability, it ensures that UNDERFLOW encodes the entirety of INSECSL in a semantically complete way.

PULSE-INSECSL takes a different design to UNDERFLOW, and makes maximum advantage of the fact that INSECSL is purposefully designed to be very similar to ISL [17], allowing its symbolic execution procedure (Sect. 5) to very closely resemble that for ISL also [12].

PULSE-INSECSL implements a non-trivial fragment of INSECSL. In this fragment, there are only two security levels ℓ: **low** (bottom) and **high** (top). The level of the attacker is **low**. Insecurity assertions $b \not\preceq \mathbf{low}$ appear only over boolean expressions b and mention only the security level **low**. Security assertions $e :: \mathbf{low}$ do not appear directly. Instead, whenever an expression e is to be treated as **low** ($e :: \mathbf{low}$), the expression e is concretised, i.e. replaced by a concrete value (a constant). We refer to this process as *low concretisation*. Since constants are **low** by definition, concretising **low** expressions e ensures that PULSE-INSECSL treats them as **low** without having to perform a relational encoding of the security assertion $e :: \mathbf{low}$. In our current implementation, constants for concretisation are not chosen randomly, ensuring determinism.

Likewise, PULSE-INSECSL avoids having to perform relational encoding of insecurity assertions $b \not\preceq \mathbf{low}$ by soundly encoding them as follows. In particular:

$$\mathbf{sat}\ b \not\preceq \mathbf{low} \iff \mathbf{sat}\ b\ \text{and}\ \mathbf{sat}\ \neg b.$$

Thus satisfiability of insecurity assertions over boolean conditions b can be checked via unary (non-relational) satisfiability checking.

With these two techniques, PULSE-INSECSL automates INSECSL reasoning directly within the existing symbolic execution framework for ISL with minimal modifications, inheriting Infer's highly optimised implementation and scalability. In this implementation, PULSE-INSECSL performs symbolic execution in a bottom-up fashion: each function is analysed in isolation from all others to produce summaries. Loops are unrolled up to a fixed bound, making symbolic execution entirely deterministic.

7   Evaluation

We evaluate both UNDERFLOW and PULSE-INSECSL on the programs, listed in Table 1. The `auction` sample is the synthetic auction case study from Fig. 1. The samples `ctselect`, `ctsort`, `haclpolicies`, `kremlib`, `libsodiumutils`, `opensslutil`, `ssl3cbcrem`, `tls1lucky13`, `tls1patched` are cryptographic library code, drawn from benchmarks for the Binsec/Rel tool [7]. Samples `ctselect`, `ctsort` and `tls1lucky13` contain known vulnerabilities. Most are libraries of basic helper routines, except for `ssl3cbcrem`, `tls1lucky13` and `tls1patched`. The latter two are the vulnerable and patched versions of the infamous "Lucky13" TLS

Table 1. Tool evaluation results. For each sample we record its size in (SLOC) and the number of *top-level* functions analysed (# funs). The third column (sec?) indicates whether the sample had no security vulnerabilities known a-priori. Analysis time of UNDERFLOW for each sample is reported in seconds. PULSE-INSECSL analysed each sample in less than one second. The unique top-level bugs reported we break down into memory safety errors (# err, for UNDERFLOW) and information leaks (# insec, for both). (†) indicates samples that were analysed in PULSE-INSECSL with a manually set loop unrolling bound. (‡) indicates samples that were analysed in UNDERFLOW with an increased symbolic execution pruning and SMT timeout of 600 s.

				UNDERFLOW			PULSE-INSECSL
Sample	SLOC	# funs	sec?	time (s)	# err	# insec	# insec
auction (†)	172	1	✗	195	0	1	1
ctselect	27	5	✗	1	0	1	1
ctsort	57	3	✗	5	0	2	7
cttkinner	77	3	✓	5	0	0	0
haclpolicies	34	1	✓	50	0	0	0
hex	178	2	✓	80	0	1	1
int31 (‡)	1923	60	✓	708	1	2	-
kremlib	68	10	✓	2	0	0	0
libsodiumutils	115	3	✓	380	0	1	1
opensslutil	84	7	✓	1	0	0	0
oram1	167	4	✓	27	0	1	1
ssl3cbcrem	111	1	✓	10	0	0	0
tls1lucky13	122	1	✗	119	1	4	6
tls1patched	229	1	✓	192	2	2	0

vulnerability [1]. The remaining samples are drawn from the Constant-Time Toolkit (CTTK) (https://github.com/pornin/CTTK): cttkinner is a library of basic helper functions, hex is purportedly constant-time routines for converting to/from binary and hexadecimal strings; int31 is drawn from big integer library; oram1 is a basic oblivious RAM (ORAM) library.

Accuracy and Bug Discovery. For the known vulnerable samples, UNDER-FLOW and PULSE-INSECSL correctly detect the known vulnerabilities. UNDER-FLOW additionally identifies an out-of-bounds array access in the big integer library int31. This vulnerability we confirmed by fuzzing the affected code with libFuzzer and AddressSanitizer enabled, and was subsequently confirmed by the developer of the CTTK library. UNDERFLOW also identified an undocumented information leak in the hex CTTK sample, which leaks the location of non-hex characters in strings. Upon reporting this issue to the developer, we were informed it was intended behaviour. This behaviour was also detected by PULSE-INSECSL. UNDERFLOW identified two information leaks also in the int31 library in routines for copying one big integer to another. In particular, if the destination big integer is not initialised, then these routines can leak information about the destination memory contents. Limitations in PULSE-INSECSL's current implementation prevent it from running on int31 at the time of writing.

The information leak identified by UNDERFLOW in libsodiumutils is similar to that in hex and occurs in a routine for converting hex strings to binary, leaking information if the hex string contains non-hex characters. Both tools correctly identify the "Lucky13" vulnerability in tls1lucky13. UNDERFLOW additionally identifies an out-of-bounds array access in this legacy (now patched) code, heretofore undiagnosed. The two information leaks that UNDERFLOW identifies in the patched "Lucky13" code tls1patched are due to if-conditions that branch on secrets but, which many compilers optimise away and hence why this sample is considered to have no known vulnerabilities. Thus whether one regards these reports as true or false positives depends on how the code is compiled.

In two samples, PULSE-INSECSL reports additional information leaks not reported by UNDERFLOW (bold entries). These arise because PULSE-INSECSL treats expressions like (a > b) - 1 as if they branch on the boolean condition a > b. Indeed, gcc 13.1 will compile such code to a conditional jump when compiled at the lowest optimisation level -O0 for x86-64, so we regard these reports as true positives; however we note that on all higher optimisation levels all modern C compilers will compile such expressions to straight line code that doesn't leak.

Performance. PULSE-INSECSL is orders of magnitude faster than UNDERFLOW, in general. In particular, while UNDERFLOW can take minutes to run on some samples, PULSE-INSECSL takes no more than a second to analyse each sample. This should be expected, for a number of reasons. Firstly, recall that UNDERFLOW uses a timeout mechanism to prune paths during symbolic execution in which paths are pruned when symbolic execution of individual statements becomes too slow. On the other hand PULSE-INSECSL uses a deterministic strategy to prune paths, by choosing to unroll loops up to a fixed bound only (by default, once). Thus programs with unbounded loops, like auction, take a long time for UNDERFLOW to analyse because it keeps unrolling the main loop until symbolic execution becomes sufficiently slow due to the growing size of the path condition. This also means that UNDERFLOW may explore loops many more times (and so uncover more behaviours) than PULSE-INSECSL in general, so the amount of symbolic execution that the former performs on a given program is often much greater than the second. To scale UNDERFLOW to the int31 sample required increasing its default path pruning timeout. Thus we might expect that scaling UNDERFLOW beyond samples of this size may be challenging. PULSE-INSECSL on the other hand suffers no such scalability challenges.

Secondly, UNDERFLOW makes use of an external SMT solver in which all non-spatial assertions are given a relational (i.e. two-execution) encoding to SMT, with very little simplification before formulae are encoded to SMT. On the other hand, PULSE-INSECSL is designed to avoid the need for relational assertion encoding and in any case uses a highly performant in-built satisfiability checking library while continually performing aggressive formula simplification. PULSE-INSECSL benefits from many years of development effort and optimisation, while having a much simpler problem to solve (unary symbolic execution). UNDER-

FLOW on the other hand has far fewer optimisations and has not been designed for speed, while solving a much harder problem (relational symbolic execution).

We note that the analysis times of PULSE-INSECSL also dwarf the reported analysis times of the relational symbolic executor Binsec/Rel [7] which, like UNDERFLOW, takes minutes to analyse some samples (e.g. the "Lucky13" sample for which it requires over an hour of execution time [7, Table III]).

8   Related Work and Conclusion

Our logic INSECSL is the relational analogue of ISL [17], in the same way that Security Concurrent Separation Logic (SECCSL) [10] is the relational analogue of traditional separation logic [15,18]. INSECSL can also be seen as the under-approximate dual of SECCSL, in the same way that Incorrectness Logic [16] is the under-approximate dual of Hoare logic. Despite INSECSL being relational, our symbolic execution procedure is purposefully essentially identical to that for ISL [12,17]. This allowed us to implement it as an extension of the existing symbolic execution implementation for ISL in the Infer tool.

Our symbolic execution procedure is also somewhat similar to relational symbolic execution [11] (RSE). However, RSE is not defined for programs with nondeterminism (including from dynamic memory allocation or external input, both of which we support). Indeed, RSE was proved sound with respect to over-approximate Relational Hoare logic [4], whereas ours is based on our under-approximate logic INSECSL. We conjecture that extending RSE to handle nondeterminism would be non-trivial, not least because over-approximate logics cannot precisely describe errors in nondeterministic programs (as we noted in Sect. 1). Unlike RSE, which is a whole-program analysis, our method is compositional, allowing it also be applied incrementally.

The recently developed Outcome Logic [21] unifies underapproximative and overapproximative reasoning within a uniform framework. It would be interesting to instantiate this approach with our relational setting.

Declassification is the act of intentionally revealing sensitive information in a controlled way. This aspect is orthogonal to the contribution of INSECSL and could be incorporated with standard approaches [2].

We have presented INSECSL, a logic that soundly discovers insecurities in program code. The logic strikes a particular balance: Despite being based on a relational semantic foundation, it is fairly straight-forward to automate and inherits many strengths of comparable approaches like ISL, foremost being compositional. We have demonstrated that it is capable of precise reasoning about real insecurities (and errors) in C source code.

References

1. Al Fardan, N.J., Paterson, K.G.: Lucky thirteen: breaking the TLS and DTLS record protocols. In: IEEE Symposium on Security and Privacy, pp. 526–540. IEEE (2013)

2. Banerjee, A., Naumann, D.A., Rosenberg, S.: Expressive declassification policies and modular static enforcement. In: IEEE Symposium on Security and Privacy, pp. 339–353. IEEE (2008)
3. Barthe, G., et al.: Formal verification of a constant-time preserving C compiler. PACMPL 4(POPL), 1–30 (2020)
4. Benton, N.: Simple relational correctness proofs for static analyses and program transformations. In: POPL, pp. 14–25 (2004)
5. Calcagno, C., Distefano, D., O'Hearn, P., Yang, H.: Compositional shape analysis by means of Bi-abduction. In: POPL, pp. 289–300 (2009)
6. Clarkson, M.R., Schneider, F.B.: Hyperproperties. J. Comput. Secur. 18(6), 1157–1210 (2010)
7. Daniel, L.A., Bardin, S., Rezk, T.: BINSEC/REL: efficient relational symbolic execution for constant-time at binary-level. In: IEEE Symposium on Security and Privacy, pp. 1021–1038. IEEE (2020)
8. De Vries, E., Koutavas, V.: Reverse Hoare logic. In: SEFM, pp. 155–171 (2011)
9. Eilers, M., Müller, P., Hitz, S.: Modular product programs. In: ESOP, pp. 502–529 (2018)
10. Ernst, G., Murray, T.: SecCSL: security concurrent separation logic. In: Dillig, I., Tasiran, S. (eds.) CAV 2019. LNCS, vol. 11562, pp. 208–230. Springer, Cham (2019). https://doi.org/10.1007/978-3-030-25543-5_13
11. Farina, G.P., Chong, S., Gaboardi, M.: Relational symbolic execution. In: PPDP, pp. 1–14 (2019)
12. Le, Q.L., Raad, A., Villard, J., Berdine, J., Dreyer, D., O'Hearn, P.W.: Finding real bugs in big programs with incorrectness logic. PACMPL 6(OOPSLA1), 1–27 (2022)
13. Molnar, D., Piotrowski, M., Schultz, D., Wagner, D.: The program counter security model: automatic detection and removal of control-flow side channel attacks. In: Won, D.H., Kim, S. (eds.) ICISC 2005. LNCS, vol. 3935, pp. 156–168. Springer, Heidelberg (2006). https://doi.org/10.1007/11734727_14
14. Murray, T., Yan, P., Ernst, G.: Compositional vulnerability detection with insecurity separation logic(extended version) (2023). https://covern.org/insecurity.html
15. O'Hearn, P.W.: Resources, concurrency and local reasoning. In: Gardner, P., Yoshida, N. (eds.) CONCUR 2004. LNCS, vol. 3170, pp. 49–67. Springer, Heidelberg (2004). https://doi.org/10.1007/978-3-540-28644-8_4
16. O'Hearn, P.W.: Incorrectness logic. PACMPL 4(POPL), 1–32 (2019)
17. Raad, A., Berdine, J., Dang, H.-H., Dreyer, D., O'Hearn, P., Villard, J.: Local reasoning about the presence of bugs: incorrectness separation logic. In: Lahiri, S.K., Wang, C. (eds.) CAV 2020. LNCS, vol. 12225, pp. 225–252. Springer, Cham (2020). https://doi.org/10.1007/978-3-030-53291-8_14
18. Reynolds, J.C.: Separation logic: a logic for shared mutable data structures. In: LICS, pp. 55–74. IEEE (2002)
19. Sabelfeld, A., Myers, A.C.: Language-based information-flow security. IEEE J. Sel. Areas Commun. 21(1), 5–19 (2003)
20. Yang, H.: Relational separation logic. Theoret. Comput. Sci. 375(1–3), 308–334 (2007)
21. Zilberstein, N., Dreyer, D., Silva, A.: Outcome logic: a unifying foundation for correctness and incorrectness reasoning. PACMPL 7(OOPSLA1), 522–550 (2023)

Dynamic Extrapolation in Extended Timed Automata

Nicolaj Ø. Jensen$^{(\boxtimes)}$, Peter G. Jensen, and Kim G. Larsen

Department of Computer Science, Aalborg University, Selma Lagerløfs Vej 300,
9220 Aalborg, Denmark
{noje,pgj,kgl}@cs.aau.dk

Abstract. Abstractions, such as extrapolation, ensure the termination of timed automata model checking. However, such methods are normally only defined for classical timed automata, whereas modern tools like UPPAAL take as input timed automata extended with discrete data and C-like language constructs (XTA) making classical extrapolation excessively over-approximating if even applicable. In this paper, we propose a new dynamic extrapolation technique for XTAs that utilizes information from the immediate state of the search to find more precise extrapolation values. We determine which code snippets are relevant to obtain the extrapolation values ahead of verification using static analysis and then execute these dynamically during verification. We implement our novel extrapolation technique in UPPAAL and find that it reduces the zone graph sizes by 34.7% overall compared to a classic location-clock-based extrapolation. The best case is an 82.7% reduction and the worst case is a surprising 8.2% increase.

Keywords: Extended timed automata · Extrapolation · Program analysis · Graphs

1 Introduction

Model checking and verification [2,9] are powerful tools to ensure the correctness of systems with critical requirements. However, verification of real-time systems relies on abstractions due to the infinite state space of the models. Timed automata, first introduced by R. Alur and D. Dill in [11], is one type of model for time-real systems and it is popular due to the various tools which exist for it today: UPPAAL [10], TCHECKER [18], PAT [15], etc. In timed automata, a countable representation of the state space is achieved using regions, sets of which can be represented as zones, and finiteness is typically achieved with extrapolation. Proposed in [11], a simple form of extrapolation finds a value k such that once the value of a clock x is greater than k, then the exact value of x no longer matter, only that it is greater than k matters. This technique can be extended by finding extrapolation values on a clock- and a location basis as seen in [3].

Funded by the VILLUM INVESTIGATOR project S4OS.

However, some of the aforementioned tools use more expressive timed automata known as extended timed automata (XTA), where edges are decorated with C-like code and timing constraints can be expressions with integer variables.

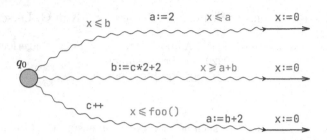

Fig. 1. Extrapolation of clock x in location q_0 depends on all reachable constraints on x between q_0 and resets of x. In XTAs, these constraints may be dynamic and involve expressions.

Consider Fig. 1 showing a fragment of an XTA and paths from location q_0 to resets of clock x. We cannot use typical extrapolation directly since the timing constraints are dynamic and depend on the integer variables a, b, c and the function foo. One solution is to estimate the maximal value of each integer variable and thus each expression. In UPPAAL, the maximal value of variables is computed from type information, which defaults to a large value if not specified by the user. This allows us to find a value k sufficient to achieve a finite verification. However, the lower k is the fewer zones in the zone graph. So we propose a more precise technique. During verification, the exact values of all variables are known in the immediate state of the search. Hence, we can evaluate the expressions to obtain exact extrapolation values. If a timing constraint is not local, we apply the updates along the path to the timing constraint first and then evaluate the expression. For instance, the extrapolation value for clock x in location q_0 in Fig. 1 is the greatest value among the results of evaluating b, evaluating $a := 2$ and then a, evaluating $b := c \cdot 2 + 2$ and then $a + b$, and evaluating $c ++$ and then $foo()$. While we are not able to find exact extrapolation values in general due to updates in cycles, we can identify such cases ahead of verification using static analysis. In fact, we can find all relevant updates and expressions ahead of verification, avoiding the overhead of locating relevant constraints whenever extrapolation is needed. When it is not feasible to find exact extrapolation values, we fall back to existing techniques.

Related Work. The efficient zone-based abstraction was introduced in [11]. Research has since been exploring ways to ensure the termination of the forward analysis with coarser abstractions and extrapolation techniques. As mentioned, natural extensions include per-clock and per-location extrapolation values [3]. The current implementation of UPPAAL uses LU-extrapolation in the form of the $Extra_{LU}^+$ operator [4] which differentiates upper- and lower bounds as well. The limitations of extrapolation have been investigated in [6,7]. In [13] the $\mathfrak{a}_{\preceq_{LU}}$ abstraction from [4] is shown to be the biggest abstraction based on LU bounds that is sound and complete for reachability. Additionally, they show how to use non-convex abstractions while working with zones by using the abstractions indirectly. In [12] they use a similar idea for a new simulation relation in order to tackle diagonal constraints, which was shown to be problematic in [6]. See [8] for a survey by P. Bouyer et al. Parametric timed automata (PTA) allow for unknown timing constants to parameterize the model at the cost of undecidability. Recent work [1] investigates several definitions of extrapolation in PTA and finds methods to enhance efficiency and the chance of termination. However, the constant parameters in PTA are not comparable to the discrete variable data in XTA, so the techniques do not transfer. All of the aforementioned work is on timed automata without discrete variable data. The closest related work is therefore in [16] where the authors approximate the ranges of integer variables and thus expressions in XTAs using abstract interpretation. This removes the reliance on users to define accurate ranges, but they are limited to linear expressions. We refine their work by employing a more exact method that partially runs at verification time.

Our Contributions. In this paper, we focus on XTAs from UPPAAL [10]. We define a clock- and location-based M-extrapolation for XTAs using an arbitrary domain analysis. We then define the dynamic $DynM$-extrapolation which gives more accurate extrapolation values in XTAs by taking advantage of the current state. We show how the relevant paths used in $DynM$-extrapolation can be found ahead of verification and discuss simple extensions which reduce the number of paths, updates, and expressions that need to be evaluated during verification. Finally, we show the effectiveness of our $DynM$-extrapolation by implementing it in UPPAAL and experimenting on XTA families with dynamic constraints. We find that $DynM$ reduces the zone graph by up to 82.7% compared to M-extrapolation in non-artificial models while being almost on par with M in other cases. Across all experiments, we explore 34.7% fewer zones and use 3.3% less time when using our $DynM$-extrapolation.

Outline. The outline of the paper is as follows. In Sect. 2, we recall the definition of XTAs and their semantics. We also define the zone abstraction and M-extrapolation on XTAs. In Sect. 3, we present our dynamic extrapolation technique and show how it can be broken down to finding acyclic paths in the XTA and then evaluating those paths to find more accurate extrapolation values. We briefly describe extensions to the technique as well. Experiments and results are presented in Sect. 4, and finally, in Sect. 5, we conclude on our findings.

2   Preliminary

Let us recall the definition of extended timed automata and its semantics.

2.1 Extended Timed Automata

Clocks and Valuations. Let X be a set of *clock* variables. A *clock valuation* is a function $\nu : X \rightarrow \mathbb{R}_{\geq 0}$ assigning each clock to a non-negative real number. The set $\mathcal{V}(X)$ contains all clocks valuations over X. We use ν_0 to denote the clock valuation such that $\nu_0(x) = 0$ for all $x \in X$. We write $\nu + d$ with $d \in \mathbb{R}_{\geq 0}$ for a clock valuation such that $(\nu + d)(x) = \nu(x) + d$ for all clocks $x \in X$. Lastly, given a set $r \subseteq X$ of clocks to reset, we define $\nu[r]$ such that $\nu[r](x) = 0$ if $x \in r$, and $\nu[r](x) = \nu(x)$ otherwise.

Discrete Data States, Updates, and Expressions. A *discrete data state* (or simply a *data state*) is denoted using σ, and Σ is the set of all data states. An *update* is a function $u : \Sigma \rightarrow \Sigma$ which transforms data states to data states and $\mathcal{U}$ is the set of all updates. We use $e, b : \Sigma \rightarrow \mathbb{Z}$ to denote *expressions* which evaluates to an integer given a data state. Expressions denoted b represent boolean expressions for which evaluation to 0 (false) is of interest. Let E be the set of all expressions. The definition of the discrete data states, updates, and expressions are simplifications of the formalism in UPPAAL. Yet, the definitions provided are sufficient to underpin our method. Our implementation fully supports the imperative language of UPPAAL, including its arrays, functions, and record types.

Constraints. The set $G(X)$ contains clock constraints generated from the grammar $g ::= 1 \mid g_1 \wedge g_2 \mid x \bowtie e$ where $x \in X$, $\bowtie \in \{<, \leq, =, \geq, >\}$, and $e \in E$. If $g \in G(X)$, we write $(x \bowtie e) \in g$ when $x \bowtie e$ is one of the terms of the conjunction g. Given a data state σ, we write $g(\sigma)$ to denote a conjunction similar to g, but where all right-hand sides of the constituent constraints have been evaluated, i.e. each $(x \bowtie e) \in g$ has been replaced by $x \bowtie e(\sigma)$. The satisfaction relation $\vDash$ is defined naturally for clock valuations and evaluated clock constraints, i.e. $\nu \vDash g(\sigma)$ iff $\forall (x \bowtie c) \in g(\sigma)$ we have $\nu(x) \bowtie c$.

Definition 1 (Extended Timed Automata (XTA)). *An extended timed automaton $\mathcal{A}$ is a 6-tuple $(Q, q_0, \sigma_0, T, X, I)$ where*

- Q *is a finite set of locations,*
- $q_0 \in Q$ *is the initial location,*
- σ_0 *is the initial discrete data state,*
- $T \subseteq Q \times [G(X) \times E \times \mathcal{U} \times \mathcal{P}(X)] \times Q$ *is a set of edges between locations such that if $(q, g, b, u, r, q') \in T$ then q and q' are respectively source and target locations, g is a clock constraint (also called guard), b is a data condition, u is an update, and r is a subset of clocks to be reset,*
- X *is a non-empty set of clocks, and*
- $I : Q \rightarrow G(X)$ *assigns clock invariants to locations.*

Given any XTA $\mathcal{A}$, we assume that all data states produced by updates in $\mathcal{A}$ fall within a finite domain which we call $\Sigma_{\mathcal{A}}$ with $\sigma_0 \in \Sigma_{\mathcal{A}}$ too. However, we also assume $\Sigma_{\mathcal{A}}$ to be impractical to iterate. It follows that each expression e evaluates to value within a finite domain $\mathcal{D}_{\mathcal{A}}(e)$. We assume that $\mathcal{D}_{\mathcal{A}}(e)$ can be estimated, either from type information or as done in [16].

Definition 2 (Extended Timed Automata Semantics). *The semantics of an XTA $\mathcal{A} = (Q, q_0, \sigma_0, T, X, I)$ is given by a transitions system $\mathcal{S}_{\mathcal{A}} = (S, s_0, \rightarrow)$, where $S = Q \times \Sigma_{\mathcal{A}} \times \mathcal{V}(X)$ is the set of configurations, $s_0 = (q_0, \sigma_0, \nu_0)$ is the initial configuration, and $\rightarrow \subseteq S \times S$ is the transition relation given by:*

$$\frac{\forall 0 \leq d' \leq d : \nu + d' \vDash I(q)(\sigma)}{(q, \sigma, \nu) \rightarrow (q, \sigma, \nu + d)} \quad where\ d \in \mathbb{R}_{\geq 0},\ and \tag{1}$$

$$\frac{\nu \vDash g(\sigma) \quad b(\sigma) \neq 0 \quad \nu[r] \vDash I(q')(u(\sigma))}{(q, \sigma, \nu) \rightarrow (q', u(\sigma), \nu[r])} \quad where\ (q, g, b, u, r, q') \in T. \tag{2}$$

In order to verify interesting behavioral properties of an XTA, we must first define zones and symbolic semantics.

2.2 Symbolic Semantics

Future and Reset. Given a set of clocks X, let $W \in \mathcal{P}(\mathcal{V}(X))$ be a set of clock valuations. We define $W^{\nearrow} = \{\nu + d \mid \nu \in W, d \in \mathbb{R}_{\geq 0}\}$ as the future of W. Given a set $r \subseteq X$ of clocks to reset, we define $W[r] = \{\nu[r] \mid \nu \in W\}$ as the reset of r in W.

Zones. Given a set of clocks X, the set of zones $\mathcal{Z}(X)$ is generated from the grammar $Z ::= 1 \mid Z_1 \wedge Z_2 \mid x \bowtie c \mid x - y \bowtie c$, where $x, y \in X$, $c \in \mathbb{N}$, and $\bowtie \in \{<, \leq, =, \geq, >\}$. Given a data state σ, notice that for all $g \in G(X)$ we have $g(\sigma) \in \mathcal{Z}(X)$, and thus $g(\sigma)$ can be considered a zone. The future, reset, and intersection operations all transform zones into other zones.

Difference Bound Matrices. A zone can be represented using a *difference bound matrix* (DBM) and has been the default representation for zones since [11]. We will briefly describe DBMs and point to [5] and [7] for more details. A DBM is a square matrix $D = (c_{i,j}; \prec_{i,j})_{0 \leq i,j \leq n}$ such that $c_{i,j} \in \mathbb{N}$ and $\prec_{i,j} \in \{<, \leq\}$ or $c_{i,j} = \infty$ and $\prec_{i,j} = <$. A DBM D defines a zone $[\![D]\!]$ which is defined by $[\![D]\!] = \{\nu \mid \forall 0 \leq i, j \leq n : \nu(x_i) - \nu(x_j) \prec_{i,j} c_{i,j}\}$ where $\{x_1, \ldots, x_n\}$ is a set of clocks, and x_0 is a special clock always with the value 0, i.e. $\forall \nu : \nu(x_0) = 0$. A DBM is not a canonical representation of zones, but a normal form can be found by considering it an adjacency matrix of a weighted directed graph and computing the shortest paths closure. DBMs are a useful representation of zones since all operations presented above can be computed efficiently.

Definition 3 (Symbolic Semantics of Extended Timed Automata). *The symbolic semantics of an XTA $\mathcal{A} = (Q, q_0, \sigma_0, T, X, I)$ is given by a transitions system $\mathcal{S}_{\mathcal{A}}^{\star} = (S, s_0, \Rightarrow)$, where $S = Q \times \Sigma_{\mathcal{A}} \times \mathcal{Z}(X)$ is the set of configurations, $s_0 = (q_0, \sigma_0, \{\nu_0\})$ is the initial configuration, and $\Rightarrow \subseteq S \times S$ is the transition relation given by:*

$$\frac{Z' = (Z^{\nearrow} \cap I(q)(\sigma)) \quad Z' \neq \emptyset}{(q, \sigma, Z) \Rightarrow (q, \sigma, Z')} \quad ,\ and \tag{3}$$

$$\frac{b(\sigma) \neq 0 \quad Z' = (Z \cap g(\sigma))[r] \cap I(q')(u(\sigma)) \quad Z' \neq \emptyset}{(q, \sigma, Z) \Rightarrow (q', u(\sigma), Z')} \quad where\ (q, g, b, u, r, q') \in T. \tag{4}$$

The zone abstraction does not guarantee a finite state graph. There may be an infinite number of reachable zones. As suggested in [3], we apply an abstraction $\mathfrak{a} : \mathcal{P}(\mathcal{V}(X)) \rightarrow \mathcal{P}(\mathcal{V}(X))$ such that $W \subseteq \mathfrak{a}(W)$ and $\mathfrak{a}(W) = \mathfrak{a}(\mathfrak{a}(W))$. The abstract transition system $\Rightarrow_\mathfrak{a}$ is then given by the induction rule:

$$\frac{(q, \sigma, W) \Rightarrow (q', \sigma', W')}{(q, \sigma, W) \Rightarrow_\mathfrak{a} (q', \sigma', \mathfrak{a}(W'))} \quad \text{where } W = \mathfrak{a}(W). \tag{5}$$

A simple way to ensure that the reachability graph induced by $\Rightarrow_\mathfrak{a}$ is finite is to establish that there is only a finite number of abstractions of sets of valuations. That is, the image of $\mathfrak{a}$ is finite. In this case, $\mathfrak{a}$ is said to be a *finite abstraction*. Moreover, $\Rightarrow_\mathfrak{a}$ is said to be sound and complete whenever:

Sound: $(q_0, \sigma_0, \{\nu_0\}) \Rightarrow_\mathfrak{a}^* (q, \sigma, W)$ implies $\exists \nu \in W : (q_0, \sigma_0, \nu_0) \rightarrow^* (q, \sigma, \nu)$

Complete: $(q_0, \sigma_0, \nu_0) \rightarrow^* (q, \sigma, \nu)$ implies $\exists W : \nu \in W \wedge (q_0, \sigma_0, \{\nu_0\}) \Rightarrow_\mathfrak{a}^* (q, \sigma, W)$

Completeness follows from the definition of abstraction. Given two abstractions $\mathfrak{a}$ and $\mathfrak{b}$ such that for any set of clock valuations W we have $\mathfrak{a}(W) \subseteq \mathfrak{b}(W)$, then we prefer abstraction $\mathfrak{b}$ because the graph induced by $\mathfrak{b}$ is smaller than the one induced by $\mathfrak{a}$.

2.3 M-Extrapolation in XTA

In extended timed automata without discrete data, finiteness is achieved with extrapolation based on the constants appearing in the constraints. Modern extrapolation techniques find different extrapolation values per clock and per location for coarser abstractions. Unfortunately, these techniques cannot be used as-is in XTAs, since bounds are expressions instead of constant values. What follows is the location-clock-based M-extrapolation from [3] extended to XTAs based on expression domains.

In XTA $\mathcal{A}$, M is given by:

$$M(q, x) = \max \begin{cases} \max \mathcal{D}_\mathcal{A}(e_1) \text{ where } (x \bowtie e_1) \in I(q), \\ \max \mathcal{D}_\mathcal{A}(e_2) \text{ where } (q, g, b, u, r, q') \in T \\ \qquad \text{and } (x \bowtie e_2) \in g, \\ M(q', x) \quad \text{where } (q, g, b, u, r, q') \in T \\ \qquad \text{and } x \notin r \end{cases} \tag{6}$$

By convention $\max \emptyset = -\infty$. The values of M can be found using fixed-point iteration.

Definition 4 M-equivalence $\equiv_M$ [3]). *Given an XTA $\mathcal{A}$ with transition system $\mathcal{S}_\mathcal{A} = (S, s_0, \rightarrow)$, then $\equiv_M \subseteq S \times S$ is a relation such that $(q, \sigma, \nu) \equiv_M (q, \sigma, \nu')$ iff for all clocks x either*

- *$\nu(x) = \nu'(x)$, or*

$-$ $\nu(x) > M(q,x)$ and $\nu'(x) > M(q,x)$.

Lemma 1. *The relation $\equiv_M$ is a bisimulation relation [3] and therefore preserves reachability, liveness, and deadlock properties.*

Definition 5 ($\mathfrak{a}_{\equiv_M,q,\sigma}$, **abstraction w.r.t.** $\equiv_M$ [3]). *Let W be a set of valuations. Then the abstraction w.r.t. $\equiv_M$ is defined as $\mathfrak{a}_{\equiv_M,q,\sigma}(W) = \{\nu \mid \exists \nu' \in W : (q,\sigma,\nu) \equiv_M (q,\sigma,\nu')\}$.*

Lemma 2. *[3] The abstraction $\mathfrak{a}_{\equiv_M,q,\sigma}$ is sound and complete.*

As M-extrapolation uses $\max \mathcal{D}_{\mathcal{A}}$, it is clear that $M(q,x)$ is an over-approximation and not necessarily the tightest bound value relevant for a given clock x in a given location q. It does not take advantage of the data state σ, which is also part of the configuration. In the following section, we will define *dynamic extrapolation*, which uses the given data state σ to evaluate expressions on-the-fly for tighter bound values.

Remark 1. The widely used LU-extrapolation technique of [4] can be extended to XTAs in a similar manner as shown above.

3 Dynamic Extrapolation

Fix an XTA $\mathcal{A}$ for this section. Dynamic extrapolation is given by a function $DynM : Q \times \Sigma_{\mathcal{A}} \times X \to \mathbb{N}$ which takes the discrete data state σ into consideration when determining the extrapolation values of a configuration (q,σ,ν).

Let us first give a recursive definition of $DynM$:

$$DynM(q,\sigma,x) = \max \begin{cases} e_1(\sigma) & \text{where } (x \bowtie e_1) \in I(q), \\ e_2(\sigma) & \text{where } (q,g,b,u,r,q') \in T \\ & \text{and } (x \bowtie e_2) \in g, \\ DynM(q',u(\sigma),x) & \text{where } (q,g,b,u,r,q') \in T \\ & \text{and } x \notin r \text{ and } b(\sigma) \neq 0 \end{cases} \quad (7)$$

However, unlike for M, it is infeasible to find a fixed-point solution for $DynM$ since, by assumption, it is impractical to iterate all data states $\Sigma_{\mathcal{A}}$. Additionally, some expressions may be expensive to evaluate. We need to deal with the recursiveness in another way.

The definition is recursive whenever there are cycles in the XTA. Trying to determine if cycles can only be repeated a finite number of times is generally undecidable [19]. By assumption of finite domains, it is not undecidable in our case, but practically infeasible. Consider the example XTA in Fig. 2a. We can easily compute $DynM(q_2,\sigma,x)$ and $DynM(q_3,\sigma,x)$ for any data state σ, but to compute $DynM(q_0,\sigma,x)$ and $DynM(q_1,\sigma,x)$ we may have to iterate a huge number of data states due to the cycle consisting of edges t_1 and t_2. This is the only cycle that is not broken up by a reset of x. We overcome this issue

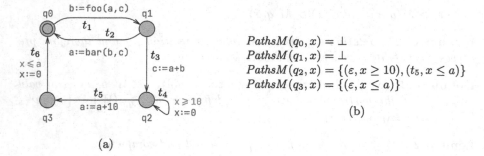

$$PathsM(q_0, x) = \bot$$
$$PathsM(q_1, x) = \bot$$
$$PathsM(q_2, x) = \{(\varepsilon, x \geq 10), (t_5, x \leq a)\}$$
$$PathsM(q_3, x) = \{(\varepsilon, x \leq a)\}$$

(b)

(a)

Fig. 2. (a) Example XTA where cycles make $DynM$ troublesome to compute. The x is a clock, a, b, c are integer variables comprising the data state, foo and bar are arbitrary functions. (b) The $PathsM$ found by Algorithms 1 and 2.

by detecting the problematic cycles and which location-clock pairs (q, x) depend on these cycles. For these cases, we fall back to M-extrapolation. In the same algorithm, we also precompute all paths to constraints relevant for each location-clock pair (q, x), such that they do not have to be found anew each time we want to compute our extrapolation values. Let us introduce some terminology.

A path $w = t_1 \ldots t_n = (q_1, g_1, b_1, u_1, r_1, q_1') \ldots (q_n, g_n, b_n, u_n, r_n, q_n')$ is a sequence of edges from T, such that for all $1 \leq i \leq n - 1 : q_i' = q_{i+1}$. We say that the path starts in q_1 and ends in q_n'. A path is cyclic if there are j, k with $j < k$ such that $q_j = q_k'$. A path resets clock x if there exists a j such that $x \in r_j$. We say that $x \bowtie e$ is a local constraint of q if $(x \bowtie e) \in I(q)$ or $(q, g, b, u, r, q') \in T$ such that $(x \bowtie e) \in g$.

Our problem at hand can now be expressed succinctly. Given a location-clock pair (q, x), we want to find all path-expression pairs (w, e) such that w is a path starting in q that does not reset x, and $x \bowtie e$ is a local constraint at the end of w. Note that w can be empty, in which case the end of w refers to q. For short, we call these *relevant* paths of (q, x). If any relevant path is cyclic, then we simply need to know that instead, such that we can fall back to M-extrapolation. We find all relevant paths for each location-clock pair using a depth-first search (DFS) and coloring. By coloring location-clock pairs as they are visited, the DFS is able to detect cycles. There are four colors with the following meanings:

- White: The location-clock pair is unexplored
- Gray: The location-clock pair is being processed
- Black: All relevant paths have been found for this location-clock pair
- Red: One or more relevant paths starting in this location-clock pair are cyclic

---

Algorithm 1: ComputePaths

Input : An XTA $(Q, q_0, \sigma_0, T, X, I)$

Output: A mapping $PathsM : Q \times X \to \mathcal{P}(T^* \times E) \cup \{\bot\}$

1 Let $PathsM$ be a new map, mapping all location-clock pairs to $\emptyset$;
2 **foreach** $x \in X$ **do**
3 | Mark all locations as white;
4 | **foreach** $q \in Q$ **do**
5 | | **if** q *is white* **then**
6 | | | Run ComputePathsRecursive($PathsM, q, x$)

7 **return** $PathsM$

Algorithm 2: ComputePathsRecursive

Input : A mapping $PathsM : Q \times X \to \mathcal{P}(T^* \times E) \cup \{\bot\}$, a location q, a clock x

Output: Modifications to $PathsM$

1 Mark q as gray;
2 $LC := \{e \mid (x \bowtie e) \in g, (q, g, b, u, r, q') \in T\} \cup \{e \mid (x \bowtie e) \in I(q)\}$;
3 **foreach** $e \in LC$ **do**
4 | $PathsM(q, x) := PathsM(q, x) \cup \{(\varepsilon, e)\}$

5 **foreach** $t = (q, g, b, u, r, q') \in T$ **do**
6 | **if** $x \in r$ **then**
7 | | Continue

8 | **if** q' *is white* **then**
9 | | Run ComputePathsRecursive($PathsM, q', x$);
10 | | // q' is now black or red

11 | **if** q' *is red or gray* **then**
12 | | // We found a cycle
13 | | $PathsM(q, x) := \bot$;
14 | | Mark q as red;
15 | | **return**

16 | **if** q' *is black* **then**
17 | | $PathsM(q, x) := PathsM(q, x) \cup \{(tw, e) \mid (w, e) \in PathsM(q', x)\}$;

18 Mark q as black;
19 **return**

The algorithm constructs a mapping $PathsM : Q \times X \to \mathcal{P}(T^* \times E) \cup \{\bot\}$ that assigns each location-clock pair to a finite set of relevant path-expression pairs or $\bot$ if the location-clock pair has a cyclic relevant path. The algorithm for finding $PathsM$ is shown in Algorithms 1 and 2. Fig. 2b shows the resulting $PathsM$ when the algorithm is run on the XTA in Fig. 2a.

Lemma 3. *Let $PathsM$ be the result of Algorithms 1 and 2. If $PathsM(q, x) \neq \bot$ then $PathsM(q, x)$ contains all relevant paths (w, e) such that w is acyclic,* *does not reset x, starts in q, and ends in q' such that $x \bowtie e$ is a local constraint to q'.*

Lemma 3 is easily proven by showing that the loop invariants induced by the definition of the colors hold at the exit of Algorithm 2, and therefore we do not include the proof in this version of the paper.

We can now define *PDynM* which approximates *DynM* by using *PathsM* and auxiliary function *eval*:

$$PDynM(q, \sigma, x) = \begin{cases} M(q,x) & \text{if } PathsM(q,x) = \bot, \\ \max_{(w,e)\in PathsM(q,x)} eval(w,e,\sigma) & \text{otherwise} \end{cases} \quad (8)$$

$$eval(tw, e, \sigma) = \begin{cases} eval(w,e,u(\sigma)) & \text{if } t = (q,g,b,u,r,q') \wedge b(\sigma) \neq 0, \\ -\infty & \text{otherwise} \end{cases} \quad (9)$$

$$eval(\varepsilon, e, \sigma) = e(\sigma) \quad (10)$$

This definition is well-defined and feasibly computable by using $M(q,x)$ as a fallback whenever $PathsM(q,x) = \bot$, i.e. in locations with cyclic paths to relevant constraints. In locations without cycles, *PDynM* is equivalent to the ideal *DynM*. We shall now argue, that *PDynM* is a valid abstraction. Specifically:

Definition 6 (PDynM-equivalence $\equiv_{PDynM}$). *Given an XTA $\mathcal{A}$ with transition system $\mathcal{S}_\mathcal{A} = (S, s_0, \rightarrow)$, then $\equiv_{PDynM} \subseteq S \times S$ is a relation such that $(q,\sigma,\nu) \equiv_{PDynM} (q,\sigma,\nu')$ iff for each clocks x either*

- $\nu(x) = \nu'(x)$, or
- $\nu(x) > PDynM(q,\sigma,x)$ and $\nu'(x) > PDynM(q,\sigma,x)$.

Lemma 4. *The relation $\equiv_{PDynM}$ is a bisimulation relation and therefore preserves reachability, liveness, and deadlock properties.*

Proof. From Lemma 3 and the definition of *PDynM*, it is clear $PDynM(q,\sigma,x)$ is either equal to $M(q,x)$ or is the greatest value obtained from evaluating the updates and data conditions along a relevant path of (q,x) and then a final bound expression, local to the end of the path. Hence, by Lemma 3, $PDynM(q,\sigma,x)$ must be equal to or greater than the greatest value which x is ever compared to before getting reset in any path starting from q. This implies that ν and ν' satisfy the same clock constraints and it follows that $\equiv_{PDynM}$ a bisimulation relation. $\square$

Definition 7 ($\mathfrak{a}_{\equiv_{PDynM}}$, abstraction w.r.t. $\equiv_{PDynM}$). *Let W be a set of valuations. Then the abstraction w.r.t $\equiv_{PDynM}$ is defined as $\mathfrak{a}_{\equiv_{PDynM},q,\sigma}(W) = \{\nu \mid \exists \nu' \in W : (q,\sigma,\nu) \equiv_{PDynM} (q,\sigma,\nu')\}$.*

Lemma 5. *The abstraction $\mathfrak{a}_{\equiv_{PDynM},q,\sigma}$ is sound and complete, and it is coarser than $\mathfrak{a}_{\equiv_{M,q,\sigma}}$*

Proof. Completeness is obvious. Soundness follows from Lemma 4. The increased coarseness follows from the definitions, where we have that $PDynM(q,\sigma,x) \leq M(q,x)$ for any location q and clock x. $\square$

The abstraction $\mathfrak{a}_{\equiv PDynM,q,\sigma}$ does not preserve convexity of valuation sets. Even if Z is a convex zone, $\mathfrak{a}_{\equiv PDynM,q,\sigma}(Z)$ is not always convex, which means it cannot be represented with a DBM. We shall therefore define a location- and data-dependent extrapolator called $Extra^+_{PDynM,q,\sigma}$ which is an operator defined on DBMs and approximates $\mathfrak{a}_{\equiv PDynM,q,\sigma}$. The naming and the definition are intentionally similar to that of $Extra^+_M$ in [4] since the only difference is that our extrapolation values come from $PDynM$ instead of M. If D is a DBM in normal form given by $(c_{i,j}; \prec_{i,j})_{0 \le i,j \le n}$, then $Extra^+_{PDynM,q,\sigma}(D)$ is defined as:

$$(c'_{i,j}; \prec'_{i,j}) = \begin{cases} (\infty; <) & \text{if } c_{i,j} > PDynM(q,\sigma,x_i) \\ (\infty; <) & \text{if } -c_{0,i} > PDynM(q,\sigma,x_i) \\ (\infty; <) & \text{if } -c_{0,j} > PDynM(q,\sigma,x_j), i \ne 0 \\ (-PDynM(q,\sigma,x_j); <) & \text{if } -c_{i,j} > PDynM(q,\sigma,x_j), i = 0 \\ (c_{i,j}; \prec_{i,j}) & \text{otherwise} \end{cases}$$

(11)

Note that $Extra^+_{PDynM,q,\sigma}(D)$ is not necessarily in normal form. From the extrapolator $Extra^+_{PDynM,q,\sigma}$ follows the abstraction $\mathfrak{a}_{Extra^+_{PDynM,q,\sigma}}$

Theorem 1. *The abstraction* $\mathfrak{a}_{Extra^+_{PDynM,q,\sigma}}$ *is sound, complete, and preserves zone convexity.*

Proof. The extrapolator $Extra^+_{PDynM,q,\sigma}$ transforms zones into larger zones, which implies completeness and zone convexity. Finiteness follows from the fact that all the DBM coefficients fall within a finite number of values. Soundness is not obvious, and we point to [4] where a similar abstraction is proven sound. □

3.1 Reducing Relevant Paths

Let us briefly describe ways to reduce the number of relevant paths.

Strongly Connected Components. So far, we have deemed all cycles as problematic based on the fact that their updates can be repeated indefinitely resulting in an infeasible number of possible data states to evaluate our constraint expression in. However, this issue does not apply to cycles where all updates are identity updates, i.e. updates u_{id} such that $u_{id}(\sigma) = \sigma$ for all $\sigma \in \Sigma_A$. Repeating u_{id} indefinitely makes no difference. Hence, we can reduce the number of cases where $PathsM(q,x) = \bot$ by essentially computing strongly connected components (SCCs) in the XTA. The internal edges of SCCs must have empty data conditions and identity updates, and cannot reset x. The latter condition implies that we must compute an SCC graph for each clock $x \in X$, but since SCCs can be constructed in linear time using Tarjan's algorithm, this is not a concern. Using the SCC graphs, we can compute $PathsM_{SCC}$ which assigns $\bot$ to fewer cases than $PathsM$. Remark that cycles of identity updates are often modeling mistakes and the models used in the experiments in Sect. 4 do not contain any such cycles.

Redundant Paths Using Expression Domains. Let $(\mathcal{P}(\mathbb{Z}), \sqsubseteq)$ be a partial order such that if $A, B \subseteq \mathbb{Z}$ then $A \sqsubseteq B$ iff $\forall a \in A. \forall b \in B : a \leq b$. We can use this to determine which bound programs will never be the greatest relevant bound expression. If a bound expression is never the greatest relevant bound, then we can discard the path leading to it, reducing the number of paths that needs to be evaluated. The function $PathsM^\star$ below is a subset of $PathsM$ without these redundant paths:

$$PathsM^\star(q, x) =$$
$$\begin{cases} \bot & \text{if } PathsM(q, x) = \bot \\ \{(w, e) \in PathsM(q, x) \mid \neg \exists (w', e') \in PathsM(q, x) : \mathcal{D}_\mathcal{A}(e) \sqsubseteq \mathcal{D}_\mathcal{A}(e')\} & \text{otherwise} \end{cases}$$
$$(12)$$

The more precise (i.e. smaller) the domains of $\mathcal{D}_\mathcal{A}$ are, the better this improvement is.

3.2 Dynamic LU-Extrapolation

We can easily extend the dynamic extrapolation in a similar manner as proposed in [4] and achieve a lower- and upper-bound aware extrapolation. We simply distinguish between bounds using $\rhd \in \{>, \geq, =\}$ and $\lhd \in \{<, \leq, =\}$ in line 2 of ComputePathsRecursive in Algorithm 2 in order to compute separate $PathsL$ and $PathsU$, which are mappings to paths respectively leading to lower- and upper-bound expressions. This allows us to create an abstraction $\mathfrak{a}_{\preceq_{PDynLU}, q, \sigma}$ based on the simulation relation $\preceq_{PDynLU, q, \sigma}$, which is correct for reachability, but not for deadlock and liveness properties. While orthogonal techniques, the resulting $PDynLU$-extrapolation is only slightly coarser than LU-extrapolation in practice, which is why we have not defined $PDynLU$ in detail.

3.3 A Note on Timed Automata Networks

In tools for modeling timed systems using timed automata, e.g. UPPAAL [10], it is common to have timed automata *networks* consisting of multiple timed automata components. The dynamic extrapolation technique presented in this paper extends to this formalism with some caveats. $PathsM$ and $PDynM$ can be found and evaluated on a component-wise basis such that for a clock x the greatest bound across all components is used, similar to M-extrapolation in [3]. This is correct for shared clocks too. Remark, however, that dynamic extrapolation cannot be done component-wise in networks with expressions relying on a globally shared data state. In networks, a relevant path of one component may be interleaved with transitions in other components. If the other components can change the globally shared state, then our assumption that the relevant path contains all updates leading up to the evaluation of the guard breaks down. If we instead attempt to find relevant paths in the composed network as opposed to the component-wise approach, the number of relevant paths increases exponentially, resulting in exponentially more work during verification whenever we extrapolate.

4   Experiments and Results

In order to test the contributions of this paper, we have implemented a prototype of our dynamic extrapolation technique in UPPAAL [10]. We use the SCC improvement and discard redundant paths as discussed in Sect. 3.1 and compute $PathsM^*_{SCC}$ once prior to verification. During verification, the paths are used to find the extrapolation values for each clock whenever a configuration is explored. We will refer to our implementation simply as *DynM* in this section.

In the experiments, various models are used. Some of the models have dynamic constraints using expressions, others have not. Our experiments show that our dynamic extrapolation never reduces the size of the zone graph compared to its non-dynamic counterpart M unless there is at least one dynamic constraint or unless data conditions can exclude bound expressions. We shall therefore delimit our results to all models in our repository with dynamic constraints such that dynamic extrapolation may take effect. These models include:[1]

- Simple (Simple-I): The artificial example from [16] designed to showcase the issues of relying purely on type information for extrapolation in XTA.
- TCP back-off protocol (TCP-V-N): In this model, N clients estimate a congestion window based on how often their messages to the server are lost/denied. They limit their rate of messaging inversely proportional to the size of the congestion window. Our experiments include both an additive-increase/multiplicative-decrease (AIMD) back-off protocol and a linear back-off protocol.
- Gossip Protocol (Gossip-V-N): In this classical model of information sharing, N components each have a secret. They can call each other and exchange their secrets. We use two variants of this model. In one variant, the duration of the call between two components is the union of their known secrets. In the other, the duration is the size of the symmetric difference of their known secrets plus one.
- Firefly synchronization (Firefly-W-H-N): In this model, N fireflies live on an W by H grid. A firefly blinks every $60 - t$ seconds, where t is the number of times it has seen another firefly in the same cell blink at least 30 s after its own latest blink. Over time this results in the fireflies blinking in synchronization.
- Leader election (Leader-N): In this model, N network nodes attempt to elect a leader by communicating with each other. The timeout deadline is dynamically calculated based on the number of hops a message do.
- Printing projects (Printing-M-P): In this model, P projects require a varying number of pieces printed. Each piece has a different size and will therefore take a different amount of time to print. There are M printers available.

All integer variables in the models use the default integer range from -32768 to 32767. There is no globally shared state. Each model is run in UPPAAL using

---

[1] The test models and results can be found at https://github.com/NicEastville/DynamicExtrapolationDataArtifact.

Table 1. Number of zones in the zone graph and time spent exploring the zone graph when using M- and $DynM$-extrapolation in various models with dynamic constraints. The better results are highlighted in bold. A dash '-' indicates that the experiment did not finish within the allocated 4 h. Time is in milliseconds.

Model	M Zones	Time	$DynM$ Zones	Time	$DynM/M\%$ Zones	Time
Simple-7	32,772	14,589	**4**	**0**	**0.01%**	**0.00%**
Simple-100	32,772	14,440	**4**	**0**	**0.01%**	**0.00%**
Simple-1000	32,772	14,675	**4**	**1**	**0.01%**	**0.01%**
Firefly-1-1-10	6,501	**176**	6,501	255	100.00%	144.89%
Firefly-1-1-15	49,233	**179,011**	49,233	180,645	100.00%	100.91%
Firefly-1-1-20	–	–	–	–	–	–
Firefly-2-1-4	167,359	**25,987**	167,359	27,345	100.00%	105.23%
Firefly-2-1-5	–	–	–	–	–	–
Gossip-symdiff-3	135	**3**	135	8	100.00%	266.67%
Gossip-symdiff-4	13,792	538	**6,972**	**356**	**50.55%**	**66.17%**
Gossip-symdiff-5	4,699,522	986,726	**919,243**	**144,123**	**19.56%**	**14.61%**
Gossip-symdiff-6	–	–	–	–	–	–
Gossip-union-3	138	3	138	3	100.00%	100.00%
Gossip-union-4	**16,536**	**99**	17,640	133	106.68%	134.34%
Gossip-union-5	**3,016,463**	**25,906**	3,264,863	35,047	108.23%	135.29%
Gossip-union-6	–	–	–	–	–	–
Leader-2	40	0	40	0	100.00%	-
Leader-3	127,537	**1,070**	127,537	1,271	100.00%	118.79%
Leader-4	–	–	–	–	–	–
Printing-2-5	**7,037**	**105**	7,257	145	103.13%	138.10%
Printing-2-6	**121,135**	3,064	125,525	4,484	103.62%	146.34%
Printing-2-7	**1,546,909**	78,747	1,601,757	108,729	103.55%	138.07%
Printing-2-8	**49,755,991**	7,914,155	51,128,387	9,448,237	102.76%	119.38%
Printing-2-9	–	–	–	–	–	–
TCP-aimd-2	66,261	385	**28,736**	218	**43.37%**	**56.62%**
TCP-aimd-3	37,528,973	807,340	**6,486,638**	**87,975**	**17.28%**	**10.90%**
TCP-aimd-4	–	–	–	–	–	–
TCP-linear-2	75,045	**307**	**62,358**	389	**83.09%**	126.71%
TCP-linear-3	46,989,547	813,729	**30,274,603**	**479,942**	**64.43%**	**58.98%**
TCP-linear-4	–	–	–	–	–	–
SUM	144,286,460	10,881,055	**94,274,934**	**10,519,305**		
% of M	100%	100%	**65.34%**	**96.68%**		

M- and $DynM$-extrapolation with a time limit of 4 h, and we measure the size of the zone graph and the time spent exploring it for each model. Many properties of these models can be verified without visiting the entire zone graph,

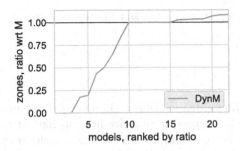

Fig. 3. Cactus plot of the number of zones in the zone graph as a ratio w.r.t. M-extrapolation

but these metrics can describe the relative coarseness and overhead of the two extrapolation techniques and give insight into their performance in a worst-case scenario. Our results can be seen in Table 1. We find that $DynM$- outperforms M-extrapolation in some families of models while being almost on par with M in others. Whenever there are improvements, those improvements are exponentially better as the parameters of the models are increased. Especially the constructed Simple-I model shows the potential of $DynM$-extrapolation. The abstract interpretation technique in [16] results in a number of zones proportional to the parameter I, while we always have 4 zones regardless of I. However, we also observe a time overhead of up to 46.3% in the worst case. The time overhead is not surprising given that $DynM$ is evaluating additional expressions during verification compared to M. There are two anomalies in our results. Specifically, we have that M-extrapolation produces fewer zones in the printing-project models and in the gossip-protocol models using union despite our Lemma 5 stating that $DynM$ is a coarser abstraction. Having confirmed that $DynM$ finds equal or smaller extrapolation values for these models, we hypothesize these anomalies occur due to how UPPAAL merges zones, and this merging happens to benefit the experiments using M in these models.

Summed across all models, $DynM$-extrapolation results in 65.3% zones and 96.7% time spent compared to M-extrapolation, a reduction of 34.6% and 3.3%, respectively. Despite anomalies and occasional increased time overhead, the $DynM$-extrapolation provides great memory savings in the general case, at least on the given benchmark set. Since memory is usually a more limited resource, this is a satisfactory outcome.

Finally, Fig. 3 is a plot of the ratios of the zone graph sizes w.r.t. M-extrapolation, where the test instances have been sorted along the x-axis based on their ratio. The graph clearly shows that $DynM$-extrapolation notably outperforms on a subset of the models, while also maintaining comparable performance on other test models. When using $DynM$-extrapolation, the number of zones in the zone graph of TCP-aimd-3 is 17.3% of what it is when using M-extrapolation, which is the greatest reduction among our experiments, if we do not consider the artificially constructed Simple model, where the reduction is close to 100%.

5   Conclusion

In this paper, we refine extrapolation techniques for extended timed automata (XTA), which is the input used in practice in tools like UPPAAL. Our technique takes advantage of the immediate state of the search to evaluate more exact extrapolation values during verification. Our experiments show that our dynamic *DynM*-extrapolation is a better abstraction for some families of XTA while being almost on par with its non-dynamic counterpart in other cases. Our summed reduction in the sizes of zone graphs is 34.7%. The best reduction of a zone graph is by 82.7% and our worst case is an increase of 8.2%. Our technique has a high time overhead, up to 46.3% slower in the worst case, but the overall time spent is reduced by 3.3%.

Future Work. Since the paths of *PathsM* are essentially programs, possible optimizations include dead-code elimination and constant propagation [14,17]. We also want to use a live variable analysis to further reduce the number of cases where $PathsM(q, x) = \perp$.

References

1. Arcile, J., André, É.: Zone extrapolations in parametric timed automata. In: Deshmukh, J.V., Havelund, K., Perez, I. (eds.) NASA Formal Methods. NFM 2022. LNCS, vol. 13260, pp. 451–469. Springer, Cham (2022). https://doi.org/10.1007/978-3-031-06773-0_24
2. Baier, C., Katoen, J.P.: Principles of Model Checking. The MIT Press, Cambridge (2008)
3. Behrmann, G., Bouyer, P., Fleury, E., Larsen, K.G.: Static guard analysis in timed automata verification. In: Garavel, H., Hatcliff, J. (eds.) TACAS 2003. LNCS, vol. 2619, pp. 254–270. Springer, Heidelberg (2003). https://doi.org/10.1007/3-540-36577-X_18
4. Behrmann, G., Bouyer, P., Larsen, K.G., Pelánek, R.: Lower and upper bounds in zone based abstractions of timed automata. In: Jensen, K., Podelski, A. (eds.) Tools and Algorithms for the Construction and Analysis of Systems, pp. 312–326. Springer, Berlin (2004). https://doi.org/10.1007/s10009-005-0190-0
5. Bengtsson, J., Yi, W.: Timed automata: semantics, algorithms and tools. In: Desel, J., Reisig, W., Rozenberg, G. (eds.) ACPN 2003. LNCS, vol. 3098, pp. 87–124. Springer, Heidelberg (2004). https://doi.org/10.1007/978-3-540-27755-2_3
6. Bouyer, P.: Untameable timed automata! In: Alt, H., Habib, M. (eds.) STACS 2003. LNCS, vol. 2607, pp. 620–631. Springer, Heidelberg (2003). https://doi.org/10.1007/3-540-36494-3_54
7. Bouyer, P.: Forward analysis of updatable timed automata. Formal Methods Syst. Des. **24**, 281–320 (2004). https://doi.org/10.1023/B:FORM.0000026093.21513.31

8. Bouyer, P., Gastin, P., Herbreteau, F., Sankur, O., Srivathsan, B.: Zone-based verification of timed automata: extrapolations, simulations and what next?. In: Bogomolov, S., Parker, D. (eds.) Formal Modeling and Analysis of Timed Systems. FORMATS 2022. LNCS, vol. 13465, pp. 16–42 (2022). Springer, Cham. https://doi.org/10.1007/978-3-031-15839-1_2

9. Clarke, E.M., Henzinger, T.A., Veith, H., Bloem, R., et al.: Handbook of model checking, vol. 10. Springer, Cham (2018). https://doi.org/10.1007/978-3-319-10575-8

10. David, A., et al.: Uppaal 4.0. In: Third International Conference on the Quantitative Evaluation of SysTems (QEST) 2006, pp. 125–126. IEEE Computer Society Press, United States (2006). https://doi.org/10.1109/QEST.2006.59

11. Dill, D.L.: Timing assumptions and verification of finite-state concurrent systems. In: Sifakis, J. (ed.) Automatic Verification Methods for Finite State Systems. pp. 197–212. Springer, Berlin (1990). https://doi.org/10.1007/3-540-52148-8_17

12. Gastin, P., Mukherjee, S., Srivathsan, B.: Fast algorithms for handling diagonal constraints in timed automata. In: Dillig, I., Tasiran, S. (eds.) Computer Aided Verification. pp. 41–59. Springer, Cham (2019). https://doi.org/10.1007/978-3-030-25540-4_3

13. Herbreteau, F., Srivathsan, B., Walukiewicz, I.: Better abstractions for timed automata. Inf. Comput. **251**, 67–90 (2016). https://doi.org/10.1016/j.ic.2016.07.004

14. Janowska, A., Janowski, P.: Slicing of timed automata with discrete data. Fundam. Informaticae **72**, 181–195 (2006)

15. Liu, Y., Sun, J., Dong, J.S.: Developing model checkers using PAT. In: Bouajjani, A., Chin, W.N. (eds.) Automated Technology for Verification and Analysis, pp. 371–377. Springer, Berlin (2010). https://doi.org/10.1007/978-3-642-15643-4_30

16. Lund, S., van Diepen, J., Larsen, K.G., Muñiz, M., Jørgensen, T.R., Andersen, T.S.D.: An integer static analysis for better extrapolation in Uppaal. In: Dima, C., Shirmohammadi, M. (eds.) Formal Modeling and Analysis of Timed Systems. pp. 84–99. Springer, Cham (2021). https://doi.org/10.1007/978-3-030-85037-1_6

17. Nielson, F., Nielson, H.R., Hankin, C.: Principles of Program Analysis. Springer Publishing Company, Incorporated (2010). https://doi.org/10.1007/978-3-662-03811-6

18. Point, G., Herbreteau, F.: The TChecker tool and librairies. https://github.com/ticktac-project/tchecker

19. Sipser, M.: Introduction to the Theory of Computability, 2nd edn. PWS Publishing Company, Computer Science Series (2006)

Formalizing Robustness Against Character-Level Perturbations for Neural Network Language Models

Zhongkui Ma[1]([✉])[iD], Xinguo Feng[1][iD], Zihan Wang[1][iD], Shuofeng Liu[1][iD], Mengyao Ma[1][iD], Hao Guan[1][iD], and Mark Huasong Meng[2,3][iD]

[1] The University of Queensland, St Lucia, QLD, Australia
{zhongkui.ma,s.feng,zihan.wang,shuofeng.liu,mengyao.ma,hao.guan}@uq.edu.au
[2] National University of Singapore, Singapore
huasong.meng@u.nus.edu
[3] Institute for Infocomm Research, A*STAR, Singapore, Singapore

Abstract. The remarkable success of neural networks has led to a growing demand for robustness verification and guarantee. However, the discrete nature of text data processed by language models presents challenges in measuring robustness, impeding verification efforts. To address this challenge, this work focuses on formalizing robustness specification against character-level perturbations for neural network language models. We introduce a key principle of three metrics, namely probability distribution, density, and diversity, for generalizing neural network language model perturbations and meanwhile, formulate the robustness specification against character-level perturbed text inputs. Based on the specification, we propose a novel approach to augment existing text datasets with specified perturbations, aiming to guide the robustness training of language models. Experimental results demonstrate that the training with our generated text datasets can enhance the overall robustness of the language model. Our contributions advance the field of neural network verification and provide a promising approach for handling robustness challenges in neural network language models.

Keywords: Neural network · Language model · Character-level perturbations · Adversarial training · Robustness

1 Introduction

The field of natural language processing (NLP) has been revolutionized by the rapid advancements in neural network language models, especially after the introduction of the Transformer architecture [28]. These models have demonstrated remarkable performance across a range of NLP tasks, including machine

---

Z. Ma and X. Feng—Equal contribution.

Y. Li and S. Tahar (Eds.): ICFEM 2023, LNCS 14308, pp. 100–117, 2023.
https://doi.org/10.1007/978-981-99-7584-6_7

translation [28], text classification [8], sentiment analysis [30], and text generation [25]. However, their vulnerability to adversarial attacks poses a significant threat to the reliability and accuracy of NLP models.

Adversarial attacks can take many forms, ranging from minor perturbations that are imperceptible to humans to more significant modifications that can result in incorrect or misleading outputs. This vulnerability brings challenges to the adoption of neural network language models in safe-critical domains such as clinical diagnosis, financial services, infrastructure, and cybersecurity [33]. To address these challenges, the training of a language model needs to take input perturbations into account and guarantee the generated model is resilient to adversarial attacks. However, discovering adversarial samples is expensive and there is an infinite number of them in specific circumstances.

Robustness is a crucial property of language models that ensures they can produce accurate or reasonable outputs even in the presence of perturbations in the input. The capacity to withstand perturbations gives rise to the ability to defend against adversarial samples, which is referred to as *robustness training*. Rather than relying solely on adversarial samples that lead to incorrect outputs, robustness training utilizes perturbed samples based on real samples to maintain the local robustness for each sample. This is an inexpensive and straightforward solution, and the challenge is to determine suitable perturbations for particular attacks. The way in which the perturbation for neural language inputs is formalized has a direct impact on the ability to protect against a particular kind of perturbed samples. Furthermore, formalizing the language model and its perturbations takes a step further towards verifying them to guarantee their practical implications. Given ϵ-perturbation has been widely adopted to measure local robustness for continuous inputs, such as numbers, images, and voice, there still lacks a measurement of the robustness specification for language models that takes text as input.

In this paper, we consider that natural language text is formed by characters as the atomic elements, and therefore we focus on robustness against character-level perturbations. Our aim is to formalize a unified concept for the imperceptible character-level perturbations. We consider perturbations of text input can be produced by three operations, namely *insertion, deletion,* and *replacement,* as demonstrated in Fig. 1. We apply the three operations in an adversarial context and propose four types of character-level attacks based on local perturbation. We then introduce a set of metrics including *probability distribution* (P), *density* (d), and *diversity* (D), to measure the perturbations, and accordingly, provide a formal definition of the robustness property against character-level perturbations. In addition to defining the robustness property, our proposed set of metrics can also be applied to augment existing text datasets by generating perturbed samples based on benign ones, which can be used to enhance the model's robustness through robustness training.

Our evaluation aims to investigate whether our proposed metrics, written as (P, d, D), can sufficiently define the robustness property against character-level attacks and, moreover, can be used to carry out robustness training. To this

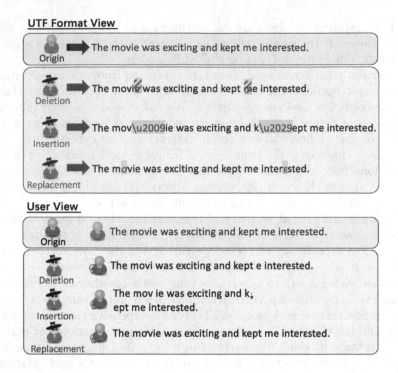

Fig. 1. Examples of character-level perturbations in English text

end, we apply the proposed metrics in augmenting existing text datasets with perturbed samples, and perform robustness training of three representative neural network language models. The experimental results show that, being guided by the defined robustness specifications, our robustness training can effectively enhance robustness for the specified perturbation while maintaining a high level of fidelity.

Contributions. Our contributions can be summarized as follows.

- We develop a canonical representation of character-level input perturbations, specifically for text and covering four types of existing attack models, with three different metrics: probability distribution, density, and diversity. Subsequently, we formalize language models and their robustness specification against character-level perturbations.
- We propose a set of perturbation generation algorithms configurable by the three metrics. We also implement a dataset augmentation tool called *PdD*, aiming to produce sufficient perturbed samples in addition to the original/real ones in the existing datasets.
- We implement adversarial training on various typical language models using *PdD*. The results demonstrate that the generated perturbed datasets are beneficial for enhancing the robustness against specified character-level perturbations.

Paper Organization. This paper is organized as follows. In Sect. 2, we provide related works. Sect. 3 formalizes the perturbation and its metrics and robustness. A formalization for language models and character-level perturbation is given. Sect. 4 presents our experiment and evaluation using generated augmented dataset by our algorithm. We conclude in Sect. 6.

Notation. We use lowercase letters, a, b, c, p, x, y to denote variables, and bold lowercase letters, x, y, to denote vectors or sequences. Sets, D, P, U, Σ, are denoted by uppercase letters. f denotes a function or model.

2   Related Work

The current work draws inspiration from existing research on adversarial attacks and the robustness of deep neural networks, with a particular focus on NLP tasks.

2.1   Adversarial Manipulations in NLP Tasks

Adversarial attacks in the NLP domain aim to manipulate systems by altering the input text, resulting in erroneous decision-making [9]. The perturbation of text inputs without prior knowledge can be achieved by utilizing special character sets, such as diacritics or invisible characters, as perturbed candidates. Boucher et al. [4] find that the injection of a single imperceptible encoding, named bad character, can lead to a remarkable decline in the performance of the targeted model, and when it comes to three injections, most models can be functionally broken. Boucher et al. [3,4] also explore a pile of adversarial attacks on NLP tasks without making any human-perceptible visual modification to inputs, and generate perturbations by uncommon encoded representations to control results across search engines and large language models (LLMs).

Performing an automatic search for adversarial samples around a given input typically requires access to gradient information from the model. This process demands additional expertise and skills, as it involves leveraging the gradient information to iteratively modify the input and search for potential adversarial examples. Behjati et al. [2] propose a gradient projection based approach to generate data-independent adversarial sequences, which can fool the classifiers into getting incorrect predictions effectively. They demonstrate that even adding one word of the adversarial sequences into the input text can downgrade the classification accuracy dramatically. Garg and Ramakrishnan [11] present BAE, a black-box attack that uses BERT masked model to hide some words of the original text with <mask> and then using BERT-MLM to predict <mask> by insertion or replacement. The usage of BAE can not only undermine the accuracy of predictions but also strengthen the grammatical and semantic coherence of the adversarial text. Morris et al. [22] propose an open-source framework called TEXTATTACK, which implements existing 16 adversarial attacks on various datasets and NLP models. Song et al. [26] develop adversarial attacks that are more like human-readable English by natural triggers and show that using such triggers together with their proposed gradient-based search can degrade the accuracy of classification tasks.

2.2 Robustness of Neural Networks

Robustness typically refers to how sensitive a model is to perturbations or noise in the input data [21,27,32]. Specifically, a model is considered robust when it is able to maintain the stability and consistency of its outputs as the input data have been changed. Several studies have been done to improve the robustness of deep learning models. Gao et al. [10] propose a mutation-based fuzzing technique to augment the training data of deep neural networks, which is capable of improving the accuracy and robustness and meanwhile, saving the training time. Zhang et al. [36] explain adversarial robustness via the sensitivity of neurons and then further analyze robustness by stabilizing the behaviors of the sensitive neurons. They reduce neuron sensitivity to improve adversarial robustness successfully. Yoo and Qi [35] propose A2T, a simple and improved vanilla adversarial training process for NLP models, that can improve the robustness of NLP models to the attack being originally trained with. Wang et al. [29] present a CAT-Gen model which mainly generates adversarial examples through controllable attributes being known to be invariant to task labels, and then fine-tune and re-train the models with adversarial examples to construct more robust NLP models. Wu et al. [34] present methods to improve robustness of NLP models from the standpoint of disentangled representation learning and shows that models trained with proposed criteria provide better robustness in many supervised learning tasks. Cheng et al. [7] address the problem of enhancing model robustness through regularization and they find for both fully supervised and semi-supervised settings, regularizing the posterior differential with f-divergence can result in well-improved model robustness.

Although there are many additional approaches to perform adversarial attacks or improve robustness [1,6,13,14,16,17,20,24,31], finding a proper representation of adversarial perturbations when it comes to NLP tasks is still an open question, due to its discrete features of the input data. Therefore, to the best of our knowledge, we are the first to explore this and provide solutions through the lens of formalization.

3 Formalization

In this section, we formulate a comprehensive framework for applying input perturbation techniques that can be extended to natural language settings. Our primary goal is to evaluate the robustness of natural language models within this framework. Throughout our analysis, we introduce three fundamental character-level operations and three metrics, namely *probability distribution*, *density* and *diversity*, to effectively control the level of input perturbation. These metrics serve as essential tools for quantifying and managing the extent of perturbation applied to the input.

3.1 Formalizing Perturbations to General Inputs

Our initial step involves considering the neighborhood of an input, as our primary objective is to formalize the local robustness of a model. Within this framework, a perturbed input is considered to be within the neighborhood of the original input vector, denoted as $x_0 \in X$. The neighborhood, denoted as U_{x_0}, is a subset of the space of all possible inputs, represented as X.

To effectively quantify the variance between the original input and its perturbed counterparts, we introduce three key metrics: probability distribution, density, and diversity. These metrics serve as valuable tools for measuring and evaluating the differences among various input samples within the neighborhood.

Probability Distribution. A discrete probability distribution is utilized to depict the probability of perturbing each item within the input vector. This distribution provides a representation of the likelihood associated with selecting each item for perturbation.

Definition 1. *The probability distribution P of a perturbation for a given input vector $x = (x_1, x_2, \cdots, x_n)$ refers to the distribution that governs the probability $P(i)$ of i-th element x_i $(1 \leq i \leq n)$ in the input vector being perturbed.*

Density. The density parameter characterizes the count of perturbed items within a given vector. It is important to emphasize that we impose a constraint where only one element can be perturbed at a time during a single perturbation. Consequently, a perturbation to the input may involve altering multiple distinct elements, but each element is perturbed individually, ensuring that only one element is modified at a time.

Definition 2. *The density d $(0 \leq d \leq 1)$ of perturbation refers to the percentage of perturbed elements in the given input vector.*

Diversity. The diversity of perturbation pertains to the collection of possible candidate characters that can be employed to perturb each original element in the input vector. This encompasses all the available choices for characters that can replace or modify the original element. The diversity metric provides a comprehensive view of the range of alternative characters that can be utilized for perturbation, offering insights into the various options for altering each element in the input vector. Notably, special character sets, such as diacritics or typos, can be utilized as candidate sets to expand the range of perturbation options.

Definition 3. *The diversity $D = \{(x_i, D_i) | 1 \leq i \leq n\}$ is a set of sets that contains all pairs (x_i, D_i), where $D_i = \{x_i', x_i'', \cdots\}$ is the set of all possible candidate elements that can be used to perturb x_i.*

Example 1: (ϵ-perturbation) When considering ϵ-perturbation, which is a common setting in verification, all elements of the input vector are available for being perturbed, resulting in a density of 1. In this case, the distribution of perturbation can be considered as any distribution. ϵ-perturbation define each input item x_i has a diversity that is a interval $[x_i - \epsilon, x_i + \epsilon]$ containing all values within a distance of ϵ to the input.

Algorithm 1: PdD(x, P, d, D)

```
   // Get the number of perturbed elements
 1 n ← floor(d * len(x));
 2 i ← 0;
 3 while i < n do
      // Choose the perturbed element
 4    while TRUE do
 5       │ j ~ P;
 6       └ if x[j] is not perturbed then break;
      // Randomly choose a perturbed candidate
 7    x' ← getPtbCandidate(D[x[j]]);
      // Perturb the specified element
 8    x[j] = x';
 9    i ← i + 1;
10 return x;
```

Example 2: (Character-level perturbation) When adding character-level perturbation to a sentence, the sentence is represented by a character vector, and the distribution describes the probability of each character being perturbed, while the density describes how many characters can be perturbed. The diversity can be a discrete character set to describe all possible replacements.

Therefore, we define the perturbation for a text input x as $U(x; P, d, D)$. Generating perturbations to an input is a process described in Algorithm 1. The algorithm takes a vector x, the probability distribution P, the density d, and the diversity parameter D as inputs and output a perturbed vector. One element of x is perturbed in one loop until the perturbed elements achieve the targeted density. When choosing a perturbed element, the distribution P is used. Choosing the perturbed candidate follows a uniform distribution.

3.2 Formalizing Language Models

In this section, our attention is directed towards formulating a specific framework for language models in the context of machine learning. We enumerate three fundamental character-level operations employed in the perturbation process. Additionally, We provide a formalized definition of robustness within this framework.

Language Model. Let L be a formal language over an alphabet Σ, which is a subset of the set of words Σ^{*1}. We begin by defining a language model in machine learning, denoted as f.

---

[1] We use Kleene star to denote the concatenation of words.

Definition 4. *(Language Model) A language model f is a function that takes a sequence of words $x \in \Sigma^*$ as input and outputs a sequence of words $y \in \Sigma^*$, where Σ^* is its finite word set.*

In practice, a language model typically uses a token-level encoding to generate a token embedding, which is then taken as a part of the model. Due to the finite memory of computers, a language model always has its own finite token set Σ^*. In cases where a token is not included in Σ^*, it is represented by a special tag/token [UNK], denoting that it is unknown. For text classification models, the output is typically binary and can be regarded as numbers in natural language. In this paper, to ease the understanding, we interchangeably use *token* and *word* to represent the basic input of a language model.

Robustness. Robustness is a critical property for neural networks, as it ensures that the network can produce accurate outputs even in the presence of perturbations. The definition highlights the importance of ensuring that the output remains within a predefined set, indicating that the network is capable of handling different types of perturbations without compromising its accuracy.

Definition 5. *Robustness is the property that, given a language model f and a input x_0 and its perturbed values set U_{x_0}, the resulting output set $f(U_{x_0})$ satisfies being a subset of the predefined set $U_{y_0} \subseteq \Sigma^*$, i.e.*

$$\forall x' \in U_{x_0}, y' = f(x') \implies y' \in U_{y_0}$$

For a classification model, it is highly desirable that the output label for a perturbed input remains consistent with the label for the original input, i.e., $U_{y_0} = \{y_0\}$. In general cases, we aim to ensure that the output for a perturbed input remains within a predefined set U_{y_0}, i.e. $f(U_{x_0}) \subseteq U_{y_0}$. Note that it is not necessary for $U_{x0} \subseteq \Sigma^*$ when considering the model f. However, it is always necessary for $U_{y_0} \subseteq \Sigma^*$ since a reasonable output under perturbed inputs is what robustness requires and expects.

3.3   Character-Level Perturbation

We note that a sequence of words can be represented as a string or a sequence of characters. We use [EMP] to denote an empty character. For example, a sequence of words $x = (x_1, x_2, \cdots, x_n)$, where x_i $(1 \leq i \leq n)$ is a word and $x_i = a_i b_i c_i \cdots$, which is composed of a finite set of characters a_i, b_i, c_i, etc., concatenated to form the word. Therefore, we consider a sequence of words in character-level as a vector $x = a_1 b_1 c_1 \cdots a_2 b_2 c_2 \cdots a_n b_n c_n \cdots$ in the following discussion. In the following discussion, we will focus on the character representation of a sequence of words and take it as a sequence of characters.

Definition 6. *(Character-level Perturbation) Given an input $x \in \Sigma^*$ for a language model L, a character-level perturbation $x' \in \tilde{\Sigma}$ ($\tilde{\Sigma}^* \supseteq \Sigma^*$) is another* *sequence of words, whose words have several characters that differ from the corresponding words in $\boldsymbol{x}$. Let $\boldsymbol{x} = a_1 b_1 c_1 \cdots a_2 b_2 c_2 \cdots a_n b_n c_n \cdots$ $(a_i, b_i, c_i \in \Sigma)$, and let $\boldsymbol{x}' = a_1' b_1' c_1' \cdots a_2' b_2' c_2' \cdots a_n' b_n' c_n' \cdots$ $(a_i', b_i', c_i' \in \tilde{\Sigma}$ and $\tilde{\Sigma} \supseteq \Sigma)$, then $\boldsymbol{x}'$ is almost the same to $\boldsymbol{x}$.*

The perturbed words need not be elements of the original word set Σ^*. Furthermore, certain types of perturbation may use characters outside of the original alphabet Σ. Therefore, for a given type of perturbation, it is necessary to have an alphabet $\tilde{\Sigma} \supseteq \Sigma$ and a word set $\tilde{\Sigma}^* \supseteq \Sigma^*$.

In the following discussion, we explore three fundamental character-level operations that can be utilized to generate perturbations: replacement, deletion, and insertion. An illustrative example of generating character-level perturbations is provided in Fig. 1.

Replacement. This operation serves as a general case encompassing all other operations. It is inherently implied in our perturbation definition. For each element x_i in the input vector $\boldsymbol{x}$, we define a finite discrete set of candidates D_i. The set D_i comprises k candidate characters, denoted as c_{ij}, where $1 \leq j \leq k$. Each c_{ij} represents a possible substitution from the candidate set D_i.

Other operations can be derived from the replacement operation. We illustrate two significant cases: deletion and insertion.

Deletion. For deletion, we set $(x_i, D_i) = (x_i, \texttt{[EMP]})$, where $\texttt{[EMP]}$ represents an empty character. This operation effectively removes the character x_i from the input.

Insertion. For insertion, we set $(x_i, D_i) = (x_i, x_i c_{ij}, c_{ij} x_i | 1 \leq j \leq k, k \in \mathbb{Z})$, where c_{ij} is defined as in the replacement operation. Here, $x_i c_{ij}$ or $c_{ij} x_i$ represents the concatenation of the original character x_i and the inserted character c_{ij}. We limit our focus to the insertion of a single character at a time in Algorithm 1 for perturbation at the character level.

It is also possible to define operations that affect subsequent characters in different sizes. Moreover, for more complex operations such as transposition or swapping two characters, a well-defined probability distribution of perturbation is required. Different operations can lead to various types of perturbations. For instance, insertion allows for the generation of diverse perturbations such as inserting invisible characters, replacing with diacritics, or introducing typos.

4   Experiments

In this section, we assess the effectiveness of our perturbation metrics on various language models and tasks trained with different perturbed datasets. Then we compare the accuracy of original or augmented trained model on original or perturbed datasets.

4.1   Experiment Setup

This section discusses the models and tasks we employed, the criteria for perturbation, the procedure for creating perturbed datasets, and the training details.

Table 1. Experimental models and datasets

Model	Dataset	Task	#Class
BERT	Rotten Tomatoes	Sentiment Analysis	2
RoBERTa	SNIL	Natural Language Inference	3
ALBERT	E-commerce	Text Classification	4

Models and Tasks. We conduct our experiments on three widely used language models, including BERT [8], RoBERTa [18], and ALBERT [15]. These models are within the Transformer Encoder family and are usually used for classification tasks. In this work, we focus on the classification task due to its well-defined measure of robustness, which is the accuracy of the classification. The task of BERT is sentiment analysis, RoBERTa is for natural language inference, and ALBERT is for text classification. Several benchmark text classification datasets, including Rotten Tomatoes [23], Stanford Natural Language Inference (SNLI) [5], and E-commerce [12], are used to evaluate the performance of the models. Table 1 displays the models and datasets evaluated in this study.

Perturbation Settings. To create augmented datasets comprising perturbed samples, we employ our formalized perturbation metrics including probability distribution, density, and diversity to define the perturbed input set $U(x_0; P, d, D)$ for each input sample x_0 by combinations of different metrics. In accordance with the definition presented in Sect. 3, the perturbations employed in our experiments are practically elaborated as follows.

- On probability distribution, we consider two probability distributions, namely the uniform distribution and the normal distribution, to deploy character-level perturbations in original input samples. Specifically for normal distribution, we select $\mu = 0.5 \times L$ and $\sigma^2 = 0.25 \times L$, where L represents the length of the input sequence.
- On density, we investigate the densities of 0.05 and 0.2, which signify a small and large number of perturbations of two levels.
- On diversity, we opt the specific perturbation generation method, encompassing deletion, keyboard typos, diacritics, invisible characters as follows, and mixed perturbation.
  - **Deletion** refers to replacing a character from the given sentence with the empty character.
  - **Keyboard typos** imitate the act of mistakenly pressing adjacent keys, whereby we consider up to 8 neighboring keys as potential candidates for a single key.
  - **Diacritics**, by definition, are characters that bear a resemblance to a specific character. In our approach, we carefully select 5 diacritics that can serve as potential replacements for a single character in the input sentence.

- **Invisible characters** encompass operational characters that are not detectable by human eyes, and we choose from a pool of 48 invisible characters to insert them behind the selected character.

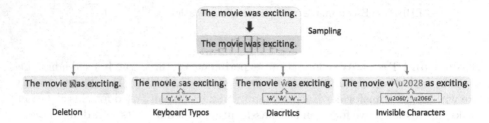

Fig. 2. Examples of four practical attacks in English text

Figure 2 demonstrates some perturbation instances generated by the four standalone attack methods. In addition to the four standalone methods, a **mixed perturbations** method is also adopted to further assess the effectiveness of the proposed adversarial training approach. It combines the aforementioned four types of perturbation and randomly applies them to the input sequence.

Table 2. Perturbation settings used in our evaluation

Metrics	Description	Setting Options
P	Probability Distribution	uniform distribution, normal distribution
d	Density	0.05, 0.2
D	Diversity	deletion, keyboard typos, diacritics, invisible characters

Augmented Datasets Generation. For each input sample, we generate 10 perturbed versions using a single perturbation setting. Consequently, an augmented dataset produced using one perturbation setting is 10 times larger than the original dataset. Using different combinations of these metrics as outlined in Table 2, we separately apply each character-level perturbation method to all samples in a dataset. We then utilize all the resulting perturbed samples to evaluate the accuracy of the language models.

Implementation Details. In our experiments, we utilize three different pre-trained large language model architectures and train them on both original training datasets and augmented training datasets. This training process results in two separate models for each model architecture, namely a clean model M_{clean}, and an augmentedly trained model M_{aug}.

To maintain consistency, we randomly choose an equivalent amount of data from the SNLI and E-commerce datasets, which are larger in size compared to the Rotten Tomatoes dataset. This selection results in 9,000 training samples and 2,000 testing samples for the original datasets. For each augmented dataset under different settings, we obtain 99,000 training samples and 22,000 testing samples, after the insertion of perturbed samples.

During the training phase, all models utilize a batch size of 16. We employ the AdamW optimizer [19] with a fixed learning rate of 2×10^{-5}. To determine the best models, we incorporate early stopping with a patience of five. On average, the training process spans approximately seven epochs. All reported experiments are conducted on a workstation equipped with an AMD Ryzen Threadripper PRO 5965WX 24-Core 4.00 GHz CPU, 252G of main memory, and one NVIDIA RTX A6000 GPU.

4.2 Evaluation

In this section, we evaluate the effectiveness of making the model more robust by using robustness training with different specified perturbations. We measure the accuracy of the models on the original datasets and the perturbed datasets to demonstrate the effectiveness of robustness for the specified perturbations.

Overall Performance. Table 3 reveals that the accuracy of the original models is lower on perturbed datasets than augmented models. This indicates that all the various perturbation types have a clear negative effect on the performance of the models when trained normally. For the models trained with perturbed datasets, their accuracy is significantly higher (up to 0.4) than those trained without perturbated samples.

The results in Table 4 demonstrate that the augmented models have a comparable or even better accuracy (ranging from −0.05 to 0.005) than the original models on the original datasets. This suggests that the augmented models are able to maintain their performance on regular samples while still being tolerant to perturbed samples.

This demonstrates the detrimental effect of character-level perturbation on models that have been trained in the usual way, and highlights the need and effectiveness for robustness training using perturbed samples.

Performance on Different Models and Tasks. We assess three cases, (1) BERT with sentiment analysis, (2) RoBERTa with natural language inference, and (3) ALBERT with text classification. For the accuracy on pertubed datasets in Table 3, cases (1) and (2) are more vulnerable to perturbed samples, with a decrease in accuracy ranging from 0.01–0.26 and 0.08–0.43, respectively. In contrast, case (3) is less affected, with a decrease ranging from 0.01–0.14.

For the accuracy on original datasets in Table 4, the augmented models show a similar accuracy (with a maximum difference of 0.01) for cases (1) and (3), but a noticeable decrease (up to 0.06) for case (2).

Table 3. Model performance (F1-scores) on augmented datasets, presented as tuples of the clean models (M_{clean}) and augmentedly trained models (M_{aug}). The improvement of model performance is displayed in **bold** font.

Deletion Perturbation

Probability Distribution	Density	BERT(SA)		RoBERTa(NLI)		ALBERT(TC)	
		M_{clean}	M_{aug}	M_{clean}	M_{aug}	M_{clean}	M_{aug}
Uniform	0.2	0.5044	**0.7499**	0.4060	**0.6769**	0.8045	**0.9443**
	0.05	0.7873	**0.8358**	0.7133	**0.8027**	0.9491	**0.9566**
Normal	0.2	0.5498	**0.7505**	0.4426	**0.6788**	0.8751	**0.9466**
	0.05	0.7901	**0.8329**	0.7241	**0.8074**	0.9533	**0.9612**

Keyboard Typos Perturbation

Probability Distribution	Density	BERT(SA)		RoBERTa(NLI)		ALBERT(TC)	
		M_{clean}	M_{aug}	M_{clean}	M_{aug}	M_{clean}	M_{aug}
Uniform	0.2	0.4963	**0.7651**	0.3625	**0.6918**	0.8095	**0.9436**
	0.05	0.7911	**0.8463**	0.7161	**0.8028**	0.9470	**0.9613**
Normal	0.2	0.5529	**0.7691**	0.3891	**0.6877**	0.8819	**0.9491**
	0.05	0.7966	**0.8471**	0.7214	**0.8058**	0.9515	**0.9627**

Diacritics Perturbation

Probability Distribution	Density	BERT(SA)		RoBERTa(NLI)		ALBERT(TC)	
		M_{clean}	M_{aug}	M_{clean}	M_{aug}	M_{clean}	M_{aug}
Uniform	0.2	0.7588	**0.8247**	0.2879	**0.7142**	0.9407	**0.9560**
	0.05	0.8404	**0.8547**	0.6799	**0.8213**	0.9588	**0.9642**
Normal	0.2	0.7727	**0.8259**	0.2978	**0.7061**	0.9485	**0.9588**
	0.05	0.8466	**0.8519**	0.6883	**0.8184**	0.9600	**0.9637**

Invisible Characters Perturbation

Probability Distribution	Density	BERT(SA)		RoBERTa(NLI)		ALBERT(TC)	
		M_{clean}	M_{aug}	M_{clean}	M_{aug}	M_{clean}	M_{aug}
Uniform	0.2	0.5336	**0.7712**	0.3630	**0.6925**	0.8380	**0.9434**
	0.05	0.7978	**0.8411**	0.7099	**0.7999**	0.9501	**0.9618**
Normal	0.2	0.5812	**0.7740**	0.3995	**0.6821**	0.8885	**0.9527**
	0.05	0.8051	**0.8442**	0.7176	**0.8063**	0.9542	**0.9612**

Mixed Perturbation

Probability Distribution	Density	BERT(SA)		RoBERTa(NLI)		ALBERT(TC)	
		M_{clean}	M_{aug}	M_{clean}	M_{aug}	M_{clean}	M_{aug}
Uniform	0.2	0.5534	**0.7630**	0.3370	**0.6750**	0.8636	**0.9477**
	0.05	0.8080	**0.8416**	0.7001	**0.8035**	0.9526	**0.9613**
Normal	0.2	0.6013	**0.7667**	0.3634	**0.6742**	0.9051	**0.9529**
	0.05	0.8128	**0.8387**	0.7097	**0.8101**	0.9563	**0.9594**

SA: Sentiment Analysis **NLI**: Natural Language Inference **TC**: Text Classification

Our perturbation has a more significant effect on the natural language inference (NLI) task than the other two tasks. This is because NLI requires a thorough analysis of each word and phrase in a sentence to create a detailed context, which is one of the most difficult areas of NLP. On the other hand, text classi-

Table 4. Model performance (F1-scores) on original datasets, presented as tuples of the clean models (M_{clean}) and augmentedly trained models (M_{aug}). The improvement of model performance is displayed in **bold** font.

Deletion Perturbation

Probability Distribution	Density	BERT(SA)		RoBERTa(NLI)		ALBERT(TC)	
		M_{clean}	M_{aug}	M_{clean}	M_{aug}	M_{clean}	M_{aug}
Uniform	0.2	0.8625	0.8611	0.8686	0.8283	0.9636	0.9599
	0.05		0.8611		0.8419		0.9620
Normal	0.2		0.8424		0.8394		0.9609
	0.05		0.8574		0.8571		**0.9644**

Keyboard Typos Perturbation

Probability Distribution	Density	BERT(SA)		RoBERTa(NLI)		ALBERT(TC)	
		M_{clean}	M_{aug}	M_{clean}	M_{aug}	M_{clean}	M_{aug}
Uniform	0.2	0.8625	**0.8672**	0.8686	0.8149	0.9636	0.9624
	0.05		**0.8653**		0.8516		0.9630
Normal	0.2		0.8621		0.8277		0.9624
	0.05		**0.8672**		0.8543		**0.9657**

Diacritics Perturbation

Probability Distribution	Density	BERT(SA)		RoBERTa(NLI)		ALBERT(TC)	
		M_{clean}	M_{aug}	M_{clean}	M_{aug}	M_{clean}	M_{aug}
Uniform	0.2	0.8625	**0.8638**	0.8686	0.8299	0.9636	0.9599
	0.05		**0.8639**		0.8568		**0.9669**
Normal	0.2		0.8601		0.8170		**0.9639**
	0.05		0.8602		0.8571		**0.9648**

Invisible Characters Perturbation

Probability Distribution	Density	BERT(SA)		RoBERTa(NLI)		ALBERT(TC)	
		M_{clean}	M_{aug}	M_{clean}	M_{aug}	M_{clean}	M_{aug}
Uniform	0.2	0.8625	**0.8681**	0.8686	0.8554	0.9636	0.9624
	0.05		**0.8658**		0.8391		**0.9644**
Normal	0.2		**0.8630**		0.8393		**0.9646**
	0.05		**0.8634**		0.8450		0.9634

Mixed Perturbation

Probability Distribution	Density	BERT(SA)		RoBERTa(NLI)		ALBERT(TC)	
		M_{clean}	M_{aug}	M_{clean}	M_{aug}	M_{clean}	M_{aug}
Uniform	0.2	0.8625	0.8564	0.8686	0.8134	0.9636	0.9627
	0.05		0.8600		0.8488		**0.9637**
Normal	0.2		0.8508		0.8510		**0.9655**
	0.05		0.8615		0.8593		0.9595

SA: Sentiment Analysis **NLI**: Natural Language Inference **TC**: Text Classification

fication models usually only consider a few keywords to determine the category of the review, resulting in a less noticeable impact. Despite the presence of perturbed characters, the model still manages to achieve a satisfactory result on text classification.

114 Z. Ma et al.

Performance on Different Perturbation Settings. Perturbations with a uniform distribution always lead to a greater decrease in accuracy (as much as 0.08) of the original models than perturbations with a normal distribution. The uniform perturbation has a greater impact on all the words of the sentence, while the normal distribution is more likely to affect words in certain positions with higher probability. . The results of augmented models demonstrate that they are able to learn the data with perturbation, regardless of the two distribution settings, with little to no impact on their accuracy.

When perturbations with a higher density of 0.2 are applied, the accuracy of the original models decreases by a range of 0.07 to 0.39, while the augmented models experience a decrease of 0.01 to 0.14. It is logical to assume that the more perturbed elements there are, the more challenging it is to make an inference.

Different types of character-level perturbations demonstrate varying levels of vulnerability for the original models. In case (1), the original models are more resilient to diacritics perturbations (with an accuracy of approximately 0.75–0.85) than to other perturbations (with an accuracy of approximately 0.5–0.8). In the second case, all types of perturbations have a similar effect on the accuracy of the original models. In the third case, the original models are more resistant to diacritics perturbations (with an accuracy of approximately 0.95) and less resistant to other perturbations (with an accuracy of approximately 0.8–0.95). The augmented models show a similar pattern when exposed to different types of perturbations, but with a higher and more stable accuracy. Moreover, the accuracy of the augmented models is not significantly affected by the various types of perturbations when tested on the original datasets. In current natural language models, the words are tokenized and converted into numerical vectors. These perturbed characters often lead to the replacement of [UNK] token. Those perturbation, causing another correct existing words, has a greater impact on the inference of models.

It is evident that models and tasks with regular training can be affected to varying degrees when exposed to different perturbations. Our three metrics show different impacts on the performance of the original models, indicating that these metrics do indeed measure the perturbation. If robustness training is used to target a particular perturbation, the robustness of the original models can be significantly improved.

5 Discussion

This study focuses on the formalization of perturbation at the natural language level, treating it as a character sequence. Our work contributes a novel endeavor by establishing a unified definition encompassing all types of inputs for neural networks. However, to comprehensively evaluate the robustness of these models, it is imperative to develop additional metrics that effectively capture the distance or dissimilarity between the original item and its perturbed counterpart. Such metrics are essential for quantifying the diversity and construction of the candidate set. Although our study provides an initial framework, further refinement is expected in this aspect.

Our experiment results demonstrate that our approach can not only significantly enhance the robustness, but also retain a high level of fidelity of the models. However, we only experiment with models of classification tasks. The robustness of models of generative tasks such as Machine Translation and Text Summarization can be further investigated.

We also remark that the robustness of neural network language models can be extended to the word level. Defining metrics of word-level robustness presents unique challenges as it entails considerations of semantic meaning and grammar and therefore, desires future efforts from the research community.

6   Conclusion

This paper introduces a generalized formalization of perturbed inputs for natural language models, offering a crucial step towards testing and verifying their robustness. We specifically focus on character-level perturbations, outlining the basic operations of replacement, deletion, and insertion. By controlling the perturbation process through principles of probability distribution, density, and diversity, we can generate different levels and types of character-level perturbations using a clean dataset.

Our approach demonstrates significant improvements in robustness against specific perturbations when training a network on a dataset perturbed by our method compared to using only clean data. Augmenting existing text datasets with adversarial perturbations, guided by our proposed approach, leads to notable enhancements in overall model robustness.

Overall, this work contributes novel insights and techniques, advancing the measurement and assurance of language model robustness. Given the critical importance of reliability and accuracy in language models, our approach holds great potential for further advancements in this area.

References

1. Bai, T., Luo, J., Zhao, J., Wen, B., Wang, Q.: Recent advances in adversarial training for adversarial robustness. arXiv preprint arXiv:2102.01356 (2021)
2. Behjati, M., Moosavi-Dezfooli, S.M., Baghshah, M.S., Frossard, P.: Universal adversarial attacks on text classifiers. In: ICASSP 2019–2019 IEEE International Conference on Acoustics, Speech and Signal Processing (ICASSP), pp. 7345–7349 (2019). https://doi.org/10.1109/ICASSP.2019.8682430
3. Boucher, N., Pajola, L., Shumailov, I., Anderson, R., Conti, M.: Boosting big brother: attacking search engines with encodings. arXiv preprint arXiv:2304.14031 (2023)
4. Boucher, N., Shumailov, I., Anderson, R., Papernot, N.: Bad characters: Imperceptible NLP attacks. In: 2022 IEEE Symposium on Security and Privacy (SP), pp. 1987–2004. IEEE (2022)
5. Bowman, S., Angeli, G., Potts, C., Manning, C.D.: A large annotated corpus for learning natural language inference. In: Proceedings of the 2015 Conference on Empirical Methods in Natural Language Processing, pp. 632–642 (2015)

6. Chakraborty, A., Alam, M., Dey, V., Chattopadhyay, A., Mukhopadhyay, D.: A survey on adversarial attacks and defences. CAAI Trans. Intell. Technol. **6**(1), 25–45 (2021)
7. Cheng, H., Liu, X., Pereira, L., Yu, Y., Gao, J.: Posterior differential regularization with f-divergence for improving model robustness. arXiv preprint arXiv:2010.12638 (2020)
8. Devlin, J., Chang, M.W., Lee, K., Toutanova, K.: Bert: pre-training of deep bidirectional transformers for language understanding. arXiv preprint arXiv:1810.04805 (2018)
9. Eger, S., et al.: Text processing like humans do: visually attacking and shielding NLP systems. arXiv preprint arXiv:1903.11508 (2019)
10. Gao, X., Saha, R.K., Prasad, M.R., Roychoudhury, A.: Fuzz testing based data augmentation to improve robustness of deep neural networks. In: Proceedings of the ACM/IEEE 42nd International Conference on Software Engineering, pp. 1147–1158 (2020)
11. Garg, S., Ramakrishnan, G.: Bae: bert-based adversarial examples for text classification. arXiv preprint arXiv:2004.01970 (2020)
12. Gautam: E commerce text dataset. https://zenodo.org/record/3355823#. ZF99xy8Rq-o (2019). Accessed 12 May 2023
13. Hendrycks, D., Mu, N., Cubuk, E.D., Zoph, B., Gilmer, J., Lakshminarayanan, B.: Augmix: a simple data processing method to improve robustness and uncertainty. arXiv preprint arXiv:1912.02781 (2019)
14. Hu, P., Wang, Z., Sun, R., Wang, H., Xue, M.: M^4i: multi-modal models membership inference. In: Advances in Neural Information Processing Systems, vol. 35, pp. 1867–1882 (2022)
15. Lan, Z., Chen, M., Goodman, S., Gimpel, K., Sharma, P., Soricut, R.: Albert: A lite bert for self-supervised learning of language representations. arXiv preprint arXiv:1909.11942 (2019)
16. Li, Y., Min, M.R., Lee, T., Yu, W., Kruus, E., Wang, W., Hsieh, C.J.: Towards robustness of deep neural networks via regularization. In: Proceedings of the IEEE/CVF International Conference on Computer Vision, pp. 7496–7505 (2021)
17. Liu, S., Lei, P., Koji, K.: LSTM based hybrid method for basin water level prediction by using precipitation data. J. Adv. Simul. Sci. Eng. **8**(1), 40–52 (2021)
18. Liu, Y., et al.: Roberta: a robustly optimized bert pretraining approach. arXiv preprint arXiv:1907.11692 (2019)
19. Loshchilov, I., Hutter, F.: Decoupled weight decay regularization. arXiv preprint arXiv:1711.05101 (2017)
20. Ma, M., et al.: Loden: Making every client in federated learning a defender against the poisoning membership inference attacks. In: 18th ACM ASIA Conference on Computer and Communications Security ASIACCS 2023, ACM (2023)
21. Meng, M.H., et al.: Adversarial robustness of deep neural networks: a survey from a formal verification perspective. IEEE Trans. Dependable Secure Comput. (2022)
22. Morris, J.X., Lifland, E., Yoo, J.Y., Grigsby, J., Jin, D., Qi, Y.: TextAttack: a framework for adversarial attacks, data augmentation, and adversarial training in NLP. arXiv preprint arXiv:2005.05909 (2020)
23. Pang, B., Lee, L.: Seeing stars: exploiting class relationships for sentiment categorization with respect to rating scales. In: Proceedings of the ACL (2005)
24. Qiu, S., Liu, Q., Zhou, S., Wu, C.: Review of artificial intelligence adversarial attack and defense technologies. Appl. Sci. **9**(5), 909 (2019)
25. Radford, A., Wu, J., Child, R., Luan, D., Amodei, D., Sutskever, I., et al.: Language models are unsupervised multitask learners. OpenAI blog **1**(8), 9 (2019)

26. Song, L., Yu, X., Peng, H.T., Narasimhan, K.: Universal adversarial attacks with natural triggers for text classification. arXiv preprint arXiv:2005.00174 (2020)
27. Subbaswamy, A., Adams, R., Saria, S.: Evaluating model robustness and stability to dataset shift. In: International Conference on Artificial Intelligence and Statistics, pp. 2611–2619. PMLR (2021)
28. Vaswani, A., et al.: Attention is all you need. In: Advances in Neural Information Processing Systems, vol. 30 (2017)
29. Wang, T., et al.: Cat-gen: Improving robustness in NLP models via controlled adversarial text generation. arXiv preprint arXiv:2010.02338 (2020)
30. Wang, Y., Huang, M., Zhu, X., Zhao, L.: Attention-based LSTM for aspect-level sentiment classification. In: Proceedings of the 2016 Conference on Empirical Methods in Natural Language Processing, pp. 606–615 (2016)
31. Wang, Z., Guo, H., Zhang, Z., Liu, W., Qin, Z., Ren, K.: Feature importance-aware transferable adversarial attacks. In: Proceedings of the IEEE/CVF International Conference on Computer Vision, pp. 7639–7648 (2021)
32. Wang, Z., et al.: Data hiding with deep learning: a survey unifying digital watermarking and steganography. IEEE Trans. Comput. Soc. Syst. 1–15 (2023). https://doi.org/10.1109/TCSS.2023.3268950
33. Waqas, A., Farooq, H., Bouaynaya, N.C., Rasool, G.: Exploring robust architectures for deep artificial neural networks. Commun. Eng. 1(1), 46 (2022)
34. Wu, J., Li, X., Ao, X., Meng, Y., Wu, F., Li, J.: Improving robustness and generality of NLP models using disentangled representations. arXiv preprint arXiv:2009.09587 (2020)
35. Yoo, J.Y., Qi, Y.: Towards improving adversarial training of NLP models. arXiv preprint arXiv:2109.00544 (2021)
36. Zhang, C., et al.: Interpreting and improving adversarial robustness of deep neural networks with neuron sensitivity. IEEE Trans. Image Process. 30, 1291–1304 (2020)

Trace Models of Concurrent Valuation Algebras

Naso Evangelou-Oost[(✉)][iD], Larissa Meinicke[(✉)][iD], Callum Bannister[(✉)][iD],
and Ian J. Hayes[(✉)][iD]

The University of Queensland, St Lucia, Australia
a.evangelouoost@uq.edu.au, {l.meinicke,C.Bannister,ian.hayes}@uq.edu.au

Abstract. This paper introduces Concurrent Valuation Algebras (CVAs), a novel extension of ordered valuation algebras (OVAs). CVAs include two combine operators representing parallel and sequential products, adhering to a weak exchange law. This development offers theoretical and practical benefits for the specification and modelling of concurrent and distributed systems. As a presheaf on a space of domains, CVAs enable localised specifications, supporting modularity, compositionality, and the ability to represent large and complex systems. Furthermore, CVAs align with lattice-based refinement reasoning and are compatible with established methodologies such as Hoare and Rely-Guarantee logics. The flexibility of CVAs is explored through three trace models, illustrating distinct paradigms of concurrent/distributed computing, interrelated by morphisms. The paper also highlights the potential to incorporate a powerful local computation framework from valuation algebras for model checking in concurrent and distributed systems. The foundational results presented have been verified with the proof assistant Isabelle/HOL.

Keywords: Concurrent valuation algebras · Concurrent systems · Distributed systems

1 Introduction

Valuation algebras are versatile algebraic structures that parameterise information across multiple domains, representing for example subsets of variables or events. These structures have been widely utilised across diverse disciplines such as database theory, logic, probability and statistics, and constraint satisfaction, among others. What sets valuation algebras apart is their robust computational theory, enabling the deployment of highly efficient distributed algorithms for addressing inference problems that involve information combination and querying [17].

In our preceding work [7], we applied ordered valuation algebras to distributed systems, demonstrating their potential as a modular framework for specifying these systems in a refinement paradigm. Moreover, we established a link between sequential consistency—a crucial correctness criterion—and contextuality, an abstract form of information inconsistency which valuation algebras capture.

Y. Li and S. Tahar (Eds.): ICFEM 2023, LNCS 14308, pp. 118–136, 2023.
https://doi.org/10.1007/978-981-99-7584-6_8

Paper Outline. In Sect. 2, we introduce ordered valuation algebras (OVAs) based on prior studies [1,9] and extend these to concurrent valuation algebras (CVAs) in Sect. 3, a structure comprising two OVA structures on a space with combine operators adhering to a weak exchange law. This design takes inspiration from *Communicating Sequential Processes (CSP)* [12], *Concurrent Kleene Algebra (CKA)* [13], *Concurrent Refinement Algebra (CRA)* [10], and *duoidal/2-monoidal categories* [2]. We also define morphisms between CVAs, and explain their alignment with the refinement reasoning methodologies of Hoare [11] and Rely-Guarantee [14] logics. Section 4 delves into tuple systems and relational OVAs, which underpin our trace models. The subsequent sections, Sects. 5 to 7, introduce and contrast various trace models, elaborating on their distinct combine operators and trace characteristics. In Sect. 8, we reflect on the potential extension of the local computation framework from valuation algebras to CVAs. Section 9 closes our paper, encapsulating our findings and suggesting avenues for future exploration.

The theoretical underpinnings detailed in Sects. 2 to 4 have been rigorously formalised using the proof assistant Isabelle/HOL, lending credibility to our study.[1] A separate formalisation of Sect. 6 is also available.[2] Proofs of omitted results can be found in the appendix of the arXiv version of this paper [6].

2   Ordered Valuation Algebras

We assume familiarity with foundational ideas in order theory and category theory, including the definitions of a category, a functor, and a natural transformation. For those interested in a more detailed understanding, please refer to [8] for an accessible introduction, or [18] as a thorough reference.

Notation. The category of sets and functions is denoted $\mathscr{S}et$. Posets (partially ordered sets) are identified with their associated (thin) categories, so that the hom-set $\mathrm{hom}(a, b)$ is a singleton when $a \leq b$ and empty otherwise, and we write $\mathscr{P}os$ for the category whose objects are posets and whose morphisms are monotone functions. A **topological space** $(X, \mathscr{T})$ is a set X equipped with a topology $\mathscr{T}$, which is a family of subsets of X, termed **open sets**, partially ordered by inclusion, and closed under arbitrary unions and finite intersections (in particular, the empty intersection, X, and the empty union, $\emptyset$, are open). For a category $\mathcal{C}$, $\mathcal{C}^{\mathrm{op}}$ denotes its **opposite category**, that is the category $\mathcal{C}$ with the direction of its arrows reversed. A **presheaf** Φ on a topological space $(X, \mathscr{T})$ is a functor with domain $\mathscr{T}^{\mathrm{op}}$. We notate the value of a presheaf Φ applied to A by Φ_A instead of $\Phi(A)$, and for $B \subseteq A$ in $\mathscr{T}$, the **restriction map** $\Phi_A \to \Phi_B$ is denoted $a \mapsto a^{\downarrow B}$. All presheaves considered are valued in $\mathscr{S}et$ or $\mathscr{P}os$, though we adopt the name **prealgebra** for a poset-valued presheaf, suggesting our intent to develop an OVA structure upon it. A **global element** of a prealgebra Φ is a natural transformation $\epsilon : \mathbf{1} \Rightarrow \Phi$ from the terminal prealgebra $\mathbf{1}$, defined

---

[1] Available at https://github.com/nasosev/cva .

[2] Available at https://github.com/onomatic/icfem23-proofs .

$\mathbf{1} := A \mapsto \{\heartsuit\}$. For such a global element ϵ, we write ϵ_A instead of $\epsilon_A(\heartsuit)$. The symbol $\mathbf{P}$ denotes the *covariant powerset functor* $\mathbf{P} : \mathcal{S}et \to \mathcal{P}os$, sending a set X to the poset of its subsets $\mathbf{P}(X)$, and sending a function $f : X \to Y$ to its *direct image* $f_* := X \mapsto \{f(x) \mid x \in X\}$. The symbol $\mathbb{N}$ denotes the set of natural numbers $\{0, 1, \ldots\}$, while $\mathbb{N}_+$ is the set of positive natural numbers $\{1, 2, \ldots\}$.

Throughout this paper, we fix a topological space $(X, \mathcal{T})$. Here, the open sets symbolise abstract *domains*, representing subsets of system elements like memory locations, resources, or events, as well as their interconnectivity.

Example 1. A network composed of three computer systems a, b, c and three network links d, e, f as pictured in Fig. 1 may be represented by the topological space generated by unions and intersections of the domains $\{d, a, e\}$, $\{e, b, f\}$, $\{f, c, d\}$. More generally, a network defined by a labelled, undirected graph converts to a finite topology where open sets are the upwards-closed sets of the network's *face poset*, i.e. the poset whose elements are the nodes n and edges e of the network, where $n \leq e$ if and only if n is a vertex of e.[3] Alternatively, a set of memory addresses X may be given the discrete topology $\mathcal{T} = \mathbf{P}(X)$.

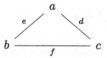

Fig. 1. A network of three computers and three links.

A prealgebra $\mathbf{\Phi} : \mathcal{T}^{op} \to \mathcal{P}os$ comprises a family of posets $\{\mathbf{\Phi}_A\}_{A \in \mathcal{T}}$ parameterised by the domains of the space $\mathcal{T}$, and a family of monotone restriction maps $\{a \mapsto a^{\downarrow B} : \mathbf{\Phi}_A \to \mathbf{\Phi}_B\}_{A, B \in \mathcal{T}, B \subseteq A}$ parameterised by the inclusions of the space.

The elements of the posets $\mathbf{\Phi}_A$ represent abstract units of information pertaining to their domain. Their ordering signifies information refinement: $a \preceq b$ means a is *more* deterministic than b, a convention that aligns with the intuitions of program refinement.

The prealgebra's restriction maps $a \mapsto a^{\downarrow B}$ serve to project or query information $a \in A$ onto a subdomain $B \subseteq A$. These mappings facilitate the extraction of specific details from a wider context. Further, restriction maps are transitive and idempotent: for $C \subseteq B \subseteq A$ and $a \in \mathbf{\Phi}_A$, we have $(a^{\downarrow B})^{\downarrow C} = a^{\downarrow C}$, and $a^{\downarrow A} = a$.

---

[3] The topology described is the *Alexandrov* topology of the face poset of the network, viewed as a simplicial complex. Another possibility is to take its geometric realisation, but this typically results in an infinite space. These spaces, however, are weakly homotopy equivalent [3].

This family of posets $\{\mathbf{\Phi}_A\}_{A \in \mathcal{T}}$ can be unified into a single poset $\int \mathbf{\Phi}$, through a canonical process known as the *Grothendieck construction* of $\mathbf{\Phi}$ (for a detailed explanation within a broader context, refer to [19]).

Definition 1 (covariant Grothendieck construction for a prealgebra). *Let* $\mathbf{\Phi} : \mathcal{T}^{\mathrm{op}} \to \mathcal{P}os$ *be a prealgebra. The* **covariant Grothendieck construction** *of* $\mathbf{\Phi}$ *is the poset* $(\int \mathbf{\Phi}, \preceq)$ *whose elements are pairs* $(A, a) \in \int \mathbf{\Phi}$ *where* $A \in \mathcal{T}$ *and* $a \in \mathbf{\Phi}_A$, *and whose ordering* $\preceq$ *is defined*

$$(A, a) \preceq (B, b) \text{ if and only if } B \subseteq A \text{ and } a^{\downarrow B} \leq_{\mathbf{\Phi}_B} b \tag{1}$$

For the projection map $\mathrm{d} : \int \mathbf{\Phi} \to \mathcal{T}^{\mathrm{op}}, (A, a) \mapsto A$, *call* $\mathrm{d}a$ *the* **domain** *of* a.

Notation. As shorthand, we suppress the domain in the first component of elements (A, a) belonging to $\int \mathbf{\Phi}$, writing a instead of (A, a).

Remark 1. In Definition 1, we apply the *covariant* Grothendieck construction to a *contravariant* functor, treating it as a covariant functor from its domain's opposite. This choice, though atypical, aligns with a semantic interpretation for refining program specifications, explained in Sect. 3.1.

Next, the concept of an *ordered valuation algebra (OVA)* is introduced, which incorporates a prealgebra $\mathbf{\Phi} : \mathcal{T}^{\mathrm{op}} \to \mathcal{P}os$, a binary operator $\otimes : \int \mathbf{\Phi} \times \int \mathbf{\Phi} \to \int \mathbf{\Phi}$, and a global element $\epsilon : 1 \Rightarrow \mathbf{\Phi}$, satisfying a number of axioms. Before delving into the formal definition, we illustrate the concept with an example.

Example 2. A familiar instance of an OVA models *relational databases*. Here, a set X of *attributes* is fixed (e.g., $X = \{$'name', 'age', 'height'$\}$). A *schema* is a subset A of X defining a table's columns, while each row defines a *tuple*: an assignment of a value to each attribute. A *relation* on X is a set a of tuples sharing a common schema $\mathrm{d}a$, and a relational database is a set of such relations.

To frame this within an OVA, we define a prealgebra $\mathbf{\Phi} : \mathbf{P}(X) \to \mathcal{P}os$, mapping a schema $A \in \mathcal{T}$ to the poset $\mathbf{\Phi}_A$ of all relations with schema A, with ordering given by inclusion. The restriction maps of $\mathbf{\Phi}$ correspond to *querying*, by projecting the tuples of a relation a to a sub-schema B; the result is the relation $a^{\downarrow B} = \{t^{\downarrow B} \mid t \in a\}$, where $t^{\downarrow B}$ is the tuple t restricted to the attributes in B.

The operator $\otimes$ is taken to be the *natural join*,

$$\bowtie : \int \mathbf{\Phi} \times \int \mathbf{\Phi} \to \int \mathbf{\Phi}$$
$$a \bowtie b := \{t \in \mathbf{\Phi}_{\mathrm{d}a \cup \mathrm{d}b} \mid t^{\downarrow \mathrm{d}a} \in a \text{ and } t^{\downarrow \mathrm{d}b} \in b\} \tag{2}$$

This operation is associative and monotone (forming an *ordered semigroup*), and the schema of $a \bowtie b$ is $\mathrm{d}a \cup \mathrm{d}b$. Moreover, the natural join satisfies the following *combination axiom*:

$$(a \bowtie b)^{\downarrow \mathrm{d}a} = a \bowtie b^{\downarrow \mathrm{d}a \cap \mathrm{d}b} \tag{3}$$

This identity is fundamental to query optimisation algorithms in relational databases, with its right-hand side referred to as a *semi-join*.

Lastly, the global element ϵ assigns to each schema A the universal relation ϵ_A on A, encompassing all possible tuples on A. These universal relations serve as units for the natural join, i.e. for all $a \in \int \Phi$, we have $a \bowtie \epsilon_{da} = a = \epsilon_{da} \bowtie a$.

Please note that our definition of an OVA below deviates from standard ones (e.g. [1,9,17]) in several ways. First, we do not mandate commutativity of the operator $\otimes$, as a sequential product of programs is noncommutative. This requires a symmetric revision Eq. (7) of the *combination axiom*. Second, constraints in the classical definition such as the existence of infima in the posets Φ_A are not imposed. Yet, we stipulate that *neutral* valuations correspond to a global element, which is tantamount to the *stability* property in [17], though we do not require neutral valuations to combine to neutral valuations—we call an algebra in which this property holds *strongly neutral* (Definition 4). Last, while Grothendieck constructions have been applied to ordered valuation algebras ([5]), their conventional definition does not involve a Grothendieck ordering.

Definition 2 (ordered valuation algebra (OVA)). *An* **ordered valuation algebra (OVA)** *is a triple* $(\Phi, \otimes, \epsilon)$*, where* Φ *is a prealgebra* $\Phi : \mathcal{T}^{\mathrm{op}} \to \mathcal{P}os$*,* $\otimes$ *is a binary operator* $\otimes : \int \Phi \times \int \Phi \to \int \Phi$*, called the* **combine operator***, and* $\epsilon : 1 \Rightarrow \Phi$ *is a global element, called the* **neutral element***, satisfying the below four axioms for all* **valuations** $a, b, c, a', b' \in \int \Phi$*:*

Ordered semigroup. *The combine operator* $\otimes$ *is associative, and monotone:*

$$a \otimes (b \otimes c) = (a \otimes b) \otimes c, \text{ and, } a \preceq a' \text{ and } b \preceq b' \implies a \otimes b \preceq a' \otimes b' \quad (4)$$

Labelling.

$$\mathrm{d}(a \otimes b) = \mathrm{d}a \cup \mathrm{d}b \quad (5)$$

Neutrality.

$$\epsilon_{da} \otimes a = a = a \otimes \epsilon_{da} \quad (6)$$

Combination.

$$(a \otimes b)^{\downarrow da} = a \otimes b^{\downarrow da \cap db}, \qquad (a \otimes b)^{\downarrow db} = a^{\downarrow da \cap db} \otimes b \quad (7)$$

Remark 2. The functor laws for Φ imply that for all $C \subseteq B \subseteq A$ and $a \in \Phi_A$, we have $(a^{\downarrow B})^{\downarrow C} = a^{\downarrow C}$, and also $a^{\downarrow A} = a$. The requirement that ϵ is a global element says for all $B \subseteq A$ in $\mathcal{T}$, we have $\epsilon_A^{\downarrow B} = \epsilon_B$.

Remark 3. Monotonicity of $\otimes$ says for $a_1 \in \Phi_{A_1}, a_2 \in \Phi_{A_2}, b_1 \in \Phi_{B_1}, b_2 \in \Phi_{B_2}$, if $a_1 \preceq b_1$ and $a_2 \preceq b_2$, then $a_1 \otimes a_2 \preceq b_1 \otimes b_2$, that is, $(a_1 \otimes a_2)^{\downarrow B_1 \cup B_2} \leq_{\Phi_{B_1 \cup B_2}} b_1 \otimes b_2$. Taking $A_1 = A_2 = B_1 = B_2$, this implies **local monotonicity**, i.e. the combine operator $\otimes$ restricted to each domain A, $\otimes_A : \Phi_A \times \Phi_A \to \Phi_A$, is monotone.

Definition 3 (commutative OVA). *We call an OVA* $(\Phi, \otimes, \epsilon)$ **commutative** *if* $\otimes$ *is commutative.*

Definition 4 (strongly neutral). *We call an OVA* $(\Phi, \otimes, \epsilon)$ **strongly neutral** *if for all inclusions* $B \subseteq A$ *in* $\mathcal{J}$, *we have* $\epsilon_B^{\uparrow A} = \epsilon_A$.

Theorem 1. *Let* $(\Phi, \otimes, \epsilon)$ *be an OVA. Then for each inclusion* $B \subseteq A$ *in* $\mathcal{J}$, *the restriction map* $a \mapsto a^{\downarrow B}$ *has a right adjoint given by* $b \mapsto \epsilon_A \otimes b$. *Moreover, these right adjoints assemble to a functor* $\mathcal{J} \to \mathcal{P}os$. *We adopt the notation* $b^{\uparrow A} := \epsilon_A \otimes b$, *and call* $b^{\uparrow A}$ *the* **extension of** b **to** A.

Proof. We must show that for all $B \subseteq A$ and all $a \in \Phi_A$ and $b \in \Phi_B$,

$$a^{\downarrow B} \leq_{\Phi_B} b \iff a \leq_{\Phi_A} \epsilon_A \otimes b$$

Assume $a^{\downarrow B} \leq_{\Phi_B} b$. Using the fact that $a \preceq a^{\downarrow B}$ and monotonicity,

$$a = \epsilon_A \otimes a \leq_{\Phi_A} \epsilon_A \otimes a^{\downarrow B} \leq_{\Phi_A} \epsilon_A \otimes b$$

Now assume $a \leq_{\Phi_A} \epsilon_A \otimes b$. Using monotonicity of restriction, the combination axiom, naturality of ϵ, and neutrality,

$$a^{\downarrow B} \leq_{\Phi_B} (\epsilon_A \otimes b)^{\downarrow B} = \epsilon_A^{\downarrow A \cap B} \otimes b = \epsilon_B \otimes b = b$$

So the adjunction holds. That extension is functorial (i.e. for $C \subseteq B \subseteq A$ and $c \in \Phi_C$, both $(c^{\uparrow B})^{\uparrow A} = c^{\uparrow A}$ and $c^{\uparrow C} = c$) is due to the composability and uniqueness of adjoints.

Corollary 1. *Let* $(\Phi, \otimes, \epsilon)$ *be a strongly neutral OVA. Then for all A, B in $\mathcal{J}$, $\epsilon_A \otimes \epsilon_B = \epsilon_{A \cup B}$. Also, $\int \Phi$ is an ordered monoid.*

Proof. We have, $\epsilon_A \otimes \epsilon_B = (\epsilon_{A \cup B} \otimes \epsilon_{A \cup B}) \otimes (\epsilon_A \otimes \epsilon_B) = (\epsilon_{A \cup B} \otimes \epsilon_A) \otimes (\epsilon_{A \cup B} \otimes \epsilon_B) = \epsilon_A^{\uparrow A \cup B} \otimes \epsilon_B^{\uparrow A \cup B} = \epsilon_{A \cup B} \otimes \epsilon_{A \cup B} = \epsilon_{A \cup B}$. If $a \in \int \Phi$, $a \otimes \epsilon_\emptyset = (a \otimes \epsilon_{da}) \otimes \epsilon_\emptyset = a \otimes (\epsilon_{da} \otimes \epsilon_\emptyset) = a \otimes \epsilon_{da} = a$. Thus, $\epsilon_\emptyset$ is a unit for $\int \Phi$.

Corollary 2. *Let* $(\Phi, \otimes, \epsilon)$ *be an OVA, and let $B \subseteq A$ in $\mathcal{J}$, $a \in \Phi_A$, and $b \in \Phi_B$. Then,*

1. *Restriction after extension is the identity map, i.e.,* $(b^{\uparrow A})^{\downarrow B} = b$.
2. *Extension after restriction is extensive, i.e.,* $a \leq_{\Phi_A} (a^{\downarrow B})^{\uparrow A}$.

Proof. For the first claim, by the neutrality and combination axioms and naturality, we have $(b^{\uparrow A})^{\downarrow B} = (\epsilon_A \otimes b)^{\downarrow B} = \epsilon_A^{\downarrow A \cap B} \otimes b = \epsilon_B \otimes b = b$. The second is always true of the composition of a right adjoint after its left adjoint.

Corollary 3. *If for each $A \in \mathcal{J}$, Φ_A is a complete lattice, then so is $\int \Phi$.*

Proof. See [19], where it is shown in more generality that completeness of the poset $\int \Phi$ follows from: (i) cocompleteness of the poset $\mathcal{J}$, (ii) completeness of each poset Φ_A, and (iii) that the restriction maps $a \mapsto a^{\downarrow B}$ have right adjoints.

Definition 5 (morphism of OVAs). *Let* $(\Phi, \otimes, \epsilon)$ *and* $(\Phi', \otimes', \epsilon')$ *be OVAs. A* **lax morphism** $f : \Phi \to \Phi'$ *is a family of monotone maps* $\{f_A : \Phi_A \to \Phi'_A\}_{A \in \mathcal{J}}$ *so that the below hold for all $a \in \Phi_A$, $b \in \Phi_B$ and $C \subseteq A$,*

Monotonicity.

$$a \preceq b \implies f_A(a) \preceq f_B(b) \tag{8}$$

Lax naturality.

$$f_A(a)^{\downarrow C} \preceq f_C(a^{\downarrow C}) \tag{9}$$

Lax multiplicativity.

$$f_A(a) \otimes' f_B(b) \preceq f_{A \cup B}(a \otimes b) \tag{10}$$

Lax unitality.

$$\epsilon'_A \preceq f_A(\epsilon_A) \tag{11}$$

Reversing the inequality directions above defines a **colax morphism**. *A morphism that is both lax and colax is termed a* **strong morphism**.

2.1 Extension of Local Operators

In the following, let Φ be a prealgebra such that for each inclusion $B \subseteq A$ in $\mathcal{T}$, the restriction map $a \mapsto a^{\downarrow B} : \Phi_A \to \Phi_B$ has a right adjoint $b \mapsto b^{\uparrow A} : \Phi_B \to \Phi_A$.

Definition 6 (extension of a family of local operators). *Assume a family of associative binary operators* $\{\odot_A : \Phi_A \times \Phi_A \to \Phi_A\}_{A \in \mathcal{T}}$. *We define the* **extension** *of* $\{\odot_A\}_{A \in \mathcal{T}}$ *to* $\int \Phi$ *to be the binary operator,*

$$\odot : \int \Phi \times \int \Phi \to \int \Phi$$
$$a \odot b := a^{\uparrow da \cup db} \odot_{da \cup db} b^{\uparrow da \cup db} \tag{12}$$

Note that a combine operator of an OVA $(\Phi, \otimes, \epsilon)$ is the extension of the family $\{\otimes_A\}_{A \in \mathcal{T}}$, where $\otimes_A$ is the restriction of $\otimes$ to $\Phi_A \times \Phi_A$, because

$$a \otimes b = (\epsilon_U \otimes \epsilon_U) \otimes (a \otimes b) = (\epsilon_U \otimes a) \otimes (\epsilon_U \otimes b) = a^{\uparrow U} \otimes_U b^{\uparrow U} \tag{13}$$

where $U = da \cup db$. Next is a key lemma establishing conditions for the reverse direction, i.e. for when a family of local operators on Φ may give rise to a combine operator.

Lemma 1. *Assume* $\{\odot_A : \Phi_A \times \Phi_A \to \Phi_A\}_{A \in \mathcal{T}}$ *is a family of local associative operators satisfying:*

Local monotonicity. *For all* $A \in \mathcal{T}$ *and* $a_1, a'_1, a_2, a'_2 \in \Phi_A$,

$$a_1 \leq_{\Phi_A} a'_1 \text{ and } a_2 \leq_{\Phi_A} a'_2 \implies a_1 \odot_A a_2 \leq_{\Phi_A} a'_1 \odot_A a'_2 \tag{14}$$

Extension-commutation. *For all* $B \subseteq A$ *in* $\mathcal{T}$ *and* $b_1, b_2 \in \Phi_B$,

$$(b_1 \odot_B b_2)^{\uparrow A} = b_1^{\uparrow A} \odot_A b_2^{\uparrow A} \tag{15}$$

Then $(\int \Phi, \odot)$ *is an ordered semigroup, where* $\odot$ *is the extension of* $\{\odot_A\}_{A \in \mathcal{T}}$.

The next lemma shows that to establish the *weak exchange* axiom for a CVA (Definition 7 below), it suffices to show a local weak exchange law on each domain.

Lemma 2. *Let* $(\Phi, \|, \mathrm{run})$ *and* $(\Phi, \mathring{,}, \mathrm{skip})$ *be OVAs whose combine operators* $\|$ *and* $\mathring{,}$ *are respectively defined as extensions of* $\{\|_A\}_{A \in \mathcal{T}}$ *and* $\{\mathring{,}_A\}_{A \in \mathcal{T}}$. *Assume that on each* $A \in \mathcal{T}$, *a weak exchange law holds: for all* $a_1, a_2, a_3, a_4 \in \Phi_A$, $(a_1 \|_A a_2) \mathring{,}_A (a_3 \|_A a_4) \leq_{\Phi_A} (a_1 \mathring{,}_A a_3) \|_A (a_2 \mathring{,}_A a_4)$. *Then the weak exchange law holds on* $\int \Phi$: *for all* $a, b, c, d \in \int \Phi$, $(a \| b) \mathring{,} (c \| d) \preceq (a \mathring{,} c) \| (b \mathring{,} d)$.

3   Concurrent Valuation Algebras

We now introduce a *concurrent valuation algebra (CVA)*, structured as two OVAs sharing the same underlying prealgebra, whose combine operators represent *parallel* and *sequential* products. These operators are interlinked via a *weak exchange law*, and their neutral elements are related by a pair of inequalities.

Definition 7 (concurrent valuation algebra (CVA)). *A concurrent valuation algebra (CVA) is a structure* $(\Phi, \mathring{,}, \mathrm{skip}, \|, \mathrm{run})$ *satisfying the four axioms:*

Sequential OVA. $(\Phi, \mathring{,}, \mathrm{skip})$ *is an OVA.*
Parallel OVA. $(\Phi, \|, \mathrm{run})$ *is a commutative OVA.*
Weak exchange. *For all* $a, b, c, d \in \int \Phi$,

$$(a \| b) \mathring{,} (c \| d) \preceq (a \mathring{,} c) \| (b \mathring{,} d) \tag{16}$$

Neutral laws. *For all* $A \in \mathcal{T}$,

$$\mathrm{skip}_A \preceq \mathrm{skip}_A \| \mathrm{skip}_A, \ and, \ \mathrm{run}_A \mathring{,} \mathrm{run}_A \preceq \mathrm{run}_A \tag{17}$$

This definition is motivated by the relationship between sequential and parallel products. Sequential product, signifying a temporal juxtaposition, is generally noncommutative. In contrast, parallel product, signifying a spatial juxtaposition, is commutative. These two interlink by the weak exchange law. It states that the sequential composite of two parallel compositions, $a \| b$ and $c \| d$, results in fewer behaviours than the parallel composite of two sequential compositions, $a \mathring{,} c$ and $b \mathring{,} d$. Pictorially, this can be represented by a diagram (Fig. 2) where, on the left, a and b must finish together, causing c and d to start simultaneously. On the right, no such constraint is applied.

The neutral element of sequential composition, skip, acts as a null specification, thus $\mathrm{skip}_A \| \mathrm{skip}_A$ must equal skip_A. Dually, the neutral element of parallel composition, run, signifies an unconstrained specification, so $\mathrm{run}_A \mathring{,} \mathrm{run}_A$ equals run_A. The proof of Proposition 1 below shows that it's enough to assume one direction of these equalities; the other is derivable.

Proposition 1. *In a CVA* $(\Phi, \mathring{,}, \mathrm{skip}, \|, \mathrm{run})$, *for all* $A \in \mathcal{T}$, *we have* $\mathrm{skip}_A \preceq \mathrm{run}_A$, $\mathrm{skip}_A \| \mathrm{skip}_A = \mathrm{skip}_A$, *and* $\mathrm{run}_A \mathring{,} \mathrm{run}_A = \mathrm{run}_A$.

Fig. 2. Graphical representation of the weak exchange law.

Proof. By neutrality and weak exchange, for each $A \in \mathcal{T}$, $\text{skip}_A = \text{skip}_A \, \mathbin{\fatsemi}$ $\text{skip}_A = (\text{run}_A \parallel \text{skip}_A) \, \mathbin{\fatsemi} (\text{skip}_A \parallel \text{run}_A) \preceq (\text{run}_A \, \mathbin{\fatsemi} \text{skip}_A) \parallel (\text{skip}_A \, \mathbin{\fatsemi} \text{run}_A) = \text{run}_A \parallel \text{run}_A = \text{run}_A$. Given the neutral laws, for the remaining two properties, it suffices to show that $\text{skip}_A \parallel \text{skip}_A \preceq \text{skip}_A$ and $\text{run}_A \preceq \text{run}_A \, \mathbin{\fatsemi} \text{run}_A$. By monotonicity of combination, we have $\text{skip}_A \parallel \text{skip}_A \preceq \text{skip}_A \parallel \text{run}_A = \text{skip}_A$. Similarly, $\text{run}_A = \text{skip}_A \, \mathbin{\fatsemi} \text{run}_A \preceq \text{run}_A \, \mathbin{\fatsemi} \text{run}_A$.

Proposition 2. *In a CVA* $(\Phi, \mathbin{\fatsemi}, \epsilon, \parallel, \epsilon)$ *in which the neutral elements of parallel and sequential product coincide, for all* $a, b \in \int \Phi$, *we have* $a \, \mathbin{\fatsemi} b \preceq a \parallel b$.

Proof. Let $a \in \Phi_A$ and $b \in \Phi_B$. We have, $a \, \mathbin{\fatsemi} b = a^{\uparrow A \cup B} \, \mathbin{\fatsemi} b^{\uparrow A \cup B} = (a \parallel \epsilon_{A \cup B}) \, \mathbin{\fatsemi}$ $(\epsilon_{A \cup B} \parallel b) \preceq (a \, \mathbin{\fatsemi} \epsilon_{A \cup B}) \parallel (\epsilon_{A \cup B} \, \mathbin{\fatsemi} b) = a^{\uparrow A \cup B} \parallel b^{\uparrow A \cup B} = a \parallel b$.

Definition 8 (morphism of CVAs).   *Let* $(\Phi, \mathbin{\fatsemi}, \text{skip}, \parallel, \text{run})$ *and* $(\Phi', \mathbin{\fatsemi}', \text{skip}', \parallel', \text{run}')$ *be CVAs. A* **lax/colax/strong morphism** $f : \Phi \to \Phi'$ *is a function* $f : \int \Phi \to \int \Phi'$ *that is both a lax/colax/strong morphism of OVAs* $(\Phi, \mathbin{\fatsemi}, \text{skip}) \to (\Phi', \mathbin{\fatsemi}', \text{skip}')$ *and a lax/colax/strong morphism of OVAs* $(\Phi, \parallel, \text{run}) \to (\Phi', \parallel', \text{run}')$.[4]

3.1   Reasoning in a CVA

Refinement. In a CVA Φ, the ordering between elements a and b in $\int \Phi$ is defined as $a \preceq b$ if and only if $\text{d}b \subseteq \text{d}a$ and $a^{\downarrow \text{d}b} \leq_{\Phi_{\text{d}b}} b$. Viewing these elements as system specifications, this ordering is interpreted as refinement: $a \preceq b$ means that all behaviour of a within domain $\text{d}b$ also exists in b, making a on $\text{d}b$ more deterministic than b. However, the domain $\text{d}a$ of a may exceed $\text{d}b$, as a refined specification may introduce constraints outside the initial domain.

Hoare Logic and Rely-Guarantee Reasoning. *Hoare triples* and *Jones quintuples* facilitate formal reasoning about program behaviour, leveraging the well-established methodologies of Hoare logic and rely-guarantee reasoning. These constructs may be realised in a CVA by adapting their definitions as framed within Concurrent Kleene Algebras [13].

Let $(\Phi, \mathbin{\fatsemi}, \text{skip}, \parallel, \text{run})$ be a CVA, and $p, a, q \in \int \Phi$. We define the **Hoare triple** of a with *precondition* p and *postcondition* q as

$$p \, \{a\} \, q := p \, \mathbin{\fatsemi} a \preceq q \tag{18}$$

---

[4] In duoidal categories, morphisms may also be lax with respect to $\mathbin{\fatsemi}$ and colax with respect to $\parallel$, but not the reverse [2].

From this definition, we may derive inference rules[5] of Hoare logic, such as:

Proposition 3 (concurrency rule). *Let* $p, p', a, a', q, q' \in \int \Phi$. *Then*

$$p \{a\} q \text{ and } p' \{a'\} q' \implies (p \parallel p') \{a \parallel a'\} (q \parallel q') \tag{19}$$

Proof. Assume $p \, \mathring{,} \, a \preceq q$ and $p' \, \mathring{,} \, a' \preceq q'$. By weak exchange and monotonicity, $(p \parallel p') \, \mathring{,} \, (a \parallel a') \preceq (p \, \mathring{,} \, a) \parallel (p' \, \mathring{,} \, a') \preceq q \parallel q'$. Thus, $(p \parallel p') \{a \parallel a'\} (q \parallel q')$.

A *Jones quintuple* with *rely* r and *guarantee* g can then be defined as[6]

$$p \, r \, \{a\} \, g \, q := p \, \{r \parallel a\} \, q \text{ and } a \preceq g \tag{20}$$

To employ the standard inference rules of rely-guarantee reasoning, constraints must be placed on the rely variable r and the guarantee variable g. Though this definition serves as a gateway to rely-guarantee reasoning in the context of a CVA, exploration of this aspect is beyond the present study's purview.

4 Tuple Systems

In Sects. 5 to 7, each CVA examined is based on an underlying OVA of a specific form—they are *OVAs of* **T**-*relations* associated to certain *tuple systems* **T**. Tuple systems are presheaves that abstract the characteristic projecting and lifting properties of ordinary tuples. For more on tuple systems and the valuation algebras they induce, please see [15, Section 6.3, p. 169] and [17, Section 7.3.2, p. 286]. A **T**-relation is a subset of these generalised *tuples* sharing a common domain. In the trace models to follow, actions, states, traces and valuations themselves are encoded as tuples within tuple systems. The structure of the tuple system **T** governs how tuples on a larger domain project to a smaller one through the presheaf's restriction maps, as well as how tuples on a smaller domain lift to a larger one via the presheaf's flasque and binary gluing properties.

Definition 9 (tuple system). *A* **tuple system** *is a presheaf* $\mathbf{T} : \mathcal{J}^{op} \to \mathcal{S}et$ *satisfying the below axioms:*

Flasque. *For all* $B \subseteq A$ *in* $\mathcal{J}$, *the restriction map* $\mathbf{T}_A \to \mathbf{T}_B$ *is surjective.*
Binary gluing. *For all* $a \in \mathbf{T}_A$ *and* $b \in \mathbf{T}_B$, *if* $a^{\downarrow A \cap B} = b^{\downarrow A \cap B}$, *then there exists* $c \in \mathbf{T}_{A \cup B}$ *so that* $c^{\downarrow A} = a$ *and* $c^{\downarrow B} = b$.

Elements of $\mathbf{T}_A$ *are called* **tuples (on** A**)** *or* A-**tuples.**

Theorem 2 (OVAs of T-relations). *Let* $\mathbf{T} : \mathcal{J}^{op} \to \mathcal{S}et$ *be a* **tuple system.** *Define the prealgebra* $\Psi := \mathbf{P} \circ \mathbf{T} : \mathcal{J}^{op} \to \mathcal{P}os$. *Then* Ψ, *equipped with the* **relational join** *as the combine operator, defined*

$$\wedge : \int \Psi \times \int \Psi \to \int \Psi$$
$$a \wedge b := \{t \in \mathbf{T}_{da \cup db} \mid t^{\downarrow da} \in a, t^{\downarrow db} \in b\} \tag{21}$$

---

[6] The guarantee requirement is stronger than required by Jones, where the guarantee only must hold while the rely does.

*is a strongly neutral commutative OVA, that we call the **OVA of T-relations**. Its local orderings $\leq_{\mathbf{T}_A}$ are given by subset inclusion $\subseteq$, and it has as neutral element $\top = A \mapsto \mathbf{T}_A$ for each $A \in \mathcal{T}$. Moreover, $\mathbf{U} \circ \mathbf{\Psi}$ is itself a tuple system, where $\mathbf{U} : \mathcal{P}os \to \mathcal{S}et$ is the forgetful functor that sends a poset to its underlying set, and a monotone map to its underlying function.*[7]

Proof. Monotonicity is easily verified. The other details are found in [15, p. 170]. $\quad\square$

It is worth noting the close resemblance of Eq. (21) with the trace semantics of the CSP parallel operator [12, Section 2.3.3, p. 53].

Proposition 4. *Extension is given by the preimage to restriction; i.e. for $a \in \mathbf{\Phi}_A$, and $B \in \mathcal{T}$ with $B \subseteq A$, we have $b^{\uparrow A} = \{t \in \mathbf{T}_A \mid t^{\downarrow B} \in b\}$.*

Proof. It is a standard proof that direct image is left-adjoint to preimage. $\quad\square$

Proposition 5. *The relational join of an OVA of relations is the extension of intersection (from Definition 6): for $a, b \in \int \mathbf{\Phi}$, $a \wedge b = a^{\uparrow \mathrm{da} \cup \mathrm{db}} \cap b^{\uparrow \mathrm{da} \cup \mathrm{db}}$. Moreover, $\int \mathbf{\Phi}$ is a complete lattice, and relational join is its meet.*

Lemma 3. *Let $\mathbf{\Omega} : \mathcal{T}^{\mathrm{op}} \to \mathcal{S}et$ be a tuple system, and let $\mathbf{L} : \mathcal{S}et \to \mathcal{S}et$ be the functor that sends a set X to the set of finite lists in X, i.e. $\mathbf{L} := X \mapsto \coprod_{n \in \mathbb{N}} X^n$, and let $\mathbf{L}_+$ be the functor that sends X to the set of nonempty finite lists in X, i.e. $\mathbf{L}_+ := X \mapsto \coprod_{n \in \mathbb{N}_+} X^n$. Then both $\mathbf{L} \circ \mathbf{\Omega}$ and $\mathbf{L}_+ \circ \mathbf{\Omega}$ are tuple systems.*

Notation. Square brackets are used to display the components of a tuple $t \in (\mathbf{\Omega}_A)^n$, i.e. we write $t = [t_1, \ldots, t_n]$. Such tuples are referred to as **traces**.

5   Action Trace Model

Let $\mathbf{\Omega}^{\mathrm{act}} : \mathcal{T}^{\mathrm{op}} \to \mathcal{S}et$ be a tuple system whose values $\mathbf{\Omega}_A^{\mathrm{act}}$ represent possible *actions* of a system in the variables A. Some concrete examples: for a semiring $\mathbb{S}$ of *values*, $\mathbf{\Omega}_A^{\mathrm{act}}$ is the set of matrices $A \times A \to \mathbb{S}$ (*linear actions*); the set of pairs $\mathbb{S}^A \times \mathbb{S}^A$ (*events*); the set of relations $\mathbf{P}(\mathbb{S}^A \times \mathbb{S}^A)$ (*events with external choice*). Let $\mathbf{T}^{\mathrm{act}} := \mathbf{L} \circ \mathbf{\Omega}^{\mathrm{act}}$, so that for each $A \in \mathcal{T}$, $\mathbf{T}_A^{\mathrm{act}}$ is the set of (possibly empty) traces of elements of $\mathbf{\Omega}_A^{\mathrm{act}}$. By Lemma 3, $\mathbf{T}^{\mathrm{act}}$ is a tuple system. Let

$$\mathbf{\Gamma} : \mathcal{T}^{\mathrm{op}} \to \mathcal{P}os$$
$$\mathbf{\Gamma} := \mathbf{P} \circ \mathbf{T}^{\mathrm{act}} = A \mapsto \mathbf{P}(\mathbf{L}(\mathbf{\Omega}_A^{\mathrm{act}})) \tag{22}$$

be the OVA of $\mathbf{T}^{\mathrm{act}}$-relations. We now develop a CVA structure on $\mathbf{\Gamma}$ that we call the **action trace model**.

For each $A \in \mathcal{T}$, define

$$\iota_A := \{[\,]_A\} \tag{23}$$

where $[\,]_A \in \mathbf{T}_A^{\mathrm{act}}$ is the unique length-0 trace with domain A. As restriction of a trace preserves length, this defines a global element $\iota : 1 \Rightarrow \mathbf{\Gamma}$.

---

[7] This last point follows from the *idempotence* property of $\wedge$ [17, Example 7.7, p. 287].

5.1 Interleaving Product

For all $p, q \in \mathbb{N}$, let $\Sigma_{p,q}$ be the set (p,q)-*shuffles*, i.e. bijections $\{1, \ldots, p+q\} \to \{1, \ldots, p+q\}$ (or permutations) such that $\sigma(1) < \cdots < \sigma(p)$ and $\sigma(p+1) < \cdots < \sigma(p+q)$. For each $A \in \mathcal{T}$, define an operator on traces,

$$\sqcup_A : \mathbf{T}_A^{\mathrm{act}} \times \mathbf{T}_A^{\mathrm{act}} \to \Gamma_A$$
$$[t_1, \ldots, t_p] \sqcup_A [t_{p+1}, \ldots, t_{p+q}] := \{[t_{\sigma(1)}, \ldots, t_{\sigma(p+q)}] \mid \sigma \in \Sigma_{p,q}\} \tag{24}$$

Then lift each $\sqcup_A$ to a local operator on valuations,

$$\sqcup_A : \Gamma_A \times \Gamma_A \to \Gamma_A$$
$$a \sqcup_A a' := \bigcup \{t_a \sqcup_A t_{a'} \mid t_a \in a, t_{a'} \in a'\} \tag{25}$$

It is well-known that $\sqcup_A$ is commutative, associative, and has unit ι_A. We then define the **interleaving product** as the extension $\sqcup$ of $\{\sqcup_A\}_{A \in \mathcal{T}}$ to $\int \Gamma$:

$$\sqcup : \int \Gamma \times \int \Gamma \to \int \Gamma$$
$$a \sqcup b := a^{\uparrow da \cup db} \sqcup_{da \cup db} b^{\uparrow da \cup db} \tag{26}$$

Note that $\sqcup$ is clearly commutative, and has as neutral element ι.

Lemma 4. *For all $t, s \in \mathbf{T}_A^{\mathrm{act}}$ and $B \subseteq A$, we have $(t \sqcup_A s)^{\downarrow B} = t^{\downarrow B} \sqcup_B s^{\downarrow B}$.*

Lemma 5. *The structure $(\int \Gamma, \sqcup)$ is an ordered semigroup.*

Proof. By Lemma 1, it suffices to show that the local monotonicity and extension-commutation properties hold. The former follows directly from the definition of $\sqcup_A$. For extension-commutation, let $B \subseteq A$, let $b, b' \in \Gamma_B$, and let $t \in b^{\uparrow A} \sqcup_A b'^{\uparrow A}$. By definition of $\sqcup_A$, there exists $r \in b^{\uparrow A}$, $s \in b'^{\uparrow A}$ so that $t \in r \sqcup_A s$. By Lemma 4, $t^{\downarrow B} \in (r \sqcup_A s)^{\downarrow B} = r^{\downarrow B} \sqcup_B s^{\downarrow B} \subseteq b \sqcup_B b'$. Thus, $t \in (b \sqcup_B b')^{\uparrow A}$. Conversely, let $t' \in (b \sqcup_B b')^{\uparrow A}$. Now there is $r \in b$, $s \in b'$ so that $t'^{\downarrow B} \in r \sqcup_B s$. We may write $r = [t_1, \ldots, t_p]$, $s = [t_{p+1}, \ldots, t_{p+q}]$, and $t'^{\downarrow B} = [t_{\sigma(1)}, \ldots, t_{\sigma(p+q)}]$ for a (p,q)-shuffle $\sigma \in \Sigma_{p,q}$. For each $1 \leq i \leq p+q$, we then have a lifting $t'_{\sigma(i)}$ of $t_{\sigma(i)}$ so that $t = [t'_{\sigma(1)}, \ldots, t'_{\sigma(p+q)}]$. Then $r' = [t'_1, \ldots, t'_p]$ is a lifting of r, $s' = [t'_{p+1}, \ldots, t'_{p+q}]$ is a lifting of s, and $t' \in r' \sqcup_A s' \in b^{\uparrow A} \sqcup_A b'^{\uparrow A}$ is exhibited as a trace associated to the same (p,q)-shuffle σ. The result follows.

Lemma 6. *The interleaving product $\sqcup$ satisfies the combination axiom.*

Proof. Let $A, B \in \mathcal{T}$, $a \in \Gamma_A$ and $b \in \Gamma_B$. Note that one direction of the combination law follows from monotonicity. It then suffices to show $a \sqcup b^{\downarrow A \cap B} \subseteq (a \sqcup b)^{\downarrow A}$ and $a^{\downarrow A \cap B} \sqcup b \subseteq (a \sqcup b)^{\downarrow B}$. Let $t \in a \sqcup b^{\downarrow A \cap B} = a \sqcup_A (b^{\downarrow A \cap B})^{\uparrow A}$. By definition of $\sqcup_A$, there exists $t_a \in a$ and $t_b \in (b^{\downarrow A \cap B})^{\uparrow A}$ so that $t \in t_a \sqcup_A t_b$. Let $t'_a \in a^{\uparrow A \cup B}$ be a lifting of t_a. Let $s := t_b^{\downarrow A \cap B} \in ((b^{\downarrow A \cap B})^{\uparrow A})^{\downarrow A \cap B} = b^{\downarrow A \cap B}$, where the equality follows by Corollary 2. There then exists $s' \in b$ so that $s'^{\downarrow A \cap B} = s$.

By binary gluing, there exists a common lifting $t'_b \in b^{\uparrow A \cup B}$ of t_b and s'. As in the proof of Lemma 5, it is easily shown that there is $t' \in t'_a \sqcup_{A \cup B} t'_b \in a \sqcup b$ (associated to the same (p, q)-shuffle as t) so that $t = t'^{\downarrow A} \in (a \sqcup b)^{\downarrow A}$. Similarly, $a^{\downarrow A \cap B} \sqcup b \subseteq (a \sqcup b)^{\downarrow B}$. The result follows.

As strong neutrality easily holds, we have the following.

Proposition 6. *The structure* $(\Gamma, \sqcup, \iota)$ *is a strongly neutral commutative OVA.*

5.2   Concatenating Product

For each $A \in \mathcal{T}$, define the associative binary operator on traces,

$$\hat{\frown}_A : \mathbf{T}_A^{\mathrm{act}} \times \mathbf{T}_A^{\mathrm{act}} \to \mathbf{T}_A^{\mathrm{act}}$$
$$[t_1, \ldots, t_n] \hat{\frown}_A [s_1, \ldots, s_m] := [t_1, \ldots, t_n, s_1, \ldots, s_m] \tag{27}$$

Then lift each $\hat{\frown}_A$ to a local operator on valuations,

$$\frown_A : \Gamma_A \times \Gamma_A \to \Gamma_A$$
$$a \frown_A a' := \{t_a \hat{\frown}_A t_{a'} \mid t_a \in a, t_{a'} \in a'\} \tag{28}$$

We call the extension $\frown$ to $\int \Gamma$ of $\{\frown_A\}_{A \in \mathcal{T}}$ the **concatenating product**.

Proposition 7. *The structure* $(\Gamma, \frown, \iota)$ *is a strongly neutral OVA.*

Proposition 8. *The structure* $(\Gamma, \frown, \iota, \sqcup, \iota)$ *is a CVA.*

Proof. Both $\frown$ and $\sqcup$ define OVA structures on Γ (Propositions 6 and 7), and the neutral laws $\iota_A \subseteq \iota_A \sqcup \iota_A$ and $\iota_A \frown \iota_A \subseteq \iota_A$ hold trivially. To show the weak exchange law, by Lemma 2, it suffices to show a local exchange law holds on each $A \in \mathcal{T}$. Let $a_1, a_2, a_3, a_4 \in \Gamma_A$ and $t \in (a_1 \sqcup_A a_2) \frown_A (a_3 \sqcup_A a_4)$. By definition of $\frown$, there is $r \in a_1 \sqcup_A a_2$ and $s \in a_3 \sqcup_A a_4$ so that $t = r \hat{\frown}_A s$. It is clear every action of t coming from a_1 precedes every action of t coming from a_3, and similarly every action of t coming from a_2 precedes every action of t coming from a_4. It follows that t is in $(a_1 \frown_A a_3) \sqcup_A (a_2 \frown_A a_4)$. The result follows.

Proposition 9. *For all* $a, b \in \int \Phi$, *we have* $a \frown b \preceq a \sqcup b$.

Proof. As the units for $\frown$ and $\sqcup$ coincide, this follows from Proposition 2.

6   State Trace Model

Here we define a CVA whose valuations consist of traces of *states* of an abstract system that progress in lockstep to an implied global clock. For each domain $A \in \mathcal{T}$, denote the hom-functor $\Omega^{\mathrm{state}} := A \mapsto (A \to \mathbb{S})$, i.e., $\Omega_A^{\mathrm{state}}$ is the set of (ordinary) A-tuples in some nonempty set $\mathbb{S}$ of *values*, and the action of Ω^{state} on inclusions in $\mathcal{T}$ is by precomposition. Notably, $\Omega_\emptyset^{\mathrm{state}}$ has a unique value $\heartsuit$, the *empty state*. By Lemma 3, $\mathbf{T}^{\text{state}} := \mathbf{L}_+ \circ \boldsymbol{\Omega}^{\text{state}}$ is a tuple system. For traces $t := [t_1, \ldots, t_n] \in \mathbf{T}_A^{\text{state}}$, a component t_i is the system's state at time i. Let

$$\boldsymbol{\Sigma} : \mathcal{T}^{\text{op}} \to \mathcal{P}os$$
$$\boldsymbol{\Sigma} := \mathbf{P} \circ \mathbf{T}^{\text{state}} = A \mapsto \mathbf{P}(\mathbf{L}_+(A \to \mathbb{S})) \tag{29}$$

be the OVA of $\mathbf{T}^{\text{state}}$-relations. The relational join $\wedge$ on $\boldsymbol{\Sigma}$ behaves as *synchronisation*, and we take this as the parallel product for a CVA structure on $\boldsymbol{\Sigma}$ that we call the **state trace model**.

Let $\lambda : \mathbf{T}_A^{\text{state}} \to \mathbb{N}_+$ denote the length function, and define

$$\tau := A \mapsto \left\{ t \in \mathbf{T}_A^{\text{state}} \mid \lambda(t) = 1 \right\} \tag{30}$$

As restriction preserves lengths of traces, this defines a global element $\tau : 1 \Rightarrow \boldsymbol{\Sigma}$.

6.1   Gluing Product

Let $A \in \mathcal{T}$. For a trace $t \in \mathbf{T}_A^{\text{state}}$, let t^-, t^+ respectively denote the first and last components of t. Define an associative binary operator $\smile_A$ on each $\mathbf{T}_A^{\text{state}}$ by

$$\smile_A : \mathbf{T}_A^{\text{state}} \times \mathbf{T}_A^{\text{state}} \to \mathbf{T}_A^{\text{state}}$$
$$t \smile_A s := (t_1, \ldots, t_{\lambda(t)-1}, s_1, \ldots, s_{\lambda(s)}) \tag{31}$$

This then lifts to an associative binary operator on valuations,

$$\smile_A : \boldsymbol{\Sigma}_A \times \boldsymbol{\Sigma}_A \to \boldsymbol{\Sigma}_A$$
$$a \smile_A a' := \left\{ t_a \smile_A t_{a'} \mid t_a \in a, t_{a'} \in a', t_a^+ = t_{a'}^- \right\} \tag{32}$$

We call the extension $\smile$ to $\int \boldsymbol{\Sigma}$ of the family $\{\smile_A\}_{A \in \mathcal{T}}$ the **gluing product**.

Proposition 10. *The structure* $(\boldsymbol{\Sigma}, \smile, \tau)$ *is a strongly neutral OVA.*

Proposition 11. *The structure* $(\boldsymbol{\Sigma}, \smile, \tau, \wedge, \top)$ *is a CVA.*

Proof. The neutral equalities are clear, and both $\wedge$ and $\smile$ define OVAs on $\boldsymbol{\Sigma}$ by Theorem 2 and Proposition 10. By Lemma 2, it suffices to show an exchange law holds on each $A \in \mathcal{T}$. Noting that $\wedge$ is the extension of intersection by Proposition 5, let $a_1, a_2, a_3, a_4 \in \boldsymbol{\Sigma}_A$ and let $t \in (a_1 \cap a_2) \smile_A (a_3 \cap a_4)$. By local monotonicity of $\smile_A$, both $t \in a_1 \smile_A a_3$ and $t \in a_2 \smile_A a_4$. Thus, $t \in (a_1 \smile_A a_3) \cap (a_2 \smile_A a_4)$, and the result follows.

6.2   Strong Morphisms Between $\boldsymbol{\Gamma}$ and $\boldsymbol{\Sigma}$

There are no interesting strong morphisms between the action trace model $\boldsymbol{\Gamma}$ and the state trace model $\boldsymbol{\Sigma}$. As the neutral elements for parallel and sequential coincide in $\boldsymbol{\Gamma}$ but not in $\boldsymbol{\Sigma}$, there are no strong morphisms $\boldsymbol{\Gamma} \to \boldsymbol{\Sigma}$. On the other hand, a strong morphism $f : \boldsymbol{\Sigma} \to \boldsymbol{\Gamma}$ must map $\top_A$ to ι_A, and by monotonicity this implies that $f_A(a) \subseteq \iota_A$ for all $a \in \boldsymbol{\Sigma}_A$. Whether there are interesting (co)lax morphisms between $\boldsymbol{\Gamma}$ and $\boldsymbol{\Sigma}$ is an open question.

7   Relative State Trace Model

We introduce a variant, Σ^{rel}, of the state trace model from Sect. 6, that we refer to as the **relative state trace model**. In this model, traces are *stuttering-reduced*, meaning they do not contain duplicate adjacent components. Consequently, only the relative order of the indices in the trace components is significant, indicating independence from a global clock. This may lead to intriguing phenomena like *sequential inconsistency* [7].

An essentially equivalent construction of the underlying relational OVA was already presented in [7] using simplicial sets. Here, we offer a more concise and direct method using *free semigroups with idempotent generators*, previously applied to concurrency theory and quantum computation [4].

Let S be a set. Construct a semigroup $\mathbf{I}(S)$ as the free semigroup on S modulo the relation $x^2 = x$ for all $x \in S$. This is known as the **free semigroup on S with idempotent generators**. For example, if $S := \{0,1\}$, then $\mathbf{I}(S) = \{0, 1, 01, 10, 010, 101, 0101, \ldots\}$, and the semigroup product is concatenation modulo this congruence; e.g., $010 \cdot 01 = 0101$. Given a function $f : S \to S'$, there is a semigroup homomorphism $\mathbf{I}(f) : \mathbf{I}(S) \to \mathbf{I}(S')$, defined by $\mathbf{I}(f)(x_1 \cdots x_n) := f(x_1) \cdots f(x_n)$, and moreover, this construction is functorial. Let $\mathbf{U} : \mathcal{S}emi \to \mathcal{S}et$ be the forgetful functor from the category of semigroups to the category of sets, that sends a semigroup to its underlying set, and a semigroup homomorphism to its underlying function. As in Sect. 6, let Ω^{state} be the contravariant hom-functor $\Omega^{\text{state}} = A \mapsto (A \to \mathbb{S})$ where $\mathbb{S}$ is a fixed set of values. We then define $\mathbf{T}^{\text{rel}} := \mathbf{U} \circ \mathbf{I} \circ \Omega^{\text{state}} : \mathcal{T}^{\text{op}} \to \mathcal{S}et$.

Proposition 12. *The presheaf $\mathbf{T}^{\text{rel}}$ is a tuple system.*

Proof (sketch). This is essentially equivalent to [7, Theorem 2]. There, empty traces were included in the tuple system by use of the *augmented* simplicial nerve functor. If the ordinary nerve were used, the same proof goes through, and we would exclude empty traces (problematic here in defining gluing product), yielding a tuple system isomorphic to the one described here with semigroups.

Now let $\Sigma^{\text{rel}} := \mathbf{P} \circ \mathbf{T}^{\text{rel}}$ be the OVA of $\mathbf{T}^{\text{rel}}$-relations, and denote the relational join $\wedge^{\text{rel}}$ and its neutral element $\top^{\text{rel}} = A \mapsto \mathbf{T}_A^{\text{rel}}$. Note that while $\top_\emptyset = \mathbf{T}_\emptyset^{\text{state}}$ has infinitely many elements $[\heartsuit], [\heartsuit, \heartsuit], \ldots$, the neutral component $\top_\emptyset^{\text{rel}} = \mathbf{T}_\emptyset^{\text{rel}}$ has only one, namely $[\heartsuit]$. We define a local operator on valuations,

$$
\smile_A^{\text{rel}} : \Sigma_A^{\text{rel}} \times \Sigma_A^{\text{rel}} \to \Sigma_A^{\text{rel}}
$$
$$
a \smile_A^{\text{rel}} a' := \left\{ t_a \cdot_A t_{a'} \mid t_a \in a, t_{a'} \in a', t_a^+ = t_{a'}^- \right\} \tag{33}
$$

where $\cdot_A$ is the product[8] of the semigroup $\mathbf{I}(\Omega_A^{\text{state}})$, and λ and $t \mapsto t^+, t^-$ are defined as in Sect. 6. We call the extension $\smile^{\text{rel}}$ of $\left\{ \smile_A^{\text{rel}} \right\}_{A \in \mathcal{T}}$ to $\int \Sigma^{\text{rel}}$ the **relative gluing product**. Let $\tau^{\text{rel}} := A \mapsto \left\{ t \in \mathbf{T}_A^{\text{rel}} \mid \lambda(t) = 1 \right\}$. We then have,

---

[8] To avoid excessive notation, we apply the semigroup products $\cdot_A$ directly to traces, although their semigroup structure was forgotten by $\mathbf{U}$.

Proposition 13. *The structure* $(\Sigma^{\mathsf{rel}}, \smile^{\mathsf{rel}}, \tau^{\mathsf{rel}})$ *is an OVA.*

Unlike the models Γ and Σ of Sects. 5 and 6, we have the following.

Proposition 14. *The OVA* $(\Sigma^{\mathsf{rel}}, \smile^{\mathsf{rel}}, \tau^{\mathsf{rel}})$ *is not strongly neutral.*

Proof. We have $\top^{\mathsf{rel}}_\emptyset = \tau^{\mathsf{rel}}_\emptyset$ and yet $\top^{\mathsf{rel}} \neq \tau^{\mathsf{rel}}$. The result follows.

Proposition 15. *The structure* $(\Sigma^{\mathsf{rel}}, \smile^{\mathsf{rel}}, \tau^{\mathsf{rel}}, \wedge^{\mathsf{rel}}, \top^{\mathsf{rel}})$ *is a CVA.*

Proof. The neutral laws are immediate, and we are only obliged to show the local weak exchange laws hold by Proposition 5 and Lemma 2. Locally $\wedge^{\mathsf{rel}}{}_A = \wedge_A = \cap$, and also $\smile_A$ and $\smile^{\mathsf{rel}}_A$ have the same effect on traces, i.e. the gluing of two stuttering-reduced traces is already stuttering-reduced, so the proof of Proposition 11 goes through unchanged.

7.1 Colax Morphism from Σ to Σ^{rel}

Define the free semigroup functor $\mathbf{F} : \mathcal{S}et \to \mathcal{S}emi$ mapping set $S \in \mathcal{S}et$ to finite lists of its elements, using concatenation as the semigroup product. Please note there is an evident isomorphism $\mathbf{L}_+ \cong \mathbf{U} \circ \mathbf{F}$ that we will apply implicitly. The universal property of the free semigroup leads to a surjective map $q_S : \mathbf{F}(S) \twoheadrightarrow \mathbf{I}(S)$ for each set S, which acts to eliminate duplicated adjacent elements in a list. This process defines a natural transformation $q : \mathbf{F} \Rightarrow \mathbf{I}$, allowing us to obtain another natural transformation by whiskering[9] on both sides of q.

$$
\mathcal{T}^{\mathsf{op}} \xrightarrow{\Omega^{\mathsf{state}}} \mathcal{S}et \underset{\substack{\nearrow \\ \mathbf{I}}}{\overset{\substack{\mathbf{L}_+ \\ \searrow \\ \mathbf{F} \quad \| \mathsf{R} \\ \Downarrow q}}{}} \mathcal{S}emi \xrightarrow{\mathbf{U}} \mathcal{S}et \xrightarrow{\mathbf{P}} \mathcal{P}os
\tag{34}
$$

We denote this composite $f := (\mathbf{P} \circ \mathbf{U}) \circ q \circ \Omega^{\mathsf{state}} : \Sigma \to \Sigma^{\mathsf{rel}}$.

Proposition 16. *The map* $f : \Sigma \to \Sigma^{\mathsf{rel}}$ *is a colax morphism of CVAs.*

Proposition 16 effectively realises the relative trace model Σ^{rel} as a quotient of the state trace model Σ.

8 Local Computation

Valuation algebras provide a foundation for practical computation through a suite of distributed *local computation* algorithms. These algorithms are designed to resolve *inference problems* that arise in the context of valuation algebras. A comprehensive reference to this topic is [17].

---

[9] See [18, Remark 1.7.6., p.46].

Definition 10. *Let* Φ *be an OVA. A* **knowledgebase** *is a finite subset of valuations* $K \subseteq \int \Phi$. *Let* $\mathcal{A} := \{A_i \in \mathcal{T}\}_{i \in I}$ *be a finite family of domains, so that for each* $i \in I$, *we have* $A_i \subseteq \bigcup_{a \in K} da$. *Then the task of computing* $\left(\bigotimes_{a \in K} a\right)^{\downarrow A_i}$ *for each* $i \in I$, *is called the* **inference problem for** $(K, \mathcal{A})$. *In this context,* $\bigotimes_{a \in K} a$ *is called the* **joint valuation**, *and the domains* A_i *are called* **queries**.

In distributed systems, an inference problem corresponds to determining the local behaviours of a composite system of interacting components. For example, sequential consistency of a specification, as shown in [7], can be framed as an inference problem. The key to local computation is the combination axiom $(a \otimes b)^{\downarrow da} = a \otimes b^{\downarrow da \cap db}$. However, traditional theory falls short in our setting as it presumes a single commutative combine operator. Though the generalised combination axiom of Definition 2 supports local computation for CVAs, further exploration in this area is called for.

9 Conclusion

In this work, we have introduced the *concurrent valuation algebra (CVA)*, a new algebraic structure that expands upon *ordered valuation algebras (OVAs)* by incorporating parallel and sequential products. This integration places the theory of concurrent and distributed systems within the expansive scope of valuation algebras.

Our CVAs draw inspiration from existing algebraic frameworks in concurrency theory such as *Communicating Sequential Processes (CSP)* [12], *Concurrent Kleene Algebra (CKA)* [15], *Concurrent Refinement Algebra (CRA)* [10], and *duoidal/2-monoidal categories* [2]. They also facilitate key reasoning methodologies for program specification, like Hoare logic [11], and rely-guarantee reasoning [14].

Within the framework of CVAs, we explored three trace models, each representing distinct computational paradigms, and related them by morphisms.

This research marks a promising pathway to practical applications, particularly through the potent *local computation* framework described in Sect. 8. Looking ahead, our work will focus on several key areas. We aim to explore a wider range of CVA models, including the trace semantics of CSP, as well as examples founded on different structures, like trees or transition systems, instead of traces. Our study will further involve deepening the understanding of the general theory of CVAs, including the exploration of their categorical structure, and the ways CVAs on different spaces relate via the pull-back and push-forward mechanisms of their underlying presheaves. Of special interest is the examination of potential links between OVAs and *the monoidal Grothendieck construction* [16].

Acknowledgements. We convey our sincere gratitude to the following for their valuable insights and support: Alexander Evangelou, Brae Webb, Christina Vasilakopoulou, Cliff Jones, Des FitzGerald, Dylan Braithwaite, Brijesh Dongol, Graeme Smith, Igor Dolinka, James East, Jesse Sigal, Joe Moeller, John Baez, Juerg Kohlas, Kait Lam, Kirsten Winter, Luigi Santocanale, Marc Pouly, Mark Utting, Martti Karvonen, Matt

Garcia, Matteo Capucci, Michael Robinson, Mike Shulman, Morgan Rogers, Nick Coughlin, Peter Hoefner, Ralph Sarkis, Reid Barton, Rob Colvin, Scott Heiner, Sori Lee, Ted Goranson, Yannick Chevalier, and the Zulip category theory community. We are thankful for the support of the Australian Government Research Training Program Scholarship of Naso, and funding from the Australian Research Council (ARC) through the Discovery Grant DP190102142. We gratefully acknowledge the use of GitHub Copilot and OpenAI ChatGPT software in refining the readability of this paper, though their contribution did not extend to the semantic substance of the research.

References

1. Abramsky, S., Carù, G.: Non-locality, contextuality and valuation algebras: a general theory of disagreement. Philos. Trans. Roy. Soc. A **377**(2157), 20190036 (2019). https://doi.org/10.1098/rsta.2019.0036
2. Aguiar, M., Mahajan, S.: Monoidal functors, species and Hopf algebras, CRM Monograph Series, vol. 29. American Mathematical Society, Providence, RI (2010). https://doi.org/10.1090/crmm/029
3. Barmak, J.A.: Algebraic topology of finite topological spaces and applications, Lecture Notes in Mathematics, vol. 2032. Springer, Heidelberg (2011). https://doi.org/10.1007/978-3-642-22003-6
4. Bertoni, A., Mereghetti, C., Palano, B.: Trace monoids with idempotent generators and measure-only quantum automata. Nat. Comput. **9**(2), 383–395 (2010). https://doi.org/10.1007/s11047-009-9154-8
5. Chen, L.-T., Roggenbach, M., Tucker, J.V.: An algebraic theory for data linkage. In: Fiadeiro, J.L., Tutu, I. (eds.) WADT 2018. LNCS, vol. 11563, pp. 47–66. Springer, Cham (2019). https://doi.org/10.1007/978-3-030-23220-7_3
6. Evangelou-Oost, N., Bannister, C., Meinicke, L., Hayes, I.J.: Trace models of concurrent valuation algebras. arXiv:2305.18017 (2023)
7. Evangelou-Oost, N., Bannister, C., Hayes, I.J.: Contextuality in distributed systems. In: Glück, R., Santocanale, L., Winter, M. (eds.) Relational and Algebraic Methods in Computer Science, pp. 52–68. Springer International Publishing, Cham (2023). https://doi.org/10.1007/978-3-031-28083-2_4
8. Fong, B., Spivak, D.I.: Seven sketches in compositionality: an invitation to applied category theory. LibreTexts (2022)
9. Haenni, R.: Ordered valuation algebras: a generic framework for approximating inference. Int. J. Approx. Reason. **37**(1), 1–41 (2004). https://doi.org/10.1016/j.ijar.2003.10.009
10. Hayes, I.J., Meinicke, L.A., Winter, K., Colvin, R.J.: A synchronous program algebra: a basis for reasoning about shared-memory and event-based concurrency. Formal Aspects Comput. **31**(2), 133–163 (2018). https://doi.org/10.1007/s00165-018-0464-4
11. Hoare, C.A.R.: An axiomatic basis for computer programming. Commun. ACM **12**(10), 576–580 (1969). https://doi.org/10.1145/363235.363259
12. Hoare, C.A.R.: Communicating Sequential Processes. Prentice-Hall, Upper Saddle River (1985)
13. Hoare, T., Möller, B., Struth, G., Wehrman, I.: Concurrent Kleene algebra and its foundations. J. Log. Algebraic Methods Program. **80**(6), 266–296 (2011). https://doi.org/10.1016/j.jlap.2011.04.005
14. Jones, C.B.: Development methods for computer programs including a notion of interference. Oxford University Computing Laboratory, Oxford (1981)

15. Kohlas, J.: Information algebras - generic structures for inference. Springer, Discrete mathematics and theoretical computer science (2003)
16. Moeller, J., Vasilakopoulou, C.: Monoidal Grothendieck construction (2021)
17. Pouly, M., Kohlas, J.: Generic Inference: a Unifying Theory for Automated Reasoning. Wiley, Hoboken (2012)
18. Riehl, E.: Category Theory in Context. Courier Dover Publications, Mineola (2017)
19. Tarlecki, A., Burstall, R.M., Goguen, J.A.: Some fundamental algebraic tools for the semantics of computation: Part 3: indexed categories. Theor. Comput. Sci. **91**(2), 239–264 (1991). https://doi.org/10.1016/0304-3975(91)90085-G

Branch and Bound for Sigmoid-Like Neural Network Verification

Xiaoyong Xue and Meng Sun[✉]

School of Mathematical Sciences, Peking University, Beijing 100871, China
{xuexy,sunm}@pku.edu.cn

Abstract. The robustness of deep neural networks has received extensive attention and is considered to need guarantees by formal verification. For ReLU neural network verification, there are abundant studies and various techniques. However, verifying sigmoid-like neural networks still relies on linear approximation, which inevitably introduces errors and leads to imprecise results. To reduce error and get better results, we present a branch and bound framework for sigmoid-like neural network verification in this paper. In this framework, we design a neuron splitting method and a branching strategy. The splitting method can split neurons with non-linear sigmoid-like activation functions, and the branching strategy reduces the size of the branch and bound tree, which improves the verification performance. We implement our verification framework as SIGBAB and evaluate its performance on open source benchmarks. Experiment results show that our method can produce more precise verification results than other state-of-the-art methods and our branching strategy shows superior performance compared to other strategies.

Keywords: Robustness · Verification · Neural network

1 Introduction

While deep neural networks play a growing role in safety-critical fields [4,9], their robustness is becoming a major concern. Studies show that deep neural networks are vulnerable to adversarial attacks. Small and imperceptible perturbations may lead to completely different prediction result from the original image [7,10,17]. To address this problem, verification techniques are leveraged to make a rigorous guarantee on the robustness of neural networks.

Formal verification of neural networks has been well studied recent years. Numerous techniques, such as satisfiability modulo theory [5], mixed integer linear programming [13], abstract interpretation [15,16], linear approximation [19,22], branch and bound [2,14,18], are applied to verify the robustness of neural networks with ReLU activation function. For sigmoid-like activation functions, their non-linearity makes the verification far more complicated, and thus formal verification of sigmoid-like neural networks mostly relies on linear approximation [1,8,12,20,22], which adopts a lower linear relaxation and an upper linear relaxation for the activation function. These works use different

© The Author(s), under exclusive license to Springer Nature Singapore Pte Ltd. 2023
Y. Li and S. Tahar (Eds.): ICFEM 2023, LNCS 14308, pp. 137–155, 2023.
https://doi.org/10.1007/978-981-99-7584-6_9

linear relaxations for sigmoid-like activation functions, such as tangent lines at an end point or the mid point [1,22], parallel lines [20], and lines with minimal enclosed area [8].

Linear approximation can be efficiently obtained through propagation based methods [22]. But it is well known that this method inevitably introduces deviations regardless of the choice of linear relaxations, which means a neural network may be robust even if linear approximation fails to prove that. Moreover, linear approximation can not refine its results by itself, *i.e.* it is unable to produce more precise result even if more time is invested, since the linear relaxations for each neuron remain unchanged during the computation.

In order to refine the results of linear approximation, we propose a branch and bound verification framework for sigmoid-like neural networks in this paper. For a verification problem that linear approximation fails to prove, we divide it into several sub-problems by splitting some hidden neurons. If all sub-problems are proved to be true, the answer to the parent problem is true. If one of the sub-problems is proved to be false, the answer to the parent problem is false. Otherwise, we continue to divide problems with unknown results.

Our verification framework contains a neuron splitting method and a branching strategy. The neuron splitting method splits a non-linear sigmoid-like function into several segments, and computes a lower linear relaxation and an upper linear relaxation for each of them. These relaxations are computed based on linear relaxations of the parent problem and the convexity of activation functions, which ensures the solutions of the sub-problems are at least as good as those of the parent problem. The branching strategy applies a heuristic scoring function to make branching decisions. The scoring function assigns a score to each neuron, which estimates the potential improvement obtained by splitting the neuron. The score for each neuron is computed locally, enabling the entire scoring process to be completed in one backward propagation. Our strategy chooses a neuron with the highest score to split. The new branching strategy can reduce the size of the branch and bound search tree, and thus improves the efficiency of our framework. Besides, we can generate possible counterexamples for each sub-problem, which may detect unsatisfiable properties.

We have made an implementation of this framework, called SIGBAB. Different from other verification tools for sigmoid-like neural networks, it runs in parallel and is amenable to GPU acceleration. We compare it with three representative tools, DEEPCERT [20], VERINET [8], CROWN [22], and NEWISE [23]. The experiments show that SIGBAB can produce more precise verification results. Compared to other tools, SIGBAB an average improvement of 34.9% and a maximum improvement of up to 160.9% in terms of the number of verified properties.

The rest of the paper is organized as follows. Section 2 provides the preliminaries on robustness properties and linear approximations of neural networks. Section 3 presents the branch and bound verification framework for sigmoid-like neural networks. In Sect. 4 and Sect. 5, we introduce the splitting method and the branching strategy, respectively. Section 6 shows the experimental results. Finally, we conclude in Sect. 7.

2 Preliminaries

In this section, we briefly introduce some background knowledge about neural networks, robustness property of neural networks, and linear relaxations of sigmoid-like activation functions.

2.1 Neural Networks

A neural network is formed by sequentially connected layers, consisting of one input layer, one output layer and multiple hidden layers. Formally, a neural network with n-dimensional input and m-dimensional output can be regarded as a function $f : \mathbb{R}^n \to \mathbb{R}^m$. The connections between layers in the neural network can be formulated as follows:

$$z_{0,i} = x_i \qquad\qquad \forall i = 1 \ldots n \qquad (1)$$

$$\hat{z}_{l,i} = \sum_{j=1}^{n_{l-1}} w_{i,j}^l z_{l-1,j} + b_i^l \qquad\qquad \forall l = 1 \ldots L, i = 1 \ldots n_l \qquad (2)$$

$$z_{l,i} = \sigma(\hat{z}_{l,i}) \qquad\qquad \forall l = 1 \ldots L-1, i = 1 \ldots n_l \qquad (3)$$

$$y_i = \hat{z}_{L,i} \qquad\qquad \forall i = 1 \ldots m \qquad (4)$$

This neural network has $L - 1$ hidden layers and n_l neurons for layer l. The behaviors of the input layer and the output layer are represented in Eq. (1) and Eq. (4), respectively. The i-th dimension of the output is denoted as y_i or $f_i(x)$. We use $\hat{z}_{l,i}$ as the i-th pre-activation neurons in layer l and $z_{l,i}$ as the corresponding post-activation neuron. The weighted-sum is described in Eq. (2), where $w_{i,j}^l$ and b_i^l denote weights and biases respectively. We also use w^l and w_i^l to represent the weight matrix and the i-th row of w^l. Equation (3) describes the activation layer, where $\sigma(x)$ is the activation function. In this paper, we focus on sigmoid-like activation functions, such as Sigmoid and Tanh:

$$\sigma(x) = \frac{1}{1 + e^{-x}} \qquad\qquad \sigma(x) = \frac{e^x - e^{-x}}{e^x + e^{-x}}$$

In classification tasks, for a given input x, the neural network determines that x belongs to class t if and only if (iff) for any $k \neq t$ ($1 \le k \le m$), $f_t(x) > f_k(x)$.

2.2 Robustness Property

Local robustness property [23] is an important and widely studied property, which means that the prediction label stays unchanged when a small perturbation is added to a given input. Formally, *local robustness* is defined as follows:

Definition 1 (Local robustness). *Let f be a neural network with m-dimensional output. Given an input x_0 with ground-truth label l and a perturbation radius ϵ under ℓ_p norm, the neural network f is* local robust *at x_0 within the radius of ϵ iff*

$$\forall x' \in \{x' \mid ||x' - x_0||_p \le \epsilon\}, \quad \bigwedge_{j \neq l} f_l(x') > f_j(x').$$

It can be observed that the constraint on the output layer is a conjunction of a set of atomic formulas. Each atomic formula means that the neural network is robust to a certain dimension of the output. We call the property represented by an atomic formula *targeted robustness*.

Definition 2 (Targeted robustness). *Let f be a neural network. Given an input x_0 with ground-truth l, one certain dimension t of the output and a perturbation radius ϵ under ℓ_p norm, the neural network f is* targeted robust *for t at x_0 within the radius of ϵ iff*

$$\forall x' \in \{x' \mid ||x' - x_0||_p \leq \epsilon\}, \quad f_l(x') > f_t(x') \tag{5}$$

In practice, the local robustness property is examined by checking all targeted robustness properties derived from it. In this paper, we consider the verification of targeted robustness in the sense of ℓ_∞ norm, which the most general case.

2.3   Linear Relaxation of Sigmoid-Like Functions

A widely adopted method to verify targeted robustness (5) is transforming itself into the following optimization problem:

$$
\begin{aligned}
\min \;\; & y_l - y_t \\
\text{s.t.} \;\; & y_l = w_l^L z_{L-1} + b_l^L, \; y_t = w_t^L z_{L-1} + b_t^L, \\
& \hat{z}_k = w^k z_{k-1} + b_k && k = 1 \ldots L-1, \\
& z_k = \sigma(\hat{z}_k) && k = 1 \ldots L-1, \\
& ||z_0 - x_0||_p \leq \epsilon.
\end{aligned}
\tag{6}
$$

If the optimal value of this optimization problem is greater than zero, we have $f_l(x') > f_t(x')$, and then the targeted robustness is satisfied.

The main obstacle in solving (6) is the non-linearity of activation functions. Linear approximation addresses this by finding a lower linear relaxation h_L and an upper linear relaxation h_U for each activation function $\sigma(x)$, which satisfies

$$h_L(x) \leq \sigma(x) \leq h_U(x).$$

In our framework, we apply the linear relaxation method used in DEEP-CERT [20]. Assume that the input interval of $\sigma(x)$ is $[l, u]$. Let $k = \frac{\sigma(u) - \sigma(l)}{u - l}$. The method computes linear relaxations in three categories:

(1) If $\sigma'(l) < k$ and $\sigma'(u) > k$, the linear relaxations are $h_L(x) = kx + \sigma(d) - kd$ and $h_U(x) = kx + \sigma(l) - kl$, where $\sigma'(d) = k$ and $l < d < u$.
(2) If $\sigma'(l) > k$ and $\sigma'(u) < k$, the linear relaxations are $h_L(x) = kx + \sigma(l) - kl$ and $h_U(x) = kx + \sigma(d) - kd$, where $\sigma'(d) = k$ and $l < d < u$.
(3) If $\sigma'(l) < k$ and $\sigma'(u) < k$, the linear relaxations are $h_L(x) = \sigma'(d_1)x + \sigma(u) - \sigma'(d_1)u$ and $h_U(x) = \sigma'(d_2)x + \sigma(l) - \sigma'(d_2)l$, where $\sigma'(d_1) = \frac{\sigma(d_1) - \sigma(u)}{d_1 - u}$ and $\sigma'(d_2) = \frac{\sigma(d_2) - \sigma(l)}{d_2 - l}$.

3   Branch and Bound for Sigmoid-Like Neural Networks

In this section, we propose a branch and bound framework to verify neural networks with sigmoid-like activation functions. This starts with a high level overview, followed with step-by-step explanation.

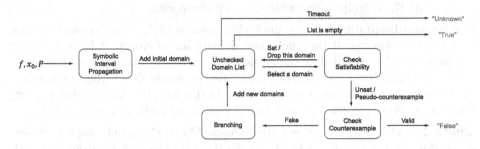

Fig. 1. Verification framework

The overall framework is depicted in Fig. 1. The input of the framework includes a neural network f, a data vector x_0 and a targeted robustness property P. In order to examine the robustness property, f must be a white box, which means that all information about weights, biases and activation functions is provided to the framework.

In the first step of our framework, we use symbolic interval propagation to compute bounds and linear relaxations for each hidden neuron. The bounds of each neuron determine the initial feasible domain of each neuron. Using the relaxations, we check the satisfiability of property P by finding the lower bound of problem (6) on the feasible domain. If the property is satisfied, our framework terminates and return "True". Otherwise, we divide the initial feasible domain into several smaller domains. The satisfiability of P is checked on every domain, and those domains on which property P is verified are discarded. The results of satisfiability checking for the rest domains are used to generate pseudo-counterexamples. If one of the pseudo-counterexamples is valid, property P is proved to be unsatisfiable and our framework returns "False". Otherwise, we perform branching on these domains and continue this process until all domains have been verified and "True" is returned, or the time limit is reached and "Unknown" is returned.

The rest of the section provides a detailed explanation of each step.

Symbolic Interval Propagation. Symbolic interval propagation computes bounds and linear relaxations for each hidden neuron. The computation starts from the first hidden layer and proceeds layer by layer. For the first hidden layer, we first compute a lower bound l and an upper bound u for every pre-activation neuron by interval arithmetic, and then use l and u to calculate linear relaxations of activation functions using the method proposed in [20] (see Sect. 2.3 for more details). For every remaining hidden layer, l and u are computed based on linear relaxations of all preceding layers, and we use l and u to calculate linear relaxations in the same way.

Remark that the tool presented in [20] for computing linear relaxations of sigmoid-like activation functions is limited to be executed on CPU. To improve the efficiency of symbolic interval propagation, we leverage a modern deep learning library to compute linear relaxations in parallel, which enables GPU acceleration and thus significantly reduces time consumption.

Unchecked Domain List. The unchecked domain list is used to store domains that need to checked. If the unchecked domain list is empty, it indicates that the property P is satisfied across all domains, and thus our framework returns "True". Domains in the unchecked domain list are sorted descendingly according to bounding results of their parent domain. In this way, the domain that is most likely to be proved is selected first, thereby reducing memory usage.

Check Satisfiability. We check the satisfiability of the input property P for every domain via transforming the verification problem into an optimization problem. To get over the non-linearity of the activation function, the constraints on activation functions in problem (6) are replaced with linear relaxations. The lower and upper linear relaxations for the activation function in layer k are denoted as $\alpha_k^L x + \beta_t^L$ and $\alpha_k^U x + \beta_k^U$, respectively, where α_k^L and α_k^U (β_k^L and β_k^U) are constants representing the slops (intercepts) of linear relaxations. The optimization problem for an domain is formally written as:

$$
\begin{aligned}
\min \;\; & D\hat{z}_L \\
s.t. \;\; & \hat{z}_k = w^k z_{k-1} + b_k & k = 1\ldots L, \\
& \alpha_k^L \hat{z}_k + \beta^L k \le z_k \le \alpha_k^U \hat{z}_k + \beta^U k & k = 1\ldots L-1, \qquad (7) \\
& l'_{k,i} \le \hat{z}_{k,i} \le u'_{k,i} & i \in S_k, \; k = 1\ldots L-1, \\
& \|z_0 - x_0\| \le \epsilon.
\end{aligned}
$$

where D is the coefficient vector of the linear constraints on the output layer, and S_k is the set of neurons that are split in this domain. The bound constraints $l'_{k,i} \le \hat{z}_{k,i} \le u'_{k,i}$ are generated by the neuron splitting method. For neurons that are not in S_k, the bound constraints are omitted because they can be inferred from the linear relaxations. As the optimal value of problem (7) serves as a lower bound for the optimal value of problem (6), property P is satisfiable on this domain if the optimal value of problem (7) is greater than 0.

For the initial domain, S_k is empty, and the optimization problem can be solved by backward propagation. For other domains, we use Lagrange Relaxation [18] to transform problem (7) into a simpler problem:

$$
\begin{aligned}
\max_{\mu,\lambda} \min_{\mathbf{z}} \;\; & D\hat{z}_L + \sum_{k=1}^{L-1} \sum_{i \in S_k} (\mu_{k,i}(l'_{k,i} - \hat{z}_{k_i}) + \lambda_{k,i}(\hat{z}_{k,i} - u'_{k,i})) \\
s.t. \;\; & \hat{z}_k = w^k z_{k-1} + b_k & k = 1\ldots L, \qquad (8) \\
& \alpha_k^L \hat{z}_k + \beta^L k \le z_k \le \alpha_k^U \hat{z}_k + \beta^U k & k = 1\ldots L-1, \\
& \|z_0 - x_0\| \le \epsilon, \; \lambda_{k,i} \ge 0, \; \mu_{k,i} \ge 0 & i \in S_k, k = 1\ldots L-1.
\end{aligned}
$$

Algorithm 1: Solving the optimization problem (8)

Input: Optimization problem (8), number of iterations T.
Output: The optimal value γ

1   Initialize all μ, λ to positive values;
2   **for** $t \leftarrow 1$ **to** T **do**
3     $R_{L-1}, c_{L-1} \leftarrow D \cdot w^L, D \cdot b^L$;
4   **for** $k \leftarrow L-1$ **to** 1 **do**
5       $c'_k \leftarrow [R_k]_+ \beta_k^L + [R_k]_+ \beta_k^U + c_k$;
6       $R'_k \leftarrow [R_k]_+ \alpha_k^L + [R_k]_+ \alpha_k^U$;
7   **for each** $i \in S_k$ **do**
8         $R'_{k,i} \leftarrow R'_{k,i} + \lambda_{k,i} - \mu_{k,i}$;
9         $c'_k \leftarrow c'_k + \mu_{k,i} l'_{k,i} - \lambda_{k,i} u'_{k,i}$;
10       $c_{k-1} \leftarrow R_k \cdot b^k + c_k$;
11       $R_{k-1} \leftarrow R_k \cdot w^k$;
12     $\gamma \leftarrow$ the minimum value of $R_0 \cdot z_0 + c_0$ subject to $||z_0 - x_0|| \leq \epsilon$;
13   Update μ, λ according to the gradient;

14 **return** γ

The bound constraints on neurons in S_k are incorporated into the objective function with the multipliers λ and μ, which must be non-negative. In this way, the problem (8) can be solved with multiple iteration of backward propagation, which is shown in Algorithm 1.

Algorithm 1 adopts projected gradient ascent to solve the outer maximization problem. The multipliers λ and μ are initialized as positive values (Line 1) and updated according to the gradient (Line 13), which is computed according to the inner minimization problem. For any specific μ and λ, the inner minimization problem can be solved with backward propagation (Line 3–Line 12). For layer k, the backward propagation use the constraints on weights and relaxations to replace variables $\hat{z}_k$ in the objective function with $\hat{z}_{k-1}$. We use R_k and c_k to represent the coefficient vector and constant term of the objective function for layer k. When the propagation reaches the input layer, we just need to find the minimum value of $R_0 z_0 + c$ subject to $||z_0 - x_0|| \leq \epsilon$.

By exploiting weak duality, we can get that the optimal value to the inner minimization problem is a valid lower bound of problem (7) for any μ and λ that are greater than 0. Therefore, the soundness of Algorithm 1 is guaranteed regardless of whether the outer maximization problem converges. This means that if the result γ returned by Algorithm 1 is greater than zero, the input property P is satisfied on the domain corresponding to the optimization problem.

Counterexample. If the result returned by Algorithm 1 is less than zero, we cannot determine the input property is unsatisfiable because of the relaxations in problem (8). But we can derive a pseudo-counterexample from Algorithm 1. The optimum point of inner minimization problem is regarded as a pseudo-counterexample and checked for validity. If it is valid, the input property P is unsatisfiable. Otherwise, the branch and bound framework continues to split more neurons.

4   Neuron Splitting

In this section, we propose a new neuron splitting method for sigmoid-like activation functions.

For a neuron with a piece-wise linear activation function like ReLU, there exists a natural splitting method, that is, splitting at the breakpoints of the piece-wise function. However, for a neuron with a sigmoid-like activation function, there are an infinite number of ways to split it due to the non-linearity of the sigmoid-like function. A direct method is to split at the middle point, which has two disadvantages. First, the linear relaxations of the created subdomains may require computing tangent lines with given slops, which needs time-consuming iterative calculation. Second, splitting at the middle point may generate looser linear relaxations, which makes the produced subdomains worse than the original one. The two weaknesses are illustrated by the following example.

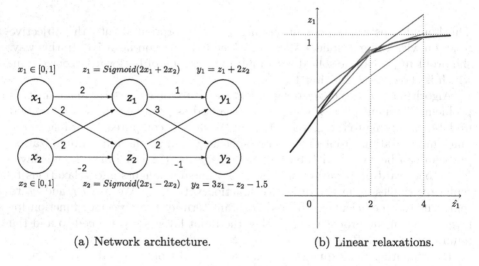

(a) Network architecture.   (b) Linear relaxations.

Fig. 2. An example of splitting neuron at the middle point.

Example 1.   Consider a neural network shown in Fig. 2(a), which has only one hidden layer. The input layer contains two neurons x_1 and x_2, where $x_1 \in [0,1]$ and $x_2 \in [0,1]$. We want to check whether this neural network satisfies the property $y_1 \geq y_2$. This requires finding the minimum value of $y_1 - y_2$. Using interval arithmetic, we get a lower bound 0 and an upper bound 4 for the pre-activation neuron $\hat{z}_1$. Linear relaxations of z_1 are represented as blue lines in Fig. 2(b). With these relaxations, we get the minimal value of $y_1 - y_2$ is -0.071.

If we split neuron z_1 at the middle point of its range $[0,4]$, two subdomains are obtained: $\hat{z}_1 \in [0,2]$ and $\hat{z}_1 \in [2,4]$. Linear relaxations for these two domains are depicted as red lines in Fig. 2(b). Note that computing the upper linear relaxations for these two domains requires finding tangent lines with given slops, which is accomplished through iterative computation and takes a lot of time. We also notice that the region enclosed by the red lines is not entirely contained within the region enclosed by the blue lines. The gray region in Fig. 2(b) is an additional part introduced by splitting. The additional part may make the verification of the two new domains more difficult than that of the parent domain. In fact, the minimal value of $y_1 - y_2$ on these two domains are -0.1502 and -0.1115. Both are less than the minimal value -0.071 of the parent domain, which means that the produced subdomains are worse than the parent domain.

We propose a new neuron splitting method, which overcomes the two weaknesses. Consider splitting a neuron with a sigmoid-like activation function $\sigma(x)$, whose feasible domain is $[l, u]$. The original lower and upper linear relaxations for σ on $[l, u]$ are $\alpha^L x + \beta^L$ and $\alpha^U x + \beta^U$, respectively. According to the following three cases, we split the parent domain $[l, u]$ into several subdomains and give the lower and upper linear relaxations for σ on every part. The lower and upper linear relaxations on the i-th subdomain are denoted as h_i^L and h_i^U, respectively. In Fig. 3–Fig. 5, we depict relaxations for the parent domain using blue lines, relaxations for subdomains using red lines and the regions enclosed by red lines using grey regions.

(1) If $l < 0 < u$, we split the domain $[l, u]$ into two parts: $[l, 0]$ and $[0, u]$. We use $\alpha^L x + \beta^L$ and $\alpha^U x + \beta^U$ as the lower linear relaxation on $[l, 0]$ and the upper linear relaxation on $[0, u]$, respectively. Remark that a sigmoid-like activation function is convex on the negative axis $(-\infty, 0)$ and concave on the positive axis $(0, +\infty)$. So, we set the line connecting the points $(l, \sigma(l))$ and $(0, \sigma(0))$ as the new upper linear relaxation on $[l, 0]$, and the line connecting the points $(0, \sigma(0))$ and $(u, \sigma(u))$ as the new lower linear relaxation on $[0, u]$. That is,

$$h_1^L(x) = \alpha^L x + \beta^L, \qquad h_1^U(x) = -\frac{\sigma(0) - \sigma(l)}{l}x + \sigma(0),$$

$$h_2^L(x) = \frac{\sigma(u) - \sigma(0)}{u}x + \sigma(0), \qquad h_2^U(x) = \alpha^U x + \beta^U.$$

(2) If $l \geq 0$, there are two subcases. The first subcase is that the intersection point of the activation function σ and the original upper linear relaxation is neither the left endpoint $(l, \sigma(l))$ nor the right endpoint $(u, \sigma(u))$, which is equivalent to $\alpha^U \neq \sigma'(l)$ and $\alpha^U \neq \sigma'(u)$. The second subcase is that the intersection point of them is one of the endpoints, which is equivalent to $\alpha^U = \sigma'(l)$ or $\alpha^U = \sigma'(u)$. For the first subcase, as shown in Fig. 4(a), we first compute the intersection point d_1 (d_2) of the original upper linear relaxation and the tangent line of σ at l (u), where

$$d_1 = -\frac{\sigma(l) - \sigma'(l)l - \beta^U}{\sigma'(l) - \alpha^U} \quad \text{and} \quad d_2 = -\frac{\sigma(u) - \sigma'(u)u - \beta^U}{\sigma'(u) - \alpha^U}.$$

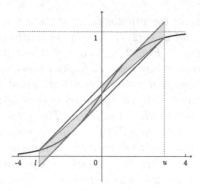

Fig. 3. Neuron splitting on $l < 0 < u$.

Then, we split the domain $[l, u]$ into three parts: $[l, d_1]$, $[d_1, d_2]$ and $[d_2, u]$. Recall that σ is concave on $(0, +\infty)$. So, we have (1) the line connecting the left endpoint and the right endpoint of each part is a lower linear relaxation on the part; and (2) the tangent lines at point l and at point u are upper linear relaxations on $[l, d_1]$ and $[d_2, u]$, respectively. We set the original upper linear relaxation as the upper linear relaxation on $[d_1, d_2]$. Namely, we have

$$h_1^L(x) = \frac{\sigma(d_1) - \sigma(l)}{d_1 - l}(x - l) + \sigma(l), \qquad h_1^U(x) = \sigma'(l)(x - l) + \sigma(l),$$

$$h_2^L(x) = \frac{\sigma(d_2) - \sigma(d_1)}{d_2 - d_1}(x - d_1) + \sigma(d_1), \quad h_2^U(x) = \alpha^U x + \beta^U,$$

$$h_3^L(x) = \frac{\sigma(u) - \sigma(d_2)}{u - d_2}(x - u) + \sigma(u), \qquad h_3^U(x) = \sigma'(u)(x - u) + \sigma(u).$$

For the second subcase, we only explain the case where the intersection point is the right endpoint u, as shown in Fig. 4(b), since the other case where the intersection point is the left endpoint is the same. We first compute the intersection point d of two tangent lines at point l and at point u, where

$$d = -\frac{(\sigma(l) - \sigma'(l)l) - (\sigma(u) - \sigma'(u)u)}{\sigma'(l) - \sigma'(u)}. \tag{9}$$

Then, we split the domain $[l, u]$ into two parts: $[l, d]$ and $[d, u]$. Similar to the first subcase, we set (1) the line connecting the left endpoint and the right endpoint of each part as the lower linear relaxation on the part; and (2) the tangent lines at point l and at point u as the upper linear relaxations on $[l, d]$ and $[d, u]$, respectively. We have

$$h_1^L(x) = \frac{\sigma(d) - \sigma(l)}{d - l}(x - l) + \sigma(l), \qquad h_1^U(x) = \sigma'(l)(x - l) + \sigma(l),$$

$$h_2^L(x) = \frac{\sigma(u) - \sigma(d)}{u - d}(x - u) + \sigma(u), \qquad h_2^U(x) = \sigma'(u)(x - u) + \sigma(u).$$

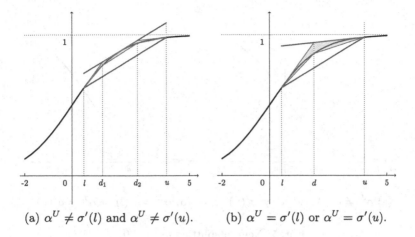

(a) $\alpha^U \neq \sigma'(l)$ and $\alpha^U \neq \sigma'(u)$.   (b) $\alpha^U = \sigma'(l)$ or $\alpha^U = \sigma'(u)$.

Fig. 4. Neuron spliting for $l \geq 0$.

(3) If $u \leq 0$, there are two subcases, which are similar to the subcases for $l \geq 0$. For the first subcase where the intersection point is not an endpoint, as shown in Fig. 5(a), we again compute the intersection point d_1 (d_2) of the original upper linear relaxation and the tangent line at point l (u), where

$$d_1 = -\frac{\sigma(l) - \sigma'(l)l - \beta^L}{\sigma'(l) - \alpha^L} \quad \text{and} \quad d_2 = -\frac{\sigma(u) - \sigma'(u)u - \beta^L}{\sigma'(u) - \alpha^L}.$$

We divide the domain $[l, u]$ at point d_1 and point d_2 to get three parts. Recall that σ is convex on $(-\infty, 0)$. So, we have (1) the line connecting the left endpoint and the right endpoint of each part is an upper linear relaxation on the part; and (2) the tangent lines at point l and at point u are lower linear relaxations on $[l, d_1]$ and $[d_2, u]$, respectively. We set the original lower linear relaxation as the lower linear relaxation on $[d_1, d_2]$. That is, we have

$$h_1^L(x) = \sigma'(l)(x - l) + \sigma(l), \quad h_1^U(x) = \frac{\sigma(d_1) - \sigma(l)}{d_1 - l}(x - l) + \sigma(l),$$

$$h_2^L(x) = \alpha^L x + \beta^L, \quad h_2^U(x) = \frac{\sigma(d_2) - \sigma(d_1)}{d_2 - d_1}(x - d_1) + \sigma(d_1),$$

$$h_3^L(x) = \sigma'(u)(x - u) + \sigma(u), \quad h_3^U(x) = \frac{\sigma(u) - \sigma(d_2)}{u - d_2}(x - u) + \sigma(u).$$

For the second subcase where the intersection point is an endpoint, we only explain the case where the intersection point is the left endpoint l, as shown in Fig. 5(b). Similarly, we divide the domain $[l, u]$ at point d to get two parts $[l, d]$ and $[d, u]$, where d is shown in Equation (9). We set (1) the line connecting the left endpoint and the right endpoint of each part as the upper linear relaxation on the part; and (2) the tangent lines at point l and at point u as

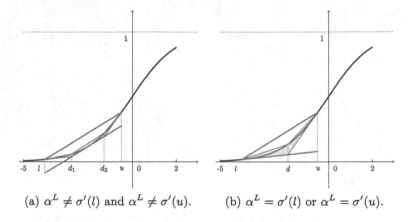

(a) $\alpha^L \neq \sigma'(l)$ and $\alpha^L \neq \sigma'(u)$.   (b) $\alpha^L = \sigma'(l)$ or $\alpha^L = \sigma'(u)$.

Fig. 5. Neuron splitting for $u \leq 0$.

the lower linear relaxations on $[l, d]$ and $[d, u]$, respectively. We have

$$h_1^L(x) = \sigma'(l)(x - l) + \sigma(l), \qquad h_1^U(x) = \frac{\sigma(d) - \sigma(l)}{d - l}(x - l) + \sigma(l),$$

$$h_2^L(x) = \sigma'(u)(x - u) + \sigma(u), \qquad h_2^U(x) = \frac{\sigma(u) - \sigma(d)}{u - d}(x - u) + \sigma(u).$$

Remark that in each of the three cases, the region enclosed by relaxations of the subdomains is contained in the region enclosed by original relaxations (see Fig. 3–Fig. 5). This ensures that the subdomains produced by splitting are not worse than their parent domain. Moreover, we only need to compute the tangent lines at endpoints, which is more efficient than computing tangent lines with given slops.

5   Branching Strategy

In this section, we present a novel branching strategy for neural networks with sigmoid-like activation functions.

Recall the verification framework presented in Fig. 1. We need to perform branching on domains where the input property fails to be verified. This requires the branching strategy to decide which neuron to split. Ideally, we hope that the branching strategy takes the neuron that maximizes the improvements of the produced subdomains, which are measured by the change of the result computed by Algorithm 1. However, due to the vast number of neurons in a network, computing the exact improvement for each neuron is impractical and usually replaced by approximation methods such as BaBSR [2] and FSB [14]. These two methods were originally designed for ReLU neural networks and show poor compatibility with our splitting method. We propose a novel branching strategy called *Neuron Improvement* (NI), which estimate the branching improvement for each neuron and choose a neuron with the maximum estimated improvement as the branching decision.

Splitting a neuron to branching a domain creates multiple subdomains. We first introduce how to estimate the improvement of one subdomain. To approximate the result of Algorithm 1, we set all all λ and μ to 0 and cease their updates. In this way, Algorithm 1 only involves the inner backward propagation. Assume that the branching is taken on the i-th neuron in layer k. It directly changes the linear relaxations for neuron $\hat{z}_{k,i}$. As a result, the computation in layers k' is changed for all $k' < k$. If we want to get the result, we need the full backward propagation. To improve efficiency, we make a rough estimation by terminating the backward propagation and computing the minimal value at layer k. Because relaxations of all neurons except $\hat{z}_{k,i}$ are the same, we only need to consider the contribution of neuron $z_{k,i}$ to the optimal value. For the parent domain, denoting the lower and upper bound of $z_{k,i}$ as $l_{k,i}$ and $u_{k,i}$ respectively, the contribution of neuron $z_{k,i}$ is

$$[R_{k,i}]_+(\alpha_{k,i}^L l_{k,i} + \beta_{k,i}^L) + [R_{k,i}]_-(\alpha_{k,i}^U u_{k,i} + \beta_k^U),$$

where (1) $\alpha_{k,i}^L \hat{z}_{k,i} + \beta_{k,i}^L$ and $\alpha_{k,i}^U \hat{z}_{k,i} + \beta_{k,i}^U$ are the linear relaxations of $\hat{z}_{k,i}$, and (2) $l_{k,i}$ and $u_{k,i}$ are the lower and upper bounds, respectively. The $R_{k,i}$ is computed according to Line 6 and Line 11 in Algorithm 1. For the subdomain, suppose the linear relaxations of neuron $\hat{z}_{k,i}$ are $\tilde{\alpha}_{k,i}^L \hat{z}_{k,i} + \tilde{\beta}_{k,i}^L$ and $\tilde{\alpha}_{k,i}^U \hat{z}_{k,i} + \tilde{\beta}_{k,i}^U$. The contribution of neuron $z_{k,i}$ is

$$[R_{k,i}]_+(\tilde{\alpha}_{k,i}^L l_{k,i} + \tilde{\beta}_{k,i}^L) + [R_{k,i}]_-(\tilde{\alpha}_{k,i}^U u_{k,i} + \tilde{\beta}_k^U).$$

As the linear relaxations for other neurons in layer k remain unchanged, the estimated improvement for a subdomain is the difference between the above two formulas, which is

$$imp_{k,i} = \begin{cases} R_{k,i}(\tilde{\alpha}_{k,i}^L - \alpha_{k,i}^L)l_{k,i} + R_{k,i}(\tilde{\beta}_{k,i}^L - \beta_{k,i}^L), & R_{k,i} \geq 0, \\ R_{k,i}(\tilde{\alpha}_{k,i}^U - \alpha_{k,i}^U)u_{k,i} + R_{k,i}(\tilde{\beta}_{k,i}^U - \beta_{k,i}^U), & R_{k,i} < 0. \end{cases} \tag{10}$$

After computing the estimated improvement for a subdomain, we show how to compute the estimated improvement for a neuron. Recalling the neuron splitting method in Sect. 4, splitting neuron $z_{k,i}$ may produce two or three subdomains. We take all of them into consideration by calculating the average estimated improvements of all subdomains. The neuron improvement score NI of neuron $z_{k,i}$ is

$$NI_{k,i} = \frac{1}{n}(imp_{k,i}^{[1]} + imp_{k,i}^{[2]} + \cdots + imp_{k,i}^{[n]}),$$

where $imp_{k,i}^{[i]}$ is the estimated improvement of the i-th subdomain created by branching neuron $z_{k,i}$.

Notice that the computation of estimated improvement only needs $R_{k,i}$ and linear relaxations of $z_{k,i}$ in the parent domain and subdomains, and branching the neuron $z_{k,i}$ does not change the value of R_j for all $j > k$. Thus, the computation is local and we can use one backward propagation to get the estimated

Table 1. Number of proved properties of fully connected neural networks.

Model	ϵ	SigBab	DeepCert	VeriNet	CROWN	NeWise	Falsified
MNIST 3×50	0.01	**800**	759	753	544	436	23
	0.02	**248**	162	148	34	25	146
MNIST 3×100	0.01	**826**	805	803	626	625	12
	0.02	**343**	266	247	47	53	114
MNIST 5×100	0.01	**619**	577	574	120	611	89
	0.02	**73**	52	46	0	33	342
MNIST 6×500	0.08	**709**	626	607	9	10	9
	0.12	**132**	59	34	0	2	18
Fashion 3×50	0.01	**735**	713	710	581	370	34
	0.02	**345**	233	218	66	8	143
Fashion 5×100	0.01	**533**	493	479	202	404	89
	0.02	**146**	117	105	2	5	294
CIFAR10 3×50	0.005	**360**	303	298	166	98	94
	0.01	**60**	23	19	1	0	275
CIFAR10 5×100	0.005	**213**	176	160	23	99	141
	0.01	**7**	3	3	2	0	346

improvement for each neuron. After computing NI for all neurons, a neuron with the highest NI is chosen as the branching decision.

6   Experiments

We implement our branch and bound verification framework as SIGBAB, which is available at https://github.com/xue-xy/SigBaB. To show the effectiveness of our branch and bound verification framework and branching strategy, the experiments contain two parts. In the first part, we evaluate SIGBAB against other state-of-the-art verification tools to demonstrate the effectiveness of our tool. In the second part, we compare different branching strategies in our branch and bound framework to show the effectiveness of our branching strategy.

6.1   Experimental Setup

Datasets and Networks. Our experiments are conducted on fully connected neural networks (FNNs) and convolutional neural networks (CNNs). The neural networks are taken from publicly available benchmarks ERAN [6] and NeWise [23] with Sigmoid activation function. These neural networks are well trained on MNIST [11], Fashion MNIST [21] and CIFAR10 [3] datasets, and the accuracy on the corresponding test sets is around 0.95, 0.85 and 0.4, respectively.

Table 2. Number of proved properties of convolutional neural networks.

Network	ϵ	SigBaB	VeriNet	DeepCert	CROWN	NeWise	Falsified
MNIST 3-2-3	0.12	**276**	271	270	254	202	503
MNIST 6-5-3	0.12	**196**	190	188	47	10	390
Fashion 4-5-3	0.08	**482**	478	479	450	262	211
Fashion 6-5-3	0.08	**413**	407	404	228	105	158
CIFAR10 3-2-3	0.02	**294**	**294**	**294**	286	290	73
CIFAR10 6-5-3	0.02	**200**	199	199	149	166	100

Metric. We use the number of proved targeted properties to measure the effectiveness. For each neural network, we take the first 100 images from the corresponding test set and filter out the misclassified images. As the output dimensions of all networks are 10, there are at most 900 targeted robustness properties to be checked.

Competitors. We consider four representative verification tools for neural networks with sigmoid-like activation functions: DEEPCERT [20], VERINET [8], CROWN [22], and NEWISE [23]. They use different linear relaxations for activation functions, and achieve state-of-the-art performance in different neural networks. It is worth noting that NEWISE is specially designed for neural networks with only one single hidden layer or neural networks that all weights are positive. It may show worse performance in general neural networks [23]. However, because it is a recent work, we still compared with it.

Implementation. We use PyTorch to implement SIGBAB so as to accelerate the computation process with GPU. However, the original implementations of those four competitors does not support GPU acceleration. To make a fair comparison, we re-implement tools according to the formulas and algorithms given in their papers [8,20,22,23] and make them compatible with GPU acceleration.

6.2 Experimental Results

Experiments Results for FNNs. Table 1 shows the experiment results for 8 fully connected neural networks. The first word of the model name indicates the training dataset, and $a \times b$ denotes that this network has a hidden layers and each layer has b neurons. For each network, we conduct experiments on different ϵ to show the performance on large radius and small radius. The time limit for each property in SIGBAB is 5 min.

In almost all cases, our method achieves significant improvement over other methods. On average, SIGBAB proves 34.9% more properties than DEEPCERT and 62.6% more than VERINET. And it is obvious that SIGBAB outperforms CROWN by a large margin. NEWISE also shows poor performance due to its special linear relaxation design for neural networks with only positive weights, which compromises its performance on general neural networks. Compared with

Table 3. Number of proved properties for different branching strategies.

Model	ϵ	NI	BaBSR	Max
MNIST 3*50	0.01	**800**	**800**	774
	0.02	**248**	235	148
MNIST 3*100	0.01	**826**	823	813
	0.02	**343**	329	285
MNIST 5*100	0.01	**619**	611	602
	0.02	**73**	66	55
MNIST 6*500	0.08	**709**	699	674
	0.12	**132**	123	91
Fashion 3*50	0.01	**735**	734	720
	0.02	**345**	325	283
Fashion 5*100	0.01	**533**	519	504
	0.02	**146**	137	121
CIFAR 3*50	0.005	**360**	350	318
	0.01	**60**	53	26
CIFAR 5*100	0.005	**213**	200	182
	0.01	**7**	6	**7**

small radius, our method has better performance on large radius. For example, the improvement over DEEPCERT is 123.7% on MNIST 6×500 $\epsilon = 0.12$ and 160.8% on CIFAR10 3×50 $\epsilon = 0.01$. The reason is that the linear approximation method has relative tighter relaxations in smaller radius and is able to prove most properties, which leaves little room for improvement. We also show the number of falsified properties by SIGBAB in the "Falsified" column. Notice that most properties from CIFAR10 5×100 $\epsilon = 0.01$ are unsatisfiable. This explains why number of proved properties are limited in those cases.

Experiments Results for CNNs.

Table 2 presents the experiment results for 6 convolutional neural networks. The network "Fashion 4-5-3" denotes a CNN trained on FashionMNIST dataset with 4 convolution layers, each with 5 filters of size 3×3, and the same for other networks. For experiments on convolutional neural networks, the time limit for each property in SIGBAB is 10 min.

The experiment results show that SIGBAB outperforms other tools in most cases. Although the improvement is not as significant as on fully connected neural networks, it shows that we can improve the verification precision with more time, which cannot be achieved by other linear approximation methods.

In addition, the number of falsified properties by SIGBAB is presented in the "Falsified" column in Table 2. Notice that a large amount of properties are proved to be false. This leaves little room for the improvement in the number of proved properties.

6.3 Experiments on Branching Strategy

We compare our branching strategy NI with BaBSR [2] and Max. BaBSR focuses on the influence of bias terms in linear approximation. It is originally designed for ReLU neural networks, but can be directly applied to sigmoid-like activation functions. The strategy "Max" means maximum range, which takes the neuron with the maximum value range as the branching decision because larger range usually indicates looser relaxation. We did not compare with FSR [14] because it is not compatible with our neuron splitting method.

The experiments are conducted on fully connected neural networks with 5 min time limit. We use different branching strategies in our branch and bound framework and compare the number of proved properties. The results are shown in Table 3. In all cases, NI proves more properties than the other two strategies, which demonstrates the superiority of our branching strategy.

7 Conclusion

In this paper, we present a branch and bound verification framework for neural networks with sigmoid-like activation functions. This framework includes a new neuron splitting method and a new branching strategy. The splitting method allows us to split neurons with sigmoid-like activation functions while ensuring the created subdomains are not worse than the parent domain. The branching strategy improves the performance of the framework by choosing a neuron with the maximum estimated improvement. We implement our framework and evaluate it on a set of neural networks with different architectures. Experiment results demonstrate the effectiveness of our methods. In the future, we would like to investigate branching strategies that are based on neural network architectures to further improve the verification efficiency.

Acknowledgements. This research was sponsored by the National Natural Science Foundation of China under Grant No. 62172019.

References

1. Boopathy, A., Weng, T., Chen, P., Liu, S., Daniel, L.: CNN-Cert: an efficient framework for certifying robustness of convolutional neural networks. In: The Thirty-Third AAAI Conference on Artificial Intelligence, AAAI 2019, pp. 3240–3247. AAAI Press (2019)
2. Bunel, R., Lu, J., Turkaslan, I., Torr, P.H.S., Kohli, P., Kumar, M.P.: Branch and bound for piecewise linear neural network verification. J. Mach. Learn. Res. **21**, 1–39 (2020)

3. Carlini, N., Wagner, D.: Towards evaluating the robustness of neural networks. In: 2017 IEEE Symposium on Security and Privacy (SP), pp. 39–57. IEEE (2017)
4. Chen, Z., Huang, X.: End-to-end learning for lane keeping of self-driving cars. In: 2017 IEEE Intelligent Vehicles Symposium (IV), pp. 1856–1860. IEEE (2017)
5. Ehlers, R.: Formal verification of piece-wise linear feed-forward neural networks. In: D'Souza, D., Narayan Kumar, K. (eds.) ATVA 2017. LNCS, vol. 10482, pp. 269–286. Springer, Cham (2017). https://doi.org/10.1007/978-3-319-68167-2_19
6. Gagandeep, S., et al.: ERAN verification dataset. https://github.com/eth-sri/eran. [online]
7. Goodfellow, I.J., Shlens, J., Szegedy, C.: Explaining and harnessing adversarial examples. In: 3rd International Conference on Learning Representations (ICLR), Conference Track Proceedings (2015)
8. Henriksen, P., Lomuscio, A.R.: Efficient neural network verification via adaptive refinement and adversarial search. In: Giacomo, G.D., et al. (eds.) ECAI 2020. Frontiers in Artificial Intelligence and Applications, vol. 325, pp. 2513–2520. IOS Press (2020)
9. Julian, K.D., Lopez, J., Brush, J.S., Owen, M.P., Kochenderfer, M.J.: Policy compression for aircraft collision avoidance systems. In: 2016 IEEE/AIAA 35th Digital Avionics Systems Conference (DASC), pp. 1–10. IEEE (2016)
10. Kos, J., Fischer, I., Song, D.: Adversarial examples for generative models. In: 2018 IEEE Security and Privacy Workshops (SPW), pp. 36–42. IEEE (2018)
11. LeCun, Y., Bottou, L., Bengio, Y., Haffner, P.: Gradient-based learning applied to document recognition. Proc. IEEE **86**(11), 2278–2324 (1998)
12. Lin, W., et al.: Robustness verification of classification deep neural networks via linear programming. In: IEEE Conference on Computer Vision and Pattern Recognition, CVPR, pp. 11418–11427. Computer Vision Foundation / IEEE (2019)
13. Lomuscio, A., Maganti, L.: An approach to reachability analysis for feed-forward ReLU neural networks (2017). https://arxiv.org/abs/1706.07351
14. Palma, A.D., et al.: Improved branch and bound for neural network verification via Lagrangian decomposition (2021). https://arxiv.org/abs/2104.06718
15. Singh, G., Ganvir, R., Püschel, M., Vechev, M.: Beyond the single neuron convex barrier for neural network certification. In: Advances in Neural Information Processing Systems (NeurIPS), vol. 32, pp. 15072–15083 (2019)
16. Singh, G., Gehr, T., Püschel, M., Vechev, M.: An abstract domain for certifying neural networks. Proc. ACM Programm. Lang. **3**(POPL), 1–30 (2019)
17. Szegedy, C., et al.: Intriguing properties of neural networks. In: 2nd International Conference on Learning Representations (ICLR), Conference Track Proceedings (2014)
18. Wang, S., et al.: Beta-CROWN: efficient bound propagation with per-neuron split constraints for neural network robustness verification. In: Advances in Neural Information Processing Systems (NeurIPS), vol. 34, pp. 29909–29921 (2021)
19. Wong, E., Kolter, J.Z.: Provable defenses against adversarial examples via the convex outer adversarial polytope. In: Proceedings of the 35th International Conference on Machine Learning, ICML 2018, Stockholmsmässan, Stockholm, Sweden, 10–15 July 2018. Proceedings of Machine Learning Research, vol. 80, pp. 5283–5292. PMLR (2018)
20. Wu, Y., Zhang, M.: Tightening robustness verification of convolutional neural networks with fine-grained linear approximation. In: Thirty-Fifth AAAI Conference on Artificial Intelligence, AAAI 2021, pp. 11674–11681. AAAI Press (2021)
21. Xiao, H., Rasul, K., Vollgraf, R.: Fashion-MNIST: a novel image dataset for benchmarking machine learning algorithms. CoRR abs/1708.07747 (2017)

22. Zhang, H., Weng, T.W., Chen, P.Y., Hsieh, C.J., Daniel, L.: Efficient neural network robustness certification with general activation functions. In: Advances in Neural Information Processing Systems (NeurIPS), vol. 31, pp. 4944–4953 (2018)
23. Zhang, Z., Wu, Y., Liu, S., Liu, J., Zhang, M.: Provably tightest linear approximation for robustness verification of sigmoid-like neural networks. In: 37th IEEE/ACM International Conference on Automated Software Engineering, ASE 2022, pp. 1–13. ACM (2022)

Certifying Sequential Consistency of Machine Learning Accelerators

Huan Wu[1]([✉]), Fei Xie[1]([✉]), and Zhenkun Yang[2]([✉])

[1] Portland State University, Portland, OR 97201, USA
{wuhuan,xie}@pdx.edu
[2] Intel Corporation, Hillsboro, OR 97124, USA
zhenkun.yang@intel.com

Abstract. Machine learning accelerators (MLAs) are increasingly important in many applications such as image and video processing, speech recognition, and natural language processing. To achieve the needed performances and power efficiencies, MLAs are highly concurrent. The correctness of MLAs hinges on the concept of sequential consistency, i.e., the concurrent execution of a program by an MLA must be equivalent to a sequential execution of the program. In this paper, we certify the sequential consistency of modular MLAs using theorem proving. We first provide a formalization of the MLAs and define their sequential consistency. After that, we introduce our certification methodology based on inductive theorem proving. Finally, we demonstrate the feasibility of our approach through the analysis of the NVIDIA Deep Learning Accelerator and the Versatile Tensor Accelerator.

Keywords: Machine Learning Accelerator · Sequential Consistency · Theorem Proving

1 Introduction

Advances in machine learning have led to the widespread adoption of deep learning models in various applications, such as image and video processing, voice recognition, and natural language processing. Existing processors often struggle to meet the computational demands of large-scale machine learning models in terms of training time, inference latency, and power consumption. It has motivated the development of Machine learning accelerators (MLAs) that speed up machine learning in training and inference while lowering power consumption, e.g., Google's Tensor Processing Unit [5], Intel's Nervana Neural Network Processor [13], NVIDIA Deep Learning Accelerator (NVDLA) [11] and Versatile Tensor Accelerator (VTA) [10]. To achieve the required performance and power efficiency, MLAs are highly concurrent and utilize design features such as multi-core and pipelining. However, these concurrent designs may lead to potential issues like race conditions, deadlocks, and non-deterministic outputs. Furthermore, in the MLA ecosystem, the software stack generates sequential workloads

Y. Li and S. Tahar (Eds.): ICFEM 2023, LNCS 14308, pp. 156–171, 2023.
https://doi.org/10.1007/978-981-99-7584-6_10

that are compiled and executed by hardware. This transition from sequential software execution to concurrent hardware processing potentially introduces data inconsistencies and race conditions.

Therefore, central to the correctness of MLAs is the concept of sequential consistency, that is, a concurrent execution of a program must be equivalent to a sequential execution of the same program. Sequential consistency essentially maps the executions of an MLA to the executions of its sequential reference design. This greatly reduces the complexities in validating the MLA's design. Properties that can be established on the executions of the sequential reference design also hold on to the executions of the concurrent MLA design if the sequential consistency is maintained.

Two major methods are widely used for design validation: simulation-based validation and formal verification. Simulation-based validation exercises the behavior of a design with a series of tests and compares the test results against expectations. However, exhaustive simulation is prohibitively expensive in time and space, and this method only covers a limited set of execution paths, potentially allowing design errors to go undetected. In contrast, formal verification uses a set of formal models, tools, and techniques to mathematically reason about the design and prove its correctness. Theorem proving is a crucial technique in formal verification. It is powerful, imposes no a priori limit on the design size or complexity, and tends to suffer fewer machine-scaling issues than more automated techniques. Nonetheless, it does often require significant human efforts.

In this paper, we present our approach to certifying the sequential equivalence of modular MLAs using inductive theorem proving. Firstly, we propose a formalization of MLAs by formalizing the instruction-driven accelerator design based on the control data flow graph (CDFG). Then, based on this formalization, we prove the sequential consistency of the MLA through induction on the instruction sequence of a program being executed by MLA. Furthermore, we conduct case studies focusing on VTA and NVDLA, demonstrating the feasibility of our approach. Our contributions can be summarized as follows:

1. Formalization of the modular MLAs and their sequential consistency;
2. An inductive theorem proving method to prove the sequential consistency of modular instruction-driven MLAs;
3. Case studies of applying our method to the VTA and NVDLA designs.

The remainder of this paper is organized as follows. Section 2 provides background information on the CDFG, VTA, and NVDLA. Section 3 focuses on the formalization of the modular MLA and its sequential consistency. In Sect. 4, the proof sketch is presented. The case studies conducted on VTA and NVDLA are discussed in Sect. 5. Section 6 explores relevant prior work in this area. Finally, Sect. 7 concludes the study and discusses future work.

2   Background

2.1   Control Data Flow Graph

CDFG combines the concepts of control flow graphs and data flow graphs to model the behavior of a program. Each instruction in a programming language can be decomposed into a series of primitive operations. This set of operations includes assignments, comparisons, arithmetic, logical operations, classic if-then-else, while-loop, and for-loop structures, etc. The control flow represents the sequence of operations performed in a program, organized into basic blocks with distinct entry and exit points. The data flow represents how data is used and modified within a program.

The state of a CDFG is a list of all variables with their corresponding values. To formally define CDFG, let V_{op} be a set of operations involving variables, and V_{bb} be a set of basic blocks, each consisting of a sequence of operations from V_{op}.

Definition 1 (Control Flow and Data Flow Graphs). *A data flow graph is a directed acyclic graph defined as $G_D \triangleq (V_{op}, E_d)$, where an edge $e \in E_d$ from operation op_1 to op_2 represents a data dependency of op_1 on op_2. Similarly, a control flow graph is denoted as $G_C \triangleq (V_{bb}, E_c)$, where an edge $e \in E_c$ from basic block bb_0 to bb_1 represents a control dependency of bb_0 on bb_1.*

Definition 2 (CDFG). *A CDFG is a triple $G \triangleq (G_D, G_C, R)$, where G_D is the data flow graph, G_C is the control flow graph, and R is a mapping $R : V_{op} \to V_{bb}$ such that $R(V_{op_i}) = V_{bb_j}$ if and only if V_{op_i} occurs in V_{bb_j}.*

2.2 Versatile Tensor Accelerator

VTA [10] is an open-source, customizable hardware platform for accelerating tensor-based computations. Figure 1 gives a high-level overview of the VTA architecture. It comprises four modules: fetch, load, compute, and store. Together,

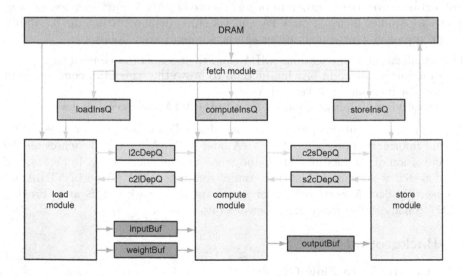

Fig. 1. VTA architecture

these modules define a task pipeline, which enables high compute resource utilization and high memory bandwidth utilization. These modules communicate
via first-in-first-out (FIFO) queues (*l2cDepQ*, *c2lDepQ*, *c2sDepQ*, *s2cDepQ*)
and on-chip shared memories (*inputBuf*, *weightBuf*, *outputBuf*) that act as unidirectional data channels. The memory accesses are synchronized through the
dependency FIFO queues to prevent data hazards.

2.3 NVIDIA Deep Learning Accelerator

NVDLA is an open-source, scalable deep learning accelerator architecture developed by NVIDIA [11]. It has a modular architecture that can be customized
and optimized for specific use cases. The architecture consists of multiple modules working together in a pipeline to perform convolution operations, as shown
in Fig. 2, including Convolution Direct Memory Access (CDMA), Convolution
Buffer (CBUF), Convolution Sequence Controller (CSC), Convolution Multiply-
Accumulate (CMAC), and Convolution Accumulator (CACC). Configuration
Space Bus (CSB) serves as an interface that connects the host system with
NVDLA.

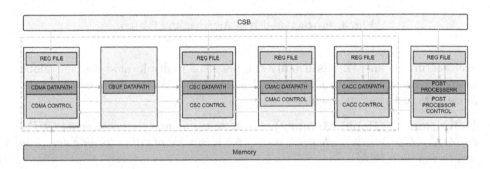

Fig. 2. NVDLA architecture

3 Formalization

To perform verification on an MLA such as VTA, we formalize its design and
the desired property into mathematical specifications for theorem proving. MLAs
are hardware accelerators designed to speed up machine learning tasks, and they
rely on instructions provided by the software to execute these tasks efficiently.
These instructions can encompass various aspects, such as defining the model
layers and operations to be executed, configuring parameters, and managing
data transfers between the host system and the accelerator.

Given the significance of instructions in driving MLA behavior, we propose an
instruction-driven architectural pattern (IAP), as depicted in Fig. 3. Within the
IAP, we define the components involved and establish the necessary constraints.
Furthermore, we specify the specific property of sequential consistency.   The

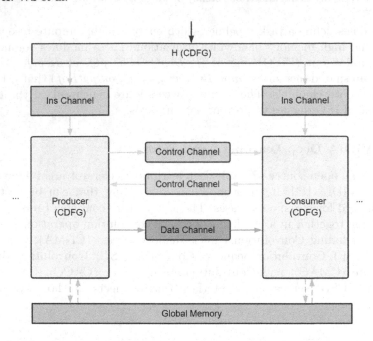

Fig. 3. Instruction-driven Architectural Pattern

architecture of an MLA is usually composed of multiple modules and global memory. Each module can be viewed as a CDFG. All modules can load and store data in the global memory.

Definition 3 (Global Memory). *Let M be the memory between some CDFGs $G_1, G_2, ..., G_N (N \in \mathbb{N})$, where $G_n (0 < n \leq N)$ is capable of either loading data from or storing data to M.*

Data exchange and communication often occur between various modules. To describe these interactions, we introduce the notion of a 'channel'.

Definition 4 (Channel). *A channel, denoted as $c(G_1, G_2)$, represents a dedicated pathway between CDFGs G_1 and G_2 for transmitting data. Each channel is unidirectional, allowing data exchange from source G_1 to destination G_2.*

Channels can be classified based on the transmitted data type: instruction channels for instructions, control channels for control information, and data channels for input and weight data. We now provide a formal definition of the instruction, which is the critical element driving the functionality of MLAs.

Definition 5 (Instruction). *An instruction is defined as $i = \{opcode, memspace, option\}$, where opcode identifies the CDFG to be controlled by this instruction; memspace specifies the address and size of data when the CDFG performs data loading or storing operations; option provides flexibility for accommodating design-specific requirements or custom functionalities.*

Let $(i_n)_{n=1}^N = \{i_1, i_2, ..., i_N | 1 \leq n \leq N, N \in \mathbb{N}\}$ be an instruction sequence, and s_0 be the initial state of an MLA. We formally define the function $isRunToComplete(s_0, (i_n)_{n=1}^N)$ to determine, starting from s_0, whether all instructions $(i_n)_{n=1}^N$ can be executed sequentially and completely, resulting in a final state. The function returns a Boolean value, where the true value indicates that all instructions can be executed completely.

Definition 6 (Valid Instruction Sequence). *A valid instruction sequence is a sequence of instructions $(i_n)_{n=1}^N$ satisfying the following conditions:*

1. *The function $isRunToComplete(s_0, (i_n)_{n=1}^N)$ returns true.*
2. *If there exist i_{k_1} and $i_{k_2}(1 \leq k_1 < k_2 \leq N)$, having the same opcodes and memspace, and no instruction between them has the same opcodes and memspace, and they control the same CDFG to write data in the same space, then there exists $i_{k_3}(k_1 < k_3 < k_2)$ with a different opcode but the same memspace. i_{k_3} controls another CDFG to read the data written by i_{k_1}.*
3. *If multiple instructions that control different CDFGs perform load and store operations on the global memory, their access locations are distinct.*

Now, we formalize the IAP. As depicted in Fig. 3 and defined by $\Gamma \triangleq \{(H, G_1, G_2, ..., G_n), \mathcal{C}, M | n \in \mathbb{N}\}$, the IAP encompasses the following components: H, which represents a special CDFG; G_k $(1 \leq k \leq n)$, representing a CDFG, where n denotes the total number of CDFGs excluding H; $\mathcal{C}$, a set of edges representing channels connecting these CDFGs; and M, the global memory. The IAP satisfies the following conditions:

1. Instruction-driven. The CDFG H is responsible for fetching the sequence of instructions $(i_n)_{n=1}^N$ from the global memory and distributing them to CDFGs $(G_1, G_2, ..., G_n)$ through the channels $c(H, G_1), c(H, G_2), ..., c(H, C_n)$. Each CDFG G_k $(1 \leq k \leq n)$ executes under the control of these instructions.
2. Producer and consumer pattern. If there exists a data channel between two CDFGs G_1 and G_2, a producer and consumer pattern is established between them. There are two control channels, $p2cCtrlC$ and $c2pCtrlC$, and at least a data channel, $dataC$, between G_1 and G_2. An instruction channel, $pInsC$, exists between H and G_1, and another one, $cInsC$ exists between H and G_2.

Algorithm 1. Producer(pInsC, p2cCtrlC, c2pCtrlC, dataC)	Algorithm 2. Consumer(cInsC, p2cCtrlC, c2pCtrlC, dataC)
1: **var** pIns = pInsC.read() 2: **var** memSpace = pIns.memSpace 3: **var** readySig = c2pCtrlC.read() 4: **while** isFalse(readySig) **do** 5: skip dataC.write(data,memSpace) 6: p2cCtrlC.write(validSig)	1: **var** cIns = cInsC.read() 2: **var** memSpace = cIns.memSpace 3: **var** validSig = p2cCtrlC.read() 4: **while** isFalse(validSig) **do** 5: skip 6: dataC.read(data,memSpace) 7: c2pCtrlC.write(readySig)

Algorithm 1 demonstrates the producer mode. Initially, an instruction $pIns$ is read from $pInsC$. To produce and transmit new data to the consumer via $dataC$, it is crucial to check if there is available space for production. This is determined by reading a ready signal from $ctrlC_2$, indicating the consumer's readiness to receive new data. If the consumer is ready to receive the new data, the producer writes data to $dataC$ and sets a valid signal in $ctrlC_1$ to inform the consumer of the availability of consumable data. If the consumer is not ready, the producer waits until space becomes available for production.

Algorithm 2 illustrates the consumer mode. Initially, an instruction $cIns$ is read from $cInsC$. To consume data through $dataC$, it is necessary to check if the producer has produced data in this space. This is determined by reading a valid signal from $ctrlC_1$, indicating the presence of new data from the producer. If new data is available, the consumer reads the data from $dataC$ and sets a ready signal into $ctrlC_2$ to notify the producer of its readiness to receive new data. If the producer has not yet produced new data, the consumer waits until the data becomes available for consumption.

The IAP has two execution semantics: sequential and concurrent.

Definition 7 (Sequential Semantics). *The instruction sequence $(i_n)_{n=1}^N$ distributed by CDFG H is executed in the exact order of $(i_n)_{n=1}^N$. Each step involves the execution of a single instruction.*

Definition 8 (Concurrent Semantics). *The instruction sequence $(i_n)_{n=1}^N$ distributed by CDFG H is executed concurrently, allowing only those instructions that have no dependencies on each other to be executed concurrently in a single step.*

The state of IAP includes the content of the global memory M, channels $\mathcal{C}$, and the state of all CDFGs $H, G_1, G_2, ..., G_n$. We define $SeqM(s, (i_n)_{n=1}^N)$ and $ConM(s, (i_n)_{n=1}^N)$ as the state of the IAP obtained from the initial state s after executing the instruction sequence $(i_n)_{n=1}^N$ sequentially and concurrently, respectively. Now we specify the property of sequential consistency:

Definition 9 (Sequential Consistency). *Given a valid instruction sequence $(i_n)_{n=1}^N$, the initial state s_0, and the IAP Γ, $ConM(s_0, (i_n)_{n=1}^N)$ is equivalent to $SeqM(s_0, (i_n)_{n=1}^N)$.*

4   Proof Sketch

We use an induction based on the instruction sequence to prove sequential consistency. In conjunction with the formalization presented in the previous section, we introduce seven auxiliary theorems that are integral to our proof. Figure 4 shows the relationship between these theorems and their role in establishing sequential consistency. Figure 4(a) depicts that sequential consistency is established based on the core step. This core step is to prove that the state obtained after executing a valid instruction sequence $(i_n)_{n=1}^{k+1}$ concurrently is equivalent to the state obtained by executing the first k instructions concurrently and then executing the last instruction i_{k+1}. The proof process of this core step is detailed in Fig. 4(b).

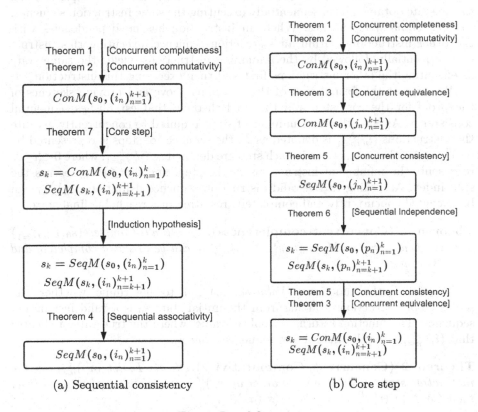

(a) Sequential consistency   (b) Core step

Fig. 4. Proof Overview

To prove the core step, we introduce the following six theorems. (1) *Concurrent completeness.* A valid instruction sequence can be executed concurrently and completely, reaching a reachable final state. Otherwise, there may be deadlocks. (2) *Concurrent commutativity.* The instructions in each concurrent step can be executed in any order without affecting the final state of each step. Concurrency improves performance while preserving correctness. Concurrent completeness and commutativity are the fundamental properties of concurrent execution and are the premise of other theorems. (3) *Concurrent equivalence.* The state resulting from executing a valid instruction sequence concurrently is consistent with the state obtained from concurrently executing the corresponding instruction sequence rearranged in the concurrent step order of execution. Although the instruction order may differ, the final state remains the same. (4) *Sequential associativity.* The state obtained from sequentially executing all instructions is equivalent to executing the preceding instructions sequentially and then the remaining instructions sequentially. It allows instructions to be grouped or associated differently without affecting the final state. (5) *Concurrent consistency.* The state obtained by concurrently executing the instruction sequence, sorted according to the order of concurrent execution steps, is equal to the state obtained from sequentially executing the same instruction sequence. (6) *Sequential independence.* When an instruction has no dependencies with the other instructions within an instruction sequence, executing this instruction sequentially, followed by the remaining instructions, yields the same state as executing the other instructions first and then executing this instruction.

We present the formulation of the theorems above and provide sketches of the proof for the core step and the final theorem that establishes sequential consistency. Assume the total number of steps required to concurrently execute the instructions $(i_n)_{n=1}^N$ is denoted as T, the sequence of steps is represented by $(t_n)_{n=1}^T$, and the instructions in each step are denoted as $(r_n^t)_{n=1}^R$, where $0<R\leq N$ represents the number of instructions in the step, and $0<t\leq T$ represents the step index. According to the valid instruction sequence definition, $(i_n)_{n=1}^N$ can be executed concurrently and completely, resulting in a reachable final state.

Theorem 1 (Concurrent completeness). *If $isRunToComplete(s_0, (i_n)_{n=1}^N)$ is true, then $s_f = ConM(s_0, (i_n)_{n=1}^N))$, $(i_n)_{n=1}^N$ can be executed completely and s_f is reachable.*

We define the function $isValid(s_0, (i_n)_{n=1}^N)$ to determine whether the sequence of instructions starting from the initial state s_0 is a valid instruction sequence. The function returns a Boolean value, where the true value indicates that $(i_n)_{n=1}^N$ is a valid instruction sequence from s_0.

Theorem 2 (Concurrent Commutativity). *$\forall 0<t\leq T$, let $(a_n^t)_{n=1}^R$ be the instruction sequence with random order of $(r_n^t)_{n=1}^R$. If $isValid(s, (r_n^t)_{n=1}^R)$ is true, then $ConM(s, (r_n^t)_{n=1}^R)) = ConM(s, (a_n^t)_{n=1}^R))$.*

Let the instruction sequence $(j_n)_{n=1}^N$ be the collection of concurrently executed instructions $(i_n)_{n=1}^N$ arranged in the order of steps. By the concurrent semantics, the concurrent equivalence theorem follows.

Theorem 3 (Concurrent Equivalence). *If $isValid(s, (i_n)_{n=1}^N)$ is true, then $ConM(s, (i_n)_{n=1}^N)) = ConM(s, (j_n)_{n=1}^N)$.*

Based on the sequential semantics, if there are N instructions, executing N instructions sequentially results in a state consistent with executing the first A instructions $(A<N)$ sequentially and then executing the remaining instructions sequentially.

Theorem 4 (Sequential Associativity). *If $A\leq N$ and $isValid(s, (i_n)_{n=1}^N)$ is true, then $s_a = SeqM(s, (i_n)_{n=1}^A)$, $SeqM(s, (i_n)_{n=1}^N) = SeqM(s_a, (i_n)_{n=A+1}^N)$.*

The concurrent execution of $(j_n)_{n=1}^N$ can be viewed as the sequential execution of the instructions within each concurrent step.

Theorem 5 (Concurrent Consistency). *If* $isValid(s, (i_n)_{n=1}^N)$ *is true, then* $ConM(s, (j_n)_{n=1}^N)) = SeqM(s, (j_n)_{n=1}^N)$.

To determine whether there is a dependency relationship between instruction i_{k_1} and all instructions in $(i_n)_{n=k_2}^{k_3}$, we use the function $dep(i_{k_1}, (i_n)_{n=k_2}^{k_3})$. Here, $k_1 \neq k_2$, $k_1 \neq k_3$, and $k_2 \leq k_3$. The function returns a Boolean value. If the return value is false, it indicates that i_{k_1} and $(i_n)_{n=k_2}^{k_3}$ can run simultaneously without causing a deadlock, thereby implying that i_{k_1} has no dependencies with any of the instructions in $(i_n)_{n=k_2}^{k_3}$. If the first instruction i_1 has no dependence on the remaining instructions in $(i_n)_{n=2}^N$, then i_1 can be scheduled to be executed in the last step without changing the final state obtained by executing $(i_n)_{n=1}^N$ sequentially.

Theorem 6 (Sequential Independence). *If* $N > 1$, $isValid(s, (i_n)_{n=1}^N)$ *is true and* $dep(i_1, (i_n)_{n=2}^N)$ *is false, then* $s_t = SeqM(s, (i_n)_{n=2}^N)$, $SeqM(s, (i_n)_{n=1}^N) = SeqM(s_t, (i_n)_{n=1}^1)$.

Based on the previous theorems, we prove the core step theorem:

Theorem 7 (Core Step). *If* $isValid(s, (i_n)_{n=1}^{N+1})$ *is true, then* $s_1 = ConM(s, (i_n)_{n=1}^N)$, $ConM(s, (i_n)_{n=1}^{N+1})) = SeqM(s_1, (i_n)_{n=N+1}^{N+1})$.

Proof. As shown in Fig. 4(b), based on Theorem 3 (concurrent equivalence), the original instruction sequence $(i_n)_{n=1}^{N+1}$ can be converted to an instruction sequence $(j_n)_{n=1}^{N+1}$ arranged according to the step order of concurrent execution while preserving the final state. Then according to Theorem 5 (concurrent consistency), where $ConM(s, (j_n)_{n=1}^{N+1}) = SeqM(s, (j_n)_{n=1}^{N+1})$, the concurrent execution can be substituted with the sequential execution. Next, let's consider the last instruction i_{N+1} in $(i_n)_{n=1}^{N+1}$, which is also present in $(j_n)_{n=1}^{N+1}$. Assume $(p_n)_{n=1}^N$ is the instruction sequence that preserves the order of the remaining instructions after removing i_{N+1} from $(j_n)_{n=1}^{N+1}$, with $p_{N+1} = i_{N+1}$. Applying Theorem 6 (sequential independence), the sequential execution can be divided into two parts: executing $(p_n)_{n=1}^N$ sequentially and then executing p_{N+1}. Additionally, due to Theorem 5 and Theorem 3, the state obtained from executing $(p_n)_{n=1}^N$ sequentially is the same as that obtained by executing $(i_n)_{n=1}^N$ concurrently.

Finally, we prove the theorem of sequential consistency:

Theorem 8. *if* $isValid(s, (i_n)_{n=1}^N)$ *is true, then*
$$ConM(s, (i_n)_{n=1}^N) = SeqM(s, (i_n)_{n=1}^N).$$

Proof. As shown in Fig. 4(a), by induction on the sequence of instructions.

Base case: if $N = 1$, it is true trivially.

Inductive case: assume $ConM(s, (i_n)_{n=1}^k) = SeqM(s, (i_n)_{n=1}^k)$ holds, we need to prove $ConM(s, (i_n)_{n=1}^{k+1}) = SeqM(s, (i_n)_{n=1}^{k+1})$. Let $s_1 = ConM(s, (j_n)_{n=1}^k)$, since

$ConM(s, (i_n)_{n=1}^{k+1})) = SeqM(s_1, (i_n)_{n=k+1}^{k+1})$ (Theorem 4.8),

$SeqM(s_0, (i_n)_{n=1}^{k+1}) = SeqM(s_1 (i_n)_{n=k+1}^{k+1})$ (Theorem 4.5)

Therefore, this theorem holds.

5   Case Studies

For case studies, we utilize VTA and NVDLA to illustrate how these accelerators align with our previously formalized IAP architectural pattern. When the architectures of MLAs adhere to IAP, the proof process outlined in Sect. 4 can be applied to establish the sequential consistency of the MLA. Our analysis primarily evaluates how well these accelerators adhere to the specifications and characteristics defined in our formalization.

5.1   Case Study 1: VTA

The VTA architecture is an instruction-driven architecture. Each instruction in VTA is encoded with specific fields to indicate the type of operation, control flags, memory addresses, data sizes, and other relevant information. The VTA architecture consists of four functional modules shown in Fig. 1, each designed to handle specific tasks. The fetch module, represented by CDFG H in IAP, retrieves an instruction stream from DRAM and decodes the instructions. It routes the instructions to one of three instruction FIFO queues. Within VTA, there are two sets of producer and consumer models, and between each set, there exist two control FIFO queues and at least a data buffer.

The load and compute modules follow the producer and consumer pattern. There are two control FIFO queues $l2cDepQ$ and $c2lDepQ$, and two buffers $inputBuf$ and $weightBuf$ between the load and compute modules. The data and control communication process between these modules is as follows:

- The load module operates by reading an instruction from the load instruction FIFO queue. Each load instruction contains flags associated with control FIFO queues, indicating dependencies on the compute module. If the flag corresponding to $c2lDepQ$ is set, the load module checks the status of $c2lDepQ$ to determine if it's empty. In the event that $c2lDepQ$ is empty, indicating that the consumer is not ready to receive new data, the load module waits for the compute module to write the control information into $c2lDepQ$. Otherwise, the load module proceeds to load input or weight tensors from DRAM into $weightBuf$ or $inputBuf$. Additionally, if the flag corresponding to the control queue $l2cDepQ$ is set, the load module writes control information into $l2cDepQ$.
- The compute module reads an instruction from the compute instruction FIFO queue. Each compute instruction has flags associated with control FIFO queues, indicating dependencies on the load module. If the flag for $l2cDepQ$ is set, the compute module checks the status of $l2cDepQ$. If $l2cDepQ$ is found to be empty, indicating that there is no new data available for consumption, the compute module waits for the load module to write the control information into $l2cDepQ$. Otherwise, the compute module proceeds to read data from buffers and performs various computations on the input data. Furthermore, if the flag corresponding to the control queue $c2lDepQ$ is set, the compute module writes control information into $c2lDepQ$.

The compute and store models also function following the producer and consumer pattern. Similarly, they have two control FIFO queues, *c2sDepQ* and *s2cDepQ*, and a buffer, *outputBuf*, between them. Similar to the communication process described above between the load and compute modules, both the compute and store modules follow a similar procedure. They start by reading an instruction from their respective instruction queues and then check the corresponding control queue based on the flag specified in the instruction. The compute module stores the computed data in the buffer *outputBuf*, while the store module reads data from *outputBuf* and stores it in DRAM. Finally, they write control information to each control queue based on the flag in the instruction.

The VTA architecture and IAP demonstrate a strong alignment in terms of their instruction-driven nature and the communication between different models. In both cases, there is a module for acquiring instructions and effectively distributing them to their respective instruction channels. Additionally, the communication patterns within VTA exhibit a clear producer-consumer relationship, where data flows from one module to another in a coordinated manner. This correspondence further solidifies the compatibility between the VTA architecture and IAP, reinforcing the effectiveness and accuracy of the formalized model in capturing the essential aspects of the accelerator architecture.

Mechanized Proof in Dafny. We use Dafny [9] as our theorem prover to certify the sequential consistency of VTA. Table 1 summarizes the statistics about our Dafny implementation. The "Formalization" column shows the lines of code, including the formalization of the instruction definition, the valid instruction sequence, VTA, and sequential consistency. The "Proof" column shows lines of code of all proofs we need to certify the sequential consistency. The overall verification time for proof-checking all Dafny code is about 35 min.

Table 1. Code size and verification time

Formalization (LoC)	Proof (LoC)	Verification Time (Min)
1788	14274	35

We illustrate the implementation details with the theorem that ultimately proves sequential consistency. Figure 5 shows the proof of Theorem 8 in Dafny. The input of lemma function *theorem8* includes: the instruction sequence *insSeq1*; the global memory *gsmem*; the buffers *InputB*, *WeightB*, and *OutputB*; and FIFO queues *L2CQ*, *C2LQ*, *C2SQ*, and *S2CQ*. The precondition requires a valid instruction sequence, denoted as *validInsSeq*, while the property to be proven is sequential consistency, represented as *seqConsistency*. The proof follows an induction method based on the input sequence of instructions. The base case involves only one instruction, and the property holds trivially. In the inductive step, sequential consistency is proved by leveraging *theorem 7*, the induction hypothesis *theorem8*, and *theorem4*. Overall, Theorem 8 is certified by Dafny.

```
lemma theorem8(insSeq1: seq<ins>, gsmem:seq<nat>, InputB: seq<int>,
    WeightB: seq<int>, OutputB: seq<int>, L2CQ:seq<nat>, C2LQ:seq<nat>,
    C2SQ:seq<nat>, S2CQ:seq<nat>)
  requires validInsSeq(insSeq1, L2CQ, C2LQ, C2SQ, S2CQ)
  ensures seqConsistency(insSeq1, gsmem, InputB, WeightB, OutputB,
            L2CQ, C2LQ, C2SQ, S2CQ)
{ var length := |insSeq1|;
  if length <= 1
  { assert true;
  }else{
    assert seqConsistency(insSeq1, gsmem, InputB, WeightB, OutputB,
        L2CQ, C2LQ, C2SQ, S2CQ) by {
      theorem7(insSeq1, gsmem, InputB, WeightB, OutputB,
        L2CQ, C2LQ, C2SQ, S2CQ);
      theorem8(insSeq1[..length-1], gsmem, InputB, WeightB, OutputB,
        L2CQ, C2LQ, C2SQ, S2CQ);
      theorem4(insSeq1, gsmem, InputB, WeightB, OutputB,
        L2CQ, C2LQ, C2SQ, S2CQ);}
  }}
```

Fig. 5. Mechanized Proof of Theorem 8 in Dafny

5.2   Case Study 2: NVDLA

NVDLA also follows an instruction-driven architecture. The CSB module facilitates communication between the host system and NVDLA, allowing the host system to send commands and configuration parameters to define the behavior and settings of NVDLA. CSB acts as the CDFG H in IAP and distributes instructions to the register file in various modules within NVDLA. These instructions can include configuration parameters, control commands, memory addresses, and other information for configuring and controlling the accelerator. The specific instructions that CSB distributes depend on the desired operation and functionality of NVDLA, as specified by the host system.

The NVDLA convolution core pipeline consists of 5 stages that work together to perform convolution operations efficiently. The CDMA is responsible for fetching input and weights from memory and storing the data in CBUF, which acts as a buffer for holding the received data. The CSC controls the sequencing of convolution operations. It takes input and weights from CBUF and distributes them to the relevant CMAC units for processing. The CMAC performs the convolutions, receiving CSC data and executing the multiply and accumulate operations. The CACC accumulates the results from CMAC by collecting the partial products generated and combining them to produce the final output. There are two sets of producers and consumers.

The CDMA and CSC follow the producer and consumer pattern. There are two ports, $sc2cdmaC$ and $cdma2scC$, and a buffer CBUF between CDMA and CSC. These ports facilitate the transmission of CBUF's status between CDMA and CSC. The communication process follows these steps:

- The CDMA reads the instruction from the register file to determine the data and weights to be fetched from memory. It checks the status of the CBUF using port $sc2cdmaC$ to determine if there is available space in the CBUF to store the data. If space is available, the CDMA writes the data into the CBUF and sends the current status of the CBUF to the CSC through port $cdma2scC$, informing the CSC about the data availability. If there is no space, the CDMA waits until space becomes available.
- The CSC reads the instruction from the register file to determine which data to retrieve from the CBUF. It checks the status of the CBUF using the port $cdma2scC$ to determine if there is data available in CBUF for processing. If data is available in the CBUF, the CSC reads the data from the CBUF for further processing and sends the updated status of the CBUF to the CDMA through the port $sc2cdmaC$. This status update informs the CDMA about the current status of the CBUF after data retrieval. If no data is available, the CSC waits until data becomes available.

The CSC, CMAC, and CACC also follow the producer and consumer pattern. The CSC serves as the producer model, while the combined CMAC and CACC modules function as the consumer model. There is a data port $sc2macDC$ and a control port $sc2macC$ between the CSC and the CMAC. Similarly, there is a data port $mac2accDC$ and a control port $mac2accC$ between the CMAC and the CACC. Additionally, there is a control port $acc2scC$ between CACC and CSC. The communication process follows these steps:

- The CSC reads the instruction from the register file. It checks the credit signal from the CACC through $acc2scC$ to determine if there is available space for the CACC to perform computations. If space is available, the CSC sends the data to the CMAC through $sc2macDC$ and sends the valid signal to the CMAC through $sc2macC$. If no space is available, the CSC waits until space becomes available.
- The CMAC reads the instruction from the register file. It checks the valid signal from CSC through $sc2macC$ to determine if there is valid data to receive. If there is valid data, the CMAC gets the data and performs the convolution computation, producing intermediate results. The intermediate data is then sent to the CACC through $mac2accDC$, and the valid signal is sent to the CACC through $mac2accC$. If there is no valid data, the CMAC waits until valid data is available.
- The CACC reads the instruction from the register file. It checks the valid signal from CMAC through $mac2accC$ to determine if there is valid data to receive. If there is valid data, the CACC gets the data and performs the accumulated operations. The CACC sends a credit signal to the CSC through $acc2scC$, indicating the space available for the CSC. If there is no valid data, the CACC waits until valid data is available.

The NVDLA architecture aligns with IAP. The CSB plays the role of CDFG H in the pattern. Within NVDLA, there are two sets of producers and consumers. In one set, the CDMA is the producer, while the CSC is the consumer. In the other set, the CSC is the producer, and the CMAC and CACC act as consumers. Using Theorem 7, Theorem 4, and the induction method, we can establish the sequential consistency of NVDLA.

6   Related Work

There have been many approaches to certifying concurrent processor features using theorem proving techniques. For example, Kroening et al. [8] demonstrate the correctness of generating a pipelined microprocessor from an arbitrary sequential specification. They employ the PVS proof assistant [2] to implement this proof. Sawada et al. [14] verify the equivalent of the state transitions of pipelined and non-pipelined machines in the presence of external interrupts. They create a table-based model of pipeline execution and achieve this proof in the ACL2 theorem prover [6]. Damm et al. [3] establish the property that out-of-order execution produces the same final state as a purely sequential machine running the same program. Their proof is based on the semantic model of synchronous transition systems [12]. Vijayaraghavan et al. [15] develop a modular proof structure to prove that the distributed shared-memory hardware system implements sequential consistency. This method is based on labeled transition systems (LTSes) theory [7], and the proof is carried out using the Coq proof assistant [1].

The statement of correctness in our work is sequential consistency; that is, the MLA produces the same final state as the same design with sequential semantics. The formalization follows the style of Communicating Sequential Processes (CSP) [4] and adds features to formalize MLA designs. CDFG is used to realize the process in CSP. Since CDFG contains data and control dependencies, it helps prove the properties of the corresponding sequential design. Moreover, the data communication between models adheres to the producer-consumer pattern, ensuring the proper synchronization and communication between them.

7   Conclusions and Future Work

This paper presents a comprehensive formalization of MLAs and specifies and certifies their sequential consistency, that is, the concurrent execution of a program by the MLA is equivalent to a sequential execution of the program by its sequential reference design. This finding is crucial as it paves the way for simplifying the verification process of concurrent MLAs by leveraging their sequential counterparts. Building upon the foundation of sequential consistency, in future work, we can explore and validate various properties of concurrent MLAs, such as correctness, optimizations, resource utilization, or novel execution models.

Acknowledgment. This research is partially supported by a gift from Intel Corporation.

References

1. Bertot, Y., Castéran, P.: Interactive Theorem Proving and Program Development: Coq'Art: the Calculus of Inductive Constructions. Springer, Heidelberg (2013). https://doi.org/10.1007/978-3-662-07964-5
2. Cyrluk, D., Rajan, S., Shankar, N., Srivas, M.K.: Effective theorem proving for hardware verification. In: Kumar, R., Kropf, T. (eds.) TPCD 1994. LNCS, vol. 901, pp. 203–222. Springer, Heidelberg (1995). https://doi.org/10.1007/3-540-59047-1_50
3. Damm, W., Pnueli, A.: Verifying out-of-order executions. In: Advances in Hardware Design and Verification. IAICT, pp. 23–47. Springer, Boston, MA (1997). https://doi.org/10.1007/978-0-387-35190-2_3
4. Hoare, C.A.R.: Communicating sequential processes. Commun. ACM **21**(8), 666–677 (1978)
5. Jouppi, N.P., et al.: In-datacenter performance analysis of a tensor processing unit. In: Proceedings of the 44th Annual International Symposium on Computer Architecture, pp. 1–12 (2017)
6. Kaufmann, M., Moore, J.S.: ACL2: an industrial strength version of Nqthm. In: Proceedings of 11th Annual Conference on Computer Assurance. COMPASS 1996, pp. 23–34. IEEE (1996)
7. Keller, R.M.: Formal verification of parallel programs. Commun. ACM **19**(7), 371–384 (1976)
8. Kroening, D., Paul, W.J., Mueller, S.M.: Proving the correctness of pipelined micro-architectures. In: MBMV, pp. 89–98 (2000)
9. Leino, K.R.M.: Dafny: an automatic program verifier for functional correctness. In: Clarke, E.M., Voronkov, A. (eds.) LPAR 2010. LNCS (LNAI), vol. 6355, pp. 348–370. Springer, Heidelberg (2010). https://doi.org/10.1007/978-3-642-17511-4_20
10. Moreau, T., et al.: A hardware-software blueprint for flexible deep learning specialization. IEEE Micro **39**(5), 8–16 (2019)
11. Nvidia: Nvidia deep learning accelerator (2018). http://nvdla.org/primer.html
12. Pnueli, A., Shankar, N., Singerman, E.: Fair synchronous transition systems and their liveness proofs. In: Ravn, A.P., Rischel, H. (eds.) FTRTFT 1998. LNCS, vol. 1486, pp. 198–209. Springer, Heidelberg (1998). https://doi.org/10.1007/BFb0055348
13. Rao, N., et al.: Intel Nervana: a next-generation neural network processor. In: Proceedings of the 2017 IEEE Hot Chips Symposium on High Performance Chips (HOTCHIPS), pp. 1–28. IEEE, Cupertino, CA, USA, August 2017
14. Sawada, J., Hunt, W.A. Jr.: Processor verification with precise exceptions and speculative execution. In: CAV, vol. 98, pp. 135–146 (1998)
15. Vijayaraghavan, M., Chlipala, A., Dave, N.: Modular deductive verification of multiprocessor hardware designs. In: Kroening, D., Păsăreanu, C. (eds.) Computer Aided Verification. CAV 2015. LNCS, San Francisco, CA, USA, July 18–24, 2015, Proceedings, Part II 27, vol. 9207, pp. 109–127. Springer, Cham (2015). https://doi.org/10.1007/978-3-319-21668-3_7

Guided Integration of Formal Verification in Assurance Cases

Irfan Sljivo[✉], Ewen Denney, and Jonathan Menzies

KBR/NASA Ames Research Center, Moffett Field, CA, USA
{irfan.sljivo,ewen.denney,jonathan.j.menzies}@nasa.gov

Abstract. Assurance cases are being increasingly acknowledged as a way to build trust in complex systems with autonomous capabilities. An assurance case is a comprehensive, defensible, and valid justification that a system will function as intended for a specific mission and operating environment. Formal verification is often reserved for the most critical components of such systems. However, formal verification tools are themselves often complex, and their usage is subject to many constraints and contextual dependencies. This can raise challenges both for performing the verification and reflecting the verification results appropriately in the assurance case, especially for non-expert users of the formal tool.

To address these challenges, we present a tool-supported methodology for integrating formal verification into an assurance case by capturing key verification method information in a rigorously constructed assurance case. In particular, we capture the tool specifications in terms of its inputs, outputs, and assurance constraints as assumptions over inputs and guarantees provided over its outputs. The tool specifications are parametrized over the inputs and outputs to both guide the intended application of the tool, and to check that the tool has been applied following the stated assumptions and that the guarantees hold. We define a generic tool assurance argument pattern that enables integration of the verification in the assurance case through custom refinement and automated instantiation for each tool use. We demonstrate our methodology on two formal verification tools and their applications to the verification of neural network properties for the aircraft domain.

Keywords: Assurance Cases · Formal Verification · Tool Assurance

1 Introduction

Even though formal tools have been shown to be effective at finding defects in safety-critical systems, their adoption in industry is much slower than the pace of research in formal verification [21]. One of the main reasons for this is being able to assure trustworthiness of the tools in terms of their design, implementation and correct usage. The issue from the developer side is the prescriptive nature of the tool qualification standards and a lack of assurance understanding. The issue from the user side is the lack of the tool understanding due to its complexity, which hinders integration with non-formal parts of the system development process. The issue for the certification experts of the formal tool qualification is the lack of expertise in the formal method qualification.

Standards such as DO-333 [19] offer a process for qualifying a formal tool. DO-333 requires evidence that any formal method to be used will never provide unwarranted confidence. However, constructing such evidence and following the prescriptive requirements can make it difficult for tools that originate in a research environment to achieve qualification [21]. Even when the tool qualification is achieved, it does not help the user to integrate the results with the non-formal parts of the development process, nor does it assist the certification experts to review the tool qualification and accept its usage in a safety-critical setting.

Assurance cases are increasingly acknowledged as a way to build trust in complex systems [2]. An assurance case is a comprehensive, defensible, and valid justification that a system will function as intended for a specific mission and operating environment [8]. In this paper, we propose to complement the prescriptive tool qualification with assurance cases in order to ease adoption of formal methods in critical applications. We present a tool-supported methodology that assists both the formal tool developer to prepare the formal tool for assurance in advance, and the user applying a formal tool to safely use and assure the tool results. The result of following the proposed methodology is an assurance case argument that clearly communicates the tool trustworthiness. We demonstrate the proposed methodology in two case studies performed using different formal verification tools. Finally, we describe the tool support for our methodology in the Assurance Case Automation Toolset (AdvoCATE) [8].

In prior work, assurance case arguments have been used to automatically integrate output from a formal verification tool [3,7,9,12], though the focus there was on converting individual reasoning steps and assumptions from verification artifacts into corresponding fragments of an assurance case, rather than assembling results from multiple tools. [5] describes a case study in constructing an assurance case based on verifications from a set of verification tools. In this work, in contrast, we provide a systematic methodology that guides both tool developers and users to assure tools and their application, while constructing an assurance case. We do not focus on integration of a particular formal verification tool in an assurance case, but provide a generic methodology that could be used for any formal verification tool. Considering the approach [20] for tool qualification of a model checker according to DO-333, we do not aim to replace the prescribed tool qualification process, but rather to complement it and offer ways to ease the issues that different stakeholders of formal tool assurance have.

The Evidential Tool Bus (ETB) [6] provides a formal way for tools to collaborate in creation and management of evidence, out of which claims can be derived for their inclusion in an assurance case. While the ETB focuses on evidence, the Structured Assurance Case Metamodel (SACM) [18] defines a metamodel covering different assurance aspects with the aim of supporting structured creation and reuse of assurance cases across different tools. In contrast, in this work, we provide a methodology that integrates not only input and output evidence of tools, but confidence in the tools and their uses as well. Both of these concepts are complementary with the AdvoCATE methodology and the proposed methodology for integration of formal verification in assurance cases.

Though not directly addressing assurance cases, there have been several attempts to create general frameworks for tools. Wildmoser et al. [22] give a model of tool chains and a confidence model, incorporating notions of tool fault, error, and failure (based on ISO 26262), which allows them to generate review checklists and evaluation reports, and compute tool confidence levels. The SAMATE (Software Assurance Metrics and Tool Evaluation) project from NIST [17] has created a tool taxonomy covering concepts such as static analysis tools, functionalities, and weaknesses.

2   Background

2.1   AdvoCATE

AdvoCATE (Assurance Case Automation Toolset [8]) is a tool that supports the development and management of safety assurance cases. A safety assurance case comprises all the artifacts that are created during system development and verification that are needed to assure that the system is acceptably safe for its intended operation. Assurance cases are often represented and documented in the form of a graphical argument that presents how the system safety goals have been achieved and supported by the various items of *evidence*, such as test results, simulations, and formal verifications. AdvoCATE supports a range of notations and modeling formalisms, including Goal Structuring Notation (GSN) [1] to document the safety cases. To enable automation of the development and management of assurance cases, AdvoCATE implements an assurance metamodel that allows all the artifacts relevant from the safety assurance perspective can be explicitly defined and their relations captured.

AdvoCATE Assurance Methodology. The high level AdvoCATE assurance methodology is presented in Fig. 1. The rounded rectangles represent the different activities and arrows the data flow. Briefly, the AdvoCATE assurance methodology starts by defining the physical decomposition of the system in terms of its components and their failure modes, followed by the functional decomposition of the system in terms of the system functions and their deviations. Each system function captures intended (logical) behavior of the system based on a set of functional requirements. Then, hazard analysis is performed based on the system definition and recorded in the *hazard log*. Each hazard, along with its causes, consequences, and their mitigations, is depicted in a *bow tie diagram* that is used for risk modelling and control. The composition of all bow tie diagrams comprises the *safety architecture* of the system. Information from the safety architecture and evidence artefacts is used to construct structured arguments presenting the system assurance rationale.

AdvoCATE Metamodel. Figure 2 presents an excerpt of the AdvoCATE metamodel, focusing on the Requirements, Evidence and Tools Logs. System requirements are defined as a part of mitigation planning and are stored in the

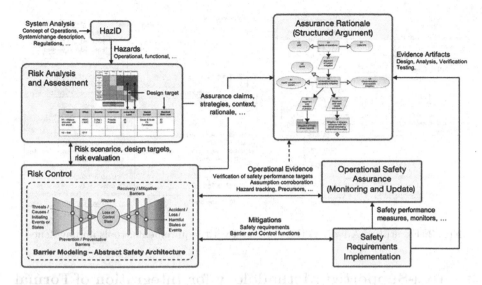

Fig. 1. Overview of the AdvoCATE assurance methodology [10]

Requirements Log. Each requirement has a *verification method*, which can be a *tool* that indicates the way the requirement is to be verified, and a *verification allocation* that represents the result of the verification method (e.g., tool output), and serves as evidence artifact that verifies the requirement.

The *Evidence Log* records all the evidence artifacts (evidence for short) used in the assurance case, as well as any evidence that is planned for use in future. Evidence can be designated as pending, to indicate that it is anticipated that it will eventually be obtained. Self-contained evidence artifacts will have no dependencies on other evidence, but often evidence is created from other evidence artifacts using some tool, e.g., simulation results are created using a simulator from a model and an initial configuration, and these relations are recorded.

The *Tools Log* is used to record external tools which are used to create evidence artifacts. The tools and evidence logs are interrelated and capture the chain of dependencies through which evidence is constructed, along with the supporting assumptions. Tools are characterized in terms of their inputs and outputs, each of which is either an evidence artifact or value of primitive type. *Tool specifications* give assumptions on the inputs and guarantees on the outputs. A *tool use* represents an application of the tool to concrete evidence artifacts.

Structured Assurance Arguments. In this work, we use GSN [1] to represent assurance arguments. Figure 4 shows a simple argument pattern on the left and the core GSN elements used in this paper on the right. An argument pattern represents a pattern of reusable reasoning, which contains variables in its nodes that need to be instantiated, e.g., *Guarantee1* and *Guarantee2* being two variables used in the top node in Fig. 4. By instantiating all the variables within an argument pattern, we create arguments that aim to establish the top-level claim by supporting it with other claims, evidence and contextual information.

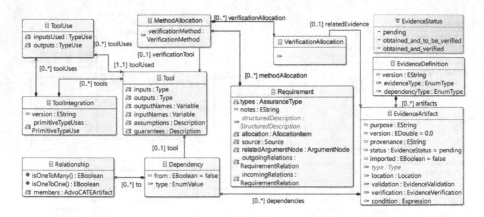

Fig. 2. Excerpt of AdvoCATE metamodel with requirements, tools and evidence

3   Tool-Supported Methodology for Integration of Formal Verification in Assurance Cases

In this section, we present our methodology for integration of formal verification in assurance cases. We also describe the tool support in AdvoCATE.

3.1   Methodology

When integrating formal verification into an assurance case, it is not only that the result of verification is being integrated, but also the assurance that communicates confidence in the tool and its result. Assuring that the tool methodology is sound and that it has been implemented correctly is independent of a particular tool application and is reusable whenever the tool is used. We refer to this setting independent of a specific application as *out-of-context* (similar to the safety element out-of-context notion used in ISO 26262 [15]). In contrast, the *in-context* setting represents the development and assurance of a specific system, including application of a verification tool for that system.

An overview of the methodology is shown in Fig. 3. The out-of-context steps are applied in advance and are generally performed just once for each tool. The in-context steps are performed every time a tool is used in the context of a specific system, and they aim at assuring the specific tool application, building on the tool assurance information that is prepared in advance. Out of context of a particular application, we perform the following steps:

Step 1: Create the tool assurance case. This step aims to capture the reusable tool trustworthiness assurance argument. It can be supported by a certificate of qualification, verification report, or an assurance case for the tool, itself. To prepare a tool assurance case, we follow these steps:

– identify the tool functions and create the tool functional decomposition,

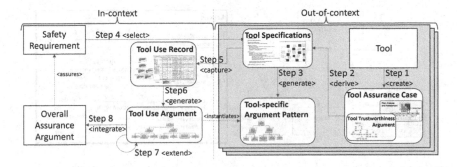

Fig. 3. Overview of the proposed verification tool assurance methodology

- define deviations for each function,
- perform hazard analysis based on the functional decomposition,
- identify hazards mitigated by the tool and those that remain,
- create an assurance argument describing all the hazards that have been mitigated and provide evidence to support the mitigation means.

Step 2: Derive the tool specifications. In this step we capture the tool specifications in terms of an informal tool description, its input and output types, and constraints over those input/output types as assumptions over inputs, and guarantees expressed as relations between inputs and outputs. The main challenge with creating tool specifications is identifying all the prerequisites that need to hold to ensure the result is trustworthy. To this end, we use the systematic hazard analysis of the tool from *Step 1* to identify all the remaining conditions not covered by the internal mitigation mechanisms that the user should satisfy in order to produce a trustworthy result. These conditions are captured in the tool assumptions. The assumptions and guarantees are parametrized using variables of specific type for each input and output, so that once the tool is applied, these variables are instantiated so that the assumptions and guarantees refer to the concrete evidence artefacts. Considering that a single verification tool can often be used in different use cases, e.g., VerifAI [11] can be used for testing and training of NNs, we define one tool specification for each verification tool use case. This is because different guarantees are offered by the tool in different use cases, and also different assumptions need to be met for those guarantees to hold.

Step 3: Generate the tool assurance argument pattern. In this step, we refine the generic assurance argument pattern (Fig. 4) for the specific tool based on its tool specifications. This generic assurance pattern uses the tool specification guarantees as the top assurance claim and uses support from two assurance strategies, the satisfaction of the tool specification assumptions and the trustworthiness of the tool. This pattern communicates that the guarantees of the tool hold if all of the tool assumptions are met and the tool justifications are trustworthy. For each tool specification, we refine this generic pattern to create a more tool-specific argument pattern. The parametrized tool specifica-

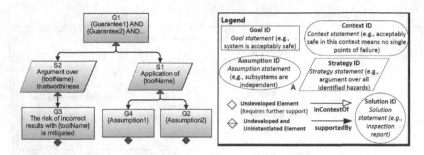

Fig. 4. Generic tool assurance pattern and a legend of the core GSN elements

tion guarantees become the top assurance claim, while each parametrized tool specifications assumption is transformed into an assurance claim needing further support under the S1 strategy. The G3 goal deals with the tool assurance justifications and includes the evidence specified in the first step of this methodology.

In context of a particular application and assurance case, we perform the following steps that guide the application and integration of the verification tool in the assurance case:

Step 4: Select the verification method. Given a library of predefined verification tool specifications, we can select which verification tool will be used to verify the corresponding system requirement. By checking the offered tool guarantees, we can evaluate whether the tool can be used to support the requirement.

Step 5: Capture the tool application record. Before applying a verification tool, we need to prepare and record the input evidence artefacts according to the tool specifications, and make sure that all the assumptions over those inputs are met. We record the outputs from the tool as evidence artefacts. We allocate this output to the corresponding requirement based on *Step 4.*

Step 6: Generate the tool assurance argument. Once a tool application is recorded, we use that information to instantiate the corresponding tool-specific assurance pattern. The resulting assurance argument gives us the top assurance claim that can be used to support higher-level claims in terms of requirements and hazards, and it leaves the assumption-related claims undeveloped, to indicate that evidence is needed to assure those claims.

Step 7: Extend the tool assurance argument. In this step, we further extend the instantiated argument to support all the undeveloped goals and provide contextual information relevant for the particular tool application.

Step 8: Integrate the assurance argument. Once the tool application assurance argument is finalized, it can be integrated in the overall assurance argument to support the requirements associated with the verification tool.

3.2 Tool Support in AdvoCATE

The methodology for integrating formal verification results into an assurance case extends the AdvoCATE methodology presented in Sect. 2.1. In particular, it provides greater support for planning, performing, and documenting requirement verification in an assurance case. In the reminder of the section, we will highlight the tool support in AdvoCATE for each step of the methodology.

To prepare a tool for future application and integration in an assurance case, a subset of the AdvoCATE assurance methodology can be used to perform *Step 1* and assure trustworthiness in each tool. To support *Step 2*, we have extended the tool specifications to include assumptions over its inputs and guarantees over its inputs and outputs, as shown in Fig. 2. We have embedded the basic tool assurance pattern in AdvoCATE to support *Step 3* and enable automated refinement of tool-specific argument patterns using the tool specification.

As a part of creating an assurance case for a specific system in AdvoCATE, we create Tools log where we include Tool Specifications of different verification tools that we may use to support safety requirements. To support *Step 5* and verification method selection, we connect Requirements and tools from the tools log in AdvoCATE and allow the user to indicate which tool is planned for verification of the specific requirement. Performing the verification and recording the Tool Use as part of *Step 5* is currently a manual process in AdvoCATE where for each tool application we record which inputs evidence have been used to run the tool and which output evidence have been obtained. To support *Step 6*, for each tool use, we enabled automated instantiation of the tool-specific assurance pattern. When a chain of tools is specified in the tools log, and output evidence from one tool is used to perform verification with another tool, AdvoCATE supports recursive instantiation of tool use assurance arguments to generate a single argument that integrates information from all the tools in the verification chain. The assurance argument editor in AdvoCATE supports *Steps 7 and 8*, where the generated tool argument can be manually refined and inserted into a specific place in an overall system argument.

4 Application Examples

In this section, we demonstrate our methodology on the application of two formal verification tools to the verification of neural network (NN) properties.

4.1 Application Example 1: Venus for Object Detection

Venus [4] is a verification toolkit for ReLU-based feed-forward NNs. Given a feed-forward NN, Venus answers the verification problem whether for every input within a linearly definable set the output is always contained within some other linearly definable set. To optimize the verification, Venus decomposes the verification problem into smaller, more manageable tasks so that they can be executed in parallel. Each subproblem is encoded as a Mixed Integer Linear Program

```
function VENUS "Venus verification engine" system {deviations [value_inverted]
    function splitter "Input domain splitter" system {deviations [improper_value,values_added,values_ommitted]}
    function MILP_encoder "MILP Encoder using big-M method" system {deviations [improper_value]}
    function MILP_solver "Venus MILP solver" system {deviations [value_inverted]
        function GUROBI "GUROBI MILP solver" system {deviations [value_inverted]}
        function dependency_analyzer "Dependency Analyzer" system {deviations [values_added,values_ommitted]}
    }
    function integrator "Results integrator" system {deviations [values_ommitted]}
}
```

Fig. 5. Venus functional decomposition

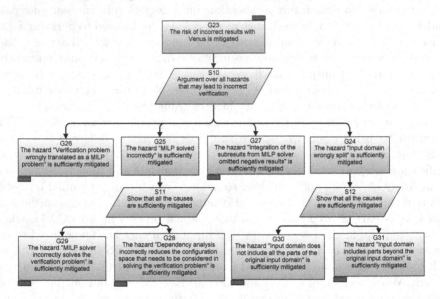

Fig. 6. A portion of the Venus assurance argument

(MILP). An external MILP solver is called to solve each subproblem independently. Due to the high dimensionality of inputs that the MILP solver would have to handle, Venus implements a dependency analyzer as a callback function supplied to the MILP solver, to reduce the dimensionality of inputs that need to be verified. An example of a local robustness verification problem with Venus is verifying a NN image classifier for open object detection. Answering the local robustness problem requires establishing whether the NN correctly classifies all perturbations of the input image within a specific perturbation radius. In the reminder of this section, we first present the out-of-context assurance of Venus, and then we present the assurance of its application on a concrete system.

Preparing the Out-of-Context Assurance for Venus

Step 1: Create the tool assurance case. To assure the trustworthiness of Venus, we have developed an assurance case to capture its internal structure, risks, and how these risks are mitigated. We have represented the internal structure of Venus using a hierarchical functional decomposition in AdvoCATE, consisting of input domain splitter, MILP encoder, MILP solver, dependency analyzer, and results

```
tool A2 {
    description "DataSetVerification"
    inputs [
        input_CNN : ev.EvidenceType.mnist_NN ,
        perturbation_radius : real ,
        image_dataset : ev.EvidenceType.ImageDataSet ,
        selection_count : int]
    assumptions [
        { image_dataset } + " is representative of the operational context " ,
        "Images in " + { image_dataset } + " are correctly classified" ,
        "Selection of " + { selection_count } + " images for verification is acceptable
            compared to the size of the " + { image_dataset } ,
        { selection_count } + " selected images correctly represent " + { image_dataset } ,
        "The input 1EC " + { input_CNN } + " is a feed-forward ReLU neural network" ,
        "Image perturbations within the defined radius" + { perturbation_radius } + " represent
            the likely perturbations for the given operational context"]
    outputs [
        results_dataset : ev.EvidenceType.venus_dataset_results ,
        robustness_level : real]
    guarantees [
        { input_CNN } + " is " + { robustness_level } + "% robust with respect to the perturbation
        radius " + { perturbation_radius } + " in the operational context defined by " + { image_dataset }]
}
```

Fig. 7. Venus tool specifications for verification of an object detection ReLU NN

integrator (Fig. 5). Then we performed hazard analysis and identified hazards as functional deviations, e.g., the input domain splitter can split the domain to exclude certain parts or include parts that are not in the initial domain specification. We have used the hazard analysis results to identify the mitigated hazards and those that are yet to be mitigated. A portion of the assurance argument highlighting the mitigated hazards is shown in Fig. 6.

Step 2: Derive the tool specifications. We focus on deriving the tool specifications for verifying an image classifier for object detection system with Venus. While Venus answers the verification problem for a single image serialized in the pickle format, the verification use case here is to work on a set of images representing the operational domain and determine the robustness level of the NN for that data-set. We define the Venus tool specification for verifying the image data-set in Fig. 7. We derived the tool specifications based on the Venus assurance case from *Step 1*. For example, to use the Venus guarantee and its calculated robustness level to support satisfaction of a requirement or a hazard, we need to make sure that the data-set on which the verification is performed is representative of the operating environment of the system, and if the entire data-set has not been verified, we need to make sure that the subset of selected images for verification is representative of the initial data-set. Such assurance aspects are captured in the Venus tool assumptions, while the guarantee constrains the achieved robustness level to the specific perturbation radius and image data-set.

Step 3: Generate the tool assurance argument pattern. Given the generic tool assurance pattern in Fig. 4, AdvoCATE automatically generates a Venus-specific version of that pattern by including the Venus tool specification assumptions and guarantees, as shown in Fig. 8. We further extend the pattern with additional contextual information (nodes C1 and C2 in Fig. 8) to clarify the notions of what robustness means for the top assurance claim.

Assurance of the Venus Application for Object Detection

In this section, we analyse the application of Venus for verification of an object detection NN for the aircraft domain [16]. The Venus developers specified the verification problem as a local robustness problem of the provided NN. For a correctly classified image, the local robustness problem is to check that the NN returns the same result for all the images within a specified perturbation radius. Venus was run for a set of correctly classified images from the provided data-set. Each image was verified for different perturbation radii, to determine how robust the NN is for different perturbation radii. For each of the images and perturbation radii, the NN and the verification problem are encoded as a MILP, and then solved using splitting and dependency optimization. The results showed that for a small perturbation radius, the NN was robust for all the images. Moreover, as the radius increases, the robustness decreases, and more misclassifications are detected. In the reminder of the section, we follow the in-context steps for integrating the Venus application in an overall assurance case. We do not present the overall assurance case here due to space constraints, but we describe the portions relevant for Venus integration.

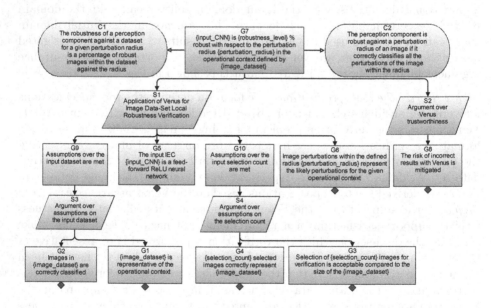

Fig. 8. Venus-specific tool assurance pattern

Step 4: Select the verification method. The aircraft level hazard analysis identified ways in which the failures of the object detection NN could contribute to different hazards. For example, misclassification of an object, or failure to detect one, can lead to a hazard *loss of separation*, where the aircraft could get closer than it should to another object, which may lead to collision. Some causes that may lead to this involve internal failures of the NN, but also conditions regarding the inputs into the NN, such as distorted images. Images can be distorted for a number of reasons, ranging from dirty camera lens, environmental conditions, to malicious actors. The level of risk associated with each of those different hazardous situations leads to requirements for how robust the NN should be to potential image distortions in order to reduce the risk of those hazards to acceptable levels. For those requirements, we can match the Venus tool specification guarantee as an assurance claim that could be used to support them, and we select Venus as a verification method for those requirements.

ID	Tool	Toolset	Input Types	Inputs	Output Types	Outputs
AU2	A2: DataSetVerification	TS1: Venus toolkit	mnist_NN	input_CNN: Input cnn	venus_dataset_results	venus_results-4: venus_results_1.0-4
			real	PTU2: 0.0001		
			ImageDataSet	Image_dataset: Original image dataset	real	PTU8: 100
			int	PTU90: 20		
AU3	A2: DataSetVerification	TS1: Venus toolkit	mnist_NN	input_CNN: Input cnn	venus_dataset_results	venus_results-3: venus_results_1.0-3
			real	PTU3: 0.001		
			ImageDataSet	Image_dataset: Original image dataset	real	PTU9: 30
			int	PTU91: 20		
AU4	A2: DataSetVerification	TS1: Venus toolkit	mnist_NN	input_CNN: Input cnn	venus_dataset_results	venus_results-2: venus_results_1.0-2
			real	PTU4: 0.01		
			ImageDataSet	Image_dataset: Original image dataset	real	PTU10: 0
			int	PTU92: 20		

Fig. 9. Venus data-set verification tool applications captured in AdvoCATE

Step 5: Capture the tool application record. Figure 9 shows several different applications of Venus for data-set verification recorded in the AdvoCATE tools log. Verification was performed on 20 images from the original image data-set for three different perturbation radii 0.0001, 0.001 and 0.01. The results showed that for the smallest perturbation radius 0.0001, the provided input NN was 100% robust, while the robustness level was 30% for perturbation radius 0.001. The NN was not robust for any of the images for the perturbation radius 0.01.

Step 6: Generate the tool assurance argument. The Venus-specific assurance pattern is instantiated with tool data to give the argument shown in Fig. 10. We show here the fragment for the verification performed with the 0.001 perturbation radius.

Step 7: Extend the tool assurance argument. We extend the argument with additional contextual information regarding the actual values of the perturbation radius and the achieved robustness level. The assumption-specific assurance claims remain undeveloped, indicating that they should be further supported with evidence. Some of them can be simply supported by reviews, e.g., making sure the type of the input NN is correct, while for others, like the process of selecting images from the data-set or the representatives of the data-set itself, may require additional assurances.

Step 8: Integrate the assurance argument. Considering the different requirements as to how robust should the object detection NN be for likely image distortions for the different causes, we can now use this argument fragment to support safety requirements addressing those causes where the likely perturbation radius is 0.001, assuming that the achieved 30% robustness level meets the corresponding hazard's risk targets. For other causes with different likely perturbation radii, arguments can be generated for the other Venus uses and further tailored in support of their corresponding requirements.

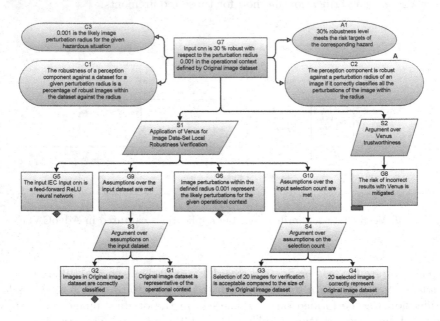

Fig. 10. Instantiated Venus assurance argument

4.2   Application Example 2: VerifAI for NN Testing

The VerifAI toolkit [11] implements a wide suite of verification tasks that together constitute a methodology for the reliable design of systems that include machine learning (ML) components. VerifAI uses an environment model specified in Scenic [14] to generate test vectors, i.e., concrete test scenes for simulation. Each Scenic feature has an assigned value based on a distribution assigned in the corresponding Scenic model. VerifAI can be coupled with different simulators. The simulator should include a model of the system, with the controller and the ML component, as well as an environmental model that is consistent with the Scenic specification. VerifAI supports monitoring metric temporal logic (MTL) properties by evaluating the property with respect to each simulation run. In the reminder of this section, we first present the out-of-context assurance of VerifAI, and then we present the assurance of its application on a concrete system.

Preparing the Out-of-Context Assurance for VerifAI

Step 1: Create the tool assurance case. Just as for Venus in Sect. 4.1, we developed an assurance case for VerifAI. We created a functional decomposition of VerifAI for NN testing consisting of the following functions: abstract feature space modelling, test case generation, X-Plane simulation, temporal logic falsification, and counterexample analysis. Then we performed hazard analysis and allocated the identified hazards to the different functions, e.g., abstract feature space modelling could omit an important feature for testing the NN, or it could model a feature differently from how it is implemented in the simulator. Based on the results of the analysis, we identified the assurance constraints that should be made on the input into the VerifAI testing to guarantee the result with sufficient confidence. We omit the VerifAI assurance case here due to space constraints.

```
tool T1 {
    description "VerifAI NN testing with X-Plane"
    inputs [
        input_NN : ev.EvidenceType.perception_NN ,
        scenic_model : ev.EvidenceType.scenic_specification ,
        runway_model : ev.EvidenceType.environment_xplane_specification ,
        plane_controller : ev.EvidenceType.controller ,
        nr_test_samples : int ,
        sim_duration : ev.EvidenceType.time ,
        property : ev.EvidenceType.formal_MTL_specification]
    assumptions [
        { scenic_model } + " is consistent with " + { runway_model } ,
        { scenic_model } + " correctly represents the operational environment in which " + { input_NN } + " is intended to operate" ,
        { runway_model } + " correctly represents the operational environment in which " + { input_NN } + " is intended to operate" ,
        { nr_test_samples } + " generated test cases is adequate to achieve sufficient test space coverage" ,
        { plane_controller } + " correctly models the plane dynamics in which " + { input_NN } + " is intended to operate" ,
        "Simulation duration of " + { sim_duration } + " per test case is representative of the operational situation in which " +
        { input_NN } + " is intended to operate" ,
        "The MTL formula " + { property } + " correctly formalizes the corresponding requirement"]
    outputs [
        success_rate : real ,
        unsafe_table_set :ev.EvidenceType.formal_verification_results]
    guarantees [
        { input_NN } + " meets the formalized requirement " + { property } + "at " + { success_rate } + "% in the simulated environment"]
}
```

Fig. 11. VerifAI tool specifications for NN testing

Step 2: Derive the tool specifications. VerifAI can be used for multiple use cases, including NN testing and (re)training. We focus on the tool specifications for testing of a NN with the X-Plane simulator (Fig. 11). The testing with VerifAI relies on a Scenic model that captures the testing environment from which the test cases are generated. Each test case is simulated for the same amount of time using the same inputs, including models of the NN, the runway, and the airplane controller. The results of each simulation are exported as a trace, and falsification is performed on each trace. Based on the results of *Step 1*, we captured some of the assumptions on the VerifAI inputs. For example, it is important to make sure that the features captured in the Scenic model are consistent with the other models of the environment, such as the runway model. The assurance guarantee that we can claim based on the VerifAI testing results is that the input NN meets the formalized property at the resulting success rate in the simulated environment.

Step 3: Generate the tool assurance argument pattern. The refined tool assurance pattern specific to VerifAI NN testing is shown in Fig. 12. We include the identified guarantees and assumptions and refine the pattern further to group the assumptions over environment models and include additional contexts.

Assurance of the VerifAI Application for Testing a NN

In this section, we analyse the application of VerifAI for testing a NN in the aircraft domain [13]. TaxiNet is an experimental autonomous aircraft taxiing system. The system uses an NN to estimate the position of the aircraft relative to the runway centerline, using images from wing-mounted cameras. A controller then steers the plane to track the centerline. In the reminder of the section, we follow the in-context steps for integrating the VerifAI application in the overall TaxiNET assurance case. We omit details of the overall assurance case due to space constraints, but we describe the portions relevant for VerifAI integration.

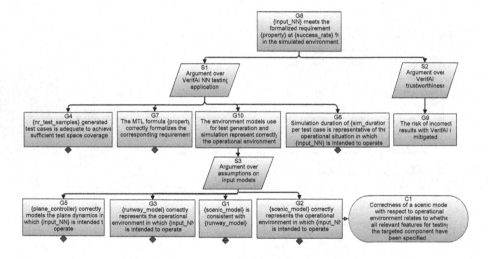

Fig. 12. VerifAI-specific tool assurance pattern

ID	Tool	Toolset	Input Types	Inputs	Output Types	Outputs
TU1	T1: VerifAI NN testing with X-Plane	TS1: VerifAI	perception_NN	EA2: TaxiNET	real	PTU2: 82
			scenic_specification	EA3: Scenic TaxiNET falsification specification		
			environment_xplane_specification	EA4: Runway model		
			controller	EA5: XPLANE aircraft dynamics	formal_verification_results	EA8: TaxiNET falsification results
			int	PTU1: 4000		
			time	EA6: 30 seconds		
			formal_MTL_specification	EA7: <>[0,10]A(CTE<=1.5)		

Fig. 13. VerifAI TaxiNet testing tool application entry captured in AdvoCATE

Step 4: Select the verification method. The main TaxiNet centerline tracking requirement is that "TaxiNet shall keep the aircraft within 1.5 m of the runway

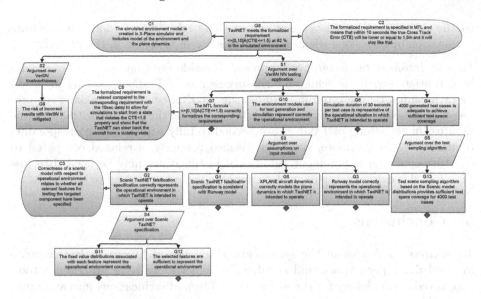

Fig. 14. Extended VerifAI assurance argument for testing of TaxiNET

centerline during taxiing". To establish the quantitative target for this requirement, we consider human pilot performance with the same aircraft. For a Cessna Caravan, the aircraft must remain within 1.5 m of the centerline 95% of the time. Hence, the probability at which the system meets the requirement should not be less than 95%. The VerifAI testing tool specifications guarantee matches this requirement and hence the tool is suitable for its verification.

Step 5: Capture the tool application record. Figure 13 shows the *tool use* of VerifAI for testing TaxiNet. The testing was performed with 4000 test cases and 30 s of simulation for each test case. The formal property was relaxed compared to the corresponding requirement to allow for the simulation to start from a position that violates the property and evaluate whether the controller will steer the aircraft to the position within 1.5 m of the centerline. The VerifAI results show that the TaxiNet managed to satisfy the property 82% of the time.

Step 6: Generate the tool assurance argument. The instantiated VerifAI argument is shown in Fig. 14. The top goal of this argument concerns the formalized requirement regarding the violation of the Cross Track Error and the success rate of the TaxiNet system in satisfying this formalized requirement.

Step 7: Extend the tool assurance argument. Some extensions of the argument in Fig. 14 are marked with orange nodes (C1, C2, C5, S4 and below, S5 and below). For example, to assure the correctness of the Scenic model, we need to argue over the set of features included in the Scenic model and the fixed value distributions of each included feature. Furthermore, we extend the argument to note that the formalized requirement verified using the tool is relaxed compared to the corresponding safety requirement. The relaxation is done to facilitate verification of situations where initial states are in violation of the property.

Step 8: Integrate the assurance argument. Considering that the top level claim is instantiated with the achieved 82% success rate of TaxiNet, this argument on its own cannot be used to fully support the TaxiNet centerline tracking requirement. Additional mitigation measures such as paring the TaxiNet with a runtime monitor or retraining of TaxiNet are needed to fully support the corresponding requirement. Furthermore, since the verified property is relaxed compared to the corresponding requirement, additional justifications may be needed to justify that this evidence is sufficient to support the more general requirement.

5   Conclusions

To address challenges in the qualification and use of formal tools that arise for tool developers, users, and certification experts, we have proposed a tool-supported methodology for the integration of formal verifications into assurance cases. The proposed methodology is implemented in the assurance case toolset AdvoCATE, guides developers to prepare tools for assurance, and helps users to safely apply tools and assure their usage. The resulting assurance case arguments are created in order to clearly communicate the trustworthiness of the tool as well as its application, and assist certification experts in reviewing the formal tool qualification. We have analysed two formal tool applications and demonstrated how each of the tools can be prepared for assurance, how they can be applied, and finally assured via structured arguments. Although the presented application examples focused on formal verification of neural network properties, the methodology is not specific to neural networks, but can be used for assurance of formal verification tools, more generally. We focus on formal verification tools because the additional effort invested can be justified, since such tools are typically used only for the most critical parts of the system and greater confidence is placed on their results. Although the methodology could be used for any verification tool, the additional effort may not always be justified. Though not described here, AdvoCATE also has the capability to generate various *views* that show architectural abstractions of the assurance case, such as the dependencies between the various tools used in the argument.

In future work, we will incorporate libraries of potential tool hazards to ease the creation of tool assurance cases. We also aim to allow direct invocation of formal tools from AdvoCATE applied to evidence artifacts stored in the evidence log, and automatically store the results as evidence in the log. We are also working on connecting the tools and the evidence artefacts with ontologies, as a basis for a structured language for tool assumptions and guarantees that will allow checking of additional properties. Finally, since tools are often used in complex workflows, we are extending the tool specifications language with the relevant constructs to support this.

References

1. GSN Community Standard Version 3. Technical report, Assurance Case Working Group of The Safety-Critical Systems Club (2021). https://scsc.uk/r141C:1
2. Asaadi, E., Denney, E., Menzies, J., Pai, G.J., Petroff, D.: Dynamic assurance cases: a pathway to trusted autonomy. Computer **53**(12), 35–46 (2020). https://doi.org/10.1109/MC.2020.3022030
3. Basir, N., Denney, E., Fischer, B.: Constructing a safety case for automatically generated code from formal program verification information. In: Harrison, M.D., Sujan, M.-A. (eds.) SAFECOMP 2008. LNCS, vol. 5219, pp. 249–262. Springer, Heidelberg (2008). https://doi.org/10.1007/978-3-540-87698-4_22
4. Botoeva, E., Kouvaros, P., Kronqvist, J., Lomuscio, A., Misener, R.: Efficient verification of relu-based neural networks via dependency analysis. In: Proceedings of the AAAI Conference on Artificial Intelligence, vol. 34, pp. 3291–3299 (2020)
5. Bourbouh, H., et al.: Integrating formal verification and assurance: an inspection rover case study. In: Dutle, A., Moscato, M.M., Titolo, L., Muñoz, C.A., Perez, I. (eds.) NFM 2021. LNCS, vol. 12673, pp. 53–71. Springer, Cham (2021). https://doi.org/10.1007/978-3-030-76384-8_4
6. Cruanes, S., Hamon, G., Owre, S., Shankar, N.: Tool integration with the evidential tool bus. In: Giacobazzi, R., Berdine, J., Mastroeni, I. (eds.) VMCAI 2013. LNCS, vol. 7737, pp. 275–294. Springer, Heidelberg (2013). https://doi.org/10.1007/978-3-642-35873-9_18
7. Denney, E., Pai, G.: Evidence arguments for using formal methods in software certification. In: 2013 IEEE International Symposium on Software Reliability Engineering Workshops (ISSREW), pp. 375–380. IEEE (2013)
8. Denney, E., Pai, G.: Tool support for assurance case development. Autom. Softw. Eng. **25**(3), 435–499 (2018)
9. Denney, E., Pai, G., Pohl, J.: Heterogeneous aviation safety cases: integrating the formal and the non-formal. In: 17th IEEE International Conference on Engineering of Complex Computer Systems (ICECCS), Paris, France, pp. 100–208 (2012)
10. Denney, E., Pai, G., Whiteside, I.: The role of safety architectures in aviation safety cases. Reliab. Eng. Syst. Saf. **191**, 106502 (2019)
11. Dreossi, T., et al.: VERIFAI: a toolkit for the formal design and analysis of artificial intelligence-based systems. In: Dillig, I., Tasiran, S. (eds.) CAV 2019. LNCS, vol. 11561, pp. 432–442. Springer, Cham (2019). https://doi.org/10.1007/978-3-030-25540-4_25
12. Foster, S., Nemouchi, Y., Gleirscher, M., Wei, R., Kelly, T.: Integration of formal proof into unified assurance cases with Isabelle/SACM. Formal Aspects Comput. **33**(6), 855–884 (2021)
13. Fremont, D.J., Chiu, J., Margineantu, D.D., Osipychev, D., Seshia, S.A.: Formal analysis and redesign of a neural network-based aircraft taxiing system with VERIFAI. In: Lahiri, S.K., Wang, C. (eds.) CAV 2020. LNCS, vol. 12224, pp. 122–134. Springer, Cham (2020). https://doi.org/10.1007/978-3-030-53288-8_6
14. Fremont, D.J., Dreossi, T., Ghosh, S., Yue, X., Sangiovanni-Vincentelli, A.L., Seshia, S.A.: Scenic: a language for scenario specification and scene generation. In: Proceedings of the 40th ACM SIGPLAN Conference on Programming Language Design and Implementation, pp. 63–78 (2019)
15. ISO 26262-10: Road vehicles – Functional safety – Part 10: Guideline on ISO 26262. International Organization for Standardization (2011)

16. Kouvaros, P., et al.: Formal analysis of neural network-based systems in the aircraft domain. In: Huisman, M., Păsăreanu, C., Zhan, N. (eds.) FM 2021. LNCS, vol. 13047, pp. 730–740. Springer, Cham (2021). https://doi.org/10.1007/978-3-030-90870-6_41
17. NIST: Metrics and measures. http://samate.nist.gov/index.php/Metrics_and_Measures.html
18. OMG: SACM: Structured Assurance Case Metamodel. Technical report, Version 2.3, OMG (2022). https://www.omg.org/spec/SACM
19. RTCA DO-333: Formal Methods Supplement to DO-178C and DO-278A. Washington, DC (2011)
20. Wagner, L., Mebsout, A., Tinelli, C., Cofer, D., Slind, K.: Qualification of a model checker for avionics software verification. In: Barrett, C., Davies, M., Kahsai, T. (eds.) NFM 2017. LNCS, vol. 10227, pp. 404–419. Springer, Cham (2017). https://doi.org/10.1007/978-3-319-57288-8_29
21. Wagner, L.G., Cofer, D., Slind, K., Tinelli, C., Mebsout, A.: Formal methods tool qualification. Technical report, NASA/CR-2017-219371 (2017)
22. Wildmoser, M., Philipps, J., Slotosch, O.: Determining potential errors in tool chains. In: Ortmeier, F., Daniel, P. (eds.) SAFECOMP 2012. LNCS, vol. 7612, pp. 317–327. Springer, Heidelberg (2012). https://doi.org/10.1007/978-3-642-33678-2_27

Validation-Driven Development

Sebastian Stock$^{(\boxtimes)}$ [ID], Atif Mashkoor [ID], and Alexander Egyed [ID]

Johannes Kepler University, Altenbergerstr. 69, 4040 Linz, Austria
{Sebastian.Stock,Atif.Mashkoor,Alexander.Egyed}@jku.at

Abstract. Formal methods play a fundamental role in asserting the correctness of requirements specifications. However, historically, formal method experts have primarily focused on verifying those specifications. Although equally important, validation of requirements specifications often takes the back seat. This paper introduces a validation-driven development (VDD) process that prioritizes validating requirements in formal development. The VDD process is built upon problem frames - a requirements analysis approach - and validation obligations (VOs) - the concept of breaking down the overall validation of a specification and linking it to refinement steps. The effectiveness of the VDD process is demonstrated through a case study in the aviation industry.

Keywords: Validation-driven development · validation obligations · formal methods · Event-B

1 Introduction

Formal methods play a crucial role when developing critical systems, allowing a correct specification of the system behavior. This specification can be checked for consistency via verification that often takes preeminence in formal development. Consequently, techniques like model checking, theorem proving, and associated toolsets such as SPIN [12] or Isabelle [20] are widely used in industry. On the other hand, the compliance of the specification with desired system behavior can be ensured via validation. Validation is supported by techniques like animation and simulation and associated toolsets like AsmetaA [5] or JeB [18]. Contrary to verification, using validation techniques and toolsets is less common, especially in state-based formal methods [16]. Even if used, they are considered a secondary activity towards the end of the development cycle.

A typical formal requirements specification process starts with a set of (natural language) requirements. Once specified, requirements undergo a stringent verification process for consistency checking. Then, the validation process follows. The whole development process is iterative. Verification is often given preeminence over validation because it does not make sense to validate something

The research presented in this paper has been conducted within the IVOIRE project, which is funded by "Deutsche Forschungsgemeinschaft" (DFG) and the Austrian Science Fund (FWF) grant # I 4744-N and has been partly financed by the LIT Secure and Correct Systems Lab sponsored by the province of Upper Austria.

Y. Li and S. Tahar (Eds.): ICFEM 2023, LNCS 14308, pp. 191–207, 2023.
https://doi.org/10.1007/978-981-99-7584-6_12

inconsistent. However, prioritizing verification over validation may lead to crucial issues, such as keeping the end users out of the loop. While specifiers create, verify, and validate specifications, the end users only give inputs at the specification process's beginning or end. Consequently, late feedback means more changes, efforts, and costs.

Many techniques have been proposed to overcome this problem. For example, Baumeister [4] suggested using test-driven development (TDD) for writing formal specifications. The author proposes generating run-time assertions from the specification to check for compliance between specification, code, and tests. Later, Bonfanti et al. [6] proposed using behavior-driven development (BDD) for a similar cause. The advantage of BDD over TDD is that it supports early collaboration among stakeholders, such as specifiers, developers, quality assurance experts, and end users, by giving low-level tests a high-level meaning. However, this reliance on tests comes with a price, and while testing is a valid means of validation, it is not necessarily exhaustive enough to cover all validation challenges. BDD restricts itself to a scenario language translated to some test in the target language (e.g., natural language to LTL formula), which may not be extensive enough to validate all properties of interest. This translation is often limited depending on the expressiveness of the target language. Furthermore, BDD is usually applied to formal specifications late in the process.

This paper proposes a validation-driven development (VDD) process for writing formal specifications that puts validation at the center of formal development. The VDD process focuses on creating validatable specifications, allowing end users to subjugate the formal specification process. Furthermore, VDD suggests a highly expressive and systematic structuring, elicitation, documentation, tracing, and maintenance process for formal requirements specifications appealing to all stakeholders.

The VDD process is built upon two well-known concepts: problem frames [13] and validation obligations (VOs) [17]. Problem frames help analyze requirements in a structured and collaborative manner. On the other hand, VOs help check the compliance of a specification concerning the stakeholders' requirements and support incremental specification writing and evolution. Analogous to proof obligations, VOs break down the overall validation of a specification and associate it with the specification's refinement steps.

The rest of the paper is structured as follows: Sect. 2 provides the necessary background to understand the content of this paper by introducing Event-B and VOs. However, note that the findings of this paper are language-independent. Section 3 introduces and exemplifies the VDD process. Section 4 demonstrates the application of the VDD process through a case study from the aviation domain. Section 5 compares the VDD process to other similar approaches. Finally, Sect. 6 concludes the paper with some proposed future work.

2   Background

2.1   Event-B

The formal language Event-B [1] is based on first-order predicate logic and set theory and helps with specification writing, verification, and proving using the platform Rodin [2]. The behavior of a specification is defined using `machines` that contain a set of `variables`, which are described in the `invariant` section. `Events` are considered state transitions, with a guard marked with the `when` clause that must be true before enabling the event. `Context` defines the static part of a specification. The Event-B language supports both vertical and horizontal refinement styles. While vertical refinement is about concretizing the abstract data structure, horizontal refinement is about introducing additional features to the specification.

2.2   Validation Obligations

Validation obligations (VOs) are logical formulas associated with the correctness claims of given validation properties. Each VO represents a requirement showing evidence of its existence in the specification. Figure 1 shows the internal components of a VO and their interplay. A validation expression (VE) is run against the specification and can consist of one or more validation tasks (VT) connected by the logical operators ∨, ∧, and ;. The semicolon operator represents a validation expression where the components before and after the semicolon share the same state space of the specification. Thus, this operator allows for complex validation expressions where steps depend logically on each other. Typical validation techniques are animation, simulation, testing, or model checking. VTs have parameters determined by the requirements and structures of the specification. VOs help us with traceability, documentation, and maintenance throughout the specification as they act as tokens documenting how a requirement is realized in a specification. Further, they indicate when a requirement is no longer satisfied.

Let us consider the following requirement in a lift example where the operator can choose between multiple floors from 0 to 2. REQ0: *The floor level will eventually equal 2.* This requirement is implemented in specification M0. Suppose we choose LTL model checking as a validation technique. In that case, we can encode the requirement into the following VO, where the parameter is an LTL formula:

$$\text{REQ0/M0} : \text{LTL1} := \text{FG}(\{x = 1\}) \tag{1}$$

3   Validation-Driven Development

VDD proposes a systematic process for requirements elicitation, documentation, tracing, and maintenance during formal developments. In the following, we discuss the workflow of the VDD process, the role of VOs in specification writing, and the structuring of the specification through problem frames.

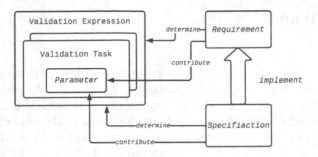

Fig. 1. Internal view of a VO

3.1 Workflow

Figure 2 shows the workflow of the VDD process, which is as follows:

1. Select a requirement.
2. Write a VO that, if successful, would give evidence for correctly implementing the requirement.
3. Implement the VO in the specification.
4. Verify the specification, e.g., check for internal consistency.
5. Run the VO, e.g., execute the associated validation task.

After satisfying a VO, the specifier can introduce a refactoring session to improve the existing specification. Overall, the approach is iterative for all requirements, and if we introduce additional VOs and change the specification, leading to other VOs failing, we have a hint of inconsistency. The VDD process also helps to keep things simple, i.e., if we need to introduce more than a handful of variables, state transitions, and invariants during the VO implementation, we most likely want too much at once. The VO makes this apparent. Checking multiple properties of one requirement hints that the requirement may be divided into sub-requirements.

Example. Let us specify `REQ0` from the previous lift example (step 1). For this, we first create the VO as shown in Eq. 1 (step 2). Now we need to implement the VO (step 3). We approach this as minimalist as possible. In the LTL formula, we need a variable `floor` which is some form of a number. Consequently, we start with x equaling 1. Then, we check the specification for internal consistency (step 4). If this is successful, we employ the LTL model checking to evaluate the VO (step 5).

3.2 Specification Structuring and Refinement

We now focus on problem structuring and refinement planning, two challenging tasks in formal developments [11]. The first challenge is to recognize what aspects of the problem are related to which other elements, i.e., eliciting the structure of

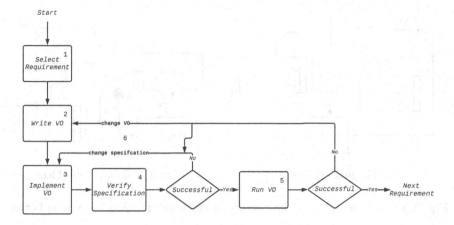

Fig. 2. VDD workflow

the specification. The second challenge is to derive a valid refinement structure from this, which supports the verification and validation process. However, both challenges require experience to master them.

Framing the Problem. We adapt the problem frame methodology [13] to structure specifications. Figure 3 shows the problem frame of the lift example. The rectangles represent the concerning domains. Each domain represents an aspect of the physical world that is observable to the stakeholders. Lines between the domains are interfaces and explain how the domains interact with each other. The rectangle with the doubled vertical stripe is the *machine domain*, the specification we want to write. Rectangles with one stripe are *designed domains* that represent the information we are free to express as we desire. This notation is for complex domains where the design is up to the specifier but where the details do not concern the global problem. Finally, rectangles with no stripe are *given domains*. Given domains are those we need to consider but cannot alter their appearance. They are usually very abstract for our specification purposes and require less attention. Our addition to the problem frames is the arrows on the interfaces indicating an information flow. Either they are uni- or bi-directional.

Example. In our running example in Fig. 3a, we want to specify a lift with three areas of concern. The `Floors` we want to navigate to are a given domain we cannot change. The lift `Doors` need to be detailed and marked as a designed domain. Finally, the `Buttons` is also a designed domain, as we have yet to get further instructions on how the buttons should look. Going into further detail, in Fig. 3b, we can see a sub-problem only concerning the lift's `Doors`. This sub-problem was separated as it would bloat Fig. 3 with information only specific to one domain. We can see that we replaced the `Doors` domain with two more specific domains related to each other. The `Outer Doors` are the doors on each floor. `Inner Door` is the lift's door and must read the outer door status to synchronize

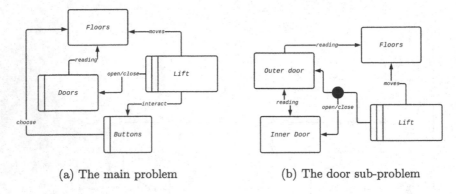

(a) The main problem   (b) The door sub-problem

Fig. 3. Problem frame of the lift problem and the sub-problem concerning `Doors`

accordingly. Furthermore, three domains share the `open/close` interface. The arrows at the interfaces show us the dependencies of their interaction, mainly the lift specification. In reality, domains are chosen and marked according to given and extracted information. This can lead to eliciting new requirements to fill gaps between the desired specification and reality. Moreover, we may involve non-technical stakeholders in the process due to a visual structure.

Structuring Specification. We use the following guidelines to structure the specification:

1. Domains sharing an interface will need to interact eventually. Therefore, they should refine each other horizontally (e.g., `Doors` is dependent on `Floors` in our problem frame and should refine it).
2. The first domain to be implemented is the one with the most connecting incoming interfaces. We then implement the domain with the second-highest incoming interfaces and proceed iteratively (e.g., specifying `Floors` before `Doors` as `Floors` has the most incoming interfaces).
3. Whenever we omit details in the main problem frame and create a sub-problem frame, we are confronted with a choice:
   (a) We can introduce the details immediately, substituting the domain with the domains introduced in the sub-problem (e.g., `Doors` is immediately specified as `Outer Doors` and `Inner Door`).
   (b) We can introduce the details later in a vertical refinement and keep the abstract domain around (e.g., `Doors` is refined to `Outer Doors` and `Inner Door`).
4. Whenever multiple domains share an interface without being connected otherwise, they may be related in a vertical refinement relationship.
5. Domains not directly connected to the machine domain are of secondary concern.

Structuring the specification further and fostering understanding for stakeholders involved, we can annotate domains with corresponding requirements extracted from the requirements document. This helps later with the elicitation of VOs. We distinguish between two types of VOs: VOs focusing on the domain and VOs focusing on the interplay of two domains. Separating both concerns helps estimate the validation effort, as VOs focusing on the domain will likely still be valid if we change unrelated domains.

Example Continued. Applying these guidelines, we can derive a specification structure. For example, to specify the lift, we would start with the floors, as they are referenced most (Guideline 1). Next, we would specify the `Doors`. Here we are confronted with a choice. We can keep the `Doors` abstract for now and move on to the `Buttons` (Guideline 3b) or detail the `Doors` before moving on (Guideline 3a). The decision for either is dependent on the requirements we want feedback on. If we keep the `Doors` abstract (Guideline 3a), we can introduce the `Buttons` and gather early feedback on the whole system and the interaction between domains. On the other hand, if we choose to introduce the details of the `Doors` (Guideline 3b), we encounter a special case of two domains sharing an interface and being connected independently. The dependency structure is that `Outer Doors` and `Inner Door` complement each other as the bidirectional interface indicates. However, as a subproblem, they refine the `Doors` domain. Consequently, both domains are introduced at the same time. Therefore the problem frame helped us to evaluate the impact of possible specification structures.

Validation and Refinement. When introducing VOs early and then applying changes to the specification due to refinement or refactoring, we must tackle the (re)validation question. We can use the problem frame to indicate where revalidation might become necessary. For example, in horizontal refinement relationships, if we have an incoming interface, i.e., we consume information from another domain and change the producing domain, we must revalidate every VO consuming from this producing domain. Analogous is true for having producing domain. Adding to the insights proposed by Stock et al. [26] if a VO only concerns a single domain and is not dependent on others, outside changes do not invalidate it. For vertical refinement, rechecking VOs depends on the specification language. If the specification language has a strict notion of refinement, such as Event-B, where we can show the preservation of safety and liveness properties, our VOs will stay intact. For specification languages featuring a liberal notion of refinement, such as ASMs, we might recheck VOs. In some cases, the VO can be transferred, preserving its insights. For example, the works of Arcaini et al. [3] and Stock et al. [25] tackle the problem of information transfer, and the insights can be applied to VOs.

4   Case Study

4.1   System Description

We exemplify the VDD process on the Arrival Manager (AMAN) case study [19]. The AMAN system focuses on developing a human-machine interface for managing aircraft arriving at an airport. The particularity lies in continuously scheduling new aircraft to land at the airport while users can interact with the schedule on a screen in three different. The first interaction to consider is dragging the aircraft to another landing slot via the mouse. The second is blocking landing slots and disallowing the computer from scheduling aircraft in this slot. The third is to put the aircraft on *hold*, meaning that the countdown till landing is not reduced for these planes. Furthermore, the user can zoom in and out on the landing schedule, thus reducing or increasing the presented slots and aircraft, respectively. Figure 4 shows the working of the AMAN system. In the middle, one can see the remaining time till landing, and the boxes on the left and right are planes. Colors indicate different statuses, for example, *hold*.

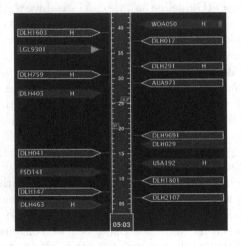

Fig. 4. Screenshot of the AMAN system [15]

4.2   Problem Structuring

This subsection demonstrates how the requirements of the AMAN system can be specified using the VDD process. We use the problem frames approach introduced in Sect. 3.2 to understand and define the problem. For brevity, only a portion of the case study and the validation process is shown here. For the complete specification and the VOs derived, please consider the work of Geleßus et al. [7].

Defining Domains of Interest. Consider Fig. 5a, the AMAN we want to specify is marked as the centerpiece by the two extra bars inside; this is the goal of the specification process. Next to the AMAN are designed domains partially mentioned in the system description. Here, we have the designed domain User, which encapsulates the user behavior. For example, the AMAN reacts to the user input. We designated User as a designed domain because we know about some user behavior, but we are unaware of the details and might want to create a sub-problem frame. Then there is the designed domain of Schedule, which encapsulates the process of the AMAN creating a schedule from aircraft and time slots. We marked Schedule as a designed domain as we are not sure of the structure and behavior of the schedule and want to investigate further. Finally, we have the designed domain Display that works as a transmitter as a physical way of transmitting user inputs to the Schedule. However, the lack of an interface with the AMAN suggests its secondary role.

Sub-problem Structure. Diving deeper into the designed domains, we start with the sub-problem shown in Fig. 5b. Focusing on the Schedule itself, we now consider the Schedule's two components: Time, which is again a designed domain, and Aircraft, a given domain. We decided here that Aircraft is a given domain as no detail about Aircraft is available. Therefore, we consider it a rather primitive datatype. On the other hand, Time is complex and might require much consideration. Both tie into the Schedule domain, which, according to the proposed guidelines, indicates a refinement. Additionally, both have the same amount of incoming interfaces. Therefore, we can start specifying with any of them.

The second sub-problem in Fig. 5c covers the topic of user interaction. Here the domain structure is simple. However, all sub-domains need the Schedule, and additional domains share the interaction interface, which indicates some interference in the domains. Otherwise, the domains remain very loosely connected. What could be a consideration is that we define abstract User interaction that interacts with the Schedule and later refines the User interaction into the three subdomains. This, again, depends on how we define the scheduling.

Final Specification Structure. We can use the proposed guidelines discussed in Sect. 3.2 to derive a specification structure from these initial problem frames. Considering incoming interfaces, starting with the Schedule seems reasonable. We must decide if we detail the Schedule before implementing User interaction. An argument for this would be that we can validate the most basic function of the AMAN and get feedback on it. Further, we tackle the difficult representation of time early. Afterward, we may implement the User interaction. We subjugate the choice of what to implement first to what needs the most investigation and validation effort, as the individual User interactions only are loosely connected. Finally, we can conclude with the specification of the Display properties. The Display has no direct connection to the primary concern of the AMAN system. Therefore, its specification is a secondary concern.

The final specification structure is as follows:

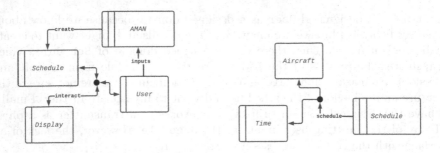

(a) Problem frame of the AMAN   (b) Sub-problem concerning the Schedule

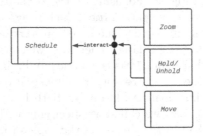

(c) Sub-problem concerning the user interaction

Fig. 5. Problem frame of the AMAN and a sub-problem frame concerning the scheduling

1. Create the Schedule (Guideline 2):
   (a) Introduce the Aircraft domain (Guideline 3a)
   (b) Vertically refine the created specification by introducing Time (Guideline 3a & 4)
2. Horizontally refine the specification by introducing User interactions (Guideline 1 & 3a) and consequently Zoom, Hold/Unhold, and Move in any order (Guideline 1)
3. Horizontally refine the specification by introducing Display (Guideline 5)

4.3   Specification and Validation

We start the specification process with the Schedule sub-problem. In the following, we refer to requirements directly derived from the specification as a direct quote: REQX with X being a number. According to the tactics presented in Sect. 3.1, we start by selecting a requirement, creating a VO, and then specifying the requirement. For example, let's assume we select the requirement of REQ1: "Planes can be added to the flight sequence, e.g., planes arriving in close range of the airport." This requirement means: a) we have aircraft, b) we have something

```
 1 machine M0_AMAN_Update sees M0_AMAN_Update_Ctx
 2
 3 variables scheduledAirplanes
 4
 5 invariants
 6   @inv0,1 scheduledAirplanes ⊆ AIRPLANES
 7
 8 events
 9   event INITIALISATION
10     then
11       @act0,1 scheduledAirplanes = ø
12   end
13
14   event AMAN_Update
15     any newScheduledAirplanes
16     where
17       @grd0,1 newScheduledAirplanes ⊆ AIRPLANES
18     then
19       @act0,1 scheduledAirplanes = newScheduledAirplanes
20   end
```

Fig. 6. The schedule sub-problem with only aircraft

to store them, and c) we can manipulate this storage by adding planes. Let's formulate this as a VO:

$$\text{REQ1/M0}: \text{GF}(\text{BA}(\text{scheduledAirplanes} \neq \text{scheduledAirplanes\$0})) \implies$$
$$\text{GF}(\text{BA}(\{\exists x.(x \in \text{scheduledAirplanes} \land x \notin \text{scheduledAirplanes\$0})\}))$$

The GF (Globally-Finally) operator indicates that the brackets' expression will eventually be true. The BA is the **before-after** operator, comparing the current version of a variable with the previous version marked with an **$0**, i.e., the difference between **scheduledAirplanes** in one step and the next step is observed. The LTL formula will ensure that our scheduled aircraft can contain an aircraft not previously in the set of scheduled aircraft. This, however, implies some state transition in our specification, going from an initial state to a state with one more aircraft that was not previously contained.

Figure 6 is an Event-B specification that attempts to satisfy the VO. We have a variable representing our **Schedule**, an **AIRPLANE** datatype, and an event creating a new schedule, eventually satisfying the VO. We could now generate more VOs to ensure soundness implementation regarding the amount of added planes. For now, we are satisfied and proceed.

Taking a look back at Fig. 5b, we need to implement the **Time** domain to cover the **Schedule** domain fully. The corresponding requirement we want to satisfy by introducing the time is **REQ5**: "The space between two aircraft is always ≥ 3, with 3 being the time in minutes." Following is the corresponding VO.

```
1 machine M1_Landing_Sequence refines M0_AMAN_Update  sees M1_Landing_Sequence_Ctx
2
3 variables landing_sequence
4
5
6 invariants
7    @inv1,1 landing_sequence ∈ AIRPLANES ⇸ PLANNING_INTERVAL
8    @inv13,2 ∀a1,a2 · a1 ∈ dom(landing_sequence) ∧
9              a2 ∈ dom(landing_sequence) ∧ a1 ≠ a2 ⇒
10             (DIST(landing_sequence(a1) ↦ landing_sequence(a2))
11             ≥ AIRCRAFT_SEPARATION_MIN)
12    @glue1,1 scheduledAirplanes = dom(landing_sequence)
13
14 events
15    event INITIALISATION
16      then
17        @act1,1 landing_sequence = ∅
18    end
19
20    event AMAN_Update refines AMAN_Update
21      any new_landing_sequence
22      where
23        @grd1,1 new_landing_sequence ∈ AIRPLANES ⇸ PLANNING_INTERVAL
24        @inv1,2 ∀a1,a2 · a1 ∈ dom(new_landing_sequence) ∧
25                a2 ∈ dom(new_landing_sequence) ∧ a1 ≠ a2 ⇒
26                (DIST(new_landing_sequence(a1) ↦ new_landing_sequence(a2))
27                ≥ AIRCRAFT_SEPARATION_MIN)
28      with
29        @wit1,1 newScheduledAirplanes = dom(new_landing_sequence)
30      then
31        @act1,1 landing_sequence = new_landing_sequence
32    end
33 end
```

Fig. 7. The schedule sub-problem with added time

$$\text{REQ5/M1} : \forall a1, a2 \cdot a1 \in \text{dom}(\text{landing\_sequence}) \wedge$$
$$a2 \in \text{dom}(\text{landing\_sequence}) \wedge a1 \neq a2 \implies$$
$$(\text{DIST}(\text{landing\_sequence}(a1) \mapsto \text{landing\_sequence}(a2))$$
$$\geq \text{AIRCRAFT\_SEPARATION\_MIN})$$

For this VO, we assumed that we upgraded our `scheduledAirplanes` from Fig. 6 to `landing_sequence` as shown in Fig. 7, which is a mapping from aircraft to time slots. Consequently, we demand that every aircraft contained in this mapping has a distance (`DIST`) to every other aircraft of `AIRCRAFT_SEPARATION_MIN`, which in our case is 3. Consequently, we must upgrade our `scheduledAirplanes` and take care of the proof.

Figure 7 shows the corresponding specification. We introduced the mentioned `landing_sequence` and further introduced `inv13,2` to establish proof. Furthermore, we refined our **event** to use the upgraded data structure. After discharging the proof, we establish that our requirement is truly represented in the specification.

As previously established, both domains `Aircrafts` and `Time` have a connection, and therefore when creating M1, we need to show that `REQ1` is still preserved in the specification. As Rodin only supports a safety-preserving notion of refinement, re-establishing the VO must happen by re-executing the LTL formula.

After completing the scheduling sub-problem, we move on to the User interaction part. Our VOs concerning the Schedule will not be revalidated when validating the interaction. We only consume the Schedule's behavior as laid out at the end of Sect. 4.2.

5   Related Work

Several approaches have been proposed for the validation of requirements specifications. While some focus on the whole specification process, others focus only on certain aspects. We briefly introduce and compare some of them with our proposed process.

5.1   BDD Usage in Formal Requirement Specification

BDD [24] is a well-established technique in the area of software development. It is appealing due to its easy-to-follow procedure and its effectiveness in establishing that requirements are part of the code. First, a scenario is created and run (with intermediate steps) against the code. If this is successful, the next scenario is tackled. If it fails, either code or scenario has to be fixed. One strength is the imposed iterative nature, which comes naturally by adding more satisfied scenarios. Furthermore, tracing and maintaining requirements is massively simplified as every requirement has one scenario mapped to a group of tests. Naturally, attempts have been made to use BDD in formal developments.

There are many significant adaptations of the BDD approach for the formal specification community. For example, Snook et al. [23] proposed an Event-B targeting version of Cucumber [27] to describe scenarios in the Gherkin[1] language which is translated into a trace and executed against a specification. The scenario language FRETISH [9] goes in a similar direction as it can be used to express requirements which are then converted to an LTL formula with the help of the FRET [8] tool. This approach orients itself heavily on what Gehrkin does for programming examples. It provides a basic language to write scenarios, which can be (automatically) linked to LTL formulas.

While these approaches can be applied successfully, they suffer from two drawbacks. First, they consider validation after writing specifications, thus losing out on the advantages of validation-centered specifications. Doing validation last will compromise completeness due to time constraints or the complexity of the specification. Second, scenario language used in BDD causes problems of expressiveness and, therefore, suffers from a lack of completeness. Second, while these approaches work well, they only provide one solution to a validation problem. We must rely on the correct translation from the scenario language to the validation technique. Furthermore, there is no way to choose between different validation techniques to translate the scenario. This means a method like FRETISH can only react to a scenario by producing an LTL formula. However, model checking may not always be a good solution, e.g., in infinite state spaces.

---

[1] https://cucumber.io/docs/gherkin/.

VDD addresses both concerns while keeping the compact and easy-to-follow style of BDD. First, it puts validation at the center of the formal development process. Second, it offers a liberal syntax allowing for expressing and consequently validating different properties of interest with many techniques and tools.

Arcaini et al. [3] showed how BDD-like scenarios targeting ASMs can be transferred between refinement steps of abstract state machines. While the previously mentioned disadvantages to using BDD-like scenarios apply, this work highlights the importance of the transferability of validation results. In the context of VDD, with our approach, we know early when results are transferable or might be due to revalidation, as pointed out at the end of Sect. 4.2.

5.2 Bridging the Gap Between Natural Language Requirements and Formal Specification

Several efforts have been made to narrow the gap between natural language requirements and formal specifications, as it can reduce the mental load placed on the specifier, and it helps when attempting to involve non-technical stakeholders. The efforts are bidirectional: creating specifications from natural language requirements and validating natural language requirements in specifications. As discussed in Sect. 5.1, BDD for formal specifications caters to the latter concern.

Regarding creating specifications from natural language requirements, Golra et al. [10] focus on creating intermediate steps with meta-models for systematically translating requirements to formal specifications. A second work of Sayer et al. [21,22] uses translation patterns. However, as both approaches introduce intermediate layers of abstraction, they also introduce additional error sources where the translation could be wrong. Furthermore, they may suffer from the same problems discussed in Sect. 5.1, where the intermediate language might not be powerful enough to translate the constructs.

VDD does not introduce intermediate layers but changes the standard order from specification first to validation. Therefore no new error source was introduced. Furthermore, the mental load is reduced as the problem is tackled in smaller portions. Finally, with VOs, non-technical stakeholders can get a feeling for the progress the specification made and point to requirements that still need work.

5.3 Requirements Tracing

Another field of interest is systematically tracing the implementation status of requirements. Exculpatory for these efforts are, for example, the works [11,14], where a sophisticated set-theoretic representation for requirements is proposed, which is supposed to help with the tracing of requirements. Compared to our approach, the authors heavily focus on the properties of Event-B and proofing with proof obligations. Validation is a gap filler for everything that cannot be proven. While our work also contributes to traceability, it takes a more lightweight approach inspired by software development strategies and thus is more intuitive.

Furthermore, the focus is on validating and creating validatable specifications, not fitting a validation solution to an existing specification.

6   Conclusion and Future Work

This paper presents the validation-driven development process for writing formal specifications. It offers an iterative approach to formal specifications, strongly focusing on their validation. The aim is to provide a systematic process to structure, elicit, document, trace, and maintain formal requirements specifications. To this end, we employ an adapted version of problem frames complemented by validation obligations.

In the future, we want to provide tool support that helps automate the VDD process by keeping track of VOs, the specification structure, and changes. Especially the steps of VOs elicitation and creation could be fully automated.

References

1. Abrial, J.R.: Modeling in Event-B: System and Software Engineering. Cambridge University Press, Cambridge (2010)
2. Abrial, J.R., Butler, M.J., Hallerstede, S., Hoang, T.S., Mehta, F., Voisin, L.: Rodin: an open toolset for modelling and reasoning in Event-B. Int. J. Softw. Tools Technol. Transf. **12**(6), 447–466 (2010)
3. Arcaini, P., Riccobene, E.: Automatic refinement of ASM abstract test cases. In: 2019 IEEE International Conference on Software Testing, Verification and Validation Workshops (ICSTW), pp. 1–10 (2019)
4. Baumeister, H.: Combining formal specifications with test driven development. In: Zannier, C., Erdogmus, H., Lindstrom, L. (eds.) XP/Agile Universe 2004. LNCS, vol. 3134, pp. 1–12. Springer, Heidelberg (2004). https://doi.org/10.1007/978-3-540-27777-4_1
5. Bonfanti, S., Gargantini, A., Mashkoor, A.: AsmetaA: animator for abstract state machines. In: Butler, M., Raschke, A., Hoang, T.S., Reichl, K. (eds.) ABZ 2018. LNCS, vol. 10817, pp. 369–373. Springer, Cham (2018). https://doi.org/10.1007/978-3-319-91271-4_25
6. Bonfanti, S., Gargantini, A., Mashkoor, A.: Generation of behavior-driven development C++ tests from abstract state machine scenarios. In: Abdelwahed, E.H., et al. (eds.) MEDI 2018. CCIS, vol. 929, pp. 146–152. Springer, Cham (2018). https://doi.org/10.1007/978-3-030-02852-7_13
7. Geleßus, D., Stock, S., Vu, F., Leuschel, M., Mashkoor, A.: Modeling and analysis of a safety-critical interactive system through validation obligations. In: Glässer, U., Creissac Campos, J., Méry, D., Palanque, P. (eds.) ABZ 2023. LNCS, vol. 14010, pp. 284–302. Springer, Cham (2023). https://doi.org/10.1007/978-3-031-33163-3_22
8. Giannakopoulou, D., Mavridou, A., Rhein, J., Pressburger, T., Schumann, J., Shi, N.: Formal requirements elicitation with FRET. In: International Working Conference on Requirements Engineering: Foundation for Software Quality (REFSQ-2020) (2020)

9. Giannakopoulou, D., Pressburger, T., Mavridou, A., Schumann, J.: Generation of formal requirements from structured natural language. In: Madhavji, N., Pasquale, L., Ferrari, A., Gnesi, S. (eds.) REFSQ 2020. LNCS, vol. 12045, pp. 19–35. Springer, Cham (2020). https://doi.org/10.1007/978-3-030-44429-7_2

10. Golra, F.R., Dagnat, F., Souquières, J., Sayar, I., Guerin, S.: Bridging the gap between informal requirements and formal specifications using model federation. In: Johnsen, E.B., Schaefer, I. (eds.) SEFM 2018. LNCS, vol. 10886, pp. 54–69. Springer, Cham (2018). https://doi.org/10.1007/978-3-319-92970-5_4

11. Hallerstede, S., Jastram, M., Ladenberger, L.: A method and tool for tracing requirements into specifications. Sci. Comput. Program. **82**, 2–21 (2014). Special Issue on Automated Verification of Critical Systems (AVoCS'11)

12. Holzmann, G.J.: The model checker spin. IEEE Trans. Software Eng. **23**(5), 279–295 (1997)

13. Jackson, M.: Problem Frames: Analysing and Structuring Software Development Problems. Addison-Wesley, Boston (2001)

14. Jastram, M., Hallerstede, S., Leuschel, M., Russo, A.G.: An approach of requirements tracing in formal refinement. In: Leavens, G.T., O'Hearn, P., Rajamani, S.K. (eds.) VSTTE 2010. LNCS, vol. 6217, pp. 97–111. Springer, Heidelberg (2010). https://doi.org/10.1007/978-3-642-15057-9_7

15. Martinie, C., Palanque, P., Pasquini, A., Ragosta, M., Rigaud, E., Silvagni, S.: Using complementary models-based approaches for representing and analysing ATM systems' variability. In: 2nd International Conference on Application and Theory of Automation in Command and Control Systems (ATACCS 2012), Toulouse, pp. 146–157. IRIT Press (2012)

16. Mashkoor, A., Kossak, F., Egyed, A.: Evaluating the suitability of state-based formal methods for industrial deployment. Softw. Pract. Exp. **48**(12), 2350–2379 (2018)

17. Mashkoor, A., Leuschel, M., Egyed, A.: Validation obligations: a novel approach to check compliance between requirements and their formal specification. In: ICSE 2021 NIER, pp. 1–5 (2021)

18. Mashkoor, A., Yang, F., Jacquot, J.: Refinement-based validation of Event-B specifications. Softw. Syst. Model. **16**(3), 789–808 (2017)

19. Palanque, P., Campos, J.C.: Aman case study. In: Glässer, U., Creissac Campos, J., Méry, D., Palanque, P. (eds.) ABZ 2023. LNCS, vol. 14010, pp. 265–283. Springer, Cham (2023). https://doi.org/10.1007/978-3-031-33163-3_21

20. Paulson, L.C.: Isabelle: A Generic Theorem Prover. Springer, Heidelberg (1994). https://doi.org/10.1007/BFb0030541

21. Sayar, I., Souquières, J.: Bridging the gap between requirements document and formal specifications using development patterns. In: 2019 IEEE 27th International Requirements Engineering Conference Workshops (REW), pp. 116–122. IEEE (2019)

22. Sayar, I., Souquières, J.: Formalization of requirements for correct systems. In: 2020 IEEE Workshop on Formal Requirements (FORMREQ), pp. 28–34. IEEE (2020)

23. Snook, C., et al.: Behaviour-driven formal model development. In: Sun, J., Sun, M. (eds.) ICFEM 2018. LNCS, vol. 11232, pp. 21–36. Springer, Cham (2018). https://doi.org/10.1007/978-3-030-02450-5_2

24. Solis, C., Wang, X.: A study of the characteristics of behaviour driven development. In: 2011 37th EUROMICRO Conference on Software Engineering and Advanced Applications, pp. 383–387 (2011)

25. Stock, S., Mashkoor, A., Leuschel, M., Egyed, A.: Trace refinement in B and Event-B. In: Riesco, A., Zhang, M. (eds.) ICFEM 2022. LNCS, vol. 13478, pp. 316–333. Springer, Cham (2022). https://doi.org/10.1007/978-3-031-17244-1_19
26. Stock, S., Vu, F., Geleßus, D., Leuschel, M., Mashkoor, A., Egyed, A.: Validation by abstraction and refinement. In: Glässer, U., Creissac Campos, J., Méry, D., Palanque, P. (eds.) ABZ 2023. LNCS, vol. 14010, pp. 160–178. Springer, Cham (2023). https://doi.org/10.1007/978-3-031-33163-3_12
27. Wynne, M., Hellesoy, A., Tooke, S.: The cucumber book: behaviour-driven development for testers and developers. Pragmatic Bookshelf (2017)

Incremental Property Directed Reachability

Max Blankestijn and Alfons Laarman[✉]

Leiden University, Leiden Institute for Advanced Computer Science, Leiden,
The Netherlands
max@blankestijn.com, a.w.laarman@liacs.leidenuniv.nl

Abstract. Property Directed Reachability (PDR) is a widely used technique for formal verification of hardware and software systems. This
paper presents an incremental version of PDR (IPDR), which enables the
automatic verification of system instances of incremental complexity. The
proposed algorithm leverages the concept of incremental SAT solvers
to reuse verification results from previously verified system instances,
thereby accelerating the verification process. The new algorithm supports both incremental constraining and relaxing; i.e., starting from an
over-constrained instance that is gradually relaxed.

To validate the effectiveness of the proposed algorithm, we implemented IPDR and experimentally evaluate it on two different problem
domains. First, we consider a circuit pebbling problem, where the number
of pebbles is both constrained and relaxed. Second, we explore parallel
program instances, progressively increasing the allowed number of interleavings. The experimental results demonstrate significant performance
improvements compared to Z3's PDR implementation SPACER. Experiments also show that the incremental approach succeeds in reusing a
substantial amount of clauses between instances, for both the constraining and relaxing algorithm.

1 Introduction

Symbolic model checking based on satisfiability has revolutionized automated
verification. Initially, symbolic model checkers were based on (binary) decision
diagrams [13,42]. While they enabled the study of large software and hardware
systems [14,18,20], they were inevitably limited by memory constraints because
decision diagrams represent all satisfying assignments explicitly. *Bounded Model
Checking* (BMC) [5,6] alleviated the need for decision diagrams by encoding the
behavior of a system directly into propositional logic, in a way similar to the
reductions provided by Cook [19] and Levin [39] much earlier (who could have
foreseen this future application of the theory?). BMC, in turn, is limited by the
depth of the system under verification, since the encoding explicitly 'unrolls'
the transition relation for each time step of the computation and each unrolling
requires another copy of the state variables. The introduction of the IC3 algorithm [10,12], later known as Property Directed Reachability (PDR) [23,35,52],

© The Author(s), under exclusive license to Springer Nature Singapore Pte Ltd. 2023
Y. Li and S. Tahar (Eds.): ICFEM 2023, LNCS 14308, pp. 208–227, 2023.
https://doi.org/10.1007/978-981-99-7584-6_13

circumvents this unrolling by using small SAT solver queries to incrementally construct an inductive invariant from the property.

This work is inspired by the success of BMC and other verification methods based on *incremental SAT solving* [1,24,45,53]. In order to reduce the search space, modern SAT solvers learn new clauses, further constraining the original problem, from contradictions arising during the search for satisfying assignments [1,50]. BMC can exploit the power of clause learning by incrementally increasing the hardness of the problem instance, while retaining learned clauses from 'easier' instances [53]. A natural parameter here is the unrolling depth: Incremental BMC increases the unrolling bound to generate a new problem instance. This approach has shown to yield multiple orders of magnitude runtime improvements [7], which often translates into unrollings that are multiple times longer.

A natural question is whether PDR can also benefit from incremental SAT solving. However, since PDR does not unroll the transition relation, we need new parameters to gradually increase the hardness of instances and exploit incremental solvers. Moreover, the standard PDR algorithm requires an extension to reuse information learned in previous runs. We provide both these parameters and a new incremental PDR algorithm.

For instance, an increasing parameter to consider, other than the unrolling depth, is the number of parallel threads in a system. However, it is not always clear how a system with fewer threads relates to a larger one, since it is not necessarily either an over- or under-approximation: Interaction between threads can remove behavior in some systems, while the new thread also introduces new behavior. And the incremental SAT solving requires either a relaxing or a constraining of problem instances. Therefore, we focus here on bounding the number of interleavings in a parallel program. Research has shown that most bugs occur after a limited number of interleavings [29,49], so an incremental PDR algorithm can exploit this parameter by solving a 'relaxed' instance bounded to $\ell + 1$ interleavings by reusing the previous results (learned clauses in the SAT solver) from solving an instance of ℓ interleavings.

Another interesting application of incremental PDR is for optimization problems. An example is the PSPACE-complete circuit pebbling problem [40], used to study memory bounds. It asks whether a circuit, viewed as a graph, can be 'pebbled' using p pebbles and the optimization problem is to find the lowest p. These pebbles model the memory required to store signals at the internal wires of the circuit (the working memory): An outgoing wire of a gate can be 'pebbled' if its incoming wires are and pebbles can always be removed (memory erasure). In the reversible pebbling problem [2], pebbles can only be removed if all incoming wires are pebbled, is relevant for reversible and quantum computations. An incremental PDR algorithm can potentially solve a 'relaxed' instance with $p+1$ pebbles faster by reusing the results from a previous run on p pebbles. Moreover, it could approximate the number of pebbles from above by solving a 'constrained' instance with $p - 1$ pebbles, by reusing the same previous results (we could start for example with p equal the number of gates in the circuit, which is always enough to successfully pebble it).

In Sect. 3, we introduce an incremental PDR (IPDR) algorithm that can both handle relaxing, as well as constraining systems. It runs an adapted PDR algorithm multiple times on instances of increasing (or decreasing) 'constraintness'. We show how the PDR algorithm can be adapted to reuse the internal state from a previous run to achieve this. Moreover, IPDR can combine both constraining and relaxing approaches in a binary search strategy in order to solve optimization problems, such as the pebbling problem.

We emphasize here that the incremental approach of IPDR is orthogonal to the incrementality already found in the original PDR algorithm: Its original name IC3 comes from $(IC)^3$, which stands for: "Incremental Construction of Inductive Clauses for Indubitable Correctness." This refers to the internals of the PDR algorithm which maintain a sequence of increasingly constrained formulas (clause sets) which ultimately converge to the desired inductive invariant. This sequence is also extended *incrementally*. However, IPDR, in addition, incrementally grows a sequence of problem instances that are increasingly (or decreasingly) constrained. This sequence exists in between runs of the adapted PDR algorithm. Both approaches exploit incremental SAT solver capabilities: Or rather, IPDR uses incremental SAT solving in two different and orthogonal ways: inside PDR runs and in between PDR runs on incremental instances.

In Sect. 5, we give an open source implementation of an IPDR-based model checker. We experimentally compare IPDR with Z3's PDR implementation SPACER [22,36] and in our own PDR implementation. From the results, we draw two separate conclusions: 1) for the relaxing of interleavings, IPDR can reuse a large amount of information between increments, which gives roughly a 30% performance gain with respect to our own naive PDR implementation, while outperforming SPACER as well, and 2) for the pebbling problems, when gradually constraining the system, IPDR again reuses many clauses between incremental instances and can achieve performance gains of around 50% with respect to SPACER and our naive PDR implementation, but relaxing or binary search (using both relaxing and constraining) does not help.

2   Preliminaries

Given a set of Boolean variables $X = \{x_1, x_2, \ldots, x_n\}$, a propositional formula $F(X)$ represents a function $F \colon \mathbb{B}^n \to \mathbb{B}$ where $\mathbb{B} \triangleq \{0, 1\}$. A literal is a variable x_i or its negation $\neg x_i$ (also written as $\overline{x_i}$). A clause is a disjunction of literals and a cube a conjunction of literals. A formula in conjunctive normal form (CNF) is a conjunction of clauses and a formula in disjunctive normal form (CNF) is a disjunction of cubes. A (truth) assignment v is a function $v \colon X \to \mathbb{B}$, which can also be expressed as a cube $\bigwedge_{x_i \in X} x_i \Leftrightarrow v(x_i)$. Vice versa, we can think of the formula F as a set of satisfying assignments $\{v \in \mathbb{B}^X \mid F(v) = 1\}$. We often use this duality to interpret a formula $F(X)$ as both a set of system states (satisfying assignments) and its CNF description (which we may explicitly denote with $\mathcal{F}$).

In symbolic model checking, a formula can represent the current set of states of the system under analysis (each satisfying assignment of the constraint formula represents one state). To reason over the next system states, i.e., the system states after the system performs a transition, we use primed variables, e.g., $F(X\prime)$, or more concisely: F'. So F' is obtained by taking every variable x_i in F, and replacing it with the corresponding x_i'. E.g., if $F = (a \wedge b) \vee (a \wedge \neg c)$ then $F' = (a' \wedge b') \vee (a' \wedge \neg c')$. A symbolic transition system (Definition 1) describes the behavior of discrete systems in Boolean logic over a set of Boolean variables X. Example 1 shows how to encode a simple system as an STS.

Definition 1 (Symbolic Transition System (STS)). *A symbolic transition system is a tuple TS $\triangleq (X,\ I,\ \Delta)$ where:*

- $S \triangleq \mathbb{B}^X$ *is the set of all system states defined over Boolean variables* $X = \{\, x_1,\ x_2,\ \ldots,\ x_n \,\}$ *(wlog). A system state* $s \in S$ *is an assignment* $X \to \mathbb{B}$.
- $I \subseteq S$ *is a finite set of initial states of the system.*
- $\Delta \subseteq S \times S'$ *is the transition relation. Where* S' *represents the states* S *in the next state of the system. If there exists a pair of states* $(p, q) \in \Delta$*, this means that the system can go from state* p *to state* q *in a single step.*

Example 1. We construct an STS $(X,\ I,\ \Delta)$ for the system in Fig. 1b. First, we define its states over variables $X = \{\, x_1, x_2 \,\}$, denoting 00 for $x_1 = x_2 = 0$, etc. We encode its states as $a = 00$, $b = 01$, $c = 10$ and $d = 11$. The initial states can de encoded as $I(x_1, x_2) = \overline{x_1} \wedge \overline{x_2}$. Finally, the transition relation is encoded as: $\Delta(x_1, x_2, x_1', x_2') = \overline{x_1} \wedge x_1' \Leftrightarrow x_2 \wedge x_2' \Leftrightarrow \overline{x_2}$ or alternatively as $(\overline{x_1} \wedge \overline{x_2} \wedge \overline{x_1'} \wedge x_2') \vee (\overline{x_1} \wedge x_2 \wedge x_1' \wedge x_2')$. Both encodings can be efficiently transformed to CNF for use in SAT solver queries (see e.g. [47,51]).

A basic model checking task is to show that an STS $(X,\ I,\ \Delta)$ satisfies an invariant property $P \subseteq S$, i.e., that no state $s \notin P$ is reachable from the initial states I using the transitions encoded in Δ.

Image and Preimage. Given an STS $(X,\ I,\ \Delta)$, the image and preimage under $\Delta(X, X')$ can be used to reason over the reachable states of a transition system. For sets of states $A \subseteq S$, we define the (pre)image of A under Δ as the states (backwards) reachable from A-states in one step as follows.

$$A.\Delta \triangleq \{\, q \in S \mid \exists p \in A \colon \Delta(p, q) \,\}$$

$$\Delta.A \triangleq \{\, p \in S \mid \exists q \in A \colon \Delta(p, q) \,\}$$

Of course, a SAT solver can only query individual states (satisfying assignments) $s \in A, t \in B$ for formulas A, B. In practice, however, we will not compute (pre)images, but only whether the (pre)image is contained in a set of states, e.g., $A.\Delta \subseteq B$. This can be done with a SAT solver query $\text{SAT}(A \wedge \Delta \wedge B')$, which returns false iff no state in A can transit to a state in B, and otherwise returns an example $s \in A, t \in B$ such that $\Delta(s, t) = 1$.

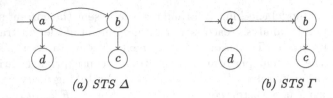

(a) STS Δ (b) STS Γ

Fig. 1. STS Δ relaxes Γ, since $\Delta \sqsupseteq \Gamma$. STS Γ constrains Δ, since $\Gamma \sqsubseteq \Delta$.

Model Checking using the Inductive Invariance Method. Given an STS (X, I, Δ) and a desired invariant property $P \subseteq S$, model checking can done by computing all reachable states $R = I \cup I.\Delta \cup I.\Delta.\Delta \cup \ldots$ and showing that $R \subseteq P$. This is the approach that BMC takes. Alternatively, Theorem 1 shows that we may also construct an *inductive invariant* (see Definition 2) $F \subseteq P$, which contains the initial states: That is, a strengthening of P, which contains I and is also inductive with respect to the transition relation Δ. E.g., the sets of states $F_1, F_2, \ldots, F_k$ in Fig. 2 prove unreachability of $\overline{P}$ provided they are inductive.

Definition 2 (Inductive Invariant). $F \subseteq S$ *is an inductive invariant for STS* (X, I, Δ) *if* $F.\Delta \subseteq F$ *(or* $F \wedge \Delta \wedge \neg F' = 0$ *as a SAT-solver query).*

Theorem 1 (Inductive Invariant Method [21,26,28]). *A property* $P \subseteq S$ *is an invariant for STS* (X, I, Δ) *if and only if there exists an inductive invariant* F *such that* $I \subseteq F$ *and* $F \subseteq P$.

In particular, R is the strongest possible inductive invariant for an STS (X, I, Δ) and all invariant properties P that hold for it. But in general, an invariant property $P \subseteq S$ is usually not initially inductive, even if it holds for the STS. For instance, in the case of a mutual exclusion protocol, the property that two processes do not end up in the critical section at the same time, can be violated in states where one process is already in the critical section and the other is about to enter it. However, in a correct protocol these states are unreachable. (And this information is contained exactly in the set of reachable states R.)

Constraining and Relaxing Symbolic Transition Systems. Consider the transition systems *(a)* and *(b)* in Fig. 1. System *(b)* can be obtained by removing transitions from system *(a)*. Intuitively speaking, system *(b)* behaves much the same as system *(a)* and if PDR were to collect clauses to describe the reachability in *(a)*, that information would seem useful when running PDR for system *(b)*. Definition 3 defines relaxing and constraining formally. For instance, if Δ encodes the transition relation of a pebbling problem with at most k pebbles, then we have $\Delta \sqsubseteq \Delta^\uparrow$ for $\Delta^\uparrow$ encoding the relaxed instance with $k+1$ pebbles.

Definition 3 (Constrained and relaxed STSs). *An STS* $M_1 = (X, I_1, \Delta_1)$ *is a constrained version of STS* $M_2 = (X, I_2, \Delta_2)$, *denoted* $M_1 \sqsubseteq M_2$, *iff* $I_1 \subseteq I_2$ *and* $\Delta_1 \subseteq \Delta_2$. *Vice versa, we say* M_2 *relaxes* M_1, *or* $M_2 \sqsupseteq M_1$.

Consequently, $\sqsubseteq$ *is a partial order, and* $M_1 = M_2$ *iff* $M_1 \sqsubseteq M_2$ *and* $M_1 \sqsupseteq M_2$. *We denote* $M_1 \sqsubset M_2$ $(M_1 \sqsupset M_2)$ *when* $M_1 \sqsubseteq M_2$ $(M_1 \sqsupseteq M_2)$ *and* $M_1 \neq M_2$.

3   Incremental Property Directed Reachability

This section introduces a simplified PDR algorithm. The full version of PDR requires intricate interactions with the SAT solver to attain efficiency (i.e., we omit *generalization* and use set-based notation instead of SAT solver calls). We emphasize that this simplified PDR is not efficient as it treats individual states (and not their generalizations); nonetheless, this description suffices to define IPDR in such a way that it is also compatible with the full version of PDR (as we discuss in Sect. 3.1). For a full description of PDR, we refer to [11,12,23].

Section 3.1 extends PDR with an internal state that Incremental PDR (IPDR) utilizes to reuse information between PDR runs. IPDR, introduced in Sect. 3.2, takes a sequence of constraining (or relaxing) STS instances $M_1, \ldots, M_z$ such that $M_{i+1} \sqsubseteq M_i$ (or $M_{i+1} \sqsupseteq M_i$), solving them one by one with the extended PDR algorithm, while passing the internal state along to speed up subsequent PDR runs. Using the properties of simplified PDR (mostly the invariants defined in Definition 5 maintained by the algorithm that also hold in the full PDR algorithm), we demonstrate how IPDR correctly instantiates incremental PDR runs.

3.1   Extending PDR with an Internal State

Given a TST (X, I, Δ) and an invariant property $P \subseteq S$, constructing an inductive invariant according to Theorem 1 is non-trivial. The PDR algorithm [10,23] approaches this problem by using the concept of *relative inductivity* (Definition 4). To construct the inductive invariant, PDR maintains a sequence $F_0, F_1, \ldots F_k \subseteq S$ of candidate inductive invariants as defined in Definition 5 and illustrated in Fig. 2. The first candidate F_0 is invariably set to the initial states. Initially, the algorithm also sets $k = 0$ and assures that $I \subseteq P$ so the Φ conditions of Definition 5 are satisfied.

By virtue of the fact that PDR maintains the Φ properties as invariants, a few observations can be made. First, the candidates are relatively inductive to their neighbors: By Φ_2, we have $F_{i+1} \cap F_i = F_i$. Paired with Φ_3, this implies

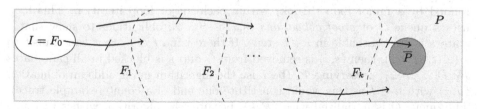

Fig. 2. The box represents all states $S = \{0, 1\}^X = 1$. The candidates F_i visualized. All F_i for $i \leq k$ are a subset of P, each F_i is a subset of F_{i+1}, and there is no transition from a state in F_i to a state in F_{i+2}.

that F_{i+1} is inductive relative to F_i. It can also be shown that each candidate F_i over-approximates the set of states reachable within i steps (only states proved unreachable in i steps are blocked in F_i). It follows in turn that, in iteration k of the PDR algorithm, all counterexamples traces (Definition 6) of length k have been eliminated, because otherwise Φ_1 would not hold. Finally, whenever $F_i = F_{i+1}$ for some $i < k$, then Φ_3 implies that F_i is an inductive invariant. Because PDR maintains the candidates F_i as CNF formulas (the candidates are refined by blocking cubes, which is the same as conjoining clauses), this termination check can be done syntactically [12] (without expensive SAT solver call).

Towards incrementing k, the algorithm initializes F_{k+1} to $1 = S = \{0,1\}^X$ for each k. To make candidate F_{k+1} satisfy Φ_1, PDR proceeds to remove states (block cubes) $s \in F_{k+1} \setminus P$ (initially $s \in \overline{P}$). But removing these states might invalidate Φ_2 and Φ_3. So the algorithm searches backwards to also refine previous candidates F_i. Once a candidate F_i (which overapproximates states reachable in i steps) is strong enough to show that some $s \in F_{i+1}$ cannot be reached in one step, F_{i+1} is refined by removing s by constraining the candidate with the negation of cube s (a clause). We now explain this process in more detail.

Definition 4 (Relative Inductivity). *A formula F is inductive relative to G under a transition relation Δ if $(F \cap G).\Delta \subseteq F$ (or $F \wedge G \wedge \Delta \wedge \neg F\prime = 0$).*

Definition 5. *The sequence of candidate inductive invariants, or simply the candidates, is defined as $F = \{F_0 = I, F_1, F_2, \ldots, F_k\}$. It has the following properties Φ [10], which are maintained throughout the PDR algorithm:*

$$F_0 = I, \tag{Φ_0}$$

$$\forall 0 \le i \le k\colon F_i \subseteq P, \tag{Φ_1}$$

$$\forall 0 \le i < k\colon F_i \subseteq F_{i+1}, \tag{Φ_2}$$

$$\forall 0 \le i < k\colon F_i.\Delta \subseteq F_{i+1} \tag{Φ_3}$$

Figure 3 gives the simplified PDR algorithm. PDR takes as inputs: an STS according to Definition 1, a property P and a sequence of candidate inductive invariants F, all initialized to 1. It then produces either an inductive invariant, which proves P to be an invariant of the system, or a *counterexample trace*, i.e., a path that shows a violation of P (see Definition 6). To do this, PDR iteratively extends the sequence of candidate inductive invariants $F_1, F_2, \ldots, F_k$ in a major loop (**pdr-main**). To maintain all invariants in Definition 5, the candidates are refined by a minor loop (**block**) within each major loop iteration. This loop uses a queue O of *proof obligations* $(s, i) \in S \times \mathbb{N}$; obligations to show that a state s is not reachable in $i + 1$ steps. If there is no $t \in F_i$ that can transit to s ($\Delta(t, s) = 1$), then (s, i) is removed from O and s is blocked in all candidates $F_1, F_2, \ldots F_{i+1}$, preserving Φ_3 (because the algorithm never adds an obligation (u, j) with $u \in I$ as this would constitute one end of a counterexample trace). The queue O is initialized with $(\overline{P}, k)$, because the algorithm wishes to refine F_{k+1} until it is a subset of P so that Φ_1 is satisfied when k is increased to $k + 1$.[1]

---

[1] Without loss of generality, we may assume that $\overline{P}$ is a single state (i.e., a sink state).

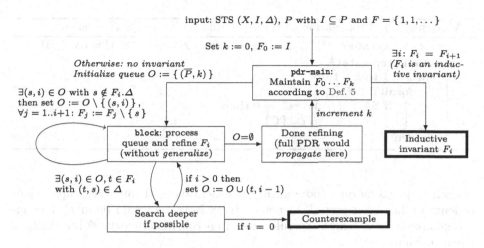

Fig. 3. A simplified PDR algorithm

Once the minor loop completes the search by refining candidates, the major loop continues by incrementing k.

Definition 6 (Counterexample trace). *A counterexample trace for an STS (X, I, Δ) and a property P is a path $\pi_0, \pi_1, \ldots, \pi_m \in S$ with $\pi_0 \in I$ and $\pi_m \in \overline{P}$.*

We now extend PDR with an internal state for restarting the algorithm. The goal of the internal state is to let PDR suspend the search upon encountering a counterexample or an inductive invariant, to restart it later on a constrained or relaxed instance of the STS. PDR uses two main data structures during its execution the sequence of candidate inductive invariants F and a priority queue O to track outstanding proof-obligations. Definition 7 gives a *valid PDR state* that also records invariants maintained by the proof obligation queue O.

Definition 7 (Valid PDR state). *Given an STS $M = (X, I, \Delta)$ and a property $P \subseteq \{0,1\}^X$, a valid PDR state is a tuple (M, P, k, F, O) that satisfies:*

- $F = F_0, F_1, \ldots, F_k$ *with* $0 \le k < 2^{|X|}$ *is a sequence of candidate invariants that adheres to the properties Φ from Definition 5, and*
- $O \subseteq S \times \mathbb{N}$ *is a queue (set) of proof obligations adhering to the properties:*

$$\forall (s,\ i) \in O: 0 < i \le k \tag{Ω_1}$$

$$\forall (s,\ i) \in O: (s,i) = (\overline{P}, k) \ \vee \ \exists (t, i+1) \in O: \Delta(s,t) = 1 \tag{Ω_2}$$

$$\forall (s,\ i) \in O: s \notin F_i \tag{Ω_3}$$

The properties Ω follow from the fact that the minor loop (**block**) basically performs a backwards search starting from $\overline{P}$ states. The property Ω_2 in particular requires that all proof obligations lead to a $\overline{P}$ state (via other proof obligations). Only Ω_3 is non-trivial in this respect: It follows from the fact that

---

Algorithm 1: Propagation at the level of formulas and SAT queries

In : A sequence $F_0, F_1, \ldots, F_k$ (in CNF form $\mathcal{F}_i$) and STS $M = (X, I, \Delta)$.

function propagate(F, TS)

1   **for** $i \leftarrow 1$ **to** $k - 1$ **do**   ▷ CNF $\mathcal{F}_i$ (set of clauses) represents F_i:
2   **forall** $\mathcal{C} \in \mathcal{F}_i \setminus \mathcal{F}_{i+1}$ **do**   ▷ Find the last $\mathcal{F}_i$ containing $\mathcal{C}$
3   **if** $\mathsf{SAT}(\mathcal{F}_i \land \Delta \land \neg\mathcal{C}') = 0$ **then**
4           $\mathcal{F}_{i+1} \leftarrow \mathcal{F}_{i+1} \cup \{\mathcal{C}\}$
5   **return** F ▷ Modified indirectly through its formula representation $\mathcal{F}$

---

in each major iteration k (**pdr-main**) the nonexistence of counterexample traces of length k has been proved, as noted above. Now if s would be in F_i, a counterexample trace of length k would exist, thus contradicting the Φ invariants of the algorithm.

The full version of PDR adds generalization of states and propagation of clauses in candidates F_i, which we briefly explain here, as IPDR uses propagation as well. In the above, the refinement of a candidate F_i is done by blocking (removing) a state $F_i := F_i \setminus \{s\}$ (in set notation). In reality, PDR maintains F_i as a CNF formula $\mathcal{F}_i$; a conjunction of clauses $\mathcal{C}$ which represent the removed states $\neg\mathcal{C}$. However, before blocking, states are first generalized by dropping literals from $\mathcal{C}$. The generalization g_s of state s can greatly strengthen a candidate F_i by blocking (removing) many states at once (since g_s is a subcube of s, we have $s \Rightarrow g_s$) that can all be proven unreachable in i steps (while taking care not to remove initial states!). So each (blocking) clause in $\mathcal{F}_i$ is a negated cube g_s, a subcube of s.

Generalization enables propagation (see Algorithm 1), as now other blocking clauses in $\mathcal{F}_i$ may be used to strengthen later candidates $\mathcal{F}_{i+1}$. Propagation pushes blocking clauses forward and is done during the minor search (**blocking**) and after it completes (see note in Fig. 3). Both generalization and propagation have been shown to preserve the Φ invariants [12]. They also do not affect the proof obligation queue. Therefore, Definition 7 holds in the full PDR algorithm.

We can now extend PDR with the internal state $Y = ((X, I, \Delta), P, k, F, O)$ from Definition 7, by modifying the inputs and initializations on the initial edge in Fig. 3. The inputs and variables are now all set to those provided by a valid internal state (obtained from a previous run). In the first **pdr-main** loop iteration, O should also not be reset to $\{(\overline{P}, k)\}$ but instead taken from Y. When the algorithm terminates with a counterexample or an invariant, it should also return the current internal PDR state. Note that the valid PDR state does not record the line at which the PDR algorithm currently is. Consequently, we will be able to restart it with a modified but valid PDR state to obtain a different result (e.g., to avoid a counterexample in the next run by further constraining the system).

3.2   Incremental Property Directed Reachability (IPDR)

IPDR takes a sequence of constraining (or relaxing) STS instances $M_1, \ldots, M_z$ such that $M_{i+1} \sqsubseteq M_i$ (or $M_i \sqsubseteq M_{i+1}$), solving them one by one with the extended PDR algorithm (`pdr-main`), while passing the internal state along to speed up subsequent PDR runs. Here we define relaxing (and constraining) IPDR as a loop around the PDR algorithm (extended with internal state). In relaxing IPDR, the outer loop terminates when PDR finds a counterexample trace. But when PDR finds an inductive invariant for the current instance M_i (wrt property P), IPDR relaxes the instance to some $M^\uparrow = M_{i+1} \sqsupseteq M$ and calls PDR iteratively. In constraining IPDR, the algorithm instead terminates when an inductive invariant is found and iterates on a constrained version of the STS when a counterexample is found. In both cases, we show how to modify the internal PDR state such that is a valid internal PDR state for the constrained or relaxed system.

Constraining IPDR Algorithm. Algorithm 2 shows constraining IPDR. Initially, `pdr-main` is called on the system M_1 wrapped in a valid PDR state (Line 5). Effectively, `pdr-main` is initialized like in Fig. 3. Then the algorithm considers the constrained systems $M_2, \ldots, M_z$ iteratively. If the previous `pdr-main` returned an inductive invariant, then the algorithm stops at Line 8, as further constraining the system is not necessary.[2] Otherwise, a more constrained system $M_i \sqsubset M$ or $M_{c+1} \sqsubset M$ is considered next (we may skip instances $M_i..M_c$ when a counterexample is found that is valid in M_c for $c \geq i$, as Line 10 does). However, we first update the PDR state for the constrained STS $M^\downarrow = M_i$ using the `constrain` operation. It resets O at Line 3 to satisfy Ω in the constrained system $M^\downarrow$ (repairing O would require at least as many operations as simply restarting the search). It also propagates blocking clauses between candidates $F_1, \ldots, F_k$ as constraining can potentially block them. Finally, `pdr-main` is called again for the updated PDR state and the IPDR continues to the next iteration (Line 12).

Constraining a system does not add behavior, therefore all the Φ invariants remain intact (intuitively: *for the constrained system, the candidates F_i still are valid over-approximations of the reachable states in i steps and they disprove counterexamples of length i*). The propagation does not change this, as it merely strengthens frames while preserving Φ. Because the queue O is emptied, Ω holds vacuously. We conclude that the `constrain` function indeed yields a new valid PDR state according to Definition 7. Consequently, the iterative call to `pdr-main` at Line 12 of Algorithm 2 can proceed incrementally checking the constrained system.

Relaxing IPDR Algorithm. Algorithm 3 shows relaxing IPDR. Like in the constraining version, initially, `pdr-main` is called on the system M_1 wrapped in a valid PDR state (Line 8). Effectively, `pdr-main` is initialized like in Fig. 3. Then

---

[2] This represents for instance the scenario when we find the minimum number of pebbles to successfully pebble a circuit by approximating the pebble count from above; reducing pebbles in each run until goal of pebbling the circuit is no longer possible.

Algorithm 2: Constraining IPDR (C-IPDR)

In : (M, P, k, F, O) with $F = \{F_0, \ldots, F_k\}$ satisfying Def. 7 and $M^\downarrow \sqsubset M$
Out: A valid PDR *state* for STS $M^\downarrow$ according to Def. 7
function constrain((M, P, k, F, O), $M^\downarrow$)

1   $\quad F^\downarrow \leftarrow \{I^\downarrow, F_1, F_2, \ldots, F_k\}$
2   $\quad F^\downarrow \leftarrow$ propagate($F^\downarrow, M^\downarrow$) $\triangleright$ See Alg. 1
3   $\quad$ **return** $(M^\downarrow, P, k, F^\downarrow, O := \emptyset)$ $\triangleright$ Repair Ω_2 from Def. 7 by setting $O := \emptyset$

In : $M_1 \sqsubset M_2 \sqsubset \cdots \sqsubset M_z$ with $M_i = (X, I_i, \Delta_i)$ and $P \subseteq \mathbb{B}^X$
Out: A counterexample trace or inductive invariant
function ipdr_constrain($M_1, M_2, \ldots M_z$, P)

4   $\quad F \leftarrow \{F_0 := I_1, F_1 := 1\}$
5   $\quad (M, P, k, F, O), result \leftarrow$ pdr-main($(M_1, P, k := 0, F, O := \emptyset)$)
6   $\quad$ **for** $M_i \in \{M_2, \ldots M_z\}$ **do**
7   $\quad\quad$ **if** *result is an inductive invariant* **then**
8   $\quad\quad\quad$ **return** *result*
9   $\quad\quad$ **if** *result is a trace valid in* M_c *for* $c \geq i$ **then**
10 $\quad\quad\quad$ **forward loop** to $M_i := M_{c+1}$
11 $\quad\quad (M, P, k, F, O)$ $\leftarrow$ constrain((M, P, k, F, O), M_i)
12 $\quad\quad (M, P, k, F, O)$, result $\leftarrow$ pdr-main((M, P, k, F, O))
13 $\quad$ **return** *result*

Algorithm 3: Relaxing IPDR (R-IPDR)

In : (M, P, k, F, O) with $F = \{F_0, .., F_k\}$ satisfying Def. 7 and
$\quad\quad M^\uparrow \sqsupset M$ with $M^\uparrow = (X, I^\uparrow, \Delta^\uparrow)$.
Out: A valid PDR *state* for STS $M^\uparrow$ according to Def. 7
function relax($(M, P, k, F, O), M^\uparrow$)

1   $\quad F^\uparrow \leftarrow \{F_0 := I^\uparrow, F_1 := 1, \ldots, F_k := 1\}$ $\triangleright$ The tautology 1 is $\emptyset$ in CNF
2   $\quad$ **for** $i \leftarrow 1$ **to** $k-1$ **do** $\triangleright$ As Alg. 1; try copy clauses from $\mathcal{F}_i$ to $\mathcal{F}_i^\uparrow$
3   $\quad\quad$ **forall** $\mathcal{C} \in \mathcal{F}_i$ **do** $\triangleright$ Access the candidates F in CNF form $\mathcal{F}$
4   $\quad\quad\quad$ **if** SAT($\mathcal{I}^\uparrow \wedge \neg\mathcal{C}$) $= 0$ **then** $\triangleright$ Does $\neg\mathcal{C}$ not block new initial states?
5   $\quad\quad\quad\quad$ **if** SAT($\mathcal{F}_i^\uparrow \wedge \Delta^\uparrow \wedge \neg\mathcal{C}'$) $= 0$ **then** $\mathcal{F}_{i+1}^\uparrow \leftarrow \mathcal{F}_{i+1}^\uparrow \cup \{\mathcal{C}\}$
6   $\quad$ **return** $(M^\uparrow, P, k := 0, F^\uparrow, O)$

In : $M_1 \sqsupset M_2 \sqsupset \cdots \sqsupset M_z$ with $M_i = (X, I_i, \Delta_i)$ and $P \subseteq \mathbb{B}^X$
Out: A counterexample trace or inductive invariant
function ipdr-relax($M_1, M_2, \ldots M_z$, P)

7   $\quad F \leftarrow \{F_0 := I_1, F_1 := 1\}$
8   $\quad (M, P, k, F, O), result \leftarrow$ pdr-main($(M_1, P, k := 0, F, O := \emptyset)$)
9   $\quad$ **for** $M_i \in \{M_2, \ldots M_z\}$ **do**
10 $\quad\quad$ **if** *result is a counterexample trace* **then**
11 $\quad\quad\quad$ **return** *result*
12 $\quad\quad$ **if** $\exists s \in I_i^\uparrow \cap \overline{P}$ **then**
13 $\quad\quad\quad$ **return** *trace* (s)
14 $\quad\quad (M, P, k, F, O)$ $\leftarrow$ relax((M, P, k, F, O), M_i)
15 $\quad\quad (M, P, k, F, O)$, result $\leftarrow$ pdr-main((M, P, k, F, O))
16 $\quad$ **return** *result*

the algorithm considers the constrained systems $M_2, \ldots, M_z$ iteratively. Now, if the previous `pdr-main` returned a counterexample trace, then the algorithm stops at Line 11, as further relaxing the system is not necessary.[3] Otherwise, the relaxed system $M_i \sqsubseteq M$ is considered next using the valid PDR state from the previous run. However, we first update the PDR state for the constrained STS $M^{\downarrow} = M_i$ using the `relax` operation. Here, it constructs a new set of candidate inductive invariants F. Finally, `pdr-main` is called again for the updated PDR state and the IPDR continues to the next iteration (Line 15).

After an instance terminates in iteration k, the `pdr-relax` function checks whether the Φ properties hold for $i = 0$ at Line 12. If not, IPDR found a short counterexample because of newly introduced (and erroneous) initial states in the relaxed instance $M^{\uparrow} = M_i$ and terminates. As relaxing introduces new transitions, the candidates F_i may no longer be strong enough to prove unreachability of states $\neg C$ for each $C \in \mathcal{F}_{i+1}$. Therefore, the new PDR-state created by the `relax` function will have to begin from $k = 0$ again in order to strengthen the frames enough to prove unreachability of $\overline{P}$ in multiple steps. Nonetheless, `relax` attempts to preserve as much as possible of the old candidate sequence in a new sequence $F^{\uparrow}$, so that once the PDR run on the relaxed system increases k, it potentially no longer starts with a frame $F_{k+1} = 1$ (or equivalently $\mathcal{F}_i = \emptyset$), but with a subset of the blocking clauses from the previous PDR run. This can be done through a mechanism similar to the propagation phase from Algorithm 1. From Line 2 in `relax`, blocking clauses C in the original candidates $\mathcal{F}_i$ (the CNF form of F_i) are inspected and copied to $\mathcal{F}_i^{\uparrow}$ if two conditions hold: 1) $\neg C$ does not block a new initial state in $I^{\uparrow}$, and 2) the candidate $\mathcal{F}_{i-1}^{\uparrow}$ is strong enough to prove unreachability of $\neg C$ in the relaxed STS (i.e., under transition relation $\Delta^{\uparrow}$).

Because k is set to 0, Φ trivially holds, but the pre-initialized frames are also sound for $\Delta^{\uparrow}$. Because relaxing IPDR only considers a PDR-state tuple when `pdr-main` terminates with an invariant, all outstanding obligations have been eliminated ($O = \emptyset$) before returning the inductive invariant (see Fig. 3). This vacuously satisfies Ω. We conclude that the `relax` function indeed yields a new valid PDR state satisfying Definition 7. Consequently, the iterative call to `pdr-main` at Line 15 of Algorithm 3 can proceed incrementally checking the relaxed system.

Binary Search with Relaxing and Constraining IPDR. Assuming the value of the target optimization parameter equals p, e.g., the minimal number of pebbles required to pebble a circuit, relaxing IPDR needs p PDR calls to find it. Assuming a sound upper bound b on p, e.g., the number of gates in the circuit, constraining IPDR takes $b-p$ calls. By combining the `pdr-relax` and `pdr-constrain` functions, a binary search algorithm takes only $\log(b)$ PDR calls, or $O(\log(p))$ in practice, since often $b = c \cdot p$ [43,48]. (We omit the details here).

---

[3] This represents for instance the scenario when we find a bug after increasing the number of interleavings in a parallel program.

4 Related Work

Well-structured transitions systems [25] provide another formalization of relaxed and constrained systems (Definition 3) that has been used to verify infinite-state systems like priced [38] and timed automata [37]. Other approaches to deal with infinite-state systems [3,8,15,30,35] extend PDR with SMT [1] using abstraction-refinement [4,17]. In the same vein, [27] extends PDR with symmetry reduction.

Context-bounded analysis [44] in concurrent programming deals with the study of programs by adding restrictions on the context switches of threads. Incrementally increasing parallel interleavings has been exploited for model checking in [29,49]. Reversible pebble game optimization was studied in [43,48].

5 Implementation and Experimental Evaluation

IPDR **Implementation.** We implemented IPDR in relaxing, constraining and binary search form. The open source implementation in C++ is available at GitHub.[4] It uses the SAT solver Z3 [22] and fully exploits its incremental solving capabilities for PDR (internally) and IPDR (in between incremental runs). It contains the following optimizations that have been discussed before for IC3 and PDR. (None of which interfere with the discussed modifications for IPDR.)

- The delta encoding of [23] avoids duplicating blocked clauses by only storing blocked clauses for the highest frame where it occurs.
- Subsumbtion checks [10,23] avoid storing redundant weaker blocked clauses.
- Generalization [10] with the later extension with the **down** algorithm [31] finds stronger clauses to block. This methods brings along some additional parameters **ctgs** and **max-ctgs**. After some preliminary testing, these parameters were set to 1 and 5 respectively; in line with the findings Bradley [31].
- Before handling a proof-obligation in the minor PDR loop, a subsumption check can quickly detect if newly added clauses already block it [23].
- We also preempt future obligations by re-queueing a proof obligation (s, i) as $(s, i + 1)$, since it will have to be proven in later iterations anyway [23].

Benchmarks. As discussed in the introduction, we choose to apply IPDR to the optimization problem of reversible circuit pebbling. We encoded the transition relations as described in [43]. For a number of pebbles p between 1 and g (the number of gates in the circuit), we encode a separate system M_p. It is easy to see that adding more pebbles relaxes the problem, i.e., $M_i \sqsubset M_{i+1}$. We took circuits from the Reversible Logic Synthesis Benchmarks website [41], which lists several "families" of circuits of increasing size and complexity. We selected those circuits that could be completed within half an hour by all benchmarked algorithms.

For experimenting with increasing the number of interleavings [16,29,49], we encoded the Peterson mutual exclusion protocol [46]. We added a scheduler [49] to the encoding to bound the number of interleavings to ℓ, starting from zero.

---

[4] https://github.com/Majeux/pebbling-pdr

Experimental Setup. All experiments were run on a computer with 16 GB of 2400 MHz DDR4 memory and an i7 6700T CPU. All benchmarks were performed ten times in a row providing a different random seed to the Z3 SAT-solver. We compare IPDR with our own naive PDR implementation that does not reuse information between runs and with the PDR implementation of Z3's [22]: SPACER [36], for which we re-encoded the systems in Horn clauses.

Results for Peterson. Figure 4 shows the runtimes for the Peterson protocol with 2, 3 and 4 processes with a timeout of four hours. The number of context switches that was feasible to run: `Peterson2` was verified up to a bound of 10 switches, `Peterson3` to a bound of 4 and `Peterson4` to 3. With our Horn clause encoding, SPACER is not competitive. With the most incremental steps, `Peterson2` achieved a speedup of almost a factor four over naive PDR. `Peterson3` and `Peterson4` both showed a similar improvement of around a factor 1,7.

Input	Naive PDR	SPACER	IPDR
Peterson2	39 s	307 s	10 s
Peterson3	599 s	15432 s	343 s
Peterson4	10321 s		6328 s

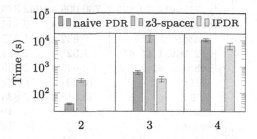

Fig. 4. Average runtimes with standard deviation for Peterson's protocol for naive PDR, SPACER and relaxing IPDR. For `Peterson4`, SPACER timed out.

Results for Pebbling. Figure 5 shows the benchmark results for the constraining (C-IPDR), relaxing (R-IPDR) and binary search versions of IPDR on the pebbling problem. In over half of the benchmarks, constraining IPDR achieves a speedup of around roughly 50% (a factor two) compared to naive PDR and SPACER. For larger benchmarks, however, SPACER has a clear advantage, reducing runtimes by a factor five, a trend that persists for the relaxing and binary search strategies as well. Relaxing IPDR appears to achieve little advantage over the other methods, a result contrary to what we observed for the Peterson protocol.

Finally, we see that speedups of the constraining version are preserved by binary search, but not improved. Internal statistics clearly show that a portion of the incremental runs complete extremely fast, because they are either over- or under-constrained. However, when the binary search approaches the optimal pebble count, the runs become expensive (a well-known threshold behavior in SAT solving [32–34]). The binary search is unable to reduce the number of expensive incremental runs close to the optimal number of pebbles, because it is now approached from both above and below.

Statistics. Figure 6 presents internal IPDR statistics for the `ham7tc` circuit (more details in [9]). These measurements reveal that constraining IPDR reduces the number of counterexamples to induction (CTIs) [10] by a factor six in incremental instances compared to naive PDR. This factor tends to reduce when approach-

	Input	Naive PDR	SPACER	IPDR	Speedup vs. naive	Speedup vs. SPACER
Constraining strategy	ham3tc	0.031 s	0.281 s	0.031 s	1%	89%
	mod5d1	1.942 s	2.850 s	1.067 s	45%	63%
	gf2^3mult_11_47	2.545 s	2.670 s	2.751 s	-8%	-3%
	nth_prime4_inc_d1	3.428 s	4.098 s	2.878 s	16%	30%
	4b15g_1	34.711 s	13.225 s	11.513 s	67%	13%
	4_49tc1	55.970 s	37.466 s	18.761 s	66%	50%
	5mod5tc	989.706 s	377.234 s	748.969 s	24%	-99%
	hwb4tc	30.292 s	30.153 s	9.865 s	67%	67%
	gf2^4mult_19_83	19.618 s	25.678 s	111.350 s	-468%	-334%
	rd73d2	836.655 s	351.181 s	499.460 s	40%	-42%
	mod5adders	57.610 s	57.699 s	34.781 s	40%	40%
	ham7tc	386.719 s	90.823 s	170.244 s	56%	-87%
	5bitadder	1396.920 s	341.008 s	964.889 s	31%	-183%
	gf2^5mult_29_129	760.006 s	242.379 s	1243.961 s	-64%	-413%
Relaxing strategy	ham3tc	0.041 s	0.144 s	0.039 s	6%	73%
	mod5d1	0.832 s	1.413 s	0.646 s	22%	54%
	gf2^3mult_11_47	1.323 s	1.416 s	1.159 s	12%	18%
	nth_prime4_inc_d1	2.647 s	2.433 s	2.806 s	-6%	-15%
	4b15g_1	16.901 s	8.773 s	19.870 s	-18%	-126%
	4_49tc1	43.018 s	19.833 s	63.133 s	-47%	-218%
	5mod5tc	845.274 s	324.640 s	747.978 s	12%	-130%
	hwb4tc	15.325 s	14.018 s	22.853 s	-49%	-63%
	gf2^4mult_19_83	5.755 s	8.441 s	5.366 s	7%	36%
	rd73d2	634.672 s	202.320 s	654.798 s	-3%	-224%
	mod5adders	45.037 s	38.639 s	28.258 s	37%	27%
	ham7tc	151.867 s	53.712 s	211.390 s	-39%	-294%
	5bitadder	639.886 s	91.152 s	474.993 s	26%	-421%
	gf2^5mult_29_129	211.999 s	64.588 s	255.076 s	-20%	-295%
Binary search strategy	ham3tc	0.135 s	0.284 s	0.043 s	68%	85%
	mod5d1	1.297 s	1.573 s	1.225 s	6%	22%
	gf2^3mult_11_47	2.124 s	1.861 s	3.169 s	-49%	-70%
	nth_prime4_inc_d1	3.776 s	4.239 s	3.041 s	19%	28%
	4b15g_1	28.433 s	10.814 s	12.944 s	54%	-20%
	4_49tc1	47.795 s	21.864 s	20.671 s	57%	5%
	5mod5tc	938.345 s	363.142 s	738.673 s	21%	-103%
	hwb4tc	19.572 s	17.900 s	8.961 s	54%	50%
	gf2^4mult_19_83	13.916 s	13.320 s	95.186 s	-584%	-615%
	rd73d2	714.732 s	279.362 s	594.911 s	17%	-113%
	mod5adders	45.037 s	39.628 s	29.790 s	34%	25%
	ham7tc	289.942 s	72.480 s	176.663 s	39%	-144%
	5bitadder	941.210 s	110.511 s	497.072 s	47%	-350%
	gf2^5mult_29_129	423.146 s	124.520 s	634.630 s	-50%	-410%

Fig. 5. Average runtimes the constraining, relaxing and binary search strategies to solve the pebbling problem with naive PDR, SPACER and IPDR. We omit standard deviations, as these are as insignificant as in Fig. 4. Speedup denotes the percentage runtime decrease or increase (gray) achieved by IPDR: $1 - \frac{\text{time(IPDR)}}{\text{time(other)}}$.

ing the optimal number of pebbles (threshold behavior that was observed elsewhere [32–34]). Nonetheless, the result is that IPDR is consistently about as fast for increment i as naive PDR for increment $i + 1$. For relaxing IPDR, we do not always observe this behavior (also not for instances with positive speedups), but R-IPDR is able to copy 60% of the blocked clauses between increments [9]. However, the copying process is expensive for the ham7tc circuit, which negates any performance benefits for the subsequent incremental IPDR run.

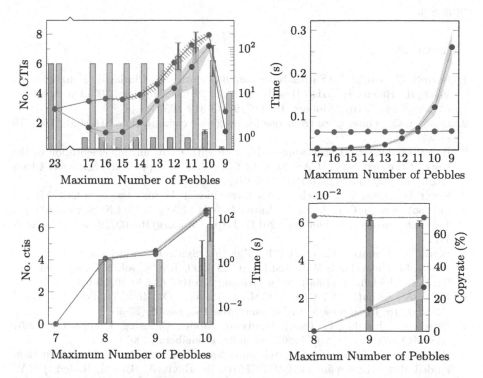

Fig. 6. Statistics for the constraining (top) and relaxing (bottom) ham7tc experiment: CTI count (bars left) and time (line left), percentage clauses copied between R-IPDR iterations (bars bottom right), copy time for R-IPDR (lines bottom right) and propagation time for C-IPDR (lines top right). For 23 pebbles, C-IPDR finds a trace with 18 pebbles, so it continues with 17 pebbles (Line 10).

6   Conclusions

We introduced Incremental Property Directed Reachability (IPDR), which harnesses the strength of incremental SAT solvers to prove correctness of parameterized systems. Since PDR does not use unrolling like in bounded model checking, we identified other structural parameters for IPDR to exploit: a bound on the number of interleavings in the parallel program and the maximum number of pebbles used to solve the pebbling game optimization problem.

With an open source implementation of IPDR, we demonstrated that the incremental approach can optimize pebbling games and model check parallel programs faster than SPACER [22,36]. Internal counters from the IPDR implementation reveal that ample of information is reused in both relaxing and constraining incremental runs. We therefore expect that further research on different parameters and other problem instances will reveal more benefits of the IPDR approach.

References

1. Barrett, C., Tinelli, C.: Satisfiability modulo theories. In: Clarke, E., Henzinger, T., Veith, H., Bloem, R. (eds.) Handbook of Model Checking, pp. 305–343. Springer, Cham (2018). https://doi.org/10.1007/978-3-319-10575-8_11
2. Bennett, C.: Time/space trade-offs for reversible computation. SIAM **18**, 766–776 (1989)
3. Beyer, D., Dangl, M.: Software verification with PDR: an implementation of the state of the art. In: TACAS 2020. LNCS, vol. 12078, pp. 3–21. Springer, Cham (2020). https://doi.org/10.1007/978-3-030-45190-5_1
4. Beyer, D., Löwe, S.: Explicit-state software model checking based on CEGAR and interpolation. In: Cortellessa, V., Varró, D. (eds.) FASE 2013. LNCS, vol. 7793, pp. 146–162. Springer, Heidelberg (2013). https://doi.org/10.1007/978-3-642-37057-1_11
5. Biere, A., Cimatti, A., Clarke, E., Zhu, Y.: Symbolic model checking without BDDs. In: Cleaveland, W.R. (ed.) TACAS 1999. LNCS, vol. 1579, pp. 193–207. Springer, Heidelberg (1999). https://doi.org/10.1007/3-540-49059-0_14
6. Biere, A., Cimatti, A., Clarke, E.M., Strichman, O., Zhu, Y.: Bounded model checking. In: Handbook of Satisfiability, vol. 185, no. 99 (2009)
7. Biere, A., Jussila, T. (eds.) Hardware Model Checking Competition 2007 (HWMCC07). LNCS, vol. 10867. Springer, Heidelberg (2007)
8. Birgmeier, J., Bradley, A.R., Weissenbacher, G.: Counterexample to induction-guided abstraction-refinement (CTIGAR). In: Biere, A., Bloem, R. (eds.) CAV 2014. LNCS, vol. 8559, pp. 831–848. Springer, Cham (2014). https://doi.org/10.1007/978-3-319-08867-9_55
9. Blankestijn, M., Laarman, A.: Incremental property directed reachability. arXiv preprint arXiv:2308.12162 (2023)
10. Bradley, A.R.: SAT-based model checking without unrolling. In: Jhala, R., Schmidt, D. (eds.) VMCAI 2011. LNCS, vol. 6538, pp. 70–87. Springer, Heidelberg (2011). https://doi.org/10.1007/978-3-642-18275-4_7
11. Bradley, A.R.: Understanding IC3. In: Cimatti, A., Sebastiani, R. (eds.) SAT 2012. LNCS, vol. 7317, pp. 1–14. Springer, Heidelberg (2012). https://doi.org/10.1007/978-3-642-31612-8_1
12. Bradley, A.R., Manna, Z.: Checking safety by inductive generalization of counterexamples to induction. In: FMCAD 2007, pp. 173–180. IEEE (2007)
13. Bryant, R.E.: Graph-based algorithms for Boolean function manipulation. IEEE Trans. Comput. **35**(8), 677–691 (1986)
14. Burch, J.R., Clarke, E.M., McMillan, K.L., Dill, D.L., Hwang, L.J.: Symbolic model checking: 10^{20} states and beyond. In: LICS, pp. 428–439 (1990)

15. Cimatti, A., Griggio, A.: Software model checking via IC3. In: Madhusudan, P., Seshia, S.A. (eds.) CAV 2012. LNCS, vol. 7358, pp. 277–293. Springer, Heidelberg (2012). https://doi.org/10.1007/978-3-642-31424-7_23

16. Clarke, E.M., Grumberg, O., Minea, M., Peled, D.: State space reduction using partial order techniques. STTT **2**, 279–287 (1999)

17. Clarke, E., Grumberg, O., Jha, S., Lu, Y., Veith, H.: Counterexample-guided abstraction refinement. In: Emerson, E.A., Sistla, A.P. (eds.) CAV 2000. LNCS, vol. 1855, pp. 154–169. Springer, Heidelberg (2000). https://doi.org/10.1007/10722167_15

18. Clarke, E., Henzinger, T., Veith, H., Bloem, R.: Handbook of Model Checking. Springer, Cham (2018). https://doi.org/10.1007/978-3-319-10575-8

19. Cook, S.A.: The complexity of theorem-proving procedures. In: STOC, STOC 1971, pp. 151–158. ACM (1971)

20. Coudert, O., Madre, J.C.: A unified framework for the formal verification of sequential circuits. In: Kuehlmann, A. (ed.) The Best of ICCAD, pp. 39–50. Springer, Boston (2003). https://doi.org/10.1007/978-1-4615-0292-0_4

21. de Bakker, J.W., Meertens, L.G.L.T.: On the completeness of the inductive assertion method. J. Comput. Syst. Sci. **11**(3), 323–357 (1975)

22. de Moura, L., Bjørner, N.: Z3: an efficient SMT solver. In: Ramakrishnan, C.R., Rehof, J. (eds.) TACAS 2008. LNCS, vol. 4963, pp. 337–340. Springer, Heidelberg (2008). https://doi.org/10.1007/978-3-540-78800-3_24

23. Een, N., Mishchenko, A., Brayton, R.: Efficient implementation of property directed reachability. In: FMCAD 2011, pp. 125–134 (2011)

24. Eén, N., Sörensson, N.: Temporal induction by incremental SAT solving. ENTCS **89**(4), 543–560 (2003)

25. Finkel, A., Schnoebelen, P.: Well-structured transition systems everywhere! Theoret. Comput. Sci. **256**(1–2), 63–92 (2001)

26. Floyd, R.: Assigning meanings to programs. In: Colburn, T.R., Fetzer, J.H., Rankin, T.L. (eds.) Program Verification, pp. 65–81. Springer, Dordrecht (1993). https://doi.org/10.1007/978-94-011-1793-7_4

27. Goel, A., Sakallah, K.: On symmetry and quantification: a new approach to verify distributed protocols. In: Dutle, A., Moscato, M.M., Titolo, L., Muñoz, C.A., Perez, I. (eds.) NFM 2021. LNCS, vol. 12673, pp. 131–150. Springer, Cham (2021). https://doi.org/10.1007/978-3-030-76384-8_9

28. Gribomont, E.P.: Atomicity refinement and trace reduction theorems. In: Alur, R., Henzinger, T.A. (eds.) CAV 1996. LNCS, vol. 1102, pp. 311–322. Springer, Heidelberg (1996). https://doi.org/10.1007/3-540-61474-5_79

29. Grumberg, O., et al.: Proof-guided underapproximation-widening for multi-process systems. In: POPL, pp. 122–131. ACM (2005)

30. Günther, H., Laarman, A., Weissenbacher, G.: Vienna verification tool: IC3 for parallel software. In: Chechik, M., Raskin, J.-F. (eds.) TACAS 2016. LNCS, vol. 9636, pp. 954–957. Springer, Heidelberg (2016). https://doi.org/10.1007/978-3-662-49674-9_69

31. Hassan, Z., Bradley, A.R., Somenzi, F.: Better generalization in IC3. In: 2013 Formal Methods in Computer-Aided Design, pp. 157–164 (2013)

32. Heule, M.: Schur number five. In: Proceedings of the AAAI Conference on Artificial Intelligence, vol. 32, no. 1 (2018)

33. Heule, M., Kullmann, O.: The science of brute force. Commun. ACM **60**(8), 70–79 (2017)

34. Heule, M.J.H., Kullmann, O., Marek, V.W.: Solving and verifying the boolean pythagorean triples problem via cube-and-conquer. In: Creignou, N., Le Berre, D. (eds.) SAT 2016. LNCS, vol. 9710, pp. 228–245. Springer, Cham (2016). https://doi.org/10.1007/978-3-319-40970-2_15

35. Hoder, K., Bjørner, N.: Generalized property directed reachability. In: Cimatti, A., Sebastiani, R. (eds.) SAT 2012. LNCS, vol. 7317, pp. 157–171. Springer, Heidelberg (2012). https://doi.org/10.1007/978-3-642-31612-8_13

36. Komuravelli, A., Gurfinkel, A., Chaki, S.: SMT-based model checking for recursive programs. In: Biere, A., Bloem, R. (eds.) CAV 2014. LNCS, vol. 8559, pp. 17–34. Springer, Cham (2014). https://doi.org/10.1007/978-3-319-08867-9_2

37. Laarman, A., Olesen, M.C., Dalsgaard, A.E., Larsen, K.G., van de Pol, J.: Multi-core emptiness checking of timed Büchi automata using inclusion abstraction. In: Sharygina, N., Veith, H. (eds.) CAV 2013. LNCS, vol. 8044, pp. 968–983. Springer, Heidelberg (2013). https://doi.org/10.1007/978-3-642-39799-8_69

38. Larsen, K., et al.: As cheap as possible: efficient cost-optimal reachability for priced timed automata. In: Berry, G., Comon, H., Finkel, A. (eds.) CAV 2001. LNCS, vol. 2102, pp. 493–505. Springer, Heidelberg (2001). https://doi.org/10.1007/3-540-44585-4_47

39. Levin, L.A.: Universal sequential search problems. Problemy Peredachi Informatsii 9(3), 115–116 (1973)

40. Lingas, A.: A PSPACE complete problem related to a pebble game. In: Ausiello, G., Böhm, C. (eds.) ICALP 1978. LNCS, vol. 62, pp. 300–321. Springer, Heidelberg (1978). https://doi.org/10.1007/3-540-08860-1_22

41. Maslov, D.: Reversible Logic Synthesis Benchmarks Page. https://reversiblebenchmarks.github.io/. Accessed 24 July 2021

42. McMillan, K.L.: Symbolic Model Checking. Springer, New York (1993). https://doi.org/10.1007/978-1-4615-3190-6

43. Meuli, G., et al.: Reversible pebbling game for quantum memory management. In: DATE, pp. 288–291. IEEE (2019)

44. Musuvathi, M., Qadeer, S.: Iterative context bounding for systematic testing of multithreaded programs. In: PLDI, pp. 446–455. ACM (2007)

45. Nadel, A., Ryvchin, V.: Efficient SAT solving under assumptions. In: Cimatti, A., Sebastiani, R. (eds.) SAT 2012. LNCS, vol. 7317, pp. 242–255. Springer, Heidelberg (2012). https://doi.org/10.1007/978-3-642-31612-8_19

46. Peterson, G.: Myths about the mutual exclusion problem. Inf. Process. Lett. 12(3), 115–116 (1981)

47. Plaisted, D.A., Greenbaum, S.: A structure-preserving clause form translation. J. Symb. Comput. 2(3), 293–304 (1986)

48. Quist, A.-J., Laarman, A.: Optimizing quantum space using spooky pebble games. In: Kutrib, M., Meyer, U. (eds.) Reversible Computation. LNCS, vol. 13960, pp. 134–149. Springer, Cham (2023). https://doi.org/10.1007/978-3-031-38100-3_10

49. Rabinovitz, I., Grumberg, O.: Bounded model checking of concurrent programs. In: Etessami, K., Rajamani, S.K. (eds.) CAV 2005. LNCS, vol. 3576, pp. 82–97. Springer, Heidelberg (2005). https://doi.org/10.1007/11513988_9

50. Silva, J.P.M., Sakallah, K.A.: Grasp – a new search algorithm for satisfiability. In: CAD, pp. 220–227 (1997)

51. Tseitin, G.S.: On the complexity of derivation in propositional calculus. In: Siekmann, J.H., Wrightson, G. (eds.) Automation of Reasoning, pp. 466–483. Springer, Heidelberg (1983). https://doi.org/10.1007/978-3-642-81955-1_28
52. Welp, T., Kuehlmann, A.: QF_BV model checking with property directed reachability. In: DATE, pp. 791–796. EDA Consortium (2013)
53. Wieringa, S.: On incremental satisfiability and bounded model checking. In: CEUR Workshop Proceedings, vol. 832, pp. 13–21 (2011)

Proving Local Invariants in ASTDs

Quelen Cartellier[1]([✉]), Marc Frappier[1][ID], and Amel Mammar[2][ID]

[1] GRIC, Université de Sherbrooke, Sherbrooke J1K2R1, QC, Canada
{Quelen.Cartellier,Marc.Frappier}@USherbrooke.ca
[2] SAMOVAR, Télécom SudParis, Institut Polytechnique de Paris, 91120 Palaiseau,
France
amel.mammar@telecom-sudparis.eu

Abstract. This paper proposes a formal approach for generating proof
obligations to verify local invariants in an Algebraic State Transition Diagram (ASTD). ASTD is a graphical specification language that allows
for the combination of extended hierarchical state machines using CSP-
like process algebra operators. Invariants can be declared at any level
in a specification (state, ASTD), fostering the decomposition of system
invariants into modular local invariants which are easier to prove, because
proof obligations are smaller. The proof obligations take advantage of
the structure of an ASTD to use local invariants as hypotheses. ASTD
operators covered are automaton, sequence, closure and guard. Proof
obligations are discharged using Rodin. When proof obligations cannot
be proved, ProB can be used to identify counter-examples to help in
correcting/reinforcing the invariant or the specification.

Keywords: ASTD · invariant · proof obligation · Rodin · ProB

1 Introduction and Related Work

ASTD [6,12] is a graphical notation that combines process algebra operators
and hierarchical state machines. It is particularly well-suited for specifying monitoring systems, like intrusion detection systems [4,18] and control systems [1,5].
ASTD allows for the combination of state transition diagrams (Statecharts-like)
with process algebra operators, drawn from CSP. Hence, ASTD takes advantage
of the strengths of both notations: graphical representation, hierarchy, orthog-
onality, compositionality, and abstraction. Statecharts-like notations offer only
two operators for decomposing behavior, OR and AND states. ASTDs support
these two operators (OR is represented by ASTD automaton; AND is represented by the flow operator), and it supports most of CSP's operators. ASTDs
differ from these notations by using simpler communication mechanisms. ASTDs
can communicate through shared state variables or through synchronisation.
Statecharts' broadcast communication is not supported.

This work was supported by the ANR projet DISCONT, Public Safety Canada and
NSERC.

In order to promote the use of ASTDs for modeling safety critical systems, it is crucial to have the ability to prove safety properties like invariants. Indeed, designing an ASTD specification is an error-prone task, *e.g.*, invariants of states can be incorrect. Model-based methods like B and Event-B offer powerful environments for proving invariants on formal specifications using refinement. But still, proving global invariants on these systems is hard [9,10]. A translation of ASTDs to B and Event-B has been proposed [5,11]. Global invariants which are associated to all states of the system can be declared and proof obligations are then generated to ensure that each event preserves the invariants. These proof obligations are hard to discharge for large specifications, due to the encoding of ASTD operators that introduces several control variables. Moreover, it does not support local invariants which are associated to some states in the system. In [1], it has been shown that the algebraic approach of ASTDs streamlines the modularisation of a large specification.

Several works have addressed the specification and verification of invariants in Statecharts-like notations (*e.g.*, [7,13,14]), but only [16,17] have addressed the proof of invariants; others are targeting model checking or assertions for run-time verification. Model-checking is often limited by state explosion (*e.g.*, [9,10]) for large specifications, whereas run-time verification is not satisfactory for safety-critical system, as it offers no insight on system correctness before deployment.

To overcome the limitations of [5,11], we propose in this paper to generate proof obligations for invariant preservation directly from an ASTD specification, in order to reduce proof complexity and make the traceability between the ASTD invariants and the produced proof obligations straightforward. An invariant can be declared by the user at any level in the specification (from complex ASTDs to elementary states of an automaton). Our work differs from [17] by permitting invariants on elementary automaton states, an important feature for critical control systems, and by supporting invariants for complex ASTDs, which amounts to supporting invariant for complex process expressions, since complex ASTDs are defined using process algebra operators. UML-B [16] supports invariants on classes and traditional states machines; a UML-B specification is translated into Event-B, and thus invariants are represented globally in the resulting Event-B machine. Our POs are local to a state, and thus simpler. They are represented as theorems of an Event-B context, and can be discharged using Rodin[1] and debugged using ProB [8], which are two industrial strengths tools supporting the B and Event-B methods.

The rest of this paper is structured as follows. Section 2 introduces a subset of the ASTD notation and its semantics. Section 3 defines the proof obligations and illustrates them on a small example. Section 4 concludes the paper.

2 Overview of the ASTD Notation

The ASTD notation includes several ASTD *types*, which are Elem, Automaton, Sequence, Kleene closure, Guard, Choice, Parameterized Synchronization, Flow,

---

[1] http://www.event-b.org/.

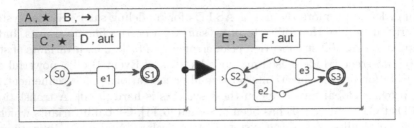

Fig. 1. ASTD Case study

Quantified choice, Quantified synchronization and Call. In this paper, we consider only the first five types. Figure 1 illustrates a simple but representative ASTD specification that is used to illustrate our approach throughout this paper. ASTDs A and C are of type Kleene closure. ASTD B is of type Sequence, and it executes ASTDs C and E in sequence. ASTD E is of type Guard. ASTDs D and F are of type Automaton. Automaton states $S0$, $S1$, $S2$, $S3$ are ASTDs of type Elem. ASTD A is a Kleene closure that allows for iteration on ASTD B. B executes C and D in sequence: when C reaches the final state $S1$, E is enabled to execute the event e2, to move from $S2$ to $S3$. Since C is a Kleene closure, it can trigger a new iteration of D when it is in the state $S1$, and execute the event e1 from the initial state $S0$. When F is in the final state $S3$, A can also trigger a new iteration of B and execute the event e1 from $S0$. Here is a possible trace of this specification:

$$[e1, e1, e1, e2, e3, e2, e1, \ldots]$$

ASTD types are organised into a type hierarchy. Specific ASTD types inherit from the top-level type ASTD, which introduces three general fields $\langle n, V, I \rangle$, where n is the name of the ASTD, V is a set of attributes and I an invariant associated to all states of the ASTD. These properties are inherited by all ASTD types. We refer to a field p of an ASTD $a \in$ ASTD using the notation $a.p$. Attributes $a.V$ are variables that are initialised a and modified in a or in its sub-ASTDs. For instance, an attribute declared in A can be modified in B, C, D, E, F. The invariant $a.I$ is a first-order logic formula on $a.V$ and on the attributes of its super-ASTDs. For instance, the invariant $F.I$ can refer to attributes $A.V, B.V, E.V$ and $F.V$. Table 1 provides the main elements of these ASTDs. If a is an elementary state, then $a.I$ applies only to this state. But if a is a complex ASTD, then $a.I$ should be fulfilled by all sub-ASTDs of a.

The execution of an ASTD is defined by a labeled transition system using a Plotkin-like operational semantics. The set of states is denoted by State. Each type of ASTD comes with its own type of states, but each state type has a property $E :$ Var $\rightarrow$ Term which represents the values of attributes declared in the ASTD. Some states may be final and enable subsequent ASTDs to start. Final states of an ASTD a are determined by the Boolean function *final* of type ASTD $\times$ State $\rightarrow$ Boolean. Function *init* of type ASTD $\times$ (Var $\rightarrow$ Term) $\rightarrow$ State returns the initial state of an ASTD. In the sequel, we use some mathematical operators from the B notation; their definition is given in Table 3.

2.1 Automaton

The ASTD type Automaton is built on a set of states related by transitions. It has the following structure: $ASTD\ Automaton \mathrel{\hat{=}} \langle$ aut, Σ, S, ν, δ, SF, DF, $n_0 \rangle$ where $\Sigma \subseteq$ Event is the alphabet and $S \subseteq$ Name is the set of state names. $\nu \in S \rightarrow$ ASTD maps each state to its sub-ASTD, which can be elementary (noted Elem) or complex (*i.e.*, of any ASTD type). An automaton transition from n_1 to n_2, labelled with $\sigma[g]/A_{tr}$, is represented in the transition relation δ as follows: $\delta(\eta, \sigma, g, A_{tr}, final?)$. Symbol η denotes the type of the transition. In this paper, we consider simple transitions of the form $\langle n_1, n_2 \rangle$, where n_1 and n_2 are respectively the source and target states of the transition. Symbol *final?* is a

Table 1. Properties of ASTDs in Fig. 1

ASTD	Attributes	Initialisation	Invariant	Guard
A	x_A	$x_A := 0$	$x_A \geq 0$	
B	x_B	$x_B := x_A + 1$	$x_B > 0$	
C	x_C	$x_C := 0$	$x_B \geq x_A$	
D	x_D	$x_D := x_C + 1$	$x_D \geq 0$	
E	x_E	$x_E := x_A$	$x_E \geq 0 \wedge x_E < x_B \wedge x_E \leq x_A$	$x_B > x_A + 4$
F	x_F	$x_F := 0$	$x_F \geq 0$	
S0			$x_D > x_C \wedge x_C \geq 0$	
S1			$x_C \geq x_D \wedge x_A > 0$	
S2			$x_F = 0 \vee x_A > x_E$	
S3			$x_F > 0 \wedge x_A > x_E$	

Table 2. Transitions of ASTDs in Fig. 1

Event	Guard	Action
e1		$x_C := x_C + x_D;\ x_B := x_B + x_C;\ x_A := x_A + 1$
e2		$x_A := x_A + x_B;\ x_F := x_F + 1$
e3	$x_A < 10000$	$x_A := x_A - x_E$

Table 3. Definitions of B operators

Description	Expression	Definition
domain antirestriction	$S \lhd\!\!\!- r$	$\{x \mapsto y \mid x \mapsto y \in r \wedge x \notin S\}$
range antirestriction	$r -\!\!\!\rhd S$	$\{x \mapsto y \mid x \mapsto y \in r \wedge y \notin S\}$
override	$r_1 \lhd\!\!\!- r_2$	$(\mathrm{dom}(r_2) \lhd\!\!\!- r_1) \cup r_2$

Boolean: when *final?* = true, the source of the transition is graphically decorated with a bullet (*i.e.*, •); it indicates that the transition can be fired only if n_1 is final. This is useful only when n_1 is not an elementary state (i.e., it is a complex ASTD). $SF \subseteq S$ is the set of shallow final states, while $DF \subseteq S$ denotes the set of deep final states, with $DF \cap SF = \varnothing$ and $DF \subseteq dom(\nu \blacktriangleright \{\text{Elem}\})$. A deep final state is final iff its sub-ASTD is final; a shallow final is final, irrespective of the state of its sub-ASTD. $n_0 \in S$ is the name of the initial state. In this paper, for the sake of simplicity, we denote by A_{tr} the sequential composition of the actions executed during a transition, that are, the actions executed when exiting the source state, on the transition and when entering the target state. The type of an Automaton state is $\langle \text{aut}_\circ, n, E, s \rangle$ where $\text{aut}_\circ$ is a constructor of the Automaton state. $n \in S$ denotes the name of the current state of the automaton. E contains the values of the Automaton attributes. $s \in \text{State}$ is state of the sub-ASTD of n, when n is a complex state; $s = \text{Elem}$ when n is elementary.

Automaton F defines the attribute x_F initialised by $(x_F := 0)$. The transition labelled with the event e2 permits to move from S2 to S3. When it is triggered, the action $(x_A := x_A + x_B; x_F := x_F + 1)$ is executed.

To define the semantics of an Automaton a, the functions *init* and *final* are defined as follows:

$$init(a, G) \mathrel{\hat{=}} (\text{aut}_\circ, a.n_0, a.E_{init}(\![G]\!), init(a.\nu(n_0), G \twoheadleftarrow a.E_{init}))$$
$$final(a, (\text{aut}_\circ, n, E, s)) \mathrel{\hat{=}} n \in a.SF \vee (n \in a.DF \wedge final(a.\nu(n), s))$$

where G and E_{init} denote respectively the environment (*i.e.*, current values of attributes defined in the enclosing ASTDs of a) and the initial values of the attributes of a, which may refer to variables declared in enclosing ASTDs, and thus they are replaced with their current values defined in G using the substitution operator $(\![\ ]\!)$ (e.g., $(x_F := x_A + 1)(\![x_A := 0]\!)) \equiv x_F := 1$). Note that the sub-ASTD of n_0 is initialised by recursively calling *init* on the ASTD of n_0.

Inference rule aut_1 defines the semantics of an automaton a for a transition between two states n_1 and n_2:

$$\text{aut}_1 \quad \frac{a.\delta((n_1, n_2), \sigma', g, A_{tr}, final?) \qquad \Psi \qquad \Omega_{loc}}{(\text{aut}_\circ, n_1, E, s_1) \xrightarrow{\sigma, E_e, E_e'}_a (\text{aut}_\circ, n_2, E', init(a.\nu(n_2), E'))}$$

The conclusion of this rule states that a transition on event σ can occur from n_1 to n_2 with before and after automaton attributes values E, E'. The sub-ASTD of n_2, denoted by $a.\nu(n_2)$, is initialised. The premise provides that such a transition is possible if there is a matching transition, which is represented by $\delta((n_1, n_2), \sigma', g, A_{tr}, final?)$. σ' is the event labelling the transition, and it may contain variables. The value of these variables is given by the environment E_e, which contains the values of variables in ASTDs enclosing the automaton (*i.e.*, the super-ASTDs of a) and attributes of a, given in by E. This match on the transition is provided by the premise Ψ defined as follows.

$$\Psi \mathrel{\hat{=}} (\ (final? \Rightarrow final(a.\nu(n_1), s)) \wedge g \wedge \sigma' = \sigma\ )(\![E_g]\!)$$

Ψ can be understood as follows. If the transition is final (*i.e.*, *final?* = true), then the current state s must be final with respect to the ASTD of n_1. The transition guard g holds. The event received, noted σ, must match the event pattern σ', which labels the automaton transition, after applying the environment E_g as a substitution. Environment E_g, defined as $E_e \triangleleft E$, denotes the list of variables of a and its super-ASTDs. The premise Ω_{loc} determines how the new values of the attributes in the environment are computed when the transition occurs; its definition is omitted for the sake of concision.

Rule aut_2 handles transitions occurring within a complex automaton state n.

$$\mathsf{aut}_2 \frac{s \xrightarrow{\sigma,E_g,E_g''}_{a.\nu(n)} s' \qquad \Theta}{(\mathsf{aut}_\circ, n, E, s) \xrightarrow{\sigma,E_e,E_e'}_a (\mathsf{aut}_\circ, n, E', s')}$$

The transition starts from a sub-state s and moves to the sub-state s' of the state n. Actions are executed bottom-up. E_g'' denotes the values computed by the ASTD of the state n. Premise Θ determines how E_g'' is computed, and it is reused in all subsequent rules where a sub-ASTD transition is involved; it is omitted here for the sake of concision and simplicity.

2.2   Kleene Closure

This operator comes from regular expressions. It allows for iteration on an ASTD an arbitrary number of times (including zero). When the sub-ASTD is in a final state, it enables to start a new iteration. The Kleene closure ASTD has the following structure:

$$\text{Kleene closure} \mathrel{\hat{=}} \langle \bigstar, b \rangle$$

where $b \in$ ASTD is the body of the closure. A Kleene closure is in a final state when it has not started or when its sub-ASTD b is in a final state. The type of a Kleene closure state is $\langle \bigstar_\circ, E, started?, s \rangle$ where $s \in$ State, *started?* is a Boolean indicating whether the first iteration has been started. It is essentially used to determine if the closure can immediately exit (*i.e.*, if it is in a final state) without any iteration. For a Kleene closure ASTD a, the initial and final states are defined as follows.

$$init(a, G) \mathrel{\hat{=}} (\bigstar_\circ, a.E_{init}(\llbracket G \rrbracket), \mathsf{false}, \bot)$$
$$final(a, (\bigstar_\circ, E, started?, s)) \mathrel{\hat{=}} \neg started? \vee final(a.b, s)$$

where $\bot$ denotes an undefined state. The semantics of a Kleene closure ASTD is defined by two inference rules: $\bigstar_1$ allows for starting a new iteration (including the first one); $\bigstar_2$ allows for execution on the sub-ASTD.

$$\bigstar_1 \frac{final(a, (\bigstar_\circ, E, started?, s)) \qquad init(a.b, E_e) \xrightarrow{\sigma,E_g,E_g''}_{a.b} s' \qquad \Theta}{(\bigstar_\circ, E, started?, s) \xrightarrow{\sigma,E_e,E_e'}_a (\bigstar_\circ, E', \mathsf{true}, s')}$$

$$\bigstar_2 \quad \frac{s \xrightarrow{\sigma, E_g, E_g''}_{a.b} s' \qquad \Theta}{(\bigstar_\circ, E, \text{true}, s) \xrightarrow{\sigma, E_e, E_e'}_a (\bigstar_\circ, E', \text{true}, s')}$$

In Fig. 1, C is a Kleene closure ASTD whose initial state is $(\bigstar_\circ, ([x_A = 0, x_B = 1, x_C = 1]), \text{false}, \bot)$; its sub-state is undefined (denoted by $\bot$). But when the first possible event is received (*i.e.*, e1), the sub-ASTD D is initialised ($x_D := x_C + 1$), the transition e1 is triggered from $S0$ and the action ($x_C = x_C + x_D; x_B = x_B + x_C; x_A = x_A + 1$) of the transition is executed. The current state is now $S1$ and the values of attributes are $([x_A = 1, x_B = 4, x_C = 3, x_D = 2])$. As $S1$ is a final state of D (*i.e.*, the sub-ASTD of C), D is final, and so is C, and a new iteration of D can be started again by receiving e1. D is reinitialised to start a new iteration, so x_D is reinitialised prior to this new transition, but the values of x_A, x_B, x_C are unaffected by the initialisation of D.

2.3   Sequence

The Sequence ASTD allows for the sequential composition of two ASTDs. When the first ASTD reaches a final state, it enables the execution of the second ASTD. In that case, it is the reception of the next event that determines which ASTD is executed: if both the first and the second can execute it, then a non-deterministic choice is made between the two. When the second ASTD starts it execution, the first ASTD becomes disabled. The Sequence ASTD enables decomposing problems into a set of tasks that have to be executed in sequence. The Sequence ASTD has the following structure:

$$\text{Sequence} \mathrel{\widehat{=}} \langle \rightarrow, \textit{fst}, \textit{snd} \rangle$$

where *fst* and *snd* are ASTDs denoting respectively the first and second sub-ASTD of the Sequence. A Sequence state is of type $\langle \rightarrow_\circ, E, [\textsf{fst} \mid \textsf{snd}], s \rangle$, where $\rightarrow_\circ$ is a constructor of the Sequence state, $[\textsf{fst} \mid \textsf{snd}]$ is a choice between two markers that respectively indicate whether the Sequence is in the first sub-ASTD or the second sub-ASTD and $s \in$ State. Since s does not indicate which ASTD is currently executed, the marker $[\textsf{fst} \mid \textsf{snd}]$ is used for that purpose. Functions *init* and *final* of a sequence ASTD are defined as follows.

$$init(a, G) \mathrel{\widehat{=}} (\rightarrow_\circ, a.E_{init}([G]), \textsf{fst}, init(a.\textit{fst}, G \twoheadleftarrow a.E_{init}))$$
$$final(a, (\rightarrow_\circ, E, \textsf{fst}, s)) \mathrel{\widehat{=}} final(a.\textit{fst}, s) \wedge final(a.\textit{snd}, init(a.\textit{snd}, E))$$
$$final(a, (\rightarrow_\circ, E, \textsf{snd}, s)) \mathrel{\widehat{=}} final(a.\textit{snd}, s)$$

The initial state of a Sequence is the initial state of its first sub-ASTD. A sequence state is final when either (*i*) it is executing its first sub-ASTD and this one is in a final state, and the initial state of the second sub-ASTD is also a final state, or (*ii*) it is executing the second sub-ASTD which is in a final state.

In Fig. 1, the ASTD B is a Sequence ASTD that allows the sequential execution of ASTDs C and E. B starts by executing C. As the initial state of E is not final, B is final only when the final state of E is reached.

Three semantic rules are necessary to define the execution of the Sequence. Rule $\rightarrow_1$ deals with transitions on the sub-ASTD fst only. Rule $\rightarrow_2$ deals with transitions from fst to snd, when fst is in a final state. Rule $\rightarrow_3$ deals with transitions on the sub-ASTD snd. Note that the arrow connecting ASTD C and E is not labeled with an event pattern, because event patterns only occur on automaton transitions; when the execution goes from C to E, it is an event of E that is executed, in this case an event of automaton F.

$$\rightarrow_1 \frac{s \xrightarrow{\sigma, E_g, E_g''}_{a.fst} s' \qquad \Theta}{(\rightarrow_\circ, E, \mathsf{fst}, s) \xrightarrow{\sigma, E_e, E_e'}_a (\rightarrow_\circ, E', \mathsf{fst}, s')}$$

$$\rightarrow_2 \frac{final(a.fst, s) \qquad init(a.snd, E_e) \xrightarrow{\sigma, E_g, E_g''}_{a.snd} s' \qquad \Theta}{(\rightarrow_\circ, E, \mathsf{fst}, s) \xrightarrow{\sigma, E_e, E_e'}_a (\rightarrow_\circ, E', \mathsf{snd}, s')}$$

$$\rightarrow_3 \frac{s \xrightarrow{\sigma, E_g, E_g''}_{a.snd} s' \qquad \Theta}{(\rightarrow_\circ, E, \mathsf{snd}, s) \xrightarrow{\sigma, E_e, E_e'}_a (\rightarrow_\circ, E', \mathsf{snd}, s')}$$

In Fig. 1, in the sequence ASTD B, the ASTD E can be executed only when the ASTD C reaches its final state, that is, it is not started at all or it is in the state $S1$. The first event executed in E is e2 because this is its only event that starts from its initial state.

2.4 Guard

A Guard ASTD defines a conditional execution of its sub-ASTD using a predicate. To be enabled, the first event executed must satisfy the Guard predicate. Once the guard has been satisfied by the first event, the sub-ASTD of the guard executes the subsequent events without further constraints from its enclosing guard ASTD. The guard predicate can only refer to attributes declared in its enclosing ASTDs. The Guard ASTD has the following structure:

$$\mathsf{Guard} \,\hat{=}\, \langle \Rightarrow, g, b \rangle$$

where $b \in \mathsf{ASTD}$ is the body of the guard. The type of a Guard state is $\langle \Rightarrow_\circ , E, started?, s \rangle$ where $started?$ states whether the first transition has been done, $s \in \mathsf{State}$. The initial and final states of a Guard ASTD a are defined as follows.

$$init(a, G) \,\hat{=}\, (\Rightarrow_\circ, a.E_{init}(\llbracket G \rrbracket, \mathsf{false}, \bot)$$
$$final(a, (\Rightarrow_\circ, E_{init}, \mathsf{false}, s)) \,\hat{=}\, final(a, s)$$
$$final(a, (\Rightarrow_\circ, E, \mathsf{true}, s)) \,\hat{=}\, final(a, s)$$

The semantic of the Guard ASTD is defined by two inference rules: $\Rightarrow_1$ deals with the first transition and the satisfaction of the guard predicate; $\Rightarrow_2$ deals with subsequent transitions.

$$\Rightarrow_1 \frac{g(\![E_e]\!]) \qquad init(a.b, E_e) \xrightarrow{\sigma, E_g, E_g''}_{a.b} s' \qquad \Theta}{(\Rightarrow_\circ, E_{init}, \mathsf{false}, init(a.b, E_e)) \xrightarrow{\sigma, E_e, E_e'} (\Rightarrow_\circ, E', \mathsf{true}, s')}$$

$$\Rightarrow_2 \frac{s \xrightarrow{\sigma, E_g, E_g''}_{a.b} s' \qquad \Theta}{(\Rightarrow_\circ, E, \mathsf{true}, s) \xrightarrow{\sigma, E_e, E_e'} (\Rightarrow_\circ, E', \mathsf{true}, s')}$$

Let us use the ASTD of Fig. 1 to explain when ASTDs are initialised in a sequence ASTD. Suppose that the system is in the state $S1$ and that the event e2 is received. Since $S1$ is a final state of D and C, the rule $\rightarrow_2$ allows for the execution of the transition e2 from the initial state of F. To trigger e2, the rule $\Rightarrow_2$ requires that the guard $(x_B > x_A + 4)$ of E must be satisfied with the current values of x_A and x_B. Finally, if the transition e2 had a guard, it should also be satisfied with the current values of its enclosing ASTDs A, B, E and F. The variables in E and F are initialised only when the transition e2 is evaluated. If the guards are satisfied, e2 is executed and the state moves to $S3$; if not, the system stays in $S1$, and then E and F will be initialised again when a new occurrence of e2 is received. In other words, E and F are initialised for good only when the first transition of F can be executed.

3   Proof Obligations for Invariant Satisfaction

In this section, we describe a systematic approach for generating the proof obligations that ensure the satisfaction of the invariants of an ASTD for its reachable states defined by the transition system. Proof obligations are generated according to the structure of the ASTD. Hereafter, we introduce the definitions of some concepts that we use in the sequel of the paper.

3.1   Definitions

We introduce the following definitions that are used as hypotheses when proving an invariant.

Definition 1. *The full invariant of an ASTD a is defined as follows:*

$$Inv_{full}(a) = \begin{cases} a.I & \text{if } type(a) = Elem \\ a.I \wedge \left(\bigvee_{s \in a.S} Inv_{full}(a.\nu(s)) \right) & \text{if } type(a) = Automaton \\ a.I \wedge \left(Inv_{full}(fst) \vee Inv_{full}(snd) \right) & \text{if } a \,\hat{=}\, (\rightarrow, fst, snd) \\ a.I \wedge Inv_{full}(b) & \text{if } a \in \{(\bigstar, b), (\Rightarrow, g, b)\} \end{cases}$$

$Inv_{full}(a)$ denotes the conjunction of $a.I$ and the invariants of its sub-ASTDs. When a contains several sub-ASTDs, we take the disjunction of their invariants, because the sub-state of a is in one of them.

Definition 2. *The invariant of the final states of an ASTD a is defined as follows:*

$$Inv_F(a) = \begin{cases} a.I & \text{if } type(a)=\text{Elem} \\ a.I \wedge \begin{pmatrix} \bigvee_{n \in a.SF} Inv_{full}(a.\nu(n)) \\ \vee \\ \bigvee_{n \in a.DF} Inv_F(a.\nu(n)) \end{pmatrix} & \text{if } type(a)=\text{Automaton} \\ a.I \wedge Inv_F(snd) & \text{if } a \mathrel{\widehat{=}} (\rightarrow, fst, snd) \\ a.I \wedge Inv_F(b) & \text{if } a \mathrel{\widehat{=}} (\Rightarrow, g, b) \\ a.I & \text{if } a \mathrel{\widehat{=}} (\bigstar, b) \end{cases}$$

$Inv_F(a)$ is the conjunction of $a.I$ and the disjunction of the invariants of its final states. A final state of an automaton can be deep or shallow. For a shallow final state n of a, we take the full invariant of n, because according to the definition of *final*, n is final irrespective of its current sub-state, so its sub-state can be in any of its sub-ASTDs. For a deep final state n, we know that it is final when its sub-ASTD is final, so we recursively call Inv_F on n to get only the invariants of its final states. For a sequence, it suffices to take into account $Inv_F(snd)$, because when a sequence is in its first ASTD, the initial state of the second ASTD must also be final, and it becomes a special of the second case. In addition, for a Kleene clsoure, the state is final while not started. Therefore, in that particular case, $Inv_F(a) = a.I$.

3.2   Proof Obligation Generation

To ensure that an ASTD is correct, we have to establish that the invariant of each reachable state is fulfilled. To generate the PO related to the correctness of an ASTD, we distinguish two cases:

– Initialisation: the state is determined by the *init* function at the initialisation of an ASTD;
– Transition: the state is reached through a transition.

We define in the following sections two functions to generate proof obligations, one for the initialisation, and another for the transitions. These functions recursively traverse an ASTD to generate POs for all of its invariants declared in its sub-ASTDs.

3.3   Proof Obligations for Initialisations

Following the semantics of ASTDs, initialisations are done from the main ASTD down to its sub-ASTDs. Therefore we introduce a recursive function $PO_i(a, J, H, Act)$ to generate proof obligations for initialisations where:

- a stands for the ASTD whose POs for initialisation are generated.
- J stands for the conjunction of all the invariants of enclosing ASTDs of a; it provides information on the values of the variables occurring in the initialisation expression Act. It will be used as an hypothesis when proving an invariant of a to provide properties of variables which are not initialised by Act.
- H contains the hypotheses obtained from enclosing ASTDs that are needed for the initialisation of the subsequent steps of a sequential execution; it is used in the Kleene closure and the sequence ASTDs, because the values of the enclosing variables are determined by the final states of the last executed ASTD.
- Act stands for all the actions that are executed before executing the initialisation of ASTD a, through the $init$ functions or the transitions that lead to a complex state of an Automaton.

To generate the PO of the initialisation of the main (*i.e.*, root) ASTD a of a specification and those of all its sub-ASTDs, the following call to PO_i is used: $PO_i(a, \text{true}, \text{true}, \text{skip})$. Hereafter, we give the definition of PO_i according to each type of ASTD. We illustrate them with the example of Fig. 1. We argue on the correction of these POs with respect to the semantics of the ASTDs.

Kleene Closure Initialisation

Let a be a Kleene closure ASTD on an ASTD b: $a \mathrel{\widehat{=}} (\bigstar, b)$. In that case, we have to prove that $a.J$ is verified and, for each iteration of the Kleene closure, the invariant of the initial state of b is verified too. This is expressed by the following proof obligation:

$$
\begin{aligned}
PO_i(a, J, H, Act) \mathrel{\widehat{=}}\ & \{H \Rightarrow [Act; Init(a)](a.I)\}\ \cup & (i)\\
& PO_i(b, (J \wedge a.I), H, (Act; Init(a)))\ \cup & (ii)\\
& PO_i(b, (J \wedge a.I), (J \wedge a.I \wedge Inv_F(b)), \text{skip}) & (iii)
\end{aligned}
$$

(i) PO (i) aims at verifying that $a.I$ holds after executing the initialisation $Init(a)$ of a following the initialisation actions Act executed in enclosing ASTDs. H provides the properties of variables which are not affected by $(Act; Init(a))$. Invariants of enclosing ASTDs do not have to be proved again, because $Init(a)$ does not modify variables of enclosing ASTDs.

(ii) PO (ii) is related to the first iteration of the ASTD b. $a.I$ is added to the invariant of enclosing ASTDs of b. $Init(a)$ is added to the sequence of actions that have been executed.

(iii) PO (iii) corresponds to the second and next iterations of b. As the next iterations will happen from the final state of b, the value of the variables of the enclosing ASTDs, which are in the initialisation of b, are described by $J \wedge a.I$ and the final values of these variables at the end of b, given by $Inv_F(b)$; thus, these two formulas are conjoined and passed as the value of H for proving the invariant of b. skip is used as the set of previous actions executed (parameter Act), because H denotes what is known about the values of the variables of the enclosing ASTDs.

To illustrate these definitions, consider the following call to compute the POs for the initialisation of ASTD A of Fig. 1: $PO_i(A, \text{true}, \text{true}, \text{skip})$. It generates the following PO:

$$\text{true} \Rightarrow [Init(A)](A.I)$$

which is reduced to $\{(0 \geq 0)\}$ after applying the substitutions. In addition, it generates the following two recursive calls:

1. $PO_i(B, A.I, \text{true}, Init(A))$
2. $PO_i(B, A.I, (A.I \wedge Inv_F(B)), \text{skip})$;

where $Inv_F(B) = B.I \wedge E.I \wedge F.I \wedge S3.I$, because B has only one final state, $S3$.

Sequence Initialisation

Let a be a Sequence ASTD: $a \mathrel{\widehat{=}} (\rightarrow, fst, snd)$. In that case, we have to prove that the invariant of the initial states of fst and snd are fulfilled when these states are reached. The generated POs are:

$$
\begin{aligned}
PO_i(a, J, H, Act) \mathrel{\widehat{=}} \ & \{H \Rightarrow [Act; Init(a)](a.I)\} \ \cup & (i) \\
& PO_i(fst, (J \wedge a.I), H, (Act; Init(a))) \ \cup & (ii) \\
& PO_i(snd, (J \wedge a.I), (J \wedge a.I \wedge Inv_F(fst)), \text{skip}) & (iii)
\end{aligned}
$$

(i) This PO follows the same pattern as case (i) of a Kleene closure.
(ii) This PO is related to the initialisation of the ASTD fst which occurs at the start of the sequence ASTD. It follows the same pattern as case (ii) of a Kleene closure.
(iii) This PO corresponds to the initialisation of the ASTD snd. According to the rule $\rightarrow_2$ (see Sect. 2.3), the initialisation of snd can occur only when fst is in a final state. Therefore, the PO is generated by taking $(J \wedge a.I \wedge Inv_F(fst))$ as hypothesis and skip as previous action since no additional action is executed when moving from the ASTD fst into snd in a sequence ASTD.

To illustrate these definitions, consider the following call to compute the POs for the initialisation of ASTD B of Fig. 1: $PO_i(B, A.I, \text{true}, Init(A))$. By applying the definitions, we obtain one generated PO and two recursive calls:

(i) $true \Rightarrow [Init(A); Init(B)] B.I)$: after substitution, we obtain the PO: $\{(0 + 1 > 0)\}$
(ii) $PO_i(C, (A.I \wedge B.I), \text{true}, (Init(A); Init(B)))$;
(iii) $PO_i(E, (A.I \wedge B.I), (A.I \wedge B.I \wedge C.I), \text{skip})$: where $C.I = Inv_F(C)$ because C is a Kleene closure.

Guard Initialisation

Let $a \mathrel{\widehat{=}} (\Rightarrow, g, b)$ be a Guard ASTD on an ASTD b. The invariant of the initial state of b is verified by the following proof obligation:

$$
\begin{aligned}
PO_i(a, J, H, Act) \mathrel{\widehat{=}} \ & \{H \Rightarrow [Act; Init(a)](a.I)\} \ \cup & (i) \\
& PO_i(b, (J \wedge a.I), H, (Act; Init(a))) & (ii)
\end{aligned}
$$

(i) This PO follows the same pattern as in case (i) for a Kleene closure.
(ii) This PO is related to the initialisation of the sub-ASTD b. It follows the same pattern as case (ii) of a Kleene closure and a sequence.

Note that the guard predicate g is not used in the generated POs. According to the guard semantics given by rules $\Rightarrow_1$ and $\Rightarrow_2$, the guard only applies to the first transition of b. The initialisation of a guard ASTD is executed before g is evaluated in the first transition of the guard body. Therefore, no information can be obtained from g in a guard ASTD initialisation. To illustrate these definitions, consider the call (iii) from the previous section:

$$PO_i(E, (A.I \wedge B.I), (A.I \wedge B.I \wedge C.I), \text{skip})$$

It generates the following PO and one recursive call:

(i) $(A.I \wedge B.I \wedge C.I) \Rightarrow [Init(E)]\ (E.I)$: After substitution, we obtain the PO:

$$(A.I \wedge B.I \wedge C.I) \Rightarrow (x_A \geq 0 \wedge x_A < x_B \wedge x_A \leq x_A)$$

(ii) $PO_i(F, (A.I \wedge B.I \wedge E.I), (A.I \wedge B.I \wedge C.I), Init(E))$;

Automaton Initialisation
Let a be an automaton with $a.n_0$ as initial state. Automaton initialisation POs are generated as follows:

$$
\begin{aligned}
PO_i(a, J, H, Act) \;\hat{=}\; &\{H \Rightarrow [Act; Init(a)](a.I)\} \cup &(i)\\
&PO_i(a.\nu(n_0), (J \wedge a.I), H, (Act; Init(a))) &(ii)
\end{aligned}
$$

(i) This PO follows the same pattern as in case (i) for a Kleene closure.
(ii) This PO is related to the initialisation of the initial state of a. This initialisation occurs at the start of the Automaton ASTD according to the syntax. It follows the same pattern as case (ii) of a Kleene closure, sequence and guard.

The initial state $a.n_0$ could be an elementary state $(i.e. \text{type}(a.n_o) = \textsf{Elem})$. Therefore we introduce a PO for a call on an elementary state n as follows:

$$PO_i(n, J, H, Act) = \{H \Rightarrow [Act](n.I)\}$$

This PO follows the same pattern as the first generated PO for a complex ASTD, except there is no additional action of initialisation. That is because an elementary state does not initialise variables.

In Fig. 1, F is an Automaton with an elementary state as initial state. With the call (ii) from the Guard initialisation:

$$PO_i(F, (A.I \wedge B.I \wedge E.I), (A.I \wedge B.I \wedge C.I), Init(E))$$

we obtain two generated POs:

(i) $(A.I \wedge B.I \wedge C.I) \Rightarrow [Init(E); Init(F)](F.I)$: After substitution, we obtain the PO:

$$(A.I \wedge B.I \wedge C.I) \Rightarrow (0 \geq 0)$$

(ii) $PO_i(S2, (A.I \wedge B.I \wedge E.I \wedge F.I), (A.I \wedge B.I \wedge C.I), (Init(E); Init(F)))$: we apply the definition of PO_i for an elementary state, generating the following formula:

$$\{ (A.I \wedge B.I \wedge C.I) \Rightarrow [Init(E); Init(F)](S2.I) \}$$

After substitution, we obtain the PO:

$$\{ (A.I \wedge B.I \wedge C.I) \Rightarrow (0 = 0 \vee x_A > x_A) \}$$

3.4 Proof Obligations for Local Transitions

When a transition t is triggered, it makes the system move from a source state n_1 to a target state n_2. So, we have to verify that the invariant of n_2 and those of its enclosing ASTDs are fulfilled. To this aim, we take as hypotheses the invariant of n_1 and those of its enclosing ASTDs. To get the set of POs associated with transitions, we introduce the recursive function $PO_{tr}(a, J)$ where:

- a stands for the ASTD whose POs for transitions are generated.
- J stands for all the invariants from the enclosing ASTD of a. Besides $a.I$, a must verify J.

The POs associated with the transitions of the main (i.e., root) ASTD a are generated by calling PO_{tr} as follows: $PO_{tr}(a, \text{true})$. Hereafter, we give the definition of PO_{tr} according to each type of ASTD:

$PO_{tr}(a, J) =$

(i) If $a \;\hat{=}\; (\rightarrow, fst, snd)$: $PO_{tr}(fst, J \wedge a.I)\; \cup PO_{tr}(snd, J \wedge a.I)$
(ii) If $a \in \{(\bigstar, b), (\Rightarrow, g, b)\}$: $PO_{tr}(b, J \wedge a.I)$
(iii) If type(a)=Automaton:

$$\bigcup s \cdot (s \in a.S \wedge a.\nu(s) \neq \text{Elem}) \mid (PO_{tr}(s, J \wedge a.I)) \tag{iii-1}$$

$$\cup \bigcup \tau \cdot (\tau \in a.\delta) \mid \tag{iii-2}$$
$$(\{J \wedge a.I \wedge H_{\tau.final?}(\tau.\eta.n_1) \wedge \tau.g \Rightarrow [\tau.A_{tr}](J \wedge a.I)\} \cup \tag{iii-2.1}$$
$$PO_i(\nu(\tau.\eta.n_2), J \wedge a.I, J \wedge a.I \wedge H_{\tau.final?}(\tau.\eta.n_1) \wedge \tau.g, \tau.A_{tr})) \tag{iii-2.2}$$

where: $H_{true} \;\hat{=}\; Inv_F$ & $H_{false} \;\hat{=}\; Inv_{full}$

(i), (ii) According to the ASTD syntax, transitions only occur in an Automaton. Thus, in a Sequence, Kleene closure or Guard ASTD, recursive calls on PO_{tr} are done on sub-ASTDs.

(iii-1) In an Automaton, there are states and transitions. For each states, if the state is a complex ASTD *i.e.*, is not elementary, then a recursive call on PO_{tr} must be done on this sub-ASTD to check all Automaton ASTD.

(iii-2) For each transition τ in an Automaton ASTD, POs have to be generated to verify that invariants of the target state are fulfilled after executing action $\tau.A_{tr}$.

(iii-2.1) This PO aims at verifying the preservation of invariants of enclosing ASTDs through the action of the transition. All invariants from the source state are gathered as hypotheses, as well as the guard $\tau.g$. A distinction is made on the *final?* property of the transition using term $H_{\tau.final?}$ because it determines if the previous state was final or not. For a final transition, we use Inv_F, providing more precise hypotheses for the proof, otherwise we use Inv_{full}.

(iii-2.2) This PO aims at verifying that the local invariant of the target state is fulfilled after the execution of the transition. A recursive call to PO_i is done because the target state could be a complex ASTD, so it is initialised with the transition as premises.

In Fig. 1, F is an Automaton ASTD. The call (obtained after going down the recursion from A)

$$PO_{tr}(F, (A.I \wedge B.I \wedge E.I))$$

We obtain four generated POs:

1. $(A.I \wedge B.I \wedge E.I \wedge F.I \wedge S2.I) \Rightarrow [Act(e2)](A.I \wedge B.I \wedge E.I \wedge F.I)$:
   After substitution, we obtain the PO:
   $(A.I \wedge B.I \wedge E.I \wedge F.I \wedge S2.I) \Rightarrow$
   $(x_A + x_B \geq 0 \wedge x_B > 0 \wedge (x_E \geq 0 \wedge x_E < x_B \wedge x_E \leq x_A + x_B) \wedge x_F + 1 \geq 0)$

2. $PO_i(S3, (A.I \wedge B.I \wedge E.I \wedge F.I), (A.I \wedge B.I \wedge E.I \wedge F.I \wedge S2.I), Act e2)$:
   We apply the formula for an elementary state:
   $(A.I \wedge B.I \wedge E.I \wedge F.I \wedge S2.I) \Rightarrow [Act(e2)](S3.I)$:
   After substitution, we obtain the PO:
   $(A.I \wedge B.I \wedge E.I \wedge F.I \wedge S2.I) \Rightarrow (x_F + 1 > 0 \wedge x_A + x_B > x_E)$

3. $(A.I \wedge B.I \wedge E.I \wedge F.I \wedge S3.I \wedge Guard(e3)) \Rightarrow [Act(e3)](A.I \wedge B.I \wedge E.I \wedge F.I)$:
   After substitution, we obtain the PO:
   $(A.I \wedge B.I \wedge E.I \wedge F.I \wedge S3.I \wedge Guard(e3))$
   $\Rightarrow (x_A - x_E \geq 0 \wedge x_B > 0 \wedge (x_E < x_B \wedge x_E \geq 0 \wedge x_E \leq x_A - x_E) \wedge x_F \geq 0)$

4. $PO_i(S2, (A.I \wedge B.I \wedge E.I \wedge F.I), (A.I \wedge B.I \wedge E.I \wedge F.I \wedge S3.I \wedge Guard(e3)), Act e3)$:
   We apply the formula for an elementary state:
   $\{(A.I \wedge B.I \wedge E.I \wedge F.I \wedge S3.I \wedge Guard(e3)) \Rightarrow [Act(e3)](S2.I)\}$:
   After substitution, we obtain the PO:
   $\{(A.I \wedge B.I \wedge E.I \wedge F.I \wedge S3.I \wedge Guard(e3)) \Rightarrow (x_F = 0 \vee x_A - x_E > x_E)\}$

3.5 Proving Proof Obligations and Strengthening Invariants

In this section, we describe how to verify the generated proof obligations using RODIN and how to reinforce invariants using ProB when POs are unprovable.

Using RODIN, proof obligations are represented as theorems of an EVENT-B contexts. Since variables of an ASTD are typed in their declaration (*i.e.*, $x : T$), we add this type in the invariant of the ASTD using $x \in T \wedge a.I$. Free variables are universally quantified in each PO when defining them as theorems.

The PO generated for the initialisation of the ASTD E is the following:

$$(A.I \wedge B.I \wedge C.I) \Rightarrow [Init(E)](E.I)$$

Adding types of variables, replacing invariants names by their definitions and adding quantifiers on free variables, we obtain the following formula which is added as a theorem in a RODIN context:

$$\forall x_A \cdot \forall x_B \cdot \forall x_C \cdot (\;((x_A \in \mathbb{Z} \wedge x_A \geq 0) \wedge (x_B \in \mathbb{Z} \wedge x_B > 0) \wedge$$
$$(x_B > x_A \wedge x_C \in \mathbb{Z}))$$
$$\Rightarrow$$
$$(x_A \in \mathbb{Z} \wedge x_A \geq 0 \wedge x_A < x_B \wedge x_A \leq x_A)))$$

This theorem is trivial to prove, since the goal consists of trivial properties or formulas available in the hypotheses.

The following PO, related to the initialisation of the ASTD D after more than one iteration of the closure ASTD C, is less trivial and requires some deduction rules which are automatically applied by the Rodin provers.

$$\forall x_A \cdot \forall x_B \cdot \forall x_C \cdot \forall x_D \cdot (\;((x_A \in \mathbb{Z} \wedge x_A \geq 0) \wedge (x_B \in \mathbb{Z} \wedge x_B > 0) \wedge$$
$$(x_C \in \mathbb{Z} \wedge x_B > x_A) \wedge$$
$$(x_D \in \mathbb{Z} \wedge x_D > 0) \wedge (x_C \geq x_D \wedge x_A > 0))$$
$$\Rightarrow$$
$$(x_C + 1 \in \mathbb{Z} \wedge x_C + 1 > 0))$$

As hypotheses, we have $x_C \in \mathbb{Z}$ and $x_C \geq x_D \wedge x_D > 0$ so the goal $(x_C + 1 \in \mathbb{Z} \wedge x_C + 1 > 0)$ is proven.

When a theorem is added to the context, RODIN will automatically try to prove it. If it fails, the user has to prove it using the interactive provers. When we fail to discharge a proof obligation, we use the model checker PROB [8] to find a possible counter-example for it. The counter-example gives the values of the different variables that violate one or several invariants. To fix this counter-example, two cases are distinguished:

1. The counter-example denotes a reachable state: it means that the invariant of a state is false and it should be corrected.
2. The counter-example is not a reachable state: in that case, the invariant that is violated is of the form P1 $\Rightarrow$ P2. This means that P1 is too weak; that is, P1 denotes an unreachable state. To fix that, we have to strengthen some state invariants to rule out this counter-example.

In Fig. 1, the generated PO for the transition e3 is not provable. The counter-example found by PROB asserts that at the state *S3*, the values of the variables are as follows: $x_A = 2; x_B = 2; x_E = 1; x_F = 1$. Then, during the transition, the substitution $x_A := x_A - x_E$ is done, setting x_A to 1, and thus, $S2.I \equiv$ $(x_F = 0 \vee x_A > x_E)$ is not satisfied. In fact, the state $S3$ is not reachable for $x_A \leq 2x_E$. That is because $S2 \equiv x_A \geq x_E \wedge x_B > x_E$ and the transition e2 does the substitution $x_A := x_A + x_B$ which leads to $x_A > 2x_E$ in state $S3$. Thus, we derive a new invariant for $S3$ that rules out the counter-example:

$$x_F > 0 \wedge x_A > 2x_E$$

It must be kept in mind that modifying an invariant modifies the generated proof obligations. The Rodin archive of the running example can be found in [3]. Proof obligations for the final version (corrected with the above new invariant) are automatically proved by Rodin.

4   Conclusion

In this paper, we have presented a systematic formal approach to verify the satisfaction of local invariants of ASTDs diagrams. Roughly speaking, an ASTDs is a set of hierarchical states (simple or complex) related by process algebra operators and transitions. Local invariants can be associated to these states. We generate proof obligations to ensure that each reachable state satisfies its invariant. To this aim, our approach consists in recursively traversing the hierarchical states and analysing state initialization and transition actions to generate appropriate proof obligations. The generated proof obligations are defined as theorems in Event-B contexts and are discharged using the Rodin platform, and debugged using PROB by using it as a model checker of first-order formulas. To show the feasibility of our approach, we have applied it on several examples which are available in [3].

We are currently working on the implementation of a tool that automatically generates the proof obligations from the ASTD specification. We are also working on the proof obligations of the remaining ASTD operators (flow, choice, synchronization and their quantified versions). Shared variables within synchronized ASTDs represent a challenge for defining proof obligations, because potential interferences between different ASTDs must be taken into account. Future work also includes considering the timed extension of ASTDs as defined on basic ASTD operators in [2]. Finally, it would be important to formally prove the correctness of our proof obligations. We intend to use the approach proposed in [15], where the theory plugin of RODIN is used to build a meta-model of a specification language (EVENT-B). We could follow a similar approach and define the semantics of ASTDs in a RODIN Theory, and then show that our proof obligations are sufficient to show that the invariants are preserved over the traces of an ASTD. This is a quite challenging task, since the semantics of ASTDs is more complex than the one illustrated in [15].

References

1. de Azevedo Oliveira, D., Frappier, M.: Modelling an automotive software system with TASTD. In: Glässer, U., Creissac Campos, J., Méry, D., Palanque, P. (eds.) Rigorous State-Based Methods (ABZ2023). LNCS, vol. 14010, pp. 124–141. Springer, Cham (2023). https://doi.org/10.1007/978-3-031-33163-3_10

2. de Azevedo Oliveira, D., Frappier, M.: TASTD: A real-time extension for ASTD. In: Glässer, U., Campos, J.C., Méry, D., Palanque, P.A. (eds.) Rigorous State-Based Methods (ABZ2023). LNCS, vol. 14010, pp. 142–159. Springer, Cham (2023). https://doi.org/10.1007/978-3-031-33163-3_11

3. Cartellier, Q.: https://gitlab.com/QCartellier/icfem2023-poastd/-/tree/main/ (2023)

4. El Jabri, C., Frappier, M., Ecarot, T., Tardif, P.M.: Development of monitoring systems for anomaly detection using ASTD specifications. In: Aït-Ameur, Y., Crăciun, F. (eds.) TASE. LNCS, vol. 13299, pp. 274–289. Springer (2022). https://doi.org/10.1007/978-3-031-10363-6_19

5. Fayolle, T.: Combinaison de méthodes formelles pour la spécification de systèmes industriels. Theses, Université Paris-Est; Université de Sherbrooke, Québec, Canada, June 2017

6. Frappier, M., Gervais, F., Laleau, R., Fraikin, B., St-Denis, R.: Extending Statecharts with process algebra operators. ISSE 4(3), 285–292 (2008)

7. Khan, A.H., Rauf, I., Porres, I.: Consistency of UML class and Statechart diagrams with state invariants. In: MODELSWARD, pp. 14–24. SciTePress (2013)

8. Leuschel, M., Butler, M.: ProB: an automated analysis toolset for the B Method. JSTTT 10(2), 185–203 (2008)

9. Mammar, A., Frappier, M.: Modeling of a speed control system using event-B. In: Raschke, A., Méry, D., Houdek, F. (eds.) ABZ 2020. LNCS, vol. 12071, pp. 367–381. Springer, Cham (2020). https://doi.org/10.1007/978-3-030-48077-6_29

10. Mammar, A., Frappier, M., Laleau, R.: An event-B model of an automotive adaptive exterior light system. In: Raschke, A., Méry, D., Houdek, F. (eds.) ABZ 2020. LNCS, vol. 12071, pp. 351–366. Springer, Cham (2020). https://doi.org/10.1007/978-3-030-48077-6_28

11. Milhau, J., Frappier, M., Gervais, F., Laleau, R.: Systematic translation rules from ASTD to event-B. In: Méry, D., Merz, S. (eds.) IFM 2010. LNCS, vol. 6396, pp. 245–259. Springer, Heidelberg (2010). https://doi.org/10.1007/978-3-642-16265-7_18

12. Nganyewou Tidjon, L., Frappier, M., Leuschel, M., Mammar, A.: Extended algebraic state-transition diagrams. In: 2018 23rd International Conference on Engineering of Complex Computer Systems (ICECCS), pp. 146–155. IEEE Computer Society (2018)

13. Porres, I., Rauf, I.: Generating class contracts from UML protocol statemachines. In: Proceedings of the 6th International Workshop on Model-Driven Engineering, Verification and Validation. MoDeVVa 2009, ACM, New York, USA (2009)

14. Porres, I., Rauf, I.: From nondeterministic UML protocol statemachines to class contracts. In: 2010 Third International Conference on Software Testing, Verification and Validation, pp. 107–116 (2010)

15. Riviere, P., Singh, N.K., Ameur, Y.A., Dupont, G.: Formalising liveness properties in event-b with the reflexive EB4EB framework. In: Rozier, K.Y., Chaudhuri, S. (eds.) NASA Formal Methods - 15th International Symposium, NFM 2023, Houston, TX, USA, May 16–18, 2023, Proceedings. Lecture Notes in Computer

Science, vol. 13903, pp. 312–331. Springer, Cham (2023). https://doi.org/10.1007/978-3-031-33170-1_19

16. Said, M.Y., Butler, M.J., Snook, C.F.: A method of refinement in UML-B. Softw. Syst. Model. **14**(4), 1557–1580 (2015)
17. Sekerinski, E.: Verifying Statecharts with state invariants. In: 13th International Conference on Engineering of Complex Computer Systems (ICECCS), pp. 7–14. IEEE Computer Society (2008)
18. Tidjon, L.N., Frappier, M., Mammar, A.: Intrusion detection using ASTDs. In: Barolli, L., Amato, F., Moscato, F., Enokido, T., Takizawa, M. (eds.) AINA 2020. AISC, vol. 1151, pp. 1397–1411. Springer, Cham (2020). https://doi.org/10.1007/978-3-030-44041-1_118

Doctoral Symposium Papers

Formal Verification of the Burn-to-Claim Blockchain Interoperable Protocol

Babu Pillai[1,2]([✉]), Zhé Hóu[1], Kamanashis Biswas[1,3],
and Vallipuram Muthukkumarasamy[1]

[1] Griffith University, Gold Coast, Australia
babu.pillai@outlook.com
[2] Southern Cross University, Lismore, Australia
[3] Australian Catholic University, Brisbane, Australia

Abstract. This paper introduces an abstract blockchain model that employs the Burn-to-Claim cross-blockchain protocol [1]. This multi-level simulator models a virtual environment of nodes running on the Ethereum Virtual Machine (EVM). Developed using the $CSP\#$ language [2], it has undergone formal verification with the model checker PAT. Focusing on inter-network operations, our model (https://github.com/b-pillai/Burn-to-Claim-formal-verification) examines the properties of correctness, security, and atomicity using PAT. Surprisingly, atomicity, assumed to be inherent in the time-lock mechanism of the Burn-to-Claim protocol, does not always hold. We establish its validity under specific assumptions while confirming the protocol's correctness and security under the added assumptions.

Keywords: Burn-to-Claim · blockchain · interoperability · formal verification

1 Introduction

Despite the recent surge in the number of proposed interoperable protocols, there is a lack of formal guarantees for the properties of those protocols. This is also a common issue in the field of (cyber)security, where much of the protocol design is proved by hand, which is error-prone. Commercial developments of such cyber and network systems are often validated by extensive software testing, but testing can only show the presence of bugs, not their absence. In recent years, formal verification has been used for verifying highly sensitive systems and protocols.

In this paper, we employ a tool named Process Analysis Toolkit (PAT) [3], which supports modelling, simulation and verification of many forms of systems. The supported modelling languages include Hoare's Communicating Sequential Processes [4] extended with C# (CSP#), timed automata, real-time systems, probabilistic systems and hierarchical systems.

The main contributions of this paper include:

© The Author(s), under exclusive license to Springer Nature Singapore Pte Ltd. 2023
Y. Li and S. Tahar (Eds.): ICFEM 2023, LNCS 14308, pp. 249–254, 2023.
https://doi.org/10.1007/978-981-99-7584-6_15

- Modelling: We build a formal model for the Burn-to-Claim blockchain inter-operable protocol [1] using CSP# that focused on inter-network operations within a network.
- Verification: Using the developed models, we specify several correctness and security properties using LTL and reachability and verify them using the PAT system.
- Findings: We discuss the verification results. In particular, the atomicity property, which contrary to the common understanding of the adopted time-lock technique, does not hold in general. However, it holds under certain assumptions.

2   An Overview of the Burn-to-Claim Protocol

At the highest level, our objective is to construct a model encompassing a scenario wherein a *user* intends to transfer an asset from one blockchain network to another. The *Burn-to-Claim* protocol [1,5] facilitates this transfer, ensuring that the asset is destroyed (or removed) from the originating blockchain network and subsequently re-created on the destination network. Within this process, the networks from which the asset is removed are termed *source* networks, while those to which the asset is transferred are labelled *destination* networks. This transfer procedure is twofold: initially, the source network produces a self-verifiable transfer-proof, and subsequently, upon verifying this proof, the destination network reconstitutes the asset.

Workflow. Upon initiating the *exitTransaction* in the source network, nodes within this network validate the transaction request. The primary objective is to generate a *proof*, which allows verification of the specific transaction without needing to reference the entire history of the associated asset. After this transaction is committed in the source chain, the *transfer-proof* triggers an *entryTransaction* in the destination network, paving the way for the asset's recreation in the recipient network. Nodes within the destination network then validate the *transfer-proof* and proceed to recreate the asset. We model the above system for formal verification in different modules described below.

Module 1—exitTransaction. This transaction triggers a transfer request on the source network, creating an exit point for an asset on the sender's blockchain through network consensus. The system's generation of a *transfer-proof* ensures security. Once the network agrees on the transaction's authenticity, a *transfer-proof* log is added to the next block, and the asset is locked to prevent further extensions.

Module 2—entryTransaction. This transaction aims to replicate the asset in the destination network. Executing the *entryTransaction* and *transfer-proof* functions from the source chain, the network validates the *transfer-proof* and reproduces the asset.

Let us assume the *exitTransaction* log and timestamp on the sender network created of t_1 time will be delivered to the recipient network through a gateway node with a time latency of t_2.

Module 3—reclaimTransaction. If the recipient does not claim the asset within the time-lock period t_2, the sender can use *reclaimTransaction* to retrieve it. The function verifies the signature and time-lock before returning the asset to the sender.

3 Specifications of the Protocol

In order to perform verification and show that the system model satisfies a set of desired requirements, we define a set of four scenarios to check the functional security of the system. 1) A sender sends a transaction and the correct recipient makes the claim. 2) A sender sends a transaction and after the time lock period reclaims the asset. 3) A sender sends a transaction and a malicious recipient tries to make the claim. 4) A malicious sender sends a transaction and tries to reclaim it within the time-lock period. Based on the above four cases, we have defined a set of properties that should hold in the Burn-to-Claim protocol [1,5].

Property 1 (Burn-Before-Claim). An asset that is transferred from the source network must be burned on the source network before the recipient can claim it on the recipient network.

Property 2 (No-Double-Spend). Double spending is not permitted in the Burn-to-Claim protocol.

Property 3 (Correctness). The Burn-to-Claim protocol only transfers an asset to the correct recipient.

Property 4 (Strong-Atomicity). The transfer operation should only obtain one of the following outcomes: either the transfer succeeds, and the asset is transferred to the recipient, or it fails, and the asset returns to the sender.

Property 5 (Weak-Atomicity). Under the assumption that either the recipient or the sender is guaranteed to make the (re)claim, a transfer operation should only have one of the following outcomes: either the transfer succeeds, and the asset is transferred to the recipient, or it fails, and the asset returns to the sender.

4 The Model for Cross-Blockchain Interactions

In this model, we focus on the inter-network events, and we only consider high level operations of transaction and mining, and leave the detailed intra-network operations to a different model that will be discussed in the next section.

The two networks are defined as constants N_1 and N_2 representing the source network as N_1 and destination network as N_2. A set of variables defined are

TxItems to hold the number of items in a transaction, *MaxTx* set the maximum number of transactions, *MaxMiners* set the number of miners, *TxAmount* to hold defaults value to transfer, *InitAmount* to hold initial wallet balance, *MaxUsers* number of users and *ChannelBufferSize* for channel buffer size.

The structure of blockchain is not critical in this model; therefore, for simplicity, we view blockchain data structure as a list of transactions as in *tx[0]*, as transactions in N_1, *tx[1]* as transactions in N_2.

Users. There are four types of users in the model: *User1, User2, Sender* and *Recipient. User1* and *User2* are network specific participants. That is, *User1* exists only in N_1 and is able to send transactions within the same network. Similarly, *User2* exists and operates only within N_2. We model the transaction as a tuple of six items in the order of *sender's network, senders address, recipient network, recipient address, beta, value, gamma, miner address.* In reference to the transaction *Tx* defined in the Burn-to-Claim paper [1], we omitted previous transaction $Tx^\dagger$ as it is not important in this model. Based on the role and requirement, the network participants send separate transactions. The *Sender* and *Recipient* are participants that can send cross network transactions to another network. The sender and recipient use separate channels to broadcast the transaction.

Miners. We model two types of miners *Miner1* and *Miner2*. Miner1 is a miner on the network N_1, listening to the channels of [*trans1, exit* and *rec*]. This miner execute a relevant function based on the channel the message is coming from. The Miner2 is mining on N_2, listening to the channels of [*trans2* and *entry*] and executes a relevant function based on the channel the message is coming from.

The Mining Process. There are five processes defined which will be executed by the miner based on the input request. The *minerVerify1* process facilitates value transfers within N_1. It first verifies conditions like transfer networks and user limits before executing the transfer. *minerVerify2* serves a similar purpose for N_2. When *exitTransaction* is invoked, miners ensure the user has sufficient funds. The *exportVerifier* process, in this model, is simplified, excluding signature verification. If conditions are met, tokens are transferred to a burn-address. For the *entryTransaction*, miners validate time-lock, burn-address status, and the provided security code. If verified, the recipient's wallet increases. For the *reclaimTransaction*, similar checks are made, and upon validation, the sender's wallet is refunded.

Process Execution. We model the execution of cross-blockchain transfer in a blockchain as a *CrossBlockchains()* process. The process is structured such that the *mining, user,* and *BurnToClaim()* processes run concurrently. The *mining* process begins with miners mining on both N_1 and N_2. Meanwhile, users process their transactions on their respective chains. The *BurnToClaim()* process then executes the defined scenarios based on the user's selection.

5 System Verification

In this section, we cover the model's targeted assertions and properties, outline the verification procedures and present results. An assertion examines system behaviours. For a given process, it checks if a state meets a specific condition. When process p runs, if e is true, then f remains true.

To verify Property 1 (Burn-Before-Claim), we define an assertion in PAT as below. This assertion verifies that an asset is burned before the recipient's claim using $[(pClaimed -> [\ ](!pBurned))]$. Results confirm the asset must be burned prior to a claim. In our model, the sender commits the transfer to a burn address, and once the network accepts it, the decision is deemed final.

```
#assert CrossChains |= [](pClaimed -> [](!pBurned));
```

We define the three assertions given below to check Property 2, *double spending*. The initial assertion examines if an asset, once claimed by the recipient, cannot be reclaimed by the sender using $[(pClaimed->\ )]$. The next assertion observes whether the recipient's wallet increases, while the sender remains unchanged using $[(recipientClaimed\ \&\ senderReclaimed)]$. Lastly, an assertion confirms against double spending scenarios, ensuring that both recipient claims and sender reclaims cannot coexist, as evidenced by $[(pReclaimed->\ )]$. Verification results from these three assertions confirm the impossibility of double spending in this model's configuration.

```
#assert CrossChains |= [](pClaimed -> [](!pReclaimed));
#assert CrossChains |= []!(rClaimed && sReclaimed);
#assert CrossChains |= [](pReclaimed -> [](!pClaimed));
```

To check the Property 3 (correctness), we define the assertion given below. This assertion examines if a burned asset remains in the burn address, is claimed by the recipient, or is reclaimed by the sender, represented by $[(pBurned -> [\ ](burnValueExists\ ||\ pClaimed\ ||\ pReclaimed))]$. Verification confirms that a burned asset consistently stays in its burn address throughout the process.

```
#assert CrossChains |=
[](pBurned -> [](burnValueExists || pClaimed || pReclaimed));
```

We define below two assertions to check strong atomicity (Property 4) and week atomicity (Property 5) atomicity:

```
#assert CrossChains|= [](rClaimed || senderReclaimed));
#assert CrossChains|= [](protocolCompleted ->
    (rClaimed || senderReclaimed));
```

The first assertion checks strong atomicity using *(recipientClaimed || sender-Reclaimed)*. The verification of Property 4 fails as PAT found a counterexample event sequence, which we analyse the explain below.

5.1 Discussion

Why General Atomicity Not Hold? Strong atomicity requires all related operations to succeed. In cross-blockchain contexts, this means assets are burned by the sender and claimed by the recipient. However, distributed environments face potential network partitions or system crashes, preventing participants from engaging. Apart from technical issues, intentional recipient inaction or incorrect asset burns by the sender can also compromise strong atomicity.

Cross-blockchain operators facilitate transactions for multiple self-interested parties. A single party's actions can have intricate impacts on others. Given the potential for malicious or irrational behaviour, the assumption is that both sender and recipient act in mutual interest. The sender burns the asset, and the recipient mints an equivalent asset. To validate weak atomicity, we use the second assertion (Property 5).

Property 5 (weak atomicity) assumes that if the sender burns the asset, the recipient must mint it. This is expressed using the second assertion *(protocol-Completed − > (RecipientClaimed || senderReclaimed))*. We introduce *protocol-Completed* to address network and node failures. This property holds.

6 Conclusion and Future Works

The current model focuses on verifying burn-before-claim (Property 1), double-spending (Property 2), correctness (Property 3), and both strong (Property 4) and weak atomicity (Property 5). While detailed transaction and block data structures are not considered, we model transaction verification's essential operations. Detailed transaction verification will be addressed in future work that incorporates a merge mining process.

References

1. Pillai, B., Biswas, K., Hóu, Z., Muthukkumarasamy, V.: Burn-to-claim: an asset transfer protocol for blockchain interoperability. Comput. Netw. **200**, 108495 (2021)
2. Sun, J., Liu, Y., Dong, J.S., Chen, C.: Integrating specification and programs for system modeling and verification. In: Third IEEE International Symposium on Theoretical Aspects of Software Engineering, pp. 127–135. IEEE (2009)
3. Sun, J., Liu, Y., Dong, J., Pang, J.: Towards flexible verification under fairness. In: CAV '09: 21th International Conference on Computer Aided Verification (2009)
4. Hoare, C.A.R.: Communicating sequential processes. Commun. ACM **21**(8), 666–677 (1978)
5. Pillai, B., Biswas, K., Hóu, Z., Muthukkumarasamy, V.: The burn-to-claim cross-blockchain asset transfer protocol. In: 2020 25th International Conference on Engineering of Complex Computer Systems (ICECCS), pp. 119–124. IEEE (2020)

Early and Systematic Validation
of Formal Models

Sebastian Stock$^{(\boxtimes)}$ (iD)

Johannes Kepler University, Altenbergerstr. 69, 4040 Linz, Austria
sebastian.stock@jku.at

Abstract. Verification and validation are equally important when creating and reasoning about formal models. Verification focuses on the consistency of a model, while validation answers whether a model appropriately represents the requirements. However, compared to verification, validation remains underrepresented in modeling activities, and one of the reasons for this underrepresentation is that the modeler postpones the validation till the end of the modeling process leading to the late discovery of mistakes. Countering this, we present a framework that integrates validation early and tightly in the modeling process.

Keywords: Validation · formal methods · formal modeling

1 Introduction

Creating a formal model can be a valuable tool in checking for the soundness and completeness of a set of natural language requirements [1] and modelers have sophisticated modeling languages like ASMs [3], Event-B [2] or TLA [10] at their disposal to express even complex requirements.

However, creating a model is not enough, as the models need to be checked for internal consistency and their ability to capture requirements adequately. For this, there is respectively verification and validation. Verification is commonly understood as checking for the internal consistency of a model, which also involves ruling out undesired states that violate predefined constraints. Over the years, the formal model community developed a broad band of techniques and tools to tackle the problem. One of the most commonly known verification techniques are model checkers, e.g., SPIN [15] or provers like Isabelle [8].

As important as the idea of verification is the idea of validation, i.e., the task of checking if the model represents the desired requirements. Validation is an intricate task. On the one hand, there is an overlap with the idea of verification, as ruling out undesired states and providing a consistent model is often

The research presented in this paper has been conducted within the IVOIRE project, which is funded by "Deutsche Forschungsgemeinschaft" (DFG) and the Austrian Science Fund (FWF) grant # I 4744-N and has been partly financed by the LIT Secure and Correct Systems Lab sponsored by the province of Upper Austria.

Y. Li and S. Tahar (Eds.): ICFEM 2023, LNCS 14308, pp. 255–260, 2023.
https://doi.org/10.1007/978-981-99-7584-6_16

within the requirements initially stated. On the other hand, validation touches upon subjects more known from the software engineering domain, e.g., checking if the model shows the desired behavior, interacting with different stakeholders, and transferring information about the requirements into the model (and the other way around). Over the years, several tools made their appearance to support the validation effort, e.g., ProB [11], however validation as a means to ensure model quality remains underrepresented, which is acknowledged within the communities publications [4, 9, 12].

One of the reasons for this phenomenon is that validation is typically applied to check on the final product while being absent from the early stages of development. The consequences are severe. Mistakes about the overall functionality of the model are often spotted too late, increasing development time and thus undermining the advantages of using a formal model in the first place. Overcoming this, we propose a framework to establish validation as an integral part of all modeling process stages. For this, we present contributions that (1) enhance state of the art in regards to structuring the validation process of a formal mode, thus enhancing reasoning about the state of the validation effort. (2) Deal with the challenges that are raised when refining validation results to transfer them between models, thus encouraging early validation as result can be kept. (3) Integrating both previous contributions in the larger framework of Validation-Driven Development (VDD) to ensure early and rigorous validation.

The rest of this paper is structured as follows: Sect. 2 will shortly introduce the necessary terms. Section 3 layout the three individual challenges in more details, and Sect. 4 will show the achievements while in Sect. 5 we conclude the paper and give an outlook to future work.

2   Background

Proof Obligations. Some modeling languages structure their verification effort and provide proof obligations (POs). POs, as the name suggests, are proofs that we are obligated to discharge to establish certain properties. There are POs for different purposes, e.g., well-definedness or deadlock freedom, of the model. In languages like Event-B, tools like Rodin [2] manage the creation and discharging of these POs.

The usage of POs is highly systematic which allows reasoning about the model and together with the syntactical rules of POs debugging models is made simple. The typical PO workflow can be described as: (1) We first model something, (2) the tool will generate POs, (3) we discharge the POs, and then we move on to the next feature. Failing POs point to missing or wrong premises in the model.

Validation Obligations. Validation Obligations (VOs) proposed by Mashkoor et al. [13] and aim to be a counterpart to POs as being a way to structure the validation effort and support the development workflow.

Refinement. Formal refinement is a means to establish a connection between two formal models. Different types and flavors are applicable under different circumstances as laid out by Derrick and Boiten [5]. Most of the time, when referring to refinement, one means that an existing model is enhanced, i.e., extended so that the refinement properties are not violated. The application of refinement is deeply entangled within the correct-by-construction idea, and both techniques are inherent to applying formal modeling languages. We start with an abstract representation of the problem, and through rigorous refinement, we create more and more concrete version representation until we capture the desired requirements in the model.

The idea of POs as a provider of structure and semantics also extends to the domain of refinement. If we use our Rodin/Event-B example again, we can see that POs cater to the Event-B refinement rules and ensure correct refinement. Within these POs, the modeler ensures that the refining machine C does not violate any POs successfully discharged in A.

3 Challenges

As stated back in Sect. 1, we have three challenges to overcome. In the following, we elaborate on these challenges and describe how we want to overcome them.

3.1 Structuring the Validation Workflow

As pointed out in Sect. 2, verification is highly systematic and structured, thus providing a range of advantages: Easy determination of whether the verification fails or succeeds. Information about completeness and coverage. Support in the development and debugging of formal models. The validation effort lacks these abilities, thus rendering it less attractive.

Goal. We want to provide these missing features to the validation effort. First, we provide a validation semantic enabling predictable behavior and easier reasoning and debugging. Also, information about coverage, completeness, and consistency is made readily available. Additionally, we want to provide tool support for generating and managing validation efforts, thus establishing validation progress as a measurement of success in the modeling process similar to verification.

3.2 Validation and Refinement

Verification is well supported by refinement as explained in Sect. 2. Once established, verification properties only need additional refinement proofs, which are often trivial and can be automatically discharged. Thus early adaptation in the development process is encouraged, as a refinement of the model is not punished by having to redo all verification efforts.

Validation, on the other hand, is missing a semantic for refinement, and additionally, many tools and techniques lack the capabilities to transfer insights between refinements. As validation can already be a cumbersome and tedious endeavor, the outlook of doing it again for each refinement step is discouraging.

Goal. Therefore, we propose to extend the semantic foundations laid in Sect. 3.1 to cater to refinement. Additionally, we want to provide techniques and tools that help transfer validation insights between refinement chains, thus encouraging early validation.

3.3   Creating the VDD Framework

As the two previous challenges show, verification is well integrated into the overall development process. We have semantics and tools that are tightly integrated into the workflow, thus delivering quick feedback on the matter. Furthermore, verification also shapes the modeling and reasoning process, as the ability to verify constructs shapes design and structuring decisions.

The goal stated for the previous two challenges is to provide the necessary foundations for a tighter validation integration in the development process of formal models. However, what is missing is a unifying rationale that lays out what a modeling process with a tightly integrated validation effort looks like.

Goal. Drawing from the contributions of Sects. 3.1 and 3.2, we propose a validation based approach to create formal models. We call this framework Validation-Driven Development (VDD) and its goal is to guide modelers to develop formal models that are complete and consistent regarding their requirements. Aiming at this, we investigate how we can integrate validation tightly into the general development process.

4   Results and Planned Contributions

The development process of the contribution can be seen in Fig. 1. Starting from semantics, we develop techniques and tools and apply them in practice. Later we draw from these practical insights to formulate a general Validation-Driven Development framework.

Validation Refinement and Domain Views. This contribution [18] focuses on two things. First, on the ability to refine VOs and, in a broader sense, combine refinement and the validation effort as laid out as a goal in Sect. 3.2. Second, it provides a unique way to create domain-specific views, enabling better communication with domain experts.

Trace Refinement. The creation and evaluation of traces is an elemental validation task. Traces check whether a state is reachable or whether a sequence of states or transitions is feasible. To encourage traces use early, this contribution [17] provides a refinement approach for traces. Thus contribution towards the goal of Sect. 3.2.

Case Study. The implementation [6] of the AMAN case study [14] not only provides valuable insides into the applicability of the VO approach but also served as a base for testing and evaluating the primary contributions. From here, we develop the VDD framework.

Validation-Driven Development. Validation-Driven development [16] (VDD) utilizes the insights gathered in the rest of the contributions to propose a complete development framework. It utilizes VOs to structure the validation and additionally draws from the contributions toward validation refinement introduced earlier. The insights are reapplied to the previously introduced case study.

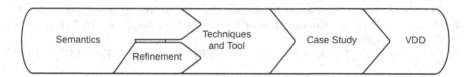

Fig. 1. Overview of dependencies in the contributed and proposed research

5 Conclusion and Future Work

In this paper we presented the progress towards developing a framework for integrating, rigorous and consistent validation into the development process of formal model. We call this framework Validation-Driven Development (VDD). In multiple contribution we lay out theoretical aspects, techniques for the transfer of validation results in refinement chains and the overall VDD framework that integrates these contributions into a bigger picture. For the future we want to contribute to two aspects of VDD:

Foundation of Validation Obligations. Yet missing from Sect. 4 and shown in Fig 1 is a contribution that lays out all basic semantics and foundations of VOs. This contribution is currently under review. It aims to tackle Sect. 3.1.

Trace Failure Refinement Checking. Trace failure refinement is a special form of refinement. Initially, it is known from process languages like CSP [7]. The idea is to transfer it to the state-based language Event-B to support the transfer of validation results, as the standard Event-B refinement focuses on verification tasks. This approach also is directed towards the goal formulated in Sect. 3.1 but is more general than the trace refinement approach.

References

1. Abran, A., Moore, J.W., Bourque, P., Dupuis, R., Tripp, L.: Software Engineering Body of Knowledge, vol. 25. IEEE Computer Society, Angela Burgess (2004)
2. Abrial, J.R.: Modeling in Event-B: System and Software Engineering. Cambridge University Press, Cambridge (2010)
3. Börger, E.: The ASM method for system design and analysis. A tutorial introduction. In: Gramlich, B. (ed.) FroCoS 2005. LNCS (LNAI), vol. 3717, pp. 264–283. Springer, Heidelberg (2005). https://doi.org/10.1007/11559306_15

4. Bowen, J., Hinchey, M.: Ten commandments of formal methods ...ten years later. Computer **39**(1), 40–48 (2006). https://doi.org/10.1109/MC.2006.35

5. Derrick, J., Boiten, E.: Refinement: Semantics, Languages and Applications, vol. 95. Springer, Cham (2018). https://doi.org/10.1007/978-3-319-92711-4

6. Geleßus, D., Stock, S., Vu, F., Leuschel, M., Mashkoor, A.: Modeling and analysis of a safety-critical interactive system through validation obligations. In: Glässer, U., Campos, J.C., Méry, D., Palanque, P.A. (eds.) ABZ 2023. LNCS, vol. 14010, pp. 284–302. Springer, Cham (2023). https://doi.org/10.1007/978-3-031-33163-3_22

7. Hoare, C.A.R., et al.: Communicating Sequential Processes, vol. 178. Prentice-Hall, Englewood Cliffs (1985)

8. Holzmann, G.J.: The model checker spin. IEEE Trans. Softw. Eng. **23**(5), 279–295 (1997)

9. Jacquot, J., Mashkoor, A.: The role of validation in refinement-based formal software development. In: Models: Concepts, Theory, Logic, Reasoning and Semantics - Essays Dedicated to Klaus-Dieter Schewe on the Occasion of his 60th Birthday, pp. 202–219 (2018)

10. Lamport, L.: The temporal logic of actions. ACM Trans. Program. Lang. Syst. (TOPLAS) **16**(3), 872–923 (1994)

11. Leuschel, M., Butler, M.: ProB: an automated analysis toolset for the B method. J. Softw. Tools Technol. Transf. **10**(2), 185–203 (2008)

12. Mashkoor, A., Kossak, F., Egyed, A.: Evaluating the suitability of state-based formal methods for industrial deployment. Softw. Pract. Exp. **48**(12), 2350–2379 (2018)

13. Mashkoor, A., Leuschel, M., Egyed, A.: Validation obligations: a novel approach to check compliance between requirements and their formal specification. In: ICSE'21 NIER, pp. 1–5 (2021)

14. Palanque, P., Campos, J.C.: Aman case study. In: Glässer, U., Creissac Campos, J., Méry, D., Palanque, P. (eds.) ABZ 2023. LNCS, vol. 14010, pp. 265–283. Springer, Cham (2023). https://doi.org/10.1007/978-3-031-33163-3_21

15. Paulson, L.C.: Isabelle: A Generic Theorem Prover. Springer, Cham (1994). https://doi.org/10.1007/BFb0030541

16. Stock, S., Mashkoor, A., Egyed, A.: Validation-driven development. In: Proceedings ICFEM (2023, to appear)

17. Stock, S., Mashkoor, A., Leuschel, M., Egyed, A.: Trace Refinement in B and Event-B. In: Riesco, A., Zhang, M. (eds.) ICFEM 2022. LNCS, vol. 13478, pp. 316–333. LNCS. Springer, Cham (2022). https://doi.org/10.1007/978-3-031-17244-1_19

18. Stock, S., Vu, F., Geleßus, D., Leuschel, M., Mashkoor, A., Egyed, A.: Validation by abstraction and refinement. In: Glässer, U., Creissac Campos, J., Méry, D., Palanque, P. (eds.) ABZ 2023. LNCS, vol. 14010, pp. 160–178. Springer, Cham (2023). https://doi.org/10.1007/978-3-031-33163-3_12

Verifying Neural Networks
by Approximating Convex Hulls

Zhongkui Ma$^{(\boxtimes)}$ (ID)

The University of Queensland, St Lucia, QLD, Australia
zhongkui.ma@uq.edu.au

Abstract. The increasing prevalence of neural networks necessitates their verification in order to ensure security. Verifying neural networks is a challenge due to the use of non-linear activation functions. This work concentrates on approximating the convex hull of activation functions. An approach is proposed to construct a convex polytope to over-approximate the ReLU hull (the convex hull of the ReLU function) when considering multi-variables. The key idea is to construct new faces based on the known faces and vertices by uniqueness of the ReLU hull. Our approach has been incorporated into the state-of-the-art PRIMA framework, which takes into account multi-neuron constraints. The experimental evaluation demonstrates that our method is more efficient and precise than existing ReLU hull exact/approximate approaches, and it makes a significant contribution to the verification of neural networks. Our concept can be applied to other non-linear functions in neural networks, and this could be explored further in future research.

Keywords: Formal Verification · Neural Networks · Convex Hull · Robustness

1 Introduction

In recent years, neural networks have become the cornerstone of artificial intelligence applications, ranging from image recognition and natural language processing to autonomous vehicles and medical diagnosis [2,3,13]. Despite of the remarkable performance, ensuring their reliability and safety is challenging [12]. Formal verification emerges to address these concerns and provide certifiable guarantees [5]. It entails the application of mathematical reasoning and logical analysis to ensure that the network's behavior aligns with desired properties, such as robustness. Unlike empirical testing, formal verification considers all possible inputs with given conditions.

Traditional methods of formal verification struggle to scale up to neural networks in high-dimensional cases. Researchers have proposed a number of successful verification frameworks for neural networks. They can be divided into two categories, *complete* [1,4,6,8] and *incomplete* [7,9,10,14,15], based on their capability. Both of these approaches are *sound*, i.e., they are an over-approximation

Y. Li and S. Tahar (Eds.): ICFEM 2023, LNCS 14308, pp. 261–266, 2023.
https://doi.org/10.1007/978-981-99-7584-6_17

to the behavior of neural networks. The fundamental idea is to build a convex polytope to encompass all potential actions of the neural network.

This work aims to construct a convex polytope to over-approximate the non-linear functions in input-output space. We have achieved or are in the process of achieving the following objectives.

- We have formalized the *ReLU hull* and developed an approximate approach, WraLU (**Wrap ReLU**), with high efficiency and precision, to over-approximate a ReLU hull. This approach detects potential constraints by known faces and vertices of the ReLU hull. We have integrated it with the state-of-the-art PRIMA framework [7] and achieved a higher efficiency and precision than the previous ones.
- We intend to extend the ReLU hull to other functions employed in neural networks, such as convex and piece-wise linear functions like max-pool or leaky ReLU, as well as S-shaped functions like sigmoid and tanh.

2   Related Work

2.1   Complete and Incomplete Approaches

Complete approaches give an exact satisfiability to the verification of neural networks solely having piece-wise linear functions, e.g. restricted linear unit (ReLU) and max-pool functions. They are based on exact approaches such as SMT [8], MILP [6], and the extended simplex method [4]. However, the NP-hardness of complete verification and these exact approaches makes the verification applicable only to decades of neurons [4]. Alternatively, a complete verification can be efficiently realized by combining fast incomplete approaches and branch-and-bound (BaB) [1].

Incomplete methods are approximate, but can be applied to large-scale networks. They are usually based on two basic techniques, optimization [7,9] and bound propagation [10,14,15]. The combination of incomplete approaches and the branch-and-bound (BaB) framework has been the main-stream advantageous approach for verification, which seeks to find a high-efficient bounding and branching strategy.

2.2   Single-Neuron and Multi-neuron Constraints

LP-based approaches verify neural networks by constructing linear constraints and solving a linear programming problem with a specified objective. Then, the focus of LP-based approaches is how to construct constraints. Single-neuron constraints can be naively determined with the lower and upper bounds of the input to the activation function, which is equal to construct a convex polyhedron that over-approximate the image of activation function in the input-output space [4]. Multi-neuron constraints consider potential dependencies that are ignored by single-neuron constraints [7,9]. Constructing multi-neuron constraints reduces to the construction of the convex hull or its over-approximation of the non-linear function in a space of multiple inputs and outputs.

3   Methodology

3.1   Formalization of Neural Network

Neural Network. Our research focuses on feedback neural networks with only fully-connected layers. We particularly discuss the neural network $y = f(x)$, which is composed of successive linear and non-linear functions, with the input vector x and the output vector y as follows. $y = W_{L+1}y_L + b_{L+1}$, $y_L = \sigma(\hat{y}_L)$, $\hat{y}_L = W_L y_{L-1} + b_L, \cdots, y_1 = \sigma(\hat{y}_1)$, $\hat{y}_1 = W_1 x + b_1$, where L is the number of hidden layers and σ is the activation function. $\hat{y}_h$ $(1 \leq h \leq L)$ and y_h are the pre-activate and post-activated variables, respectively.

Local robustness is a commonly checked property that asserts that a perturbed input will still produce the desired output. In this work, we will only discuss the local robustness of classification tasks. The perturbation of a given input x_0 is defined by a ball l_p-normal $B(x_0, \epsilon) = \{x \mid ||x - x_0||_p \leq \epsilon, \epsilon \in \mathbb{R}\}$, where ϵ is the radius of the perturbation. Local robustness holds for a sample x_0 if $\forall x \in B(x_0, \epsilon)$, $y \in \{y \mid \mathrm{argmax}_i(y) = \mathrm{argmax}_i(y_0), y = f(x), y_0 = f(x_0)\}$ holds, which means that the perturbed input x leads to the same label $\mathrm{argmax}_i(y_0)$ with the maximum logit.

3.2   Approximation of Neural Network

The verification of neural network is often transformed into an optimization problem to obtain the bounds of each output y_i (y_i is the i-th element of y). For simplicity, we only consider the case of the l_∞-norm ball for the inputs.

$$
\begin{aligned}
\text{Maximize:}\quad & y_i \text{ or } - y_i \\
\text{Subject to:}\quad & -\epsilon \leq x_j \leq \epsilon, \quad \forall 1 \leq j \leq N \\
& y = W_{L+1}y_L + b_{L+1}, \\
& \hat{y}_h = W_{h+1}y_h + b_{h+1}, \quad \forall 1 < h < L \\
& \hat{y}_1 = W_1 x + b_1, \\
& l_{hk} \leq \hat{y}_{hk} \leq u_{hk}, \quad \forall 1 \leq h \leq L, 1 \leq k \leq N_h \\
& y_l = \sigma(\hat{y}_l), \quad \forall 1 \leq l \leq L
\end{aligned}
$$

where N is the number of inputs, N_h is the number of neurons in the h-th hidden layer. The neural network's linear transformation can be exactly handled, yet the non-linear activation function must be over-approximated. $l_{hk}, u_{hk} \in \mathbb{R}$ are the lower and upper bounds of the intermediate variable $\hat{y}_{hk}$, and they are used to impose constraints on the activation functions. This process can be repeated iteratively for each variable until the bounds of the outputs are determined. The core of various strategies lies in the procedure for forming the constraints for this optimization problem.

Single-Neuron Constraints. One popular solution is to construct a set of linear constraints for the activation function only considering a pair of $\hat{y}_{hk}$ and y_{hk}. For example, for $y = \text{ReLU}(\hat{y})$ (subscripts are omitted for simplicity), its triangle relaxation consists of three constraints $y \geq 0$, $y \geq \hat{y}$, and $y \leq \frac{u}{u-l}(\hat{y}-l)$, when $l \leq y \leq u$ and $l < 0 < u$. For naive cases, $y = \hat{y}$ when $l \geq 0$ and $y = 0$ when $u \leq 0$. A similar procedure is applicable to other activation functions, and a set of linear restrictions will be formed.

Multi-neuron Constraints. To consider the potential dependency of different $\hat{y}_{hk}$s, the state-of-the-art frameworks construct an over-approximation $\widehat{\mathcal{Y}}_h$ of $\hat{y}_h$ and a convex over-approximation to $(\widehat{\mathcal{Y}}_h, \mathcal{Y}_h) = (\widehat{\mathcal{Y}}_h, \sigma(\widehat{\mathcal{Y}}_h)) = \{(\hat{y}_{hk}, y_{hk}) \mid y_{hk} = \sigma(\hat{y}_{hk})\}$. The constraints defining the over-approximation will be used in the optimization problem. Calculating the minimum convex over-approximation, i.e., convex hull, is unpractical for the high-dimensional case. Alternatively, calculating an approximation with fewer constraints is efficient.

4   Approach

The ReLU function is distinguished by its piecewise linearity. Our work defines that the corresponding convex hull with the ReLU function is called *ReLU Hull*. A ReLU hull must satisfy the constraints of $y_{hk} \geq 0$ and $y_{hk} \geq \hat{y}_{hk}$, which give the lower bound of each y_{hk} and define the faces that we call *lower faces*. With the hyperplanes determined by the constraints of $\widehat{\mathcal{Y}}_h$, we can find the boundaries of these lower faces. A group of *upper faces* crossing the boundaries of lower faces can be constructed using the following parametric function.

$$a_{hm}\hat{y}_h + d_{hm} \geq \sum_{k=1}^{N_h} \beta_{hk1}y_{hk} + \beta_{hk2}(y_{hk} - \hat{y}_{hk}),$$

where $a_{hm}\hat{y}_h + d_{hm}$ is a constraints from $\widehat{\mathcal{Y}}_h$. We designed an algorithm to iteratively determine the parameters β_{hk1} and β_{hk2} for each dimension k by the vertices of the ReLU hull.

Our algorithm is efficient, because we iteratively determine the parameters and maintain the number of constraints the same as the number of constraints of $\widehat{\mathcal{Y}}_h$. It is precise, because it contain the coherent lower faces and the constructed upper faces are identified by the boundaries of lower faces and vertices of the ReLU hull.

5   Evaluation

We have integrate our method in to the state-of-the-art PRIMA framework. Neuron grouping is used in PRIMA to group the neurons in one layer to lower-dimensional group for fast approximation of the ReLU hull. Two parameters are used, n_s denoting the size of each partition and k determine the neurons number in each group [7]. All reported experiments are conducted on a workstation equipped with one AMD EPYC 7702P 64-core 2.00 GHz CPU with 100 G of main memory. Main results are shown in Table 1. Our approach achieves an competitive number of verified samples (up to 4 more) and shorter runtime (up to 1.2X faster).

Table 1. Verifiable samples number and total runtime of different methods using multi-neuron constraints (ERAN benchmarks)

Dataset	Network	ϵ	PRIMA		PRIMA+WraLU	
			$(n_s = 20, k = 3)$	$(n_s = 100, k = 4)$	$(n_s = 20, k = 3)$	$(n_s = 100, k = 4)$
MNIST	FCTiny	0.03	$44+12(111.85\,\text{s})^a$	$44+16(258.15\,\text{s})$	$44+\mathbf{14}(\mathbf{70.19}\,\text{s})$	$44+\mathbf{18}(\mathbf{145.26}\,\text{s})$
	FCSmall	0.019	$53+7(510.56\,\text{s})$	$53+8(2649.36\,\text{s})$	$53+7(\mathbf{465.81}\,\text{s})$	$53+\mathbf{10}(\mathbf{2149.3}\,\text{s})$
	FCBig	0.012	$53+5(1799.22\,\text{s})$	$53+6(13587.90\,\text{s})$	$53+5(\mathbf{1337.65}\,\text{s})$	$53+6(\mathbf{11086.70}\,\text{s})$
	ConvSmall	0.1	$45+18(388.52\,\text{s})$	$45+20(1072.8\,\text{s})$	$45+18(\mathbf{375.34}\,\text{s})$	$45+\mathbf{21}(\mathbf{1055.21}\,\text{s})$
	ConvBig[b]	0.305	$49+6(4254.30\,\text{s})$	$46+7(4380.95\,\text{s})$	$46+5(\mathbf{3575.15}\,\text{s})$	$45+1(\mathbf{3779.91}\,\text{s})$
CIFAR10	FCTiny	0.001	$45+4(411.50\,\text{s})$	$45+4(528.23\,\text{s})$	$45+4(\mathbf{305.33}\,\text{s})$	$45+4(\mathbf{402.28}\,\text{s})$
	FCSmall	0.0007	$51+14(579.29\,\text{s})$	$51+14(791.62\,\text{s})$	$51+13(\mathbf{433.64}\,\text{s})$	$51+13(\mathbf{603.78}\,\text{s})$
	FCBig	0.0008	$53+5(3531.99\,\text{s})$	$53+6(15404.19\,\text{s})$	$53+4(\mathbf{3183.01}\,\text{s})$	$53+9(\mathbf{13176.7}\,\text{s})$
	ConvSmall	0.004	$49+8(821.59\,\text{s})$	$49+10(2131.12\,\text{s})$	$49+8(856.66\,\text{s})$	$49+10(2220.91\,\text{s})$
	ConvBig	0.007	$48+3(11029.75\,\text{s})$	$48+3(11724.91\,\text{s})$	$48+3(\mathbf{9865.48}\,\text{s})$	$48+3(\mathbf{9738.36}\,\text{s})$

[a] $m+n$ stands for n more networks are verified besides m verified by DeepPoly [11]. Numbers in brackets refer to the total runtime. Numbers in bold refer to those cases where our methods outperform PRIMA.

6 Discussion and Conclusion

6.1 Discussion

Exploring the convex approximation of other functions used in neural networks is a future research. A similar approach can be applied to leaky ReLU and max-pool functions, which are also piece-wise linear and convex. For functions that are not piece-wise linear, we construct a piece-wise linear convex or concave function as an upper or lower bound, which will enable constructing a convex polytope to over-approximate them.

Exploring the potential of our approach to scale to high-dimensional cases is another future goal. Taking advantage of the characteristics of certain special polytopes, our method can prevent exponential computation.

6.2 Conclusion

We have designed a method to give an over-approximation of the ReLU hull. The key point is to construct the adjacent faces based on the already known faces and vertices of the convex hull. This technique is both efficient and precise, and it has the potential to be extended to other functions.

References

1. Bunel, R., Turkaslan, I., Torr, P.H., Kohli, P., Kumar, M.P.: A unified view of piece-wise linear neural network verification. In: Proceedings of the 32nd International Conference on Neural Information Processing Systems, pp. 4795–4804 (2018)
2. Cao, Y., et al.: Invisible for both camera and lidar: security of multi-sensor fusion based perception in autonomous driving under physical-world attacks. In: 2021 IEEE Symposium on Security and Privacy (SP), pp. 176–194. IEEE (2021)
3. He, K., Zhang, X., Ren, S., Sun, J.: Deep residual learning for image recognition. In: Proceedings of the IEEE Conference on Computer Vision and Pattern Recognition, pp. 770–778 (2016)
4. Katz, G., Barrett, C., Dill, D.L., Julian, K., Kochenderfer, M.J.: Reluplex: an efficient SMT solver for verifying deep neural networks. In: Majumdar, R., Kunčak, V. (eds.) CAV 2017. LNCS, vol. 10426, pp. 97–117. Springer, Cham (2017). https://doi.org/10.1007/978-3-319-63387-9_5
5. Li, L., Xie, T., Li, B.: SoK: certified robustness for deep neural networks. In: 2023 IEEE Symposium on Security and Privacy (SP), pp. 94–115. IEEE Computer Society (2022)
6. Lomuscio, A., Maganti, L.: An approach to reachability analysis for feed-forward ReLU neural networks. arXiv preprint: arXiv:1706.07351 (2017)
7. Müller, M.N., Makarchuk, G., Singh, G., Püschel, M., Vechev, M.: PRIMA: general and precise neural network certification via scalable convex hull approximations. Proc. ACM Programm. Lang. 6(POPL), 1–33 (2022)
8. Pulina, L., Tacchella, A.: An abstraction-refinement approach to verification of artificial neural networks. In: Touili, T., Cook, B., Jackson, P. (eds.) CAV 2010. LNCS, vol. 6174, pp. 243–257. Springer, Heidelberg (2010). https://doi.org/10.1007/978-3-642-14295-6_24
9. Singh, G., Ganvir, R., Püschel, M., Vechev, M.: Beyond the single neuron convex barrier for neural network certification. In: Advances in Neural Information Processing Systems, vol. 32 (2019)
10. Singh, G., Gehr, T., Mirman, M., Püschel, M., Vechev, M.: Fast and effective robustness certification. In: Advances in Neural Information Processing Systems, vol. 31 (2018)
11. Singh, G., Gehr, T., Püschel, M., Vechev, M.: An abstract domain for certifying neural networks. Proce. ACM Programm. Lang. 3(POPL), 1–30 (2019)
12. Szegedy, C., et al.: Intriguing properties of neural networks. In: 2nd International Conference on Learning Representations, ICLR 2014 (2014)
13. Vaswani, A., et al.: Attention is all you need. In: Advances in Neural Information Processing Systems, vol. 30 (2017)
14. Weng, L., et al.: Towards fast computation of certified robustness for ReLU networks. In: International Conference on Machine Learning, pp. 5276–5285. PMLR (2018)
15. Zhang, H., et al.: General cutting planes for bound-propagation-based neural network verification. In: Advances in Neural Information Processing Systems, vol. 35, pp. 1656–1670 (2022)

Eager to Stop: Efficient Falsification of Deep Neural Networks

Guanqin Zhang[1,2]([✉])

[1] University of New South Wales, Kensington, Australia
Guanqin.zhang@unsw.edu.au
[2] CSIRO, Data61, Sydney, Australia

Abstract. Deep Neural Networks (DNNs), extensively used in safety-critical domains, require methods to detect misbehavior and ensure provable specifications. DNN testing encounters limitations in time and coverage, affecting effectiveness. DNN verification divides into exact and approximated approaches. Due to scalability challenges, exact methods yield precise outcomes but are suitable for smaller networks. Approximated techniques using abstractions tend to be over-approximated for soundness. Over-approximated verifiers might produce more misleading counterexamples than actual violations, impacting the identification of flaws. This paper proposes a falsifier to efficiently identify counterexamples for DNN robustness by refuting specifications. The proposed approach gradient information to fast approach local optima against specifications, collecting relevant counterexamples effectively.

Keywords: Robustness · Verification · Falsification

1 Introduction

DNNs are widely implemented and impressively deployed in the safety-critical domains, such as autonomous vehicles [1], program analysis [2,18], and airborne collision avoidance systems [9]. Although DNNs possess remarkable abilities, the growing apprehension surrounding their potentials, such as adversarial perturbations [7,12] for misclassification and unforeseeable decisions. This motivates the understanding of the reliability and quality assurance of the underlying models.

There has been a notable upsurge in the exploration and development of analysis and verification techniques for neural network robustness. Existing approaches can be mainly categorized as testing and verification. Testing [7,14,21,23] is usually providing counterexamples, such as adversaries, to reject the robustness of the DNNs. During the testing, the evaluation is based on specific test inputs and criteria, which may still lead to unforeseen issues. On the other hand, verification [5,6,8,16,20] can mathematically certify models with provably guaranteed robustness or supply a counterexample that violates the expected behaviors of models.

Y. Li and S. Tahar (Eds.): ICFEM 2023, LNCS 14308, pp. 267–272, 2023.
https://doi.org/10.1007/978-981-99-7584-6_18

2   Problem Statement and Related Work

A network model $N : \mathbb{R}^n \to \mathbb{R}^m$ maps an n-dimensional input vector to an m-dimensional output vector. The model N takes an input x and outputs $N(x)$. The typical verification problem for the network model N with a specification $\phi : \mathbb{R}^{n+m} \to \{\mathbb{T}, \mathbb{F}\}$ is a decidable problem whether there existing $x \in \mathbb{R}^n, y \in \mathbb{R}^m$ holds $(N(x) = y) \wedge \phi(x, y)$. ϕ represents the desired property that model behaviors followed human expectation. In this context, we use (l_p, ϵ)-adversary to denote a perturbed input region centered at x_0 with ϵ radius, i.e., $\{x' \mid \|x' - x_0\|_p \leq \epsilon\}$ measured by l_p norm. The satisfied results indicate the specification holds, whereas the unsatisfiability expresses the existence of a counterexample x within the (l_p, ϵ)-adversary, violates the specification.

Adversarial Examples. Adversarial robustness responds to the ML models' reliability, which has recently attracted significant attention. Some adversaries generated by attack methods can indicate the existence of a violation of the specification. Szegedy *et al.* [19] first proposed the generation method for adversarial perturbations and leveraged a hybrid loss to approximate the solution of inner maximization. Furthermore, Goodfellow *et al.* [7] introduced an efficient FGSM method to generate the adversarial inputs for misleading the model behavior. However, the efficiency property comes from the linear loss function, which leads to the vulnerability to iteration attacks. In response to this problem, Madry *et al.* [12] pushed this method into the multi-iteration attack and released their gradient-based PGD method for inner maximization solving. Following that, a line of works emerged and boosted the development of adversarial attacks [13].

Neural Network Testing. Neuron coverage [14] is utilized to count each neuron's activation status, and Ma *et al.* [11] extend with a set of test criteria for deep learning systems. Xie *et al.* [21] detect potential defects of neural networks by coverage-guided fuzzing framework with metamorphic testing. However, test-based approaches suffer from the limited number of crafted testing samples, such that they cannot enumerate all possible inputs to denote erroneous behavior of the network.

Neural Network Verification. Formal verification techniques [10] can certify neural networks based on specifications to ensure proof or identify violations. One important aspect of verification is gauging the robustness of the neural network model against input adversarial perturbations. Verification approaches fall into two main categories: (1) *Exact* verification typically utilizes mixed integer linear programming (MILP) solver [20] or satisfiability modulo theories (SMT) solvers [8], which suffers low scalability due to solving such an 'NP-hard' problem. (2) *Approximated* verification often reduces the non-linear properties into linear inequalities, such as instantiated neural network properties into the abstract domain, such as polytope [17], zonotope [16].

3   Proposed Solution

Verification to Falsification. Verifying the robustness of a model is akin to proving a theorem, which poses a significant challenge in accurately assessing a neural network. Specifically, acquiring proof for the network's robustness can be
difficult, leading to the possibility of overestimating its robustness. Ideally, a
proven robust model is necessarily reasoning *all* possible perturbation properties on a given input and indicating *non-existence* of violation. This verification is
impossible when the networks are becoming larger and deeper. Consequently, the
majority of verification methods that have been published either choose a subset
of properties to analyze or utilize approximations of the model. We propose a falsification scheme to eagerly find the counterexample within the (l_p, ϵ)-adversary
for the network model. Formally, the falsification problem keeps searching for a
falsifying x that violates the specification ϕ. Falsification shortcuts the verification processes and only supplies the rejected violations.

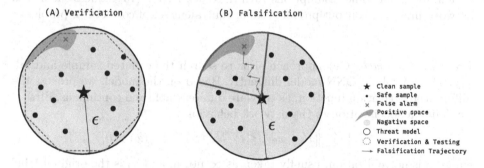

Fig. 1. Comparison between verification and falsification. We depict a threat model
(threat model refers to a specification of the potential threats by some errors) suspected
of containing positive feature space, including some false alarm samples. The false alarm
samples can fool the model into making erroneous predictions.

Figure 1 demonstrates the comparison between verification and falsification
of DNN. We construct a binary classification problem for a clean sample, which
contains a false alarm sample within a feasible set of a threat model, as shown in
(l_p, ϵ)-adversary. Verification can be described as a constraint of specifications in
a green dashed-line octagon on the left-hand side. The octagon expresses specification constraints, which cover the ample feature space for the threat model.
In practice, most of the existing exact verification methods borrowed SMT or
MILP solvers scale poorly when the size of the network is growing larger. On the
other hand, the approximated methods do not directly verify the property of the
network but reduce it to a relaxation problem. So the designed/expected specifications do not precisely formalize the threat model behaviors. As shown in Fig. 1
(A), the green octagon shape may overly cover the actual target specification
from the model and cover most of the feature space.

Falsification attempts to reject the violations by eagerly falsifying the non-robust counterexamples beyond DNN models in a smaller search space. From this perspective, we here argue for falsifying the properties of the designed specification. The falsification aims to provide a convincing *optimal* point that helps counterfeit the verification specification in a smaller region contoured with the red line in Fig. 1 (B). For a perturbation within (l_p, ϵ)-adversary to claim as a false alarm violated to a robust model specification, it is necessary to actually find a perturbed example x' that causes the model to make an error. This is similar to composing an adversary by using adversarial attack approaches. FGSM claims that linear behavior in high-dimensional spaces is sufficient to cause adversaries. However, adversarial attack approaches cannot assemble theoretic proof results to certify the model.

Falsification spreads across different domains [22], which refers to the concept that requirements (specifications) are falsified (not true). Guided by human-designed specifications, falsifiers can reach violations faster than verifiers when processing with a non-robust model. *Dohmatob* [4] finds robustness is impossible to achieve under some assumptions with the data. DNNF [15] reduces the neural network input and output property to an equivalent set of correctness problems.

Proposed Approach. Our approach aims to search the counterexample and falsify the non-robust DNN model diligently. Based on the model, we process the differential activation function, as they are differentiable and continuous. Firstly, we define a specification to the network behavior:

$$\forall x \in \{x' \mid \|x' - x_0\|_p \leq \epsilon\}, N_{s_0}(x) - N_{s_1}(x) > 0, \tag{1}$$

where p is normalization, usually taken as ∞-norm, and s_0 is the original label for x_0. Then, the model behaviour requires that for any of x within the (l_p, ϵ)-adversary should always be larger than the label value for s_1. We aim to determine whether the direction violates the specification. To decide the gradient, we use a vector Δ, that has the same dimension as the input domain, to identify the direction, namely, given an input x, it holds the objective function $N_{s_0}(x + \Delta) > N_{s_1}(x)$. The problem remains to decide Δ.

We use the line search method to start from the given direction of Δx_k to move with a step length $t > 0$ to modulate how far along this direction we proceed. The direct aim would satisfy: $f(x_k + t\Delta x_k) < f(x_k)$. Armijo [3] step size constraint is a method used in optimization algorithms to determine the step size. We use the Armijo condition to search for a sufficient decrease to our objectives. The constraint states that if the step size is small enough, the value of the objective function will decrease in gradient descent or other optimization algorithms. The Armijo step size constraint restricts the step size at each iteration to ensure the algorithm's convergence. Specifically, the Armijo step size constraint requires that the step size at each iteration satisfies the following inequality:

$$f(x_k + t\Delta x_k) \leq f(x_k) + c_1 t \nabla f_k^T \Delta x_k \tag{2}$$

Here, x_k is the current value of the optimization variable, Δx_k is the search direction, t is the step size, $f(x)$ is the objective function, ∇f_k is the gradient of the objective function at the current point, and c_1 is a constant typically chosen between 0 and 1. If the step size t satisfies the above inequality, it is considered acceptable; otherwise, the step size needs to be reduced, and the search is restarted. When we repeat and collect enough points, we can falsify the model as it is not robust.

4   Conclusion and Future Work

We propose a new falsification approach to complement the existing neural network verification approaches in searching and identifying counterexamples to prove the existence of violations in a *non-robust* model. We propose utilizing the Armijo line search method to iteratively reach the counterexample. Armijo borrows the gradient information from the network model, of which the advantage is the falsification of the specification in the smaller search space.

In our upcoming research endeavors, we intend to incorporate and examine additional elements of the network model. In our current study, we exclusively focused on the differentiable activation function. An eminent obstacle lies in dealing with piece-wise activation functions like ReLU, wherein the output lacks continuity. Addressing this challenge can facilitate the analysis of a broader range of network models.

An additional aspect involves utilizing the falsification findings for the purpose of enhancing the network model's integrity. Falsification provides prompt identification of cases where violations occur during the initial stages. Armed with these instances of violation, we can effectively identify shortcomings, subsequently enhancing both the performance and robustness of the model.

References

1. Bojarski, M., et al.: End to end learning for self-driving cars. arXiv preprint: arXiv:1604.07316 (2016)
2. Cheng, X., Zhang, G., Wang, H., Sui, Y.: Path-sensitive code embedding via contrastive learning for software vulnerability detection. In: ISSTA, pp. 519–531 (2022)
3. Dai, Y.H.: On the nonmonotone line search. J. Optim. Theory Appl. **112**, 315–330 (2002)
4. Dohmatob, E.: Generalized no free lunch theorem for adversarial robustness. In: International Conference on Machine Learning, pp. 1646–1654. PMLR (2019)
5. Fischer, M., Sprecher, C., Dimitrov, D.I., Singh, G., Vechev, M.: Shared certificates for neural network verification. In: Shoham, S., Vizel, Y. (eds.) CAV 2022. Lecture Notes in Computer Science, vol. 13371, pp. 127–148. Springer, Cham (2022). https://doi.org/10.1007/978-3-031-13185-1_7
6. Gehr, T., Mirman, M., Drachsler-Cohen, D., Tsankov, P., Chaudhuri, S., Vechev, M.: Ai2: safety and robustness certification of neural networks with abstract interpretation. In: SP, pp. 3–18. IEEE (2018)

7. Goodfellow, I.J., Shlens, J., Szegedy, C.: Explaining and harnessing adversarial examples. arXiv preprint: arXiv:1412.6572 (2014)
8. Katz, G., Barrett, C., Dill, D.L., Julian, K., Kochenderfer, M.J.: Reluplex: an efficient SMT solver for verifying deep neural networks. In: Majumdar, R., Kunčak, V. (eds.) CAV 2017. LNCS, vol. 10426, pp. 97–117. Springer, Cham (2017). https://doi.org/10.1007/978-3-319-63387-9_5
9. Katz, G., et al.: The marabou framework for verification and analysis of deep neural networks. In: Dillig, I., Tasiran, S. (eds.) CAV 2019. LNCS, vol. 11561, pp. 443–452. Springer, Cham (2019). https://doi.org/10.1007/978-3-030-25540-4_26
10. Liu, C., et al.: Algorithms for verifying deep neural networks. Found. Trends® Optim. **4**(3–4), 244–404 (2021)
11. Ma, L., et al.: DeepGauge: multi-granularity testing criteria for deep learning systems. In: Proceedings of the 33rd ACM/IEEE International Conference on Automated Software Engineering, pp. 120–131 (2018)
12. Madry, A., Makelov, A., Schmidt, L., Tsipras, D., Vladu, A.: Towards deep learning models resistant to adversarial attacks. arXiv preprint: arXiv:1706.06083 (2017)
13. Nicolae, M.I., et al.: Adversarial robustness toolbox v1.0.0. arXiv:1807.01069 (2018)
14. Pei, K., Cao, Y., Yang, J., Jana, S.: DeepXplore: automated Whitebox testing of deep learning systems. In: Proceedings of the 26th Symposium on Operating Systems Principles, pp. 1–18 (2017)
15. Shriver, D., Elbaum, S., Dwyer, M.B.: Reducing DNN properties to enable falsification with adversarial attacks. In: 2021 IEEE/ACM 43rd International Conference on Software Engineering (ICSE), pp. 275–287. IEEE (2021)
16. Singh, G., Gehr, T., Mirman, M., Püschel, M., Vechev, M.: Fast and effective robustness certification. In: Advances in Neural Information Processing Systems, vol. 31 (2018)
17. Singh, G., Gehr, T., Püschel, M., Vechev, M.: An abstract domain for certifying neural networks. Proc. ACM Programm. Lang. **3**(POPL), 1–30 (2019)
18. Sui, Y., Cheng, X., Zhang, G., Wang, H.: Flow2vec: value-flow-based precise code embedding. ACM **4**(OOPSLA), 1–27 (2020)
19. Szegedy, C., et al.: Intriguing properties of neural networks. arXiv preprint: arXiv:1312.6199 (2013)
20. Tjeng, V., Xiao, K., Tedrake, R.: Evaluating robustness of neural networks with mixed integer programming. arXiv preprint: arXiv:1711.07356 (2017)
21. Xie, X., et al.: DeepHunter: a coverage-guided fuzz testing framework for deep neural networks. In: Proceedings of the 28th ACM SIGSOFT International Symposium on Software Testing and Analysis, pp. 146–157 (2019)
22. Zhang, Z., Arcaini, P., Hasuo, I.: Constraining counterexamples in hybrid system falsification: penalty-based approaches. In: Lee, R., Jha, S., Mavridou, A., Giannakopoulou, D. (eds.) NFM 2020. LNCS, vol. 12229, pp. 401–419. Springer, Cham (2020). https://doi.org/10.1007/978-3-030-55754-6_24
23. Zhao, Z., Chen, G., Wang, J., Yang, Y., Song, F., Sun, J.: Attack as defense: Characterizing adversarial examples using robustness. In: Proceedings of the 30th ACM SIGSOFT International Symposium on Software Testing and Analysis, pp. 42–55 (2021)

A Runtime Verification Framework for Cyber-Physical Systems Based on Data Analytics and LTL Formula Learning

Ayodeji James Akande$^{(\boxtimes)}$, Zhe Hou, Ernest Foo, and Qinyi Li

Griffith University, Brisbane, Australia
ayodeji.akande@griffithuni.edu.au,
{z.hou,e.foo,qinyi.li}@griffith.edu.au

Abstract. Safeguarding individuals and valuable resources from cyber threats stands as a paramount concern in the digital landscape, encompassing realms like cyber-physical systems and IoT systems. The safeguarding of cyber-physical systems (CPS) is particularly challenging given their intricate infrastructure, necessitating ongoing real-time analysis and swift responses to potential threats. Our proposition introduces a digital twin framework built upon runtime verification, effectively harnessing the capabilities of data analytics and the acquisition of Linear Temporal Logic (LTL) formulas. We demonstrate the efficacy of our approach through an application to water distribution systems.

Keywords: Runtime verification · Linear temporal logic · Digital twins · Formal Modeling · Cyber-physical systems · Cyber-security

1 Introduction

Safeguarding users and assets from cyber-attacks within the digital realm has grown into an essential concern. This realm encompasses components such as cyber-physical systems (CPS), the metaverse, satellite communication systems, and the Internet of Things (IoT), all of which hold substantial importance in both industrial operations and the intricate tapestry of human existence. This research explores the realm of enhancing the security of cyber-physical systems, the next generation of systems combining computational and physical capabilities, enabling interaction with humans through various new modalities [1]. In Cyber-physical systems (CPS), the physical and software components are closely intertwined, capable of operating on different spatial and temporal scales, demonstrating diverse behavioural modes, and interacting with each other in context-dependent ways [5].

Incidents targeting cyber-physical systems, encompassing domains like industrial automation, smart grids, smart cities, autonomous vehicles, and agricultural precision, have the potential to result in devastating outcomes for both individuals and assets. This paper centers on attacks targeting engineering and network data, emphasizing the need to confront and counteract this threat to guarantee the safety and security of cyber-physical systems.

Securing cyber-physical systems (CPS), due to the intricate nature of their infrastructure, requires continuous real-time analysis and swift action against potential attacks. Despite the proposal of methods such as intrusion detection/prevention systems and network mapping, these approaches frequently prove insufficient or encounter constraints in effectively accessing assets. Debugging and testing CPS is widely recognized as challenging, with various techniques being questioned for their effectiveness [9].

To provide a framework capable of real-time analysis, prompt mitigation, and minimal computational burden, this paper introduces a digital twin framework based on runtime verification. This framework seamlessly integrates data analytics with the learning of Linear Temporal Logic (LTL) formulas. The framework integrates machine learning algorithms to acquire LTL formulas from past data (training data). The paper's contribution lies in designing a process to generate system-specific LTL formulas using machine learning and implementing an LTL-based runtime verification cybersecurity framework for digital twin cyberphysical systems. This framework is applicable for tackling engineering/network data-related attacks where patterns can be identified in time series. The objective of this framework is to anticipate events that precede an adverse occurrence before it actually takes place.

2   The Proposed Approach

This section presents our Linear Temporal Logic (LTL) based runtime verification digital twin framework. The systematic approach is divided into five phases; Phase I (Data Pre-processing), Phase II (Data Clustering), Phase III (Domain Expert Analysis), Phase IV (LTL Formula Learning), and Phase V (Runtime Monitoring).

Phase I: Data Pre-processing. Our framework begins with the collection of historical datasets and their pre-processing. In the process of learning Linear Temporal Logic (LTL) formulas from historical datasets, it is anticipated that the dataset encompasses both regular and anomalous events. The dataset is split into training and testing datasets. During this stage, the training dataset is used to train a model while to evaluate the model's performance after it has been trained, a testing dataset is used. With the aid of machine learning, we build a system model based on sample data, known as training data, to learn the LTL formula for the system.

First, the dataset is pre-processed which involves data cleaning, data transformation, feature selection or data reduction, handling missing data and data encoding. The data pre-processing depends on the data classification. To initiate the data pre-processing phase, we create a Python algorithm named '*LTL_Formula_Learner.py*' for learning Linear Temporal Logic (LTL) formulas.

Phase II: Data Clustering. The next phase of our methodology is data clustering, an artificial intelligence process that 'learns', that is, leverages data for improvement of performance on some set of tasks. During this stage, the goal is to recognize and categorize data into distinct clusters or groups. This process aims to distinguish clusters that correspond to favourable and unfavourable events, essential for the subsequent learning of patterns that will translate into Linear Temporal Logic (LTL) formulas.

In the case where the dataset is already labelled, the clustering algorithm may only be used to group column values into two variables 1 and 0 which is required for the generation of the LTL formula using the learning algorithm. For our research purpose, the K-means algorithm is used for data clustering.

Phase III: Domain Knowledge Expert Analysis. The third phase of our methodology is domain expert analysis. Incorporating domain-specific knowledge and expertise to select features that are known to be significant for cyber security analysis is important and crucial. Subject matter experts can offer valuable insights into pivotal system components susceptible to data modifications or anomalies. These insights aid in selecting the most informative features. For our framework, a domain knowledge expert assists in identifying which of the clusters present normal and abnormal behaviour of the system.

Phase IV: LTL Formula Learning. The next phase of our approach is the LTL formula learning. At this phase, an LTL formula is generated based on the historical data set. In order to learn the LTL formulae, we implement the samples2LTL algorithm [6]. The objective of the algorithm is to acquire an LTL formula that distinguishes between two sets of traces: positive (P) and negative (N). The resultant formula should accurately represent every trace in the positive set (P) while not being applicable to any trace within the negative set (N).

The samples2LTL algorithm takes in an input file termed as traces separated as positives (P) and negatives (N) by $---$. Each trace is a sequence of states separated by ';' and each state represents the truth value of atomic propositions. An example of a trace is $1, 0, 1; 0, 0, 0; 0, 1, 1$ which consists of two states each of which defines the values of three propositions and by default considered to be $x0, x1, x2$.

For our framework, we learn patterns by analysing rows leading to bad events to predict events before happening, therefore, the samples2LTL algorithm takes in the trace file which contains the 'n' rows leading to bad events as a set of positives (P), and 'm' rows indicative of good events as a set of negatives (N). This is stored in the samples2LTL folder as 'example' with the extension '.trace'.

Phase V: Runtime Monitoring. Runtime monitoring is the last phase of our approach. This is the process where the runtime checker verifies the real-time data against security properties for runtime checking. In runtime verification, the LTL formula is used to define a system property to verify the execution of the system.

In our previous work [4], we presented a runtime verification engine for the digital twin that can verify properties in multiple temporal logic languages. The runtime verification supports both FLTL and PTLTL in one package and is driven by the model checker Process Analysis Toolkit (PAT). In this paper, we implement the runtime verification engine with the declaration of the LTL formula as the property. This paper adopts LTL on finite trace (FLTL) with strong next, that is, $X\,A$ is true when the next state exists and makes A true; otherwise, $X\,A$ is false. In this semantics, $F\,A$ is only true when there is a future state that makes A true; otherwise, it is false. FLTL looks into the future. Also adopted in the paper is Past-time LTL (PTLTL), another useful language for specifying security-related properties [2] which has two distinct temporal operators called previously ($\mathbb{P}$) and since ($\mathbb{S}$). Their semantics are defined on past state traces, which are symmetric to FLTL. In PTLTL, $\mathbb{P}\,A$ is true when the previous state exists and makes A true; this is symmetric to $X\,A$ in FLTL. $A\,\mathbb{S}\,B$ is true if 1) the current state makes B true, or if 2) B was true sometime in the past, and since then, A has been true. The semantics of $A\,\mathbb{S}\,B$ in PTLTL is symmetric to $A\,\mathbb{U}\,B$ in FLTL.

We incorporate our runtime validation through an algorithm called execute_runtime.py, which builds upon the foundation of our previous work's runtime-monitor script. The runtime monitoring process consists of three distinct phases; the digital twin modelling, property definition and the runtime verification.

Digital Twin Modelling: We model the system using the testing dataset initially set aside to evaluate the model's performance. This serves as our digital twin model which is modelled using PAT. In our approach, we are mainly interested in verifying properties over the state variables of the system. Let us name the state variables *var1, var2,* · · ·. A state S is simply a snapshot of the values of state variables, i.e., $S ::= \{var1 = val1, var2 = val2, \cdots \}$. In PAT, we model a state via a process in Communicating Sequential Processes [3] with C# (CSP#) [7]. The process performs variable assignments as below.

$$S() = \{svar1 = val1; svar2 = val2; ...\} \rightarrow Skip;$$

A final trace T is a sequence of states, modelled as below.

$$T() = S1(); S2(); ...$$

Property Definition: The user can define properties over state variables. For example, the below code defines a proposition that states "var1 is not 0."

$$\#define\quad v1Safe\quad (var1! = 0);$$

We can then use PAT to check a safety property that "var1 should never be 0" using the temporal modality G, which is written as [].

$$\#assert\quad Trace() \models []v1Safe;$$

Verification: Given the generated LTL formula from the historical data, the property is defined for the runtime verification as the safety property in Process Analysis Toolkit (PAT) language. The foundation of our runtime verification framework is based on the observation that verifying LTL with finite traces in PAT language corresponds to verifying FLTL with strong next/future.

Utilizing this framework, we can identify data-related attacks that exhibit transient patterns in time series. This approach can be deployed in various domains, including cyber-physical systems (CPS), the metaverse, satellite communication systems, and the Internet of Things (IoT). Due to limited space, this paper focuses on a single case study related to a water distribution system.

3 Case Study: Water Distribution System

This is a main water distribution system operator of C-Town and the dataset was created and published by the BATADAL team [8]. C-Town consists of 388 nodes linked with 429 pipes and is divided into 5 district-metered areas (DMAs). The SCADA data include the water level at all 7 tanks of the network (T1-T7), the status and flow of all 11 pumps (PU1-PU11) and the one actuated valve (V2) of the network, and pressure at 24 pipes of the network that correspond to the inlet and outlet pressure of the pumps and the actuated valve. Three distinct datasets from the system generated. However, for our specific application, we focused our analysis on "training_dataset_2.csv". This dataset, which includes partially labeled data, was made available on November 28, 2016. It spans approximately six months and encompasses several attacks, some of which have approximate labels.

In the dataset are 43 columns, attack labelled using a column named 'ATT_FLAG' with a 1/0 label column, with 1 meaning that the system is under attack and 0 meaning that the system is in normal operation. After collating the dataset [8], we implement our framework to learn a pattern from the dataset indicative of the attack carried on the system. Using the observed pattern, we learn the LTL formula for the system.

The LTL runtime verification-based digital twin framework algorithm developed for this work can be accessed at the following link: https://github.com/deejay2206/LTL-based-Runtime-Verification. For further references on the LTL formula learning algorithm used in our work, see samples2LTL.

LTL-Formula Learning: Using the samples2LTL algorithm, we generate a list of the LTL formula as shown below. The LTL formula is inputted as the LTL property which is used in the runtime checker. We define the LTL formula in PAT as property.csp.

$(x20 \ U \ x37), \ X(x39), \ !(x10), \ !(x5), \ F(x28);$

Conducting runtime verification involved generating a digital twin model of the system using the testing dataset. This dataset was divided into distinct traces, each of which represented a model. These models were then fed into the runtime checker, as described in Sect. 2, to validate the adherence of the learned LTL formula set as a system property.

Result Analysis. To access the performance of our framework, we use evaluation metrics and to achieve this, we use the confusion matrix which is the calculation of number of true positives (TP), true negatives (TN), false positives (FP), and false negatives (FN) based on the predictions and the actual outcomes. In our data analysis, we considered each row within the dataset as an individual event. There were a total of 263 positive traces and 989 negative traces, resulting in a combined count of 1252 events or instances. We calculate the accuracy and precision. The result revealed TP = 242, TN = 901, FP = 54, FN = 55. The outcome demonstrated a 91% percent accuracy rate and the positive predictive value is 82% for the predictive capabilities of our framework.

4   Conclusion

Engineering or network data related attack leading to the temporal pattern of behaviour of a real critical infrastructure can cause great harm to a human being. With the concept of a runtime-based digital twin system, this temporal pattern of behaviour can be detected. In this paper, we investigated how to learn the LTL formula from historical data and evaluated our approach using a case study in cyber-physical systems.

References

1. Baheti, R., Gill, H.: Cyber-physical systems. Impact Control Technol. **12**(1), 161–166 (2011)
2. Du, X., Tiu, A., Cheng, K., Liu, Y.: Trace-length independent runtime monitoring of quantitative policies. IEEE Trans. Dependable Secure Comput. **18**(3), 1489–1510 (2019)
3. Hoare, C.A.R.: Communicating sequential processes. Commun. ACM **21**(8), 666–677 (1978)
4. Hou, Z., Li, Q., Foo, E., Song, J., Souza, P.: A digital twin runtime verification framework for protecting satellites systems from cyber attacks. In: 2022 26th International Conference on Engineering of Complex Computer Systems (ICECCS), pp. 117–122. IEEE (2022)
5. Hu, J., Lennox, B., Arvin, F.: Robust formation control for networked robotic systems using negative imaginary dynamics. Automatica **140**, 110235 (2022)
6. Neider, D., Gavran, I.: Learning linear temporal properties. In: 2018 Formal Methods in Computer-Aided Design (FMCAD), pp. 1–10. IEEE (2018)
7. Sun, J., Liu, Y., Dong, J.S., Pang, J.: PAT: towards flexible verification under fairness. In: Bouajjani, A., Maler, O. (eds.) CAV 2009. LNCS, vol. 5643, pp. 709–714. Springer, Heidelberg (2009). https://doi.org/10.1007/978-3-642-02658-4_59
8. Taormina, R., et al.: Battle of the attack detection algorithms: disclosing cyber attacks on water distribution networks. J. Water Resour. Plan. Manag. **144**(8), 04018048 (2018)
9. Zheng, X., Julien, C., Kim, M., Khurshid, S.: Perceptions on the state of the art in verification and validation in cyber-physical systems. IEEE Syst. J. **11**(4), 2614–2627 (2015)

Unified Verification of Neural Networks' Robustness and Privacy in Computer Vision

Feng Xu[1,2](✉) (iD)

[1] UNSW Sydney, Sydney, Australia
`feng.xu2@unsw.edu.au`
[2] CSIRO's Data61, Marsfield, Australia

Abstract. In recent years, extensive research efforts have delved into neural network verification, resulting in widespread deployment. Concerns have arisen regarding the robustness of neural networks and the privacy of the data they process. To address these concerns, advancements have been made in robust training, robust verification, and preserving privacy while utilizing neural networks for utility tasks. While numerous verifiers are available for verifying neural network robustness, there is still a lack of verification approaches for privacy-related properties. This paper will introduce the problem of formally verifying properties concerning the robustness and privacy of neural networks, and it will explore how existing works in robustness verification can contribute to unified verification work. Ultimately, this paper will outline a roadmap for achieving a unified verification approach encompassing both robustness and privacy concerns.

Keywords: Formal Verification · Formal Analysis · Computer Aid Verification · Neural Network

1 Introduction

The recent advancements in neural networks have led to their widespread adoption across various domains, including self-driving systems [3], medical diagnose [1, 2, 11, 12], security systems [13] and software security analysis [4,5]. These neural networks have significantly enhanced the performance of tasks within these domains. Nevertheless, recent studies have unveiled two significant shortcomings. Firstly, neural networks are vulnerable to adversarial attacks, as evidenced by instances where systems misclassify traffic signs [7] or fail to detect objects [22]. Such misclassifications or misdetections can lead to severe accidents in real-world scenarios. Secondly, the input data processed by these neural network systems is susceptible to intrusion, raising concerns about privacy breaches [14]. This vulnerability arises when data is transmitted over public networks and can be compromised through unauthorized server access. Moreover, privacy protection regulations [18] further highlight the importance of safeguarding privacy.

Various existing studies [8,24] have focused on mitigating the impact of adversarial attacks. However, these efforts typically lack a formal guarantee of

Y. Li and S. Tahar (Eds.): ICFEM 2023, LNCS 14308, pp. 279–284, 2023.
https://doi.org/10.1007/978-981-99-7584-6_20

neural network robustness. Consequently, researchers have focused on providing robustness verification for neural networks [9, 16].

Many scholars have proposed privacy-preserving techniques [19, 20] in response to concerns about privacy leakage, which involve safeguarding sensitive data while allowing for utility tasks like classification and segmentation. Notably, there is a gap in research regarding establishing privacy-preserving boundaries or certification of privacy-preserved neural networks. In exploring these areas, an opportunity arises to build upon existing robustness verification methodologies to certify these privacy-preserved neural networks. This paper aims to showcase the potential research avenues in this domain. To accomplish this objective, I will introduce definitions and their formulations to outline the problem statements in Sect. 2. Section 2 will also underscore the interrelation between these two problem domains and demonstrate current findings. Combining efforts to verify neural networks' robustness and privacy preservation is a viable direction. In Sect. 3, the proposed solutions and prospects for future research endeavors will be outlined.

2   Preliminaries and Problem Statement

Let $\mathbb{R}$ denote the set of real numbers. The function $f(\cdot)$ denotes a neural network, while $\mathbf{x}_{input} \in \mathcal{X} \to \mathbb{R}^n$ signifies the input to the neural network, which is an n-dimensional vector. Here, $\mathcal{X}$ encompasses the entire set of inputs, and $\mathbf{y}_{out} \in \mathbb{R}^m$ stands for the output of the neural network, an m-dimensional vector before applying the argmax function to the input $\mathbf{x}_{input}$. In classification tasks, $c \in C$ is the true label of $\mathbf{x}_{input}$, where C forms the set of labels for all inputs within $\mathcal{X}$. When the neural network accurately predicts a label, we have $f(\mathbf{x}_{input}) = c$ and $c = argmax(\mathbf{y}_{out})$. The symbol ϵ denotes the distance metric determined by the l_p-norm function $\|\cdot\|_p$, where $p \in \{1, 2, +\infty\}$. $B_{\epsilon,p}(\mathbf{x}_{input}) := \{\mathbf{x} : \|\mathbf{x} - \mathbf{x}_{input}\|_p \leq \epsilon\}$ designates the ball-shaped region around the point $\mathbf{x}_{input}$, with ϵ representing the radius of the ball.

2.1   Robustness Verification

Building upon the preceding definitions, $\mathbf{x}_{ptb} \in B_{\epsilon,p}(\mathbf{x}_{input})$ denotes the perturbed input within the ball region that $\mathbf{x}_{input}$ is the center.

Definition 1 ((ϵ, l_p) attack). *Given an input $\mathbf{x}_{input}$ and the true label $c \in C$ of $\mathbf{x}_{input}$, the (ϵ, l_p) adversarial attack can generate a perturbed input $\mathbf{x}_{ptb}$, where $f(\mathbf{x}_{ptb}) \neq c$. Such an $\mathbf{x}_{ptb}$ is called (ϵ, l_p) attack.*

Definition 2 (Local Robustness). *Given an input $\mathbf{x}_{input}$, the true label c and the ball area $B_{\epsilon,p}(\mathbf{x}_{input})$, for all $\mathbf{x}_{ptb} \in B_{\epsilon,p}(\mathbf{x}_{input})$, satisfy $f(\mathbf{x}_{ptb}) = c$ or there is no such an $\mathbf{x}_{ptb}$ that $f(\mathbf{x}_{input}) \neq c$, we call the network is local robust to the (ϵ, l_p) attack.*

Robustness verification aims to establish lower boundaries for the neural network model $f(\cdot)$ when subjected to (ϵ, l_p) attacks.

Definition 3 (Robustness Verification). *Given any input* $\mathbf{x}_{input} \in \mathcal{X}$ *and output label c, the robustness verification* $V(f(\cdot), \mathbf{x}_{input}, c, \epsilon)$ *is to check if there exists an* $\mathbf{x}_{ptb}$ *such that* $f(\mathbf{x}_{ptb}) \neq c$. *Ignoring the error and timeout condition, if* $V(\cdot)$ *finds such an* $\mathbf{x}_{ptb}$, $f(\cdot)$ *is not robust. If* $V(\cdot)$ *cannot find such an* $\mathbf{x}_{ptb}$, *the model is robust that* $V(\cdot)$ *can certify* $f(\cdot)$ *on* (ϵ, l_p) *attack to the input* $\mathbf{x}_{input}$ *and its true label c.*

In recent research, different $V(\cdot)$ has different performance on finding such an $\mathbf{x}_{ptb}$ because neural network verification is a NP-complete problem [9]. They pre-define a threshold, θ. $Pr(V(f(\cdot), \mathbf{x}_{input}, c, \epsilon) = False) \geq 1 - \theta$ denotes the probability of non-robust of the neural network is more than $1 - \theta$. If the verification approach can ensure $\theta = 0$, such an approach will not produce any false positives.

2.2   Privacy-Preserved Utility Task

Expanding upon the previous subsection, consider an input dataset $\mathcal{X}$ alongside a privacy budget δ and a privacy leakage function $\mathcal{M}$. Let $\mathcal{A}(\cdot)$ symbolize the optimal anonymization function that anonymizes the dataset $\mathcal{X}$, denoted as $\mathcal{A}(\mathcal{X}, \mathcal{M}, \delta)$. The resulting privacy-preserved data is $\mathcal{X}' = \mathcal{A}(\mathcal{X}, \mathcal{M}, \delta)$. $\mathcal{A}(\cdot)$ ensures that the privacy loss is less than the given privacy budget, $\mathcal{M}(\mathcal{X}') \leq \delta$. The utility task $f(\cdot)$ processes $\mathcal{X}'$, which might involve tasks such as image classification and object detection. Within the realm of privacy-preserved utility tasks, there exists a dual loss, encompassing privacy loss $\mathcal{L}_{\mathcal{A}}$ and utility task loss $\mathcal{L}_T$, with an inversely proportional relationship. Keeping privacy requires reducing the data features. The utility tasks require sufficient data features to maintain performance. Current efforts aim to minimize the cumulative loss $Sum(\mathcal{L}_{\mathcal{A}}, \mathcal{L}_T)$. However, achieving privacy preservation necessitates robust neural networks in utility tasks. This introduces a concern within the optimization target $minimize(sum(\mathcal{L}_{\mathcal{A}}, \mathcal{L}_T))$: it remains unclear how to precisely gauge the performance of both $\mathcal{A}(\cdot)$ and $f(\cdot)$, alongside their interconnection, when combined in this optimization framework.

Drawing inspiration from robustness verification, I present a novel approach: integrating privacy-preserving and robustness verification for privacy-preserved utility tasks. The primary objective is establishing a lower boundary for privacy loss and performance within the existing framework. This innovative approach comprehensively assesses the privacy-preserved utility task by considering both privacy concerns and robustness.

Definition 4 (Privacy-preserving and Robustness Verification). *Given an input* $\mathbf{x}_{input} \in \mathcal{X}$ *containing privacy information and its ground true label c, any other label* $c' \in C$, *an optimal anonymization function* $\mathcal{A}$, *a privacy budget* δ, *the utility task neural networks function* $f(\cdot)$, *The privacy-preserving and robustness verification problem is defined as a multi-objective optimization problem* $V(\cdot)$ *in Eq. (1):*

$$V(\mathbf{x}_{input}, \mathcal{A}, \delta, \mathcal{M}) = min \begin{cases} f_1 \\ f_2 \end{cases} \tag{1}$$

where $f_1 := f(\mathbf{x}_{input})_c - f(\mathcal{A}(\mathbf{x}_{input}, \mathcal{M}, \delta))_c - \delta$, $f_2 := f(\mathcal{A}(\mathbf{x}_{input}, \mathcal{M}, \delta))_c - f(\mathcal{A}(\mathbf{x}_{input}, \mathcal{M}, \delta))_{c'}$, $f(\cdot)_c$ *denotes the probability of label c produced by neural network for the input* $\cdot$. f_1 *describes the privacy-preserving level, and* f_2 *describes the robustness of the utility task. The verification result has four conditions summarized in Table 1.*

Table 1. Privacy-preserving and Robustness Verification result

Condition	Result and meaning
$f_1 \geq 0$, $f_2 \geq 0$	Data privacy is preserved, and the utility task is robust under the preserving function
$f_1 \geq 0$, $f_2 \leq 0$	Data privacy is preserved, and the utility task is not robust under the preserving function
$f_1 \leq 0$, $f_2 \geq 0$	Data privacy does not achieve the required preserved level, and the utility task is robust under the preserving function
$f_1 \leq 0$, $f_2 \leq 0$	Data privacy does not achieve the required preserved level, and the utility task is not robust under the preserving function

The core objective of this problem statement is to ascertain the effectiveness of the privacy-preserving approach and its utility task concerning data privacy preservation. Addressing this challenge will solve an optimization problem, deriving a lower performance bound for both the privacy-preserving approach and the utility task. This optimization-based approach enables the verifier to provide reliable assurance for the efficacy of these privacy-preserving utility tasks. As far as my knowledge extends, I am the originator of this research inquiry. This investigation can build upon established research methodologies in the realm of robustness verification, such as α, β-CROWN [17,21,23,25], Marabou [10] and MN-BAB [6].

3 Proposed Solutions and Future Work

To address the aforementioned research question, I have planned five coherent works. The first one was a study of existing neural network verification approaches focusing on the verification performance on accuracy and efficiency of producing $\mathbf{x}_{ptb}$. A new evaluation framework of state-of-the-art verification approaches was proposed on various datasets, perturbations and neural networks with different structures and complexity. Compared with the newest International Verification of Neural Networks Competition (VNN-COMP) report [15], the study generated a slightly different ranking result[1]. The second job was investigating how the data and configuration impacted the neural network's robustness. These two studies are the ablation study of the verification approach.

---

[1] Not include VeriNet and CGDTest, as they either did not release their code or delete their repository.

In the future, my third work will propose a state-of-the-art approach to preserve the privacy of video datasets, followed by utility tasks for the privacy-preserved data. In this work, I will utilize existing (ϵ, l_p) attack approaches to propose the privacy-preserving approach with selected utility tasks and compare it with the latest related works. The fourth work will create a benchmark for the coming VNN-COMP that utilizes the data and network from the third work. Accepting the benchmark will demonstrate the effectiveness of the unified verification problem. The fifth work will draw attention to proposing verification approaches to verify the unified verification problem.

References

1. Ahmedt-Aristizabal, D., Armin, M.A., Denman, S., Fookes, C., Petersson, L.: Graph-based deep learning for medical diagnosis and analysis: past, present and future. Sensors **21**(14), 4758 (2021)
2. Alam, M.S., Wang, D., Liao, Q., Sowmya, A.: A multi-scale context aware attention model for medical image segmentation. IEEE J. Biomed. Health Inf. (2022)
3. Badue, C., et al.: Self-driving cars: a survey. Expert Syst. Appl. **165**, 113816 (2021)
4. Cheng, X., Wang, H., Hua, J., Xu, G., Sui, Y.: DeepWukong: statically detecting software vulnerabilities using deep graph neural network. ACM Trans. Softw. Eng. Methodol. (2021). https://doi.org/10.1145/3436877
5. Cheng, X., Zhang, G., Wang, H., Sui, Y.: Path-sensitive code embedding via contrastive learning for software vulnerability detection. In: Proceedings of the 31st ACM SIGSOFT International Symposium on Software Testing and Analysis, ISSTA 2022. ACM (2022)
6. Ferrari, C., Müller, M.N., Jovanovic, N., Vechev, M.T.: Complete verification via multi-neuron relaxation guided branch-and-bound. In: The Tenth International Conference on Learning Representations, ICLR 2022, Virtual Event, 25–29 April 2022. OpenReview.net (2022). https://openreview.net/forum?id=l amHf1oaK
7. Gnanasambandam, A., Sherman, A.M., Chan, S.H.: Optical adversarial attack. In: Proceedings of the IEEE/CVF International Conference on Computer Vision, pp. 92–101 (2021)
8. Goodfellow, I., et al.: Generative adversarial nets. In: Ghahramani, Z., Welling, M., Cortes, C., Lawrence, N., Weinberger, K. (eds.) Advances in Neural Information Processing Systems, vol. 27. Curran Associates, Inc. (2014)
9. Katz, G., Barrett, C., Dill, D.L., Julian, K., Kochenderfer, M.J.: Reluplex: an efficient SMT solver for verifying deep neural networks. In: Majumdar, R., Kunčak, V. (eds.) CAV 2017. LNCS, vol. 10426, pp. 97–117. Springer, Cham (2017). https://doi.org/10.1007/978-3-319-63387-9_5
10. Katz, G., et al.: The marabou framework for verification and analysis of deep neural networks. In: Dillig, I., Tasiran, S. (eds.) CAV 2019. LNCS, vol. 11561, pp. 443–452. Springer, Cham (2019). https://doi.org/10.1007/978-3-030-25540-4_26
11. Li, X., de Belen, R.A., Sowmya, A., Onie, S., Larsen, M.: Region-based trajectory analysis for abnormal behaviour detection: a trial study for suicide detection and prevention. In: Rousseau, J.J., Kapralos, B. (eds.) International Conference on Pattern Recognition, vol. 13643, pp. 178–192. Springer, Cham (2022). https://doi.org/10.1007/978-3-031-37660-3_13

12. Li, X., Onie, S., Liang, M., Larsen, M., Sowmya, A.: Towards building a visual behaviour analysis pipeline for suicide detection and prevention. Sensors **22**(12), 4488 (2022)
13. Liang, M., Li, X., Onie, S., Larsen, M., Sowmya, A.: Improved spatio-temporal action localization for surveillance videos. In: 2021 Digital Image Computing: Techniques and Applications (DICTA), pp. 01–08. IEEE (2021)
14. Lu, D.: How abusers are exploiting smart home devices. https://www.vice.com/en/article/d3akpk/smart-home-technology-stalking-harassment
15. Müller, M.N., Brix, C., Bak, S., Liu, C., Johnson, T.T.: The third international verification of neural networks competition (VNN-COMP 2022): summary and results. arXiv preprint arXiv:2212.10376 (2022)
16. Wang, S., et al.: Beta-CROWN: efficient bound propagation with per-neuron split constraints for complete and incomplete neural network verification. In: Advances in Neural Information Processing Systems, vol. 34 (2021)
17. Wang, S., et al.: Beta-CROWN: efficient bound propagation with per-neuron split constraints for complete and incomplete neural network verification. arXiv preprint arXiv:2103.06624 (2021)
18. Weiss, M.A., Archick, K.: US-EU data privacy: from safe harbor to privacy shield (2016)
19. Wen, Y., Liu, B., Ding, M., Xie, R., Song, L.: IdentityDP: differential private identification protection for face images. Neurocomputing **501**, 197–211 (2022)
20. Wu, Z., Wang, H., Wang, Z., Jin, H., Wang, Z.: Privacy-preserving deep action recognition: an adversarial learning framework and a new dataset. IEEE Trans. Pattern Anal. Mach. Intell. **44**(4), 2126–2139 (2020)
21. Xu, K., et al.: Automatic perturbation analysis for scalable certified robustness and beyond. In: Advances in Neural Information Processing Systems, vol. 33 (2020)
22. Xu, K., et al.: Adversarial T-shirt! evading person detectors in a physical world. In: Vedaldi, A., Bischof, H., Brox, T., Frahm, J.-M. (eds.) ECCV 2020. LNCS, vol. 12350, pp. 665–681. Springer, Cham (2020). https://doi.org/10.1007/978-3-030-58558-7_39
23. Xu, K., et al.: Fast and complete: enabling complete neural network verification with rapid and massively parallel incomplete verifiers. In: International Conference on Learning Representations (2021). https://openreview.net/forum?id=nVZtXBI6LNn
24. Zhang, G., et al.: A tale of two cities: data and configuration variances in robust deep learning. arXiv preprint arXiv:2211.10012 (2022)
25. Zhang, H., et al.: General cutting planes for bound-propagation-based neural network verification. In: Advances in Neural Information Processing Systems (NeurIPS) (2022)

IoT Software Vulnerability Detection Techniques through Large Language Model

Yilin Yang(✉)

School of Computer Science and Engineering, UNSW Sydney, Sydney, Australia
Yilin1001@outlook.com

Abstract. The explosion of IoT usage provides efficiency and convenience in various fields including daily life, business and information technology. However, there are potential risks in large-scale IoT systems and vulnerability detection plays a significant role in the application of IoT. Besides, traditional approaches like routine security audits are expensive. Thus, substitution methods with lower costs are needed to achieve IoT system vulnerability detection. LLMs, as new tools, show exceptional natural language processing capabilities, meanwhile, static code analysis offers low-cost software analysis avenues. The paper aims at the combination of LLMs and static code analysis, implemented by prompt engineering, which not only expands the application of LLMs but also provides a probability of accomplishing cost-effective IoT vulnerability software detection.

Keywords: Vulnerability Detection · Large Language Model · Prompt Engineering

1 Introduction

The Internet of Things (IoT) has a proliferation of usage as an emerging technology due to its convenience and efficiency in the world, such as smart homes, industrial automation and infrastructure. However, the connectivity between devices and systems may have vulnerabilities that can be used by malicious actors, threatening personal privacy, data security and business benefits. Therefore, it is a significant problem that improves the security of IoT through the timely and accurate detection of vulnerabilities.

The traditional methods of detecting vulnerabilities are regular security audits and testing by security experts, which cost a lot and may not prompt enough when facing the increasing scale and complexity of IoT systems. Thus, it is necessary to find automatic approaches with lower costs as a substitute to detect IoT vulnerabilities.

Among detection approaches, static code analysis, which can reduce the cost of time and resources without the execution of the program [1], has the potential to detect vulnerabilities before manifesting as actual threats, minimizing the security risk. Besides, it is valuable to consider emerging tools. Large Language Models (LLMs), demonstrate outperforming capabilities. There are numerous kinds of research showing LLM-Integrated applications in different domains [2, 3]. Therefore, the combination of static code analysis and LLMs holds the potential in the field of IoT vulnerability detection.

Y. Li and S. Tahar (Eds.): ICFEM 2023, LNCS 14308, pp. 285–290, 2023.
https://doi.org/10.1007/978-981-99-7584-6_21

This research discusses the necessity of IoT vulnerability detection, explores the potential of LLM in IoT vulnerability detection through experiments and expects to provide an innovative method. The approach demonstrates more possibilities in applications of LLM and provides potential cost-effective tools for IoT vulnerability software detection.

2 Literature Review

2.1 Large Language Model

Large Language Models (LLMs) are one type of artificial intelligence language model, usually based on deep learning models and pre-trained on immense size of text data, which aim at processing and generating natural language. LLMs have become a hot topic in recent years due to their remarkable progress.

The language models in the early stage are based on statistical principles, such as n-gram models, which can just deal with short dependencies. Then with the development of Recurrent Neural Networks (RNNs), Simple Recurrent Networks (SRNs), which have the context layer to record the information in the previous timestep, are capable of learning medium-range dependencies. However, not until the introduction of gating mechanisms, the problems with long-range dependencies can be analyzed. Furthermore, Ashish Vaswani et al. proposed Transformer architecture in 2017 [4], an RNN architecture with attention mechanisms, greatly decreasing training time [5]. It positively impacts the development of LLMs since LLMs require pre-training on vast amounts of data.

On the other hand, the interpretation of LLMs remains disputation since it just predicts the next word repeatedly according to the mask of input text [6]. For specific tasks, LLMs use fine-tuning methods to get results. However, LLMs are still similar to "black boxes" when considering whether they have acquired knowledge to solve problems. There are several research discussing the mechanistic interpretability of LLMs such as analysing the approximate used algorithms for inference of LLMs [7].

2.2 Prompt Engineering

As mentioned before, LLMs get results in specific tasks through fine-tuning with high cost, however, the method can be substituted by prompt engineering in some larger-size models such as the GPT series. The prompt is text containing task descriptions in natural language, which can be commands, queries, feedback or statements including data or code, to provide keywords and additional information to LLMs. Prompt engineering is to develop and optimize prompts, which builds connections between tasks to results through in-context learning. Prompt engineering can significantly augment LLMs as tools. For example, ReAct can generate verbal reasoning and task actions by Chain-of-Thought prompting to improve the efficiency of LLMs [8].

2.3 Challenges

Although LLMs have an increasingly integrated usage in various applications, there exist challenges in the robustness of LLMs. Since LLM-integrated applications may blur the boundary between data and prompts, LLMs can be impacted by targeted adversarial prompting. According to Kai Greshake et al., adversaries can attack LLM-integrated applications without a direct interface by using Indirect Prompt Injection [9]. For this, defence systems are necessary to improve the robustness of LLM-integrated applications.

3 Proposed Approach

The research aims to develop a method with practical viability to detect potential IoT vulnerabilities through static analysis of code snippets by LLMs. The expected approach is prompt engineering built on ChatGPT-4.0 based on the principle of chain of thought [10]. The prompts can be generated by a deep-learning model automatically, which is inspired by valid experiments and based on the analysis of keywords, following a similar logical process of experiments. This prompt engineering should have a certain degree of capability of detecting potential IoT vulnerability types and related code lines when inputting code snippets.

4 Current Work

4.1 Experiments

The experiments are manually input code snippets and prompts based on the Chain-of-Thought principle, trying to get actual vulnerability types and related code lines in responses by ChatGPT using fewer prompts, which explore the potential of LLMs on IoT vulnerability detection and build the foundation of prompt engineering development. The basic logic is that constraining the scope of prompts and providing necessary additional information will get more accurate responses. The dataset used in the experiments is 60 vulnerabilities crawled from the Zephyr project, one real-world IoT system in GitHub, including the vulnerability type and related code snippets.

Constraining Vulnerability Types. The first kind of experiment constraints vulnerability types in prompts, Fig. 1 demonstrates the flow process of the experiment. Firstly, input the code snippets and ChatGPT will provide a code analysis as the default response. Then the prompt will require potential vulnerability types and the response will list several possibilities. Thirdly, inquire which line of code can cause the specific vulnerability type listed above sequentially by separate prompts and record the response to the most possible vulnerability. Finally, analyse the response and record whether the true vulnerabilities are listed and the number of used prompts.

Constraining Code Lines. The second kind of experiment constrains code lines in prompts and provides additional code by analysing the keywords in the response. The process of the experiment is shown in Fig. 2, similar to the first kind of experiment. Differently, the prompts will ask for the code relevant to vulnerabilities and if it requires

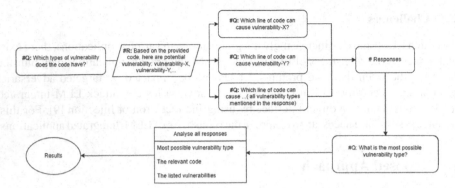

Fig. 1. Flowchart of experiments which constrain vulnerability types in prompts.

other useful additional codes. The responses will list the potential code and may include keywords that indicate the requirements of other additional code. If the responses contain keywords, search the code on the repository and input it as additional code if exists. Finally, inquire about the potential vulnerability type based on all provided codes, analyse and record the responses.

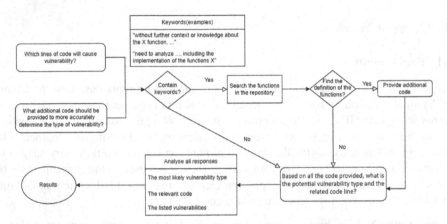

Fig. 2. Flowchart of experiments which constrain code lines in prompts.

4.2 Results and Analysis

The following Table 1 Gives a summary of the results of the first two kinds of experiments including success rate (accurate to two decimal places), where success means the true vulnerability type and related code line are included in the responses by ChatGPT, and the average number of prompts, which is the average number (integer) of used prompts in the successful experiments. It is inevitable that the results have a certain margin of error due to the slight randomness of responses by LLM.

Table 1. Results for above two experiments

Experiment	Success rate	Average number of prompts
Constraining Vulnerability Types	66.67%	9
Constraining Code Lines	83.33%	4

The results demonstrate that the experiment constraining code lines in prompts performs better than the experiment constraining vulnerability types in prompts with fewer used prompts and a higher success rate.

In the development of prompt engineering, it will be more efficient to constrain the code line and the experiments provide the reference to the process based on the chain of thought. Moreover, the identification of keywords to provide additional code will benefit the task. On the other hand, the experiments show that prompts with the same meaning in different wordings may get different responses, while the same prompts in different steps may get different responses. The facts indicate that it is necessary to use data augment such as synonyms expansion in the pre-training in prompt engineering due to the stochastic of LLMs. Besides, there exist limitations due to the small dataset, but the results still demonstrate the potential of LLM for vulnerability detection.

5 Future Work

5.1 Dataset and Experiments

As far as the dataset is concerned, it requires a larger size of data for experiments and training models of prompt engineering. Thus, future work includes gathering real-world IoT vulnerabilities. Moreover, for multiple potential vulnerabilities, ranking the result by possibility will assist in deeper analysis. Besides, repeating experiments is necessary to decrease the randomness of responses by LLM and increase the reliability of the results. These will contribute to evaluating the performance of the prompt engineering model.

5.2 Prompt Engineering

To develop prompt engineering, it is necessary to evaluate different proper deep-learning architectures and make ablation experiments on different data augment techniques. Then choose proper deep-learning architectures and data augment techniques to build models and split datasets into training data and validation data to train and evaluate the performance of the built model. Prompt engineering can achieve the aim through these works. Furthermore, it is also important to compare with other existing IoT vulnerability detection methods.

6 Conclusion

The paper demonstrates the significance of new approaches for IoT vulnerability detection and as current work, explores the potential of LLMs for detecting IoT vulnerability through static code snippet analysis. For future work, the paper first analyses the viability of prompt engineering to achieve the aim and then discusses the main techniques and steps to develop and evaluate prompt engineering. In summary, the combination of prompt engineering based on LLMs and static code analysis can benefit IoT software vulnerability detection at a lower cost.

References

1. Sözer, H.: Integrated static code analysis and runtime verification. Softw.: Pract. Exp. **45**(10), 1359–1373 (2014). https://doi.org/10.1002/spe.2287
2. Spataro, J.: Introducing Microsoft 365 Copilot – your copilot for work - The Official Microsoft Blog. The Official Microsoft Blog (2023). https://blogs.microsoft.com/blog/2023/03/16/introducing-microsoft-365-copilot-your-copilot-for-work/
3. Mehdi, Y.: Reinventing search with a new AI-powered Microsoft Bing and Edge, your copilot for the web - The Official Microsoft Blog. The Official Microsoft Blog (2023). https://blogs.microsoft.com/blog/2023/02/07/reinventing-search-with-a-new-ai-powered-microsoft-bing-and-edge-your-copilot-for-the-web/
4. Vaswani, A., et al: Attention is All you Need. arXiv (Cornell University), 30, 5998–6008 (2017). https://arxiv.org/pdf/1706.03762v5
5. Merritt, R.: What Is a Transformer Model? | NVIDIA Blogs. NVIDIA Blog (2022). https://blogs.nvidia.com/blog/2022/03/25/what-is-a-transformer-model/
6. Bowman, Samuel R.: Eight Things to Know about Large Language Models (2023). arXiv: 2304.00612
7. Nanda, N., Chan, L., Lieberum, T., Smith, J. L., Steinhardt, J.: Progress measures for grokking via mechanistic interpretability. arXiv (Cornell University) (2023). https://doi.org/10.48550/arxiv.2301.05217
8. Yao, S., et al.: ReAct: Synergizing Reasoning and Acting in Language Models (2022). https://doi.org/10.48550/arxiv.2210.03629
9. Liu, Y., et al.: Prompt Injection attack against LLM-integrated Applications (2023). https://doi.org/10.48550/arxiv.2306.05499
10. Cheung, K.S.: Real estate insights unleashing the potential of ChatGPT in property valuation reports: the "Red Book" compliance Chain-of-thought (CoT) prompt engineering. J. Property Invest. Finance (2023). https://doi.org/10.1108/JPIF-06-2023-0053

Vulnerability Detection via Typestate-Guided Code Representation Learning

Xiao Cheng[✉]⃝iD

UNSW, Kensington, Australia
`xiao.cheng@unsw.edu.au`

Abstract. Machine learning, including deep learning, has found success in various domains. Recently, the focus has shifted to using deep learning, like graph neural networks, for static vulnerability detection. Existing methods represent code as an embedding vector and train models on safe and vulnerable code patterns to predict vulnerabilities. However, these models lack precise bug detection, as they prioritize coarse-grained classification over understanding vulnerability semantics, such as typestate properties. This paper introduces an innovative typestate-guided code embedding technique for accurate static vulnerability detection. We select and retain feasible typestate sequences extracted from typestate analysis using self-supervised contrastive learning in a pretrained path embedding model. This reduces the need for labeled data in training downstream models for vulnerability detection. Evaluation on real-world projects showcases our approach's superiority over recent learning-based approaches. It outperforms them by substantial margins across various metrics like precision, recall and F1 Score.

Keywords: Typestate · code embedding · vulnerabilities

1 Introduction

Despite efforts to enhance software security, vulnerabilities persist as a significant concern in modern software development. Current static bug detectors (e.g., Checkmarx, RATs, ITS4, CoBOT, Coverity, SVF, Infer) rely heavily on user-defined rules and domain knowledge, making them labor-intensive and limited in their effectiveness. These detectors struggle to detect a broader range of vulnerabilities, often leading to false positives/negatives [2–4].

Deep learning has shown promise in learning vulnerability patterns by correlating vulnerable programs with their code features. Existing code embedding techniques aim to capture code semantics but fall short in understanding the semantics of vulnerability detection. They lack the ability to distinguish typestate properties and preserve fine-grained vulnerable paths essential for precise bug detection. To address these limitations, we propose TSVD, a

Y. Li and S. Tahar (Eds.): ICFEM 2023, LNCS 14308, pp. 291–297, 2023.
https://doi.org/10.1007/978-981-99-7584-6_22

novel typestate-guided code embedding technique for pinpointing vulnerabilities based on typestate sequences. TSVD uses self-supervised contrastive learning to train a typestate sequence encoder that retains semantically similar sequences while discarding irrelevant ones. This pretrained encoder is used to represent the semantics of typestate sequences in the compact embedding space, which is further used for precise vulnerability detection.

Our contributions include introducing TSVD, a typestate-guided code embedding technique that employs pretrained typestate sequence encoders and self-supervised learning. We formulate embedding as a reachability problem over a guarded sparse value flow graph. Experimental results demonstrate TSVD's superiority over state-of-the-art methods in terms of detecting vulnerabilities and locating buggy statements.

2   Related Work

Static Vulnerability Detection. The realm of static vulnerability detection has witnessed the development of various tools (CLANG STATIC ANALYZER, INFER, CHECKMARX, SVF [15]) aimed at identifying faulty paths within source code. Many of these tools [7–9,17,18,20] target specific vulnerabilities like memory errors, relying on traditional program analysis techniques such as abstract interpretation and symbolic execution. However, they often necessitate manual rule definitions for detecting a wider range of vulnerabilities.

Learning-Based Vulnerability Detection. Recent efforts have harnessed machine learning for automated vulnerability detection. These approaches employ diverse code representations (lexical tokens, textual slices, abstract syntax trees, control flow graphs [2], program dependence graphs [4,14]) to learn vulnerability patterns across different levels of granularity (method [2], slice [4]). Approaches like VULDEELOCATOR and IVDETECT enhance detection outcomes through post-processing techniques, interpreting the trained detection model using attention and edge-masking strategies. Despite their successes, these approaches lack path awareness, which is crucial for effective path-based vulnerability detection.

3   TSVD Approach

This section outlines our approach, which consists of three phases: Typestate Sequence Generation (Sect. 3.1), Contrastive Typestate Sequence Embedding (Sect. 3.2), Typestate Sequence Selection (Sect. 3.3), and Detection Model Training (Sect. 3.4).

3.1   Typestate Sequence Generation

Typestate represents an extension of conventional immutable types, designed to encompass the potential variability in states that can occur. This augmentation is accomplished by presenting a comprehensive depiction of the manifold states and behaviors inherent to a specific type, all within the framework of a finite-state automaton.

In the realm of typestate theory, a typestate sequence denoted as τ assumes the form of an ordered series of operations. The peculiarity of this sequence lies in its propensity to culminate in an undesirable or erroneous typestate. As each constituent instruction within τ is executed consecutively, the initial typestate under consideration undertakes a series of transitions ultimately leading to an error state. This construct enables a comprehensive study of the potential deviations from desired behaviors within the context of mutable states.

A pertinent facet of the utilization of typestate sequences pertains to the realm of analysis tools, where diverse methodologies, including but not limited to API protocol analysis, yield valuable outcomes. These outcomes function as informative artifacts, which when interpreted adeptly, can illuminate the structural patterns and potential progression paths within complex typestate sequences. Consequently, these analytical findings provide a vantage point from which the underlying typestate sequences can be inferred and subsequently harnessed for improved software design, error mitigation, and program reliability enhancement.

3.2   Contrastive Typestate Sequence Embedding

In this phase, we aim to pretrain a typestate sequence encoder (TSE) using contrastive learning. This encoder generates discriminative vector representations for typestate sequences extracted from code fragments. The embeddings are learned using a contrastive loss function that encourages similar typestate sequences to have close vector representations.

Contrastive Typestate Sequence Embedding Algorithm. The contrastive typestate sequence embedding process involves generating contrastive vector representations for typestate sequences and computing the contrastive loss. This loss is based on the similarity between embeddings of similar sequences and serves as a self-supervised objective for training the TSE.

Contrastive Typestate Sequence Representations. To create contrastive embeddings, we employ minimal data augmentation. By using independently sampled dropout masks during encoding, we generate pairs of embeddings $(\mathbf{v}_\tau, \mathbf{v}_\tau^+)$ for each typestate sequence τ. Pairs from the same sequence are considered positive, while pairs from different paths are negative.

Contrastive Typestate Sequence Embedding Loss. The Noise Contrastive Estimate (NCE) loss is used to maximize the agreement between positive typestate sequence representations. This involves measuring cosine similarity between embeddings and formulating a loss function that pushes positive pairs closer and negative pairs apart:

$$cos\_sim(\mathbf{v}_{\tau_i}, \mathbf{v}_{\tau_j}) = \frac{\mathbf{v}_{\tau_i}^\top \mathbf{v}_{\tau_j}}{||\mathbf{v}_{\tau_i}|| \cdot ||\mathbf{v}_{\tau_j}||} \tag{1}$$

The loss of τ_i is defined as :

$$loss(\tau_i) = -log\frac{exp(cos\_sim(\mathbf{v}_{\tau_i}, \mathbf{v}_{\tau_i}^+))}{\sum_{k=1}^{Batch} exp(cos\_sim(\mathbf{v}_{\tau_i}, \mathbf{v}_{\tau_k}^+))} \tag{2}$$

where $Batch$ is the batch size of typestate sequences.

The total typestate sequence contrastive loss can be computed as:

$$\mathcal{L} = \frac{1}{Batch} \sum_{i=1}^{Batch} loss(\tau_i) \tag{3}$$

Typestate Sequence Encoder. The Typestate Sequence Encoder (TSE) processes typestate sequences by first locally encoding statements using a statement encoder [5]. The local encodings are then globally encoded using Bidirectional Gated Recurrent Unit (BGRU) to capture the temporal typestate transformations. The resulting vectors represent the typestate sequence's semantics.

3.3   Typestate Sequence Selection

In this phase, we perform feasibility analysis on the selected paths by checking the reachability of control-flow paths between consecutive statements using annotated guards.

Feasibility analysis is performed on selected typestate sequences. Using guards annotated on the control-flow graph, we determine the reachability of paths between consecutive statements [16]. This is achieved by evaluating Boolean functions that consider control-flow transfer conditions. For a typestate sequence τ consisting of $s_0, s_1, \ldots, s_N$, we establish the feasibility as a Boolean function that encodes the ability to traverse control-flow paths between consecutive pairs along the path within the program, from s_0 to s_N. Thus, τ is considered feasible when the feasibility function yields a true outcome, and unfeasible otherwise.

3.4   Detection Model Training

In this phase, a detection model is trained using labeled code fragments and their selected feasible typestate sequences. The paths are encoded using the previously trained TSE and passed through a multi-head self-attention layer. A soft attention mechanism aggregates these embeddings, which are then used for vulnerability prediction. The resulting code vector is used to predict vulnerabilities using a softmax function. The top-k indexing method is employed to interpret vulnerabilities at the statement level.

4   Evaluation

Datasets. We conducted an assessment of the performance of TSVD using a dataset comprised of 288 real-world open-source projects. These projects were drawn from three distinct datasets: D2A [19], Fan [6], and the combined FFMpeg+Qemu (FQ) [21] dataset. This dataset collectively encompassed 275,000 programs with a cumulative codebase of 30 million lines.

Table 1 compares the results with the state-of-the-art vulnerability detectors. It is clear that TSVD outperforms both our baselines under the existing metrics, including F1, precision and recall.

Table 1. Comparison with the state-of-the-art under F1 Score (F1), Precision (P) and Recall (R).

Model Name	F1 (%)	P (%)	R (%)
VGDETECTOR [2]	56.7	52.6	61.4
DEVIGN [21]	58.7	54.6	63.4
REVEAL [1]	63.4	61.5	65.5
VULDEEPECKER [13]	52.3	52.2	52.4
SYSEVR [12]	55.0	54.5	55.4
DEEPWUKONG [4]	67.0	67.4	66.5
VULDEELOCATOR [11]	62.0	61.4	62.5
IVDETECT [10]	64.1	64.0	64.6
TSVD	**83.3**	**80.4**	**86.5**

As shown in Table 1, TSVD outperforms all our baselines with the highest F1 Score at 83.3%, indicating an overall better effectiveness for vulnerability detection. The precision of TSVD is the largest at 80.4%, which is more than IVDETECT at 64.0% and VULDEEPECKER at 52.2%. TSVD also has a significantly higher recall at 86.5% compared to 64.6% for IVDETECT and merely 52.4% for VULDEEPECKER. The reason for the better performance of TSVD is that it can preserve more comprehensive features of the input program by considering path-sensitive typestate sequences, which approximate the program runtime behaviour and bug semantics.

5   Conclusion and Future Work

We introduce TSVD, a novel typestate-guided code embedding method that captures path-sensitive typestate sequences in the embedding space for precise software vulnerability detection. The approach utilizes an attention-based structure-aware encoder trained with contrastive learning to retain both local and global typestate sequence semantics. The pre-trained path encoder is then employed in vulnerability detection using attention-based neural networks. The tool was assessed on a benchmark from popular open-source projects. Results demonstrate TSVD's superior performance over eight recent vulnerability detection approaches, achieving substantial improvements across various metrics. In the future, we aim to investigate code embedding on different types of program paths and produce more readable bug reports to facilitate bug fixing.

References

1. Chakraborty, S., Krishna, R., Ding, Y., Ray, B.: Deep learning based vulnerability detection: Are we there yet? CoRR (2020)
2. Cheng, X., et al.: Static detection of control-flow-related vulnerabilities using graph embedding. In: ICECCS (2019)
3. Cheng, X., Nie, X., Li, N., Wang, H., Zheng, Z., Sui, Y.: How about bug-triggering paths? - understanding and characterizing learning-based vulnerability detectors. In: TDSC (2022)
4. Cheng, X., Wang, H., Hua, J., Xu, G., Sui, Y.: Deepwukong: Statically detecting software vulnerabilities using deep graph neural network. In: TOSEM (2021)
5. Cheng, X., Zhang, G., Wang, H., Sui, Y.: Path-sensitive code embedding via contrastive learning for software vulnerability detection. In: Proceedings of the 31st ACM SIGSOFT International Symposium on Software Testing and Analysis. ISSTA '22, ACM (2022)
6. Fan, J., Li, Y., Wang, S., Nguyen, T.N.: A c/c++ code vulnerability dataset with code changes and cve summaries. In: MSR (2020)
7. Lei, Y., Sui, Y., Ding, S., Zhang, Q.: Taming transitive redundancy for context-free language reachability. In: OOPSLA (2022)
8. Lei, Y., Sui, Y., Tan, S.H., Zhang, Q.: Recursive state machine guided graph folding for context-free language reachability. In: PLDI (2023)
9. Li, T., Bai, J.J., Sui, Y., Hu, S.M.: Path-sensitive and alias-aware typestate analysis for detecting os bugs. In: ASPLOS (2022)
10. Li, Y., Wang, S., Nguyen, T.N.: Vulnerability detection with fine-grained interpretations. In: FSE (2021)
11. Li, Z., Zou, D., Xu, S., Chen, Z., Zhu, Y., Jin, H.: Vuldeelocator: A deep learning-based fine-grained vulnerability detector. In: TDSC (2021)
12. Li, Z., Zou, D., Xu, S., Jin, H., Zhu, Y., Chen, Z.: Sysevr: A framework for using deep learning to detect software vulnerabilities. In: TDSC (2018)
13. Li, Z., et al.: Vuldeepecker: A deep learning-based system for vulnerability detection. In: NDSS (2018)
14. Sui, Y., Cheng, X., Zhang, G., Wang, H.: Flow2vec: Value-flow-based precise code embedding. In: OOPSLA (2020)
15. Sui, Y., Xue, J.: SVF: Interprocedural static value-flow analysis in LLVM. In: CC (2016)
16. Sui, Y., Ye, D., Xue, J.: Static memory leak detection using full-sparse value-flow analysis. In: ISSTA (2012)
17. Sui, Y., Ye, D., Xue, J.: Detecting memory leaks statically with full-sparse value-flow analysis. In: TSE (2014)
18. Yan, H., Sui, Y., Chen, S., Xue, J.: Spatio-temporal context reduction: A pointer-analysis-based static approach for detecting use-after-free vulnerabilities. In: ICSE (2018)

19. Zheng, Y., et al.: D2a: A dataset built for AI-based vulnerability detection methods using differential analysis. In: ICSE-SEIP (2021)
20. Zhong, Z., et al.: Scalable compositional static taint analysis for sensitive data tracing on industrial micro-services. In: ICSE-SEIP (2023)
21. Zhou, Y., Liu, S., Siow, J., Du, X., Liu, Y.: Devign: effective vulnerability identification by learning comprehensive program semantics via graph neural networks. In: NIPS (2019)

Correction to: Learning Mealy Machines with Local Timers

Paul Kogel, Verena Klös, and Sabine Glesner

Correction to:
Chapter 4 in: Y. Li and S. Tahar (Eds.): *Formal Methods*
and Software Engineering, **LNCS 14308,**
https://doi.org/10.1007/978-981-99-7584-6_4

In the original version of this paper the text in Section 4.1 and the Figure 4 has been displayed incorrectly. This has been corrected.

The updated version of this chapter can be found at
https://doi.org/10.1007/978-981-99-7584-6_4

Author Index

Y. Li and S. Tahar (Eds.): ICFEM 2023, LNCS 14308, pp. 299–300, 2023.
https://doi.org/10.1007/978-981-99-7584-6

Printed in the United States
by Baker & Taylor Publisher Services